Go and Study

Go and Study

Essays and Studies in Honor of

Alfred Jospe

edited by
Raphael Jospe
and
Samuel Z. Fishman

B'nai B'rith Hillel Foundations
Washington D.C.
1980–5741

Library of Congress Cataloging in Publication Data

Main entry under title:

Go and study.

  "Alfred Jospe's writings": p.
  1. Judaism—History—Addresses, essays, lectures.
2. College students, Jewish—United States—Addresses,
essays, lectures. 3. Judaism—Study and teaching
(Higher)—United States—Addresses, essays, lectures.
4. Jews—Identity—Addresses, essays, lectures.
5. Jospe, Alfred, 1909-   —Addresses, essays, lectures. I. Jospe, Alfred, 1909-   II. Jospe, Raphael.
III. Fishman, Samuel Z.
BM42G6   909'.04924   80–20995
ISBN 0–87068–710–7

Manufactured in the United States of America

שוב מעשה בנכרי אחד שבא לפני שמאי, אמר ליה גיירני על מנת שתלמדני כל התורה כלה כשאני עומד על רגל אחת. דחפו באמת הבנין שבידו. בא לפני הלל, גייריה. אמר ליה: דעלך סני לחברך לא תעביד.
זו היא כל התורה כולה ואידך פירושה הוא. זיל גמור.
(שבת ל"א ע"א)

A gentile came to Shammai and said to him, convert me (to Judaism) on the condition that you teach me the whole Torah while I stand on one foot. He pushed him away with the builder's cubit in his hand. He came before Hillel, who converted him. He said to him: Whatever is hateful to you, do not do to your fellow.
This is the whole Torah in its entirety, and the rest is its commentary. Go and study.

(*Shabbat* 31a)

CONTENTS

ACKNOWLEDGMENTS

The publication of this volume was made possible through a fund established for the benefit of the B'nai B'rith Hillel Foundations by Isaac Wagner, and named the Isaac Wagner Educational Fund after his death in 1975 as a tribute to him for his decades of services to Hillel. The underwriting of this excellent volume expresses the high esteem of Isaac Wagner and his wife, Birdie, for Dr. Alfred Jospe.

PREFACE

Shiv'im panim la-torah—the Torah has seventy faces. In his seventy years Alfred Jospe has embodied these faces in both their practical and theoretical aspects. As Hillel's Director of Program and Resources and as its International Director, he acted to meet the functional and conceptual challenges of Hillel service to campus communities in North America and abroad. The fulfillment of these far-flung responsibilities constituted a demanding professional task; nevertheless, he maintained—and continues to maintain—an interest in scholarship by editing, writing, translating, and lecturing.

In this collection of essays and studies in Alfred Jospe's honor, we have received contributions as multi-faceted as his life and career. They reflect the dedication to pluralism within the Jewish tradition that he and the Hillel Foundations have consistently represented. The contributors differ in age by as much as half a century. They differ in their backgrounds geographically—North America, Israel, and Europe. And they differ professionally as well—rabbis, professors, communal leaders, and, of course, Hillel directors. They cover the spectrum of Jewish identity—religious, national, and cultural. But all have worked (and in some cases lived) personally, professionally, academically, and Jewishly with Alfred Jospe, and each shares his commitment to learn, to teach, and to live Judaism.

Initially, the articles for this volume were divided into three areas, a reflection of the *Ahavah Rabbah* prayer of the morning service: *lilmod, u-lelamed, lishmor ve-la'asot u-lekayyem:* to learn, to teach, to observe and to do and to fulfill "all the words of your Torah in love."

> *To learn:* — Jewish life on the contemporary campus.
> *To teach:* — Jewish education in the setting of the university.
> *To observe and to do and to fulfill:* — The shaping of contemporary Jewish identity.

xi

But consonant with Alfred Jospe's career, we had to add another category, *Torah li-shemah* (Torah for its own sake): Essays in Jewish scholarship. These four areas are not merely connected as a framework for the contributions in Alfred Jospe's honor. Like his own life's work, they constitute an organic unity which gives expression and reality to the world of Torah in all its many faces.

Raphael Jospe
Samuel Z. Fishman

Washington, D.C.
Heshvan 5740
November 1979

Alfred Jospe at 70

Benjamin M. Kahn

Washington, D.C.

"Alfred Jospe at 70" is a contradiction in terms. Although the psalmist declares that the "days of our years are but seventy" (given ten more for the mighty), Alfred's youthful vigor of body and mind belie the evidence of the calendar. His life has spanned not only two continents but various careers and several periods of Jewish history, and in each of them he has been so alive and his contributions so vital that his past and present constitute a consistently elevated continuum.

Take note of the varied fields of intellectual discipline and communal concern to which he has contributed of his vast and creative storehouse of knowledge: Jewish philosophical and religious thought, as in his writings on Moses Mendelssohn, Hermann Cohen, and *Wissenschaft des Judentums;* religious issues, as in a large number of articles dating as far back as his essay on "Religion und Erziehung" in 1938; higher education, as in his papers on religious issues in higher education and his pioneer *Academic Catalogue;* not to speak of numerous essays and monographs on the B'nai B'rith Hillel Foundations, the Jewish student, and the campus scene.

Alfred's effectiveness as a lecturer-teacher is equally recognized—never superficial, ever honest, direct and thoughtful. Not once have I heard him speak unprepared, though even his spontaneous statements are enriched by wells of knowledge and background so as to be almost indistinguishable from a written text. He captures his audiences and readers by his thoughtful content interspersed with anecdotes and inventive coinage; his original phrase "pediatric Judaism" has become a classic, often used, rarely attributed to its originator.

Whether via text or speech, Alfred serves as a bridge of communication between two sets of worlds: between the culture of Germany and that of America; between philosophy and religion, reason and faith; between the realm of the intellectual and that of the common folk; between the teacher and the student.

His orientation was largely influenced by his family background. Both grandfathers as well as his father were *ḥazanim;* his paternal grandfather was born in a suburb of Kovno, Lithuania, from where he migrated to East Prussia and later to Berlin. Alfred thus fell heir to the tradition of both the Litvak and the Yekke. He was a Zionist before he turned sixteen, and he attributes the absence of the prejudice—indeed, his intolerance of such prejudice—that frequently divided German and East European Jews to the Zionist emphasis on the unity of the Jewish people. It was not until Alfred came to the United States that he acquired first-hand knowledge of East European Jewry and its ways of life.

Alfred earned a doctorate in philosophy at the University of Breslau in 1932. Simultaneously he studied for the rabbinate at the Jewish Theological Seminary in Breslau, where he was ordained in 1935. His simultaneous enrollment in both institutions presaged Alfred's life-long role as a synthesizer of Jewish and general studies and values.

After his ordination, Alfred served for two years as District Rabbi (similar to what we know as a "circuit-riding rabbi") of the German province Grenzmark before being called to a pulpit in Berlin, where he also taught a course in Jewish history at the School for Jewish Social Work.

Following the *Kristallnacht* of 1938, Alfred was interned in the concentration camp Sachsenhausen, from which he was released for the purpose of emigration. In 1939, Eva and he landed in America with one daughter, four dollars, and a few suitcases; shortly afterwards he was elected as the first resident rabbi of the Tree of Life Congregation in Morgantown, West Virginia, which he served until 1944. In 1940, Alfred also assumed the responsibility for guiding the Hillel program at West Virginia University, initiating his career with the B'nai B'rith Hillel Foundations. After four years at West Virginia and five at Indiana University, he became Director of Program and Resources in the International Hillel Office in New York City. He welcomed the new post, partly because Bloomington, Indiana—then a tiny Jewish community—offered little opportunity for the Jewish education of his growing family, but partly also because his intellectual interests and innovative spirit sought broader fields for expression. In 1971, he was elected Hillel's

International Director, a position which he filled with distinction until his retirement in December 1974.

Alfred's career with Hillel can be reckoned not only in years but also in terms of nearly ten student generations. They came and went, each generation with its unique characteristics, problems, and needs. Through it all, Alfred maintained an equanimity and a consistency which few could equal. Though he might differ fundamentally with a colleague or a student, he remained respectful of different opinions. Even in professional judgment of someone whom he might not have liked personally, he dealt with objectivity unclouded by prejudice.

Though an intellectual, he could say that

> the emphasis on study and knowledge, on intellectual activity, should not be permitted to crowd out a genuine and authentic concern for the promotion of wholesome fellowship among our students.[1]

Though a rationalist, he deplored unconditional surrender either to emotionalism or to excessive ratiocination. "Both celebration and cerebration," he once said, "have a legitimate place, but not at the expense of the other."

Though a disciplined person himself, he was fatherly and patient with his students. In an address to his colleagues in which he decried the excesses of the sixties, he said:

> I would suggest to all of you what I am saying also to myself: be gentle with our young people . . . We must understand their anguish and what is impelling them. And some of what is impelling them is good and eminently worthwhile, even though they may go about it the wrong way . . . I am a father myself. I know you must love young people dearly in order to be be able to put up with them. But we cannot forsake them even though they might hurt us, as every young generation through the ages has hurt the older one. The world into which we have put them does not make it easy for them.[2]

Though a traditionalist at heart (not necessarily in the religious sense of the word) he consistently favored experimentation. Witness his and Richard Levy's 1973 compilation of experimental worship services, *Bridges to a Holy Time*.[3] As each decade brought forth its own concerns, Alfred's programmatic approaches responded appropriately. After World War II, he emphasized counseling techniques to meet the many troubled questions of the returning veterans. After Israel's War of Liberation, he developed enriched Israel programs for Foundations and Counselorships. In the middle fifties, he brought to their attention the world of Buber, Rosenzweig, and others. The activist sixties found Alfred encouraging his colleagues to be patient with excesses, while at the same time to represent reasonableness and perspective—a balance difficult yet necessary to achieve. As the seventies saw the hardening of denominational arteries, which he deplored as a divisive force, he nonetheless, though reluctantly, accepted the reality, yet pressed for a community of experience wherever possible. Even a decade earlier he had written:

> We cannot build a program that is to serve all segments of the Jewish community if we insist that one can be fully Jewish only in one way but not in another, and that Jewish completeness can be found only where all accept and affirm one definition, namely ours. The fundamental fact is that Jewish life is pluralistic.[4]

If we were to outline Alfred Jospe's approach to student life and Hillel, four interlocking categories could be distinguished: (1) the student, (2) the Hillel Director, (3) the Hillel movement, (4) the Jewish community.

1. *The Student:* Alfred starts his analysis of the concerns and needs of the college student by warning against generalizations. There is no such thing as *the* college student. Students change from generation to generation, and differ within each generation in a multitude of ways. At the same time (and in a sense this is a deviation from Alfred's own generalization), Jewish students share certain things. Like most young people they tend to rebel against the values and customs of the parent generation; as young Jews, they tend to question what they consider the superficialities of established institutions such as the synagogue. Of its theology and distinctive values they are frequently uninformed. Their participation in religious observance, like that of the older generation, is frequently minimal.

Yet Alfred vehemently rejects the oft-heard and quoted generalization of the campus as a "disaster area for Jewish life":

> They are not a lost generation. Students are often cynical, challenging

authority, questioning the values of preceding generations. They are impatient with the imperfections in the fabric of social or political life. Yet when it comes down to the wire, you will find that there is a deep residue of loyalty. Their basic ties to Jewish life may often be superficial, vulgar, sentimental. Indeed, they often are. Yet there is a deep-seated tenacity of Jewish belongingness that reappears under pressure and that is the soil on which we can build and must learn to build for the future of the Jewish community.[5]

Moreover, we must never forget that students change, often radically, from one generation to the other and sometimes even more frequently. Students in the seventies differ enormously from their counterparts in the fifties and sixties:

Probably at no time in the history of the American Jew has there been a greater opportunity to respond creatively to the psychological, moral, and spiritual needs of our young. We are dealing with the most intelligent, most sensitive, most serious, most questioning, and morally most committed young generation in our history. They want to learn about Judaism. But they want much more. They want the experience of being Jewish. They want to live Jewishly. They want the kind of education that will provide for them a community of meaning, the experience of belonging to a community of persons who will share their quest and search. They want and need teachers who care about young people and the problems that tear at their hearts.[6]

But Hillel's concern must, of course, be with all students and not only with those who are knowledgeable and identified:

They, too, must be our concern. Despite our efforts, they may know or acquire just a smattering of Hebrew in our courses. They may never understand Martin Buber. Yet they may also receive from their Hillel experience the stimulus to seek personal fulfillment within the Jewish community . . . We have to be concerned with both, the elite and the mass, the *rov binyan* and the *rov minyan*, the innovative function and the preservative function.[7]

But there is, nonetheless, a maximalist objective: the educated and the committed Jew. That means, for Alfred, one who has a grasp of the wholeness of Jewish life, a knowledge of the Bible, Jewish literature, the prayerbook; at-homeness in Jewish tradition and observances; an identification with the Jewish people; an acceptance of responsibility in and for the community. Utopia? No, answers Alfred, whose faith in and love for students justify his optimism.

2. *The Hillel Director.* It is a well-worn cliche that the Hillel Foundation is the shadow cast by the Hillel Director. For Hillel's 50th anniversary in 1973, many alumni wrote letters reflecting upon their Hillel experience. In his introduction to the transcript of the major papers presented at the anniversary meeting, Alfred wrote:

> The fact that we received virtually no letter that did not mention the writer's relationship to his Hillel director is, we believe, eloquent testimony to the director's role and impact as a significant model for Jewish students.[8]

True, a man's personal convictions cannot help but wield an influence on the students and the program. Yet, Alfred cautions, the Hillel Director, without forfeiting his own integrity, not only must refrain from imposing his own views on the students, but encourage and respect the expression of their legitimate differing convictions. In seeking to fulfill Hillel's tasks, two approaches are required of the director. First, he must be willing to experiment with an open mind, to accept new techniques, free himself from blind loyalty to the "way it was."
Second, Alfred sees the Hillel Director as a model:

> Techniques are important. Ultimately, however, the attitudes and values of a student are probably influenced most significantly by the educator himself—by what he says, how he acts and what he stands for, by the depth of his knowledge, the sensitivity of his empathy and understanding, and the contagion of his convictions.[9]

At the same time, the Hillel Director must be sensitive to the tensions that may arise from the potential conflict between the Director's "personal freedom and his institutional responsibility."[10] Alfred summed up his thinking on this issue in his farewell address to his colleagues on December 16, 1974:

> Nor should we allow ourselves to fall back on the principle of academic freedom to justify every view we want to express. We are *at* the university, not *of* the university. Our task is not the furtherance of dispassionate academic inquiry, the objective, assumptionless search after truth regardless of where it may lead us. Our task is to generate passionate Jewish commit-

ment, experience, self-understanding, self-identification. To be sure, study, academic inquiry, is one—though only one—of our methods but it is not our only nor our ultimate goal. Our ultimate goal is the nurture of the Jewishly informed and committed person. Hence, in the final analysis we are accountable not to the university but to Jewish history, if you will; to the Jewish people, to the living Jewish community in the time-span in which we happen to serve.[11]

Accountability to this goal must be maintained. The trust of the community can only be earned by the wisdom, integrity, and responsibility of the director-educator model.

3. *The Hillel Movement.* To be able to combine *midrash* and *ma'aseh* (thinking [study] and action) is no small feat. In his role as Director of Program and Resources and, later, as International Hillel Director, Alfred showed the capacity to institute new programs as well as to develop a philosophy of Hillel work (a phrase that often repeats itself in titles of works he wrote and edited). In the early forties he was an organizer of one of the first Hillel Leadership Institutes at his own Foundation in Indiana. It became the precursor of the National Hillel Summer Institute, from which outstanding student and community leaders have emerged.

He single-handedly produced *Clearinghouse*, a regular staff program publication, from 1949 to 1971. He had an important share in the formation on campus of "Free Jewish Universities."

His "philosophy of Hillel work?" It infuses all his writings and speeches on Hillel. Three emphases are dominant. There is his often repeated emphasis that it is the task of the responsible educator to attempt to address himself to the total personality of the student:

> I am mindful of the fact that the intellecutal transmission of information alone does not necessarily produce the committed Jew; that to know more about Judaism is not necessarily to be also more Jewish; that a person must not only *know* values but have an opportunity to *experience, feel,* and *live* them; and that Jewish values are experienced and find expression not only in study, but in worship, personal conduct, observance, and community action.[12]

A second emphasis reflects a fundamental, frequently expressed regret about the divisiveness in the Jewish community which overflowed onto the campus. Granting that diversity *per se* is wholly legitimate,

Alfred deplores the mutual intolerance of Jews of different denominational and political loyalties. He expressed it well:

> Denominationally oriented students have the right and should be encouraged to engage in activities which will meet the needs stemming from their particular backgrounds and affiliations, provided these activities do not duplicate existing Hillel programs. *But while it is not our task to reduce the pluralism that exists in the Jewish community to some spurious kind of unity, I think it is our task to reduce this pluralism to intelligibility*—to make students investigate the nature of religious faith and truth, to make them critically examine the often placid assumptions with which they are coming to us, to make them understand the real meaning and implications of their pattern of belief and practice and how it is or should be related to the totality of Jewish life.[13]

Hence, *K'lal Yisrael* is Alfred's lodestar towards a Jewish campus community—unity within diversity—his third emphasis:

> Jewish life is not monolithic but pluralistic and Jewish existence has sought and found authentic expression in numerous forms of conduct and conviction. The pluralism that has often been considered our weakness actually is our strength.
> We start from one point—that *k'lal Yisrael* includes all kinds of convictions: the religious, non-religious, and anti-religious; Zionists and non-Zionists, Hebraists and Yiddishists, secularists and folkists, the believer and the skeptic. All of them, in their many variations and orchestrations, are authentic components of *k'lal Yisrael* and constitute the Jewish community.[14]

4. *The Jewish Community:* Students do not live in a vacuum, despite the once-valid description of the university as an ivory tower. They come from the community, spend a few years in relative isolation on the campus, and eventually return to the community.

Are they prepared for Jewish living by the community and its institutions? Will they wish to participate in it once they leave the sheltered "halls of ivy?"

> Our students are a product of this community. They are the product of the synagogue with its frequent mediocrity and intellectual shallowness and its tendency to substitute social and entertainment values for spiritual quest. They are the product of the school system, the Jewish education offered by this community. As a result, thousands of students enter our universities

every year with what I call a "pediatric Judaism"—with religious notions which were arrested on the sixth or eighth grade level of intellectual development but with scholastic records which permit them to matriculate in an institution of higher learning . . . What they know of Judaism is not relevant to their thinking and needs.[15]

The Jewish community is pluralistic but weakened by fragmentation and institutional competitiveness, which, as Alfred asserts, Hillel ought not to reproduce. The problem is compounded by the fact that this orientation on the part of Hillel is generally at variance with the stance of most segments of the community. This fact is liable to impede a student's transition into the adult community. However, Alfred's hope has always been that the community might ultimately be transformed from within by the influx of a new youth population that affirms pluralism but eschews disunity and competitiveness.

And what should we expect of Jews, whether on the campus or in the community?

Judaism has laid upon us the obligation to become a kingdom of priests, and in emphasizing that all men can stand equal before God and can find God without mediation, it has safeguarded the democratic spirit in our midst and freed us from the evils of sacerdotalism and a priestly caste system. As Leo Baeck once put it, Judaism has never spoken merely of the "good Jew" but always of the "good man" and has thus taught us to accept every man of moral stature as brother even though his beliefs may differ from ours.[16]

One need not be a Jew to be concerned with service, with justice, with other human beings. But one cannot be a Jew and refrain from rendering this kind of service.[17]

I asked Alfred, my colleague and friend of almost forty years, what he had most enjoyed in his Hillel career. He answered that it was his opportunity to develop an educational and philosophical rationale for Hillel. This he did; but I believe his contributions to student life, the university community, and the concerns of the Jewish community were much greater.

When asked on another occasion what he had most enjoyed in his long Hillel experience, he answered characteristically: "It gave me a chance to learn something new or do something challenging virtually every day."

Martin Buber once said that the greatest gift Israel gave to him was the chance to make a new beginning. Alfred's seventieth birthday is for him also but a moment in his continuing service to the Jewish people and the B'nai B'rith Hillel Foundations. As a life member of the B'nai B'rith Hillel Commission, he continues his identification with the movement he loves and to which he gave of himself in abundance. May he and his family enjoy the rewards of the righteous and a long and happy life.

NOTES

1. A. Jospe, *Campus 1966: Change and Challenge*, Washington, D.C. 1965, p. 38.

2. ———, *New Frontiers for Jewish Life on the Campus*, Washington, D.C. 1967, p. 29.

3. *Bridges to a Holy Time: New Worship for the Sabbath and Minor Festivals*, ed. and with an introduction by Alfred Jospe and Richard N. Levy, New York 1973.

4. A Jospe, *Judaism on the Campus*, Washington, D.C. 1963, p. 26.

5. ———, ed., *The Test of Time*, Washington, D.C. 1974, p. 6.

6. ———, "Some Reflections on Hillel as Idea and Experience," (mimeographed), Washington, D.C. 1974.

7. ———, *New Frontiers for Jewish Life on the Campus*, p. 20.

8. ———, *The Test of Time*, p. 1.

9. ———, *Campus 1966: Change and Challenge*, p. 29.

10. ———, "Some Reflections on Hillel as Idea and Experience," p. 8.

11. *ibid.* p. 10.

12. ———, *Judaism on the Campus*, p. 19.

13. *ibid.* p. 77.

14. ———, *New Frontiers for Jewish Life on the Campus*, p. 23.

15. A. Jospe, ed., *The Sabbath as Idea and Experience*, Washington, D.C. 1962, p. 98.

16. ———, *Dimensions of Jewish Existence Today*, Washington, D.C. 1964, p. 107.

17. *The Sabbath as Idea and Experience* p. 110.

Alfred Jospe
in the German Rabbinate

Max P. Birnbaum

Jerusalem, Israel

In the summer of 1922 the Prussian Federation of Jewish Communities (Preussischer Landesverband jüdischer Gemeinden) was founded. Its main purpose was to assist hundreds of small Jewish communities in northern Germany to meet their religious requirements. It organized a network of teachers who supplied religious instruction for the children and took care of Sabbath services and related synagogue functions.

This, however was not sufficient. Of about 900 Jewish communities in Prussia, less than sixty had their own rabbi. The Federation therefore initiated the formation of District-Rabbinates in those parts of the country which did not have such institutions. This program attained added importance after the Nazis came to power in 1933.

One of the first of the newly created District-Rabbinates was for the Grenzmark, an eastern province of Prussia that had suffered the loss of its hinterland to Poland after the first World War. Many of its once flourishing Jewish communities were decimated by migration to large cities such as Berlin or Breslau. On December 2, 1934, Dr. Alfred Jospe, who had just completed his rabbinical studies at the Breslau Theological Seminary, was installed as District Rabbi in Schneidemühl, the largest city in the province with a Jewish population of about 500. Under his care were fourteen communities, many with outlying sections, altogether about 1,400 Jewish men, women, and children.

During the Nazi regime the task of the rabbi was no longer confined to spiritual and theological leadership. He became the human link between Jewish families in his district and the central self-help organizations in Berlin. His "flock" turned to him in all questions regarding emigration, re-training, liquidation of enterprises, sale of property, and the numerous juridical and practical problems connected therewith. In order to accomplish all these duties it was necessary for him to be highly organized.

Alfred Jospe was one of the pioneers in this respect. His task was facilitated by the availability of a car, which made him the first "motorized" district rabbi in Germany. He arranged regular meetings and consultation hours in all his communities and had the Jewish social worker in Schneidemühl accompany him on his rounds. He also solicited the help of a competent Jewish lawyer so that many of the pressing individual problems could be solved on the spot without undue bureaucratic delay. Aside from these tasks, which were dictated by the special circumstances of the times, he of course supervised the religious teachers and was quite often called upon to arbitrate between them and their communities. He also gave regular sermons and lectures and took care of the funerals and the few weddings and bar mitzvah celebrations: altogether a formidable array of duties. Alfred Jospe acquitted himself of these obligations so extraordinarily well that, in the fall of 1936, he was elected to one of the rabbinates of the Berlin Jewish Community which had become vacant.

It is the privilege of this writer, who was one of the officials of the Federation, to have met Alfred and Eva Jospe in connection with his first office. A lifelong friendship between both families has sprung from these beginnings.

Part I
ללמוד
Jewish Life
on the Contemporary Campus

Learning as Worship: A Jewish Perspective on Higher Education

Marver H. Bernstein

Brandeis University
Waltham, Massachusetts

1. Learning as Worship

The subject of the roots of the Jewish perspective on education does not lack for scholarly inquiry. If the depth and influence of a phenomenon can be measured by the volume of commentary upon it, then the special relationship of the Jewish people to education must rank high in the annals of interest and approbation. In some cases this unique relationship has inspired sentiments akin to awe. Nathaniel Weyl, in *The Creative Elite in America*, concludes: "Jewish intellectual eminence can be regarded as the end result of seventeen centuries of selective breeding for scholars."[1]

Beholding Jewish intellectual achievement, Weyl creates an Orwellian scenario, beginning in the third century and ending with a positive conclusion, but his judgment does not jibe with the well-known Jewish proclivity for differing views.

For the greatest part of the millenia of Jewish existence, living in the Diaspora has been the natural condition of Jews. Historically, the Jewish people have confronted issues concerning the objectives, processes, and content of higher education as small enclaves within larger societies. The dominant tension in the Jewish experience has usually come from the stresses of conflict and reconciliation between the special identity of Jews as Jews and the broader identity of Jews as part of the society around

15

them which was dominated by non-Jews and often excluded Jews from the mainstream.

Just as the Jewish experience in higher education has been traumatized but also enriched in the tensions of Diaspora life, so has Jewish survival for forty centuries often hung in the balance between the reality of exile in the Diaspora and the Messianic dream of redemption in Zion; between steadfastness to a revered heritage and to the biblical Covenant with God, and a yearning for earned status in the wider society of intellectual enlightenment.

An enduring factor in the miracle of Jewish survival has been a combative yearning for knowledge, understanding, and achievement. Whether Jewish scholars studied and taught in the established religious ways of their times or sought fruitful intellectual accommodations with the enlightened world around them, their lives were rarely quietly contemplative.

In 1938, A. Lawrence Lowell published a small book of essays entitled, *What a University President Has Learned.* In his first essay, Lowell stresses the need for a plan of university operations capable of overcoming unforeseen obstacles.[2] To emphasize the importance of flexible planning and goal-setting, he describes the university president as a general engaged in strategic military offensives. At first, one is struck by the portrait of the embattled university president seeking consensus about intangible goals under conditions of high tension. From the Jewish perspective, however, this picture of the university resident under siege evokes memories of Jewish struggles to nurture and refresh education and scholarly inquiry not only for their own sake but as the requisite instruments and processes of Jewish survival. For centuries of Jewish experience, aggressive devotion to education has been a life-sustaining imperative, a necessary condition of survival.

Ludwig Lewisohn tells about a small group of Jewish survivors making their way in 1946 from Siberian exile westward to the Polish hamlet that had been their former home:

"The town was a mass of rubble. They did not find even graves. All their kith and kin had been burned alive in the crematoriums. The synagogue was in ruins. But a stair to the cellar had been saved. Descending that stair these Jews found a few Talmudic volumes, charred and water-soaked but still usable in part. And they procured them a few tallow-candles and sat down to read a page or two. There came one running then and cried: 'Jews, do you forget that you are running for your lives? The Soviets are closing the frontiers. The American zone is still far off! Flee!' And one of the group waved the messenger aside: 'Shah!' he said gravely. 'Be still. M'darf lernen! One must learn.'"[3]

Robert M. Hutchins expressed the same idea in 1965 when he said: "The greatest contribution the Jews have made to American life is the idea that learning is a form of worship."[4]

Learning, or education, as a form of worship is an insight of the highest significance. The evolution of this concept and its implications for Jewish survival are the best guides to understanding the Jewish people's historic oneness with education. For education, purely religious at first, and later, with many secular additions, meant nothing less than salvation for Jews.

Maurice Samuel once described Judaism as "an outlook on life which is associated and interwoven ideologically with the history of a people."[5] He then distinguishes two types of knowledge of one's Jewish identity, that of the scholars and that of the folk. He writes:

"In neither of them is purely cerebral knowledge enough . . . The knowledge must be the affective kind which amounts to a renewed participation in the events — what Thomas Mann called 'the recurrent festival of present-ness.'"[6]

The affective element in Jewish knowledge is sustained by rituals in which events, their meaning and circumstances, are brought nearer to us and into us, as, for example, the story of the Exodus from Egypt, which is retold every year at the Passover Seder, with the admonition that each person round the table must see himself as if he personally had come out of Egypt. As Samuel observes:

". . . the most important part of the ritual is *study:* and the difference between Jewish and other study is clarified once for all when we remember that for others a knowledge of the history of their people is a civic duty, while for Jews it is a sacred duty."[7]

It is commonplace—but still accurate—to note that the phenomenon of the Jewish people as a race, as a culture, and as the bearers of a religion does not fit simply into any of the categories by which we try to comprehend historical phenomena. Most historians have described the

Jewish people as a unique group torn out of the general context of history. Unlike other peoples, its history runs counter to the presumed natural pattern in which a people and its culture arises, flourishes, declines, and finally disappears. Never known during 2,000 years as a people who enjoyed a flourishing position of power, Jews have episodically known violent defeat, only to arise again and again from catastrophe. To the Jewish people, learning as a form of worship has been reinforced as Jewish life persisted in an historic time-zone somewhere between the polarities of triumph and tragedy, most often closer to the latter.

Until the establishment of the State of Israel in 1948, the Jewish people had independent sovereignty only for short periods of time. Spreading from the eastern Mediterranean across North Africa to Spain and beyond, Judaism and Jewish life developed unanchored physically to a specific geographical place. Commitment to a common destiny and culture thus became of necessity the mortar of unity.

The core of this unity was the Jewish religion that did not stress theological commitment and involved far more than worship. In contradistinction to many other religions, Judaism laid central emphasis on the destinies of mankind *in this world*. It exhibited limited interest in the idea of individual life after death or resurrection. It emphasized history and the affirmation of life realized through history. In the millenia of the dispersion, the Jewish religion developed away from any particular locality and became more and more detached from the soil. It was not accidental that the Jewish people was the first to write great history. As Salo Baron notes: "Racial descent, common destiny and culture—including religion—became the uniting forces."[8]

Martin Buber states the central point most trenchantly: "The Jewish people has become the eternal people not because it was allowed to live, but because it was not allowed to live. Just because it was asked to give more than life, it won life."[9]

Against this background, it is readily apparent that education would loom large. But another important factor strengthened the position accorded to learning: the responsibility of the parent to educate. According to the Biblical story, God singled out Abraham to command his children and his household after him to keep the way of the Lord and to do righteousness and justice (Genesis 18:19). Thus, from the beginning, the instruction of children represented a momentous break with the practice of most previous and contemporaneous civilizations, which confined education generally to the classes of the priests and the scribes.

Throughout Jewish history, then, it has been considered a duty of the parent to provide for the education of children. This remains a central value of Jewish family life today, even when apparent religious underpinnings have disappeared. The respect for learning was ingrained in the Jewish people as a religious and familial imperative. The study of the Torah came to encompass all the centuries of scholastic commentary, the totality of Jewish life and lore.

The foundations of an extensive Jewish educational system were laid by the schools of wisdom and priestly training of ancient Israel. A program of primary and secondary education was formulated before the talmudic era by the Pharisaic teachers of independent Judea. After the destruction of the Temple in 70 c.e., the rabbis declared education to be a major responsibility of the community and outlined the resources required for the instruction of children. A teacher had to be supplied by the community whenever there were twenty-five children of school age, and an assistant teacher had to be added when the number increased to forty.

Talmudic learning emphasized adult education even more. Every Jew was expected to set aside for daily study as much time as possible for as long as he lived. Learning was recognized as opening opportunities for achievement in public and private life. As a rule, a rabbi as teacher had to work hard for a living. Baron finds that:

"In the period of the Talmud, Jewish learning penetrated still deeper into the masses, in a day when extreme illiteracy was widespread in the Mediterranean world and when the Imperial City had only begun to establish public schools for the wealthy and the middle class."[10]

By the early Middle Ages, Jewish education was stirring beyond its religious focus. Italian Jewish education included the broad domain of intellectual pursuits: theology, poetry, philosophy, and natural science in all its branches. In Spain, it included Aristotle's *Logic*, Euclid's *Elements*, and the mathematical works of Archimedes, as well as astronomy, music, medicine, and other natural sciences. In George Sarton's classic studies in the history of science 1,897 scholars are listed for the first 1400 years of Christendom, of whom 10.6% were Jews—at least three times their proportion in the population of Europe.

In the Middle Ages, Jewish children remained in school at least until the age of thirteen. If formal education ceased then, the child would be literate in Hebrew and Aramaic, besides the native language, and knowledgeable about the five books of Moses, the Prophets, and the *Mishnah*. This was *mass* Jewish education.

Higher education encompassed at least seven years and emphasized analytic exercises that stressed imagination and originality. The main subject was the commentaries of the greatest Jewish scholars on the *Mishnah*, by definition still open to question or they would have been incorporated in the *Mishnah*. This training ingrained a questioning, inquisitive mind. No matter how great a scholar, his words must be examined and questioned. No authority was ever taken as final. New insights were always possible, and any answer was subject to review and revision.

The most compelling and distinguished Jewish figure of the Middle Ages was Moses Maimonides (1135–1204). An extraordinary genius, he commanded every aspect of Jewish thought and of most of the science and high culture of his times. His monumental work encompassed commentary on the Mishnah, codification of Jewish law, philosophy, medicine, and science. Deeply religious, Maimonides had a practical program of survival that resisted temptations to accept fate while awaiting Messianic dreams of future reward. He advocated an education stressing science and liberal arts and rejected everything in Judaism that did not stand up to the test of reason. He embodied in one person both learning and religious law, and never doubted that these two worlds could be synthesized.

In the ghettos of Central and Eastern Europe in the 18th and 19th centuries, poverty and deprivation were accompanied nonetheless by a traditional respect and reverence for the scholar who devoted his life to study and in return was supported by his family. From the Yiddish writings of Sholem Aleichem we learn something of the cheerfulness and steady equanimity that lay behind the drab and gloomy appearance of the ghettos of Russia, Lithuania, Poland, and the Balkan countries.

These are some of the elements in the Jewish reverence for education—learning as worship. From the Renaissance to the Enlightenment, from the Emancipation which freed Jews from their ghetto existence to the mass Jewish migration to the United States, this tradition has always been part of the Jewish emotional and intellectual heritage. While religious and secular subjects remained the central curriculum in Jewish schools, Jews who arrived in the United States had also assimilated portions of the culture of their native European land. Thus, when they began to "study" to become Americans, they were becoming tri-cultural.

America's free-education system beckoned, and Jews responded. Although there was an initial period of discrimination and quota systems in higher education, there is probably no country in which Jews have been as free to develop intellectually as in the United States. By 1970, an estimated 80% of college-age Jews were enrolled in higher education, as compared to about half for the population as a whole, and Jewish students were heavily located in the more selective schools.[11] The lowering of discriminatory barriers also allowed more Jews to join university faculties.

This history has profoundly informed the general Jewish perspective on higher education in the United States; namely, reverence for learning. This reverence also characterizes many professed agnostics and atheists among Jews. Sigmund Freud best expressed this phenomenon when he was asked: "Dr. Freud, you are an atheist and do not identify with any Jewish causes. Wherein, then, lies your Jewishness?" To which Freud answered: "It is only the essential part of my personality."

II.

Given the role Jewish thought and culture has played in world history, one might surmise that its teaching has been integral to higher education. Quite the opposite is true.

The expression "Judeo-Christian tradition" is a rhetorical staple of our culture. It is universally recognized that significant elements of western civilization find their roots in the Hebrew Bible and in the literary, historical, theological, and philosophical heritage of Judaism and the Jewish people which developed out of the biblical foundations. It has become a truism to describe our culture and intellectual history as Matthew Arnold did, when he said that the twin sources from which we draw our values and life-patterns are Hebraism and Hellenism. It is, however, one of the sad facts of higher education in America that even great universities have seldom paid more than *lip service* to the importance of the Judaic component in humanistic studies. For example, while Maimonides exercised considerable influence on the Christian scholastics, such as Aquinas, hardly any attention has been given to the relationship between their philosophies. In the textbook versions, Maimonides is usually represented as concerned to reconcile Judaism with Aristotelian philosophy, with Aquinas supposedly doing the same for Christianity. This is not only a most superficial way of understanding these philosophers, but also one that is in some respects seriously mistaken.

What should be explored is the way in which these medieval figures, rooted in the same tradition, deal with common problems. With regard to ethics, for example, we would expect similar views, since for both philosophers the foundation of morality rests on Scripture. But we find a remarkable difference: Aquinas is a strong adherent of a theory of natural moral law, while Maimonides categorically rejects the idea of natural law and bases his ethics exclusively on Scripture and Rabbinic Law. Each man reads Scripture seriously and with a philosophic purpose, but with differing methods and goals. Both are concerned with the problem of divine attributes, for example. Both offer an extended treatment of the problem of creation in time vs. the eternity of the world. But here, as in ethics, their views differ in highly significant respects. What is called for is a careful examination of each philosopher in the light of the other. This would lead to a deeper understanding of the philosophical teachings of each, provide an opportunity to see how far their differing religious perspectives have philosophical consequences, and bring together two thinkers who are often mentioned in the same breath but rarely studied in a common context.

The phrase "Judeo-Christian tradition" is a serious over-simplification which ignores a rich world of Jewish creativity that requires study for its own intrinsic worth. Athens and Rome are represented today in the intellectual world of the universities. Great monuments of classical and Christian culture have been fully integrated into the academic enterprise. The achievements of Jewish learning, however, have been neglected for too long in the western academic world. The great Jewish texts must now be joined with the western humanistic tradition so that this neglected area of our common heritage may become part of the normal awareness of the educated person.

The literary scholar as well as the theologian needs to know the Hebrew Bible. The student of law and jurisprudence needs to learn something of the Talmudic tradition of legal thought. The historian of philosophy needs to be saved from the parochialism which gives Aquinas an entire volume and Maimonides a single page in a comprehensive history of philosophy.[12]

III.

What can the Jewish concept of learning contribute to our understanding of the goals of undergraduate education today? An answer to this question may yet influence the future of higher education in the United States.

During the first two-thirds of the 19th century in America, the characteristic institution of higher education was the independent college in a small town, supplemented in a few cases by fledgling advanced schools. Given relative isolation, compactness of studies, and limited numbers of students, each college developed a personality of its own—usually a blend of the robust, energetic world of the student and the austere learned formal world of the faculty. This model lingered into the 20th century, especially in small denominational colleges.

In the mid-19th century, two concurrent models arose. The negative reaction of Jacksonian democracy to the "elitist" character of the classical curriculum culminated in 1862 in the enactment of the Morrill Act, which provided for land-grant colleges stressing the teaching of agriculture and mechanics.

In the 1870's, the rapid industrialization and secularization of American society produced a need for specialists that American colleges were not meeting. German universities, however, offered such training, and many young men and women were sent off to study in Germany. The idea of the German institution was brought back to the United States and became the model for graduate work and research.

This concept was seen in the new universities which developed out of the most advanced colleges, such as Harvard, Yale, Columbia, the University of Pennsylvania, and at the leading state universities in the Middle and Far West. The 1870's were marked by the creation *de novo* of the John Hopkins University, Cornell, Stanford, and the University of Chicago. In the 1880's, the adoption of the elective system permitted colleges to add scientific studies and later social science to the classical curriculum.

The next great change in universities came during World War II with the emphasis on war-related research activities and the training of junior military officers. Since 1940, the advancement of knowledge through research rather than the teaching of undergraduates has become the primary objective of most universities.

Since World War II, disciplinary specialization in our faculties has increased and their concentration on research activity has intensified, while the liberal arts college has been torn between the values of general education and those of marketable skills. These trends have been influenced by the rapid development of federal funding for certain areas of higher education and by the sharp increase in the numbers of undergraduates, especially in public sector institutions. One consequence has been pressure on universities to respond more readily to governmental and societal demands for service and research. Another has been to give more casual attention to undergraduates, a development intensified by the rise in undergraduate enrollment, the overtaxing of the physical facilities of universities, and the persistence of high inflation.

In higher education today we are beset by gnawing doubts about the future. We agonize over the goals of liberal arts education. We are troubled by the consequences of governmental financing of higher education and the resulting intervention in the governance of universities. We fear the projected decline in enrollment of 18–22 year-olds, the deterioration of physical plants, and the growth in the proportion of faculty that is tenured. We speculate about the causes of public disenchantment with the value of a bachelor's degree and a loss of public confidence in the academic enterprise. Still other serious issues face educators and boards of trustees, especially in the independent institutions.

The primary issue among all of these vital matters is the clarification of the objectives and values of undergraduate education. The complaint is widespread that many colleges and universities do not present clear guidelines to undergraduates about what is expected of them and what they should seek to achieve in their undergraduate years. Many students, as Father Hesburgh suggests, are in an educational limbo:

> "In a world of sudden and cataclysmic change, simple sanity requires reasonably fixed points of reference. Without navigation, life today becomes irrational wandering, a journey with no homecoming, a voyage without a port of call, a story without meaning or ending."[13]

Many undergraduates today are on a whirlwind tour of random knowledge—if this is Tuesday, it must be Biology.

Above all, a university seeks to be a training ground for the mind. In Jewish experience, a 4000-year tradition of learning produces skepticism about claims of novelty and discovery in the unfettered pursuit of truth. Reinvention of the academic wheel is commonplace. In 1977, Samuel Gould recounted: "Lifelong learning, so vital a part of the American educational dream, is spoken of now as though it were something new."[14]

He then quotes William Allan Neilson writing in 1936 in the introduction to *Webster's Unabridged Dictionary:*

"Within recent years there has been a new emphasis on adult education. In spite of the multiplication of schools and the great increase in numbers of students in colleges and universities, it is more and more recognized that education does not and cannot end with attendance at institutions of learning. It is a lifelong process, in which the school or college is chiefly important in supplying tools and teaching how to use them.[15]

And Gould rightly adds:

"If we chose, we could go much further back into the past and discover statements that antedate Neilson's by decades or centuries. We might even go back to some of the original concepts of how learning takes place, concepts espoused and practiced by people like Socrates or the Talmudic scholars."[16]

One of the most cogent questions we can ask is this: What educational experience do we want graduating seniors to have? What qualities of mind and character does the university seek to nurture in them? I can think of no more pragmatic way to apply my statement of a Jewish perspective in learning than to sketch the qualities that I believe graduating seniors should have.

First, a cognitive mind. The acquisition of knowledge and information remains indispensable, provided we recognize that the learning of facts, theories, ideas, and concepts is perishable. Such knowledge illumines experience, deepens understanding, and influences judgment, provided it springs from a discipline of inquiry that demands challenge and questioning. In recollecting his childhood on New York's lower East Side, Professor Isidor I. Rabi remembers his mother greeting him when he returned from school with the question, "Did you ask any good questions today?" Similarly, the Talmudic tradition stresses a creative humility that admits to the wide variety of possible choices and truths, sometimes in conflict, sometimes even paradoxical, that are inherent in the human condition. One should act, as best as one can, after eliminating reasonable doubt. But one should always keep in mind that reasonable doubt may one day be perceived as fallacy.

A *second* goal is literacy, that is, precision, range, and style in the use of the written language to communicate knowledge and ideas. Each graduate should have analytical capacities to identify issues, collect relevant information, and marshal arguments effectively. Each should learn to read systematically about a topic and arrange knowledge in a coherent pattern. Respect for the written language should be commensurate with its place in human history as the thread of which all wisdom is sewn. The need for literacy does not stop at the threshold of English composition courses.

Because the educated person can never be a finished product, a *third* characteristic is intellectual curiosity, an awareness of the vastness of human ignorance, and an appetite for learning that is satisfied only by systematic reading and inquiry. Once instilled and nourished, these qualities serve for a lifetime of reasoned commitment, open-mindedness, and the pleasure of undiminished discovery.

Fourth is an appreciation of art as esthetic experience and a commentary on our humanity. Involvement in the nuances of art provides another critical faculty to test the validity and meaning of thought and action.

A *fifth* feature of the ideal graduate is tested experience in developing values and judgments about personal, professional, and social concerns. Each graduate should be able to demonstrate a willingness and a capacity to probe contemporary moral issues.

These capacities and skills can be stimulated and nourished by undergraduate study programs. More than ever before, learning to read and speak a foreign language is an essential mark of an educated person. Another mark is some quantitative skill—for example, in statistics, calculus, or computer science—which in a technologically advanced world facilitates problem solving and demystifies the technology upon which we daily become more dependent.

Finally, we should expect each graduate to have studied a significant portion of the world's great literature and acquired a substantial understanding of the history of the Western world and at least one other civilization. Such knowledge liberates one's perspective from the parochial boundaries of American experience and provides a practical way to develop lifelong habits of learning.

As Thorsten Veblen noted:

"The first requisite for constructive work in modern science, and indeed for any work of inquiry that shall bring enduring results, is a skeptical frame of mind . . . the skepticism that goes to make [a person] an effectual factor in the increase and diffusion of knowledge . . . involves a loss of that peace of mind that is the birthright of the safe and sane quietist. He becomes a disturber of the intellectual peace . . ."[17]

We owe much to the young men and women who spend four undergraduate years at our universities. Most important, we owe them, ourselves, and society, a graduate who is "a disturber of the intellectual peace" and whose free pursuit of truth governs professional, familial, and communal life.

David Riesman indicated recently what educational institutions need to do to meet the dilemmas that already beset them. He prescribed "'un-American' combinations of skepticism with faith, fatalism with pragmatic activism."[18]

These combinations may be more ignored than alien in American tradition, but they are acutely akin to the Jewish concept of learning as a form of worship.

Philo, according to Salo Baron, "was by no means wrong when, using Greek terminology, he called the synagogue a school where Jews gather every Sabbath to study the philosophy inherited from their forefathers, and where all kinds of virtue are taught."[19]

This merging of the house of prayer and the house of learning has profoundly affected the Jewish outlook on life through generations of Jewish dispersion. As the aggressive oneness of learning and worship helps to explain the miracle of Jewish survival, so may the Jewish concept of learning as worship stimulate universities to provide those fixed points of reference, those navigational guides which Father Hesburgh noted are so urgently needed by our students in a world of sudden and cataclysmic change.

Then will our educational institutions have earned the right to call themselves truly creative enterprises. Then will our students find that life is not irrational wandering, but a journey with a homecoming, a voyage with a port of call. So may it come to pass.

NOTES

1. Nathaniel Weyl, *The Creative Elite in America,* Washington, D.C.: Public Affairs Press, 1966, p. 92.

2. A. Lawrence Lowell, *What a University President Has Learned,* New York: The Macmillan Company, 1938.

3. Ludwig Lewisohn, *What Is This Jewish Heritage?,* Rev. ed., New York: Schocken Books, 1964, p. 48.

4. Robert Maynard Hutchins, Commencement Address, University of Judaism, Los Angeles: June 24, 1965.

5. Maurice Samuel, *The Professor and the Fossil,* New York: Knopf, 1956, p. 175.

6. *Ibid.,* p. 177.

7. *Ibid.,* p. 178.

8. Salo Wittmayer Baron, *A Social and Religious History of the Jews,* Vol. I, New York: Columbia University Press, 1937, p. 17.

9. Martin Buber, *Kampf um Israel,* p. 297; quoted in *Ibid.,* p. 19.

10. *Ibid.,* p. 289.

11. David E. Drew, *A Profile of the Jewish Freshman,* Washington, D.C.: American Council on Education, 1970.

12. This is the case, for example, in W.T. Jones' *History of Western Philosophy,* a widely used college textbook, which in its more than one-thousand pages does not mention the name of Maimonides once, to say nothing of any other Jewish philosopher. The most massive recent history of philosophy is the nine-volume work by F.C. Copleston. Two of these volumes, totalling almost eleven-hundred pages, are devoted to medieval philosophy. Medieval Jewish philosophy is treated in four pages, two of them devoted to Maimonides. In contrast, Augustine gets fifty pages, Aquinas gets one-hundred thirty-five pages, and Ockham gets one-hundred ten pages.

13. Theodore M. Hesburgh "Making Prophecies of Our Goals," *The Third Century,* New Rochelle: Change Magazine Press, p. 190.

14. Samuel Gould, "A Disease Without a Patient," *The Third Century, op. cit.,* p. 36.

15. Quoted in *Ibid.,* pp. 36–37.

16. *Ibid.,* p. 37.

17. Thorstein Veblen, "The Intellectual Pre-Eminence of Jews in Modern Europe," *Essays in Our Changing Order,* New York: The Viking Press, 1937, pp. 226–227.

18. David Riesman, "Small Steps to a Larger Vision," in *The Third Century, op. cit.,* p. 28.

19. Salo W. Baron, *op. cit.,* p. 289.

The Jewish Component
of Brandeis University

Abram L. Sachar

Brandeis University
Waltham, Massachusetts

The deep concern of Brandeis University for Jewish life and values has been demonstrated by the many special projects it has undertaken and, of course, by its emphasis on a strong Judaic curriculum. Yet it may well be that the Jewish component of Brandeis is an intangible—its unique atmosphere, an atmosphere that has been developed by the nature of its sponsorship and the students and faculty that it attracted. There are certain colleges whose history and sponsorship give them a unique character. They have a special personality, perhaps undefinable but pervasive and intellectually and socially osmotic. They defy a catalogue description because they do not depend exclusively on the courses that are listed. They are vitally influenced by the life-style or the sub-culture of the students and the faculty, the subjects that engage their interest, the causes they espouse, even the adversaries with whom they contend.

Chemistry is chemistry, or at least its basic matter is the same wherever it is taught, as is mathematics, or physics, or anthropology, or modern languages. The academic difference from one school to another comes through only in the quality of the teaching and the reaction of those taught.

When we turn to Brandeis, founded a third of a century ago, we may ask whether there has been time, in just one generation, to develop a special character. I believe there has been. I would say that it is a sensitive social consciousness, a concern for the underdog, resistance to any kind of discrimination. Some of it comes from the prophetic tradition, which has woven the passion for social justice into the warp and woof of Jewish life. Some of it comes from the economic stratum out of which most first-or-second generation immigrant groups emerge. Whatever the historical matrix, the result is plain to see. The student body is unusually activist and is very much concerned with rights. The faculty, brought together for its special skills in diverse academic areas and with no thought of personal temperament or outlook, have somehow quickly shown a more than average concern for the protection and advancement of progressive social values. Indeed, many of them may have been attracted to Brandeis because it afforded a hospitable climate for such concern. I cannot believe it is altogether accidental that the main writing and research going forward so early at Brandeis had to do with the attack on restraints on freedom, restraints that threaten the fullness of life. This would be the reason for the unusual succession of articles and books that stream from faculty who are so often involved in the attack on privilege or the abuse of power. There must be some subtle relationship with the orientation of research in the laboratories that seeks to sustain and enrich life and primarily interests such agencies as the National Institute of Health and the American Cancer Society. There is a similar relationship in the fervent concern of the young people with racial integration and Hungarian freedom fighters and Vietnam. As one of the yearbook editors put it: "At Brandeis the status is certainly not quo."

Of course Brandeis is not alone in such a concern. Fortunately many other universities are in the forefront of the battle to link truth with justice, and Brandeis gravitated naturally to this doughty band. It was not always comfortable for the administration to function in such a climate. We could become very impatient with a student newspaper that probed into every area, far beyond normal student jurisdiction, that scolded, preached, and attacked. It would be much more comfortable to deal with a conforming student leadership, quietly deferential. But these were youngsters who had cut the umbilical cord of filial obedience, and they continued to question and oppose when they reached a college where the environment was favorable for challenging all credentials and sanctions. I imagine that Hosea and Jeremiah and Ezekiel were not easy to live with either, but in the long run they were a lot more creative and valuable than the custodians of the establishment who preceded and followed them. At any rate, the educational process is expected to inflict pain, to cavil and demur and defy. The trustees have asked only that the spirit of criticism be constructive and respectful, even during the most trenchant reappraisal. All of this is in the spirit of the reforming justice for whom the University is named. "Brandeis and Holmes dissenting" was appended to hundreds of majority decisions reached in the Supreme Court. The seal of the University reads *Emeth* (Truth), and its motto comes from the psalmist, who demanded "the search for truth, even unto its innermost parts."

What I have called the special personality of Brandeis, though intangible, was a pervading presence. Every care, however, was taken to make sure that it did not affect our academic objectivity. This undoubtedly disappointed many who, because Brandeis was Jewish-founded, identified it as a Jewish parochial school on a university level. Indeed, preparatory and high school counselors, in offering advice to their graduates, often steered non-Jewish students away from Brandeis, or encouraged intensely Jewish-oriented youngsters to apply there, because it was a "Jewish university." Actually, there was no intention to develop Brandeis as such a parochial school. Its support, indeed, was to be the responsibility of its Jewish sponsors, but it was planned to serve in the tradition of the great schools, from Harvard to the present, which were the nonsectarian gifts of the religious denominations to American higher education.

Nevertheless, by virtue of its sponsorship, it was properly expected that there would be unique strength in the Judaic components (which belonged in the academic structure of any good university), particularly in the Department of Judaic Studies, the library, and in foreign studies, where Israel would be a natural magnet. In developing Judaic studies, we assigned high priority to the classical aspects of Bible, Jewish philosophy and literature, and Jewish history and archaeology. Three outstanding scholars helped to give distinction to this area: Nahum Glatzer, Simon Rawidowicz, and Alexander Altmann.

The first major appointment went to Nahum Glatzer in 1951. He was an Austro-German émigré who had come to the United States in 1938, having taught at both Frankfort and Haifa. His fields were Jewish philosophy, history, and Hebrew literature, and he wrote authoritatively on the life and thought of the German theologian Franz Rosenzweig. He had held a number of fill-in positions at the College of Jewish Studies in Chicago, at the Hebrew Teachers College in Boston, and at the Yeshiva

in New York. But he had been mainly engaged as editor-in-chief for
Schocken Books, publishers of Hebrew and German classics in English
translation. He was a quiet, modest, low-keyed man, deeply respected
by his colleagues and students. Meeting and working with him, one
thought immediately of old-world dignity, and yet the impression never
connoted pomposity. His dry humor always surprised because it usually
emerged from such a serious façade. He had the knack of transmitting
the excitement of Jewish history and literature, and was proud of the
many students whom he sent into the field of Judaic studies. As chairman of the department during its formative period, he was determined to
give it preeminent standing in the world of Jewish studies, and he was
personally involved in recruiting outstanding undergraduates and a distinguished faculty. It was significant that upon retirement, after more
than twenty years, he was the first faculty member to receive the University's honorary degree, recommended for it by his own peers; his most
devoted students presented him with a *Festschrift*.

One of Glatzer's first coups was to bring to Brandeis Simon
Rawidowicz, a Russian émigré. His erudition and the profundity of his
philosophical thinking had earned him full honors among Jewish scholars. But when he came to this country, positions worthy of his background were very difficult to find. When Glatzer called him to Brandeis,
he was filling a modest post in the College of Jewish Studies in Chicago,
then still a third-rate institution with no standing in the Jewish scholarly
world. Typical of his influence was the long ideological discussion that
he carried with the prime minister of Israel, David Ben-Gurion, who
believed that there could be no wholesome, creative Jewish life outside of
Israel, and who therefore regarded the Diaspora as vestigial. Rawidowicz
was devoted to Israel, but he passionately defended the affirmative role
of the Jewish communities in the lands where they had been rooted and
where, despite the assaults of fate, they continued to function. It was the
deep respect in which he was held by the scholarly world and by the
highest echelons of the new Israel that bespoke the influence he created
for the Department of Judaic Studies. I remember a reception at the
White House in honor of the president of Israel, the late Zalman Shazar.
When Thelma and I were presented to him, he exclaimed, "Brandeis—
that's where Rawidowicz is," and he then held up the receiving line to
explain to President Johnson what a magnificent scholar Rawidowicz
was! Tragically, he was lost to the University and the world of scholarship by an early death. He was barely sixty when he died in 1957.

Alexander Altmann was also a German-born scholar. Ordained as a rabbi, he had held one of the most distinguished pulpits in Berlin until the country was engulfed by the Nazis. He found a welcome refuge in England, where he became the chief rabbi of Manchester. When he was recruited for Brandeis, he brought with him a superb reputation for his writings in Judaeo-Arabic philosophy, rabbinical literature, Jewish mysticism, and the eighteenth-century enlightenment. As a "supplement" to his Brandeis classes, he began editing classical texts in a scholarly series, and climaxed his incumbency with a definitive two-volume work on Moses Mendelssohn. His value to the University went far beyond his teaching. In 1963, on a special grant, he made a tour of important Italian libraries and brought back duplicates of ten thousand items, including biblical commentaries, philosophical treatises, Kabbalistic texts, and other documents of priceless historic value. He had them microfilmed and they were deposited in the Goldfarb Library.

Even as the department grew in numbers and distinction, pressure mounted to supplement classical studies and research with training for contemporary Jewish affairs. There was genuine compulsion behind this pressure. It was of no small significance that it had been necessary to build our Judaic faculty almost exclusively with scholars from abroad. The American Jewish community had not yet produced many native-born specialists. Until midcentury there had been little call for them; only a few universities offered courses related to contemporary Jewish life. The upsurge of interest began, undoubtedly stimulated by the Holocaust, the role of Jews in the political and economic life of the United States and Western Europe, their changing fate in the Soviet Union, and, above all, by the emergence of a sovereign Israel. Scholars with this specialization were now very much in demand. Each year there were many offers from institutions where newly established positions now promised dignity and security. But the posts went unfilled except where rabbis were tempted away from their pulpits; they were virtually the only reservoir of competence.

The time was therefore ripe to expand the curriculum in classical studies with offerings in contemporary affairs to help meet the overwhelming need for qualified faculty. It was also important to provide a training center for service in Jewish communal life, welfare funds, philanthropic institutions, and cultural undertakings. The fulfillment came in 1965 through the generosity of a New England shoe merchant, Philip Lown, whose basic communal interest had always been the train-

ing for Jewish leadership. He had played a large role in the development
of the Boston Hebrew Teachers College and had served as its president
for many years. Early in the life of Brandeis he had established the chair
in Jewish philosophy that was held by Altmann. Now Lown provided
the endowment to launch the School of Contemporary Jewish Affairs. A
whole new component was thereby added to the service the University
could render. Additional faculty were brought in for contemporary
Jewish history, the problems of Israel and its relation to the Diaspora,
and American Jewish history. A close relationship was established with
the Florence Heller School, which looked to the Philip Lown School to
offer Jewish background for those who sought careers at the executive
level in areas of Jewish communal service. The enrollment escalated, and
within a few years Brandeis had become the most important center for
the training of Jewish communal leaders.

When the American Jewish Historical Society decided in 1966 to
establish its national headquarters on the Brandeis campus, it further
validated the symbolic central position the University had achieved in
the Jewish community. It was following the precedent of the Virginia
Historical Society and many other similar cultural agencies that had
linked up with college campuses. There were natural, mutual advantages. The Brandeis and Society libraries functioned virtually side by
side, each amplifying the other's resources. In addition, the University's
dining facilities, lectures, and colloquia were all happily merged in an
advantageous partnership with people of similar academic interests. It
should be added that while the headquarters was on campus—or, techni-
cally, contiguous to it—the Society itself was completely autonomous.

The move to Brandeis brought new life to the Society, whose membership rolls increased rapidly and whose scholarly acquisitions soared.
Indeed, much of the archival material on American Jewish history that
had been contributed to the Brandeis library was transferred, for easy
access and specialized procedures, to the headquarters of the American
Jewish Historical Society. The arrangement was permanently validated
after a seven-year trial experience.

It was inevitable that close relationships should be established with
the universities of Israel and that every encouragement be offered to
student and faculty exchanges. The precedent of study and research
relationships by American universities with their foreign counterparts
was of long standing. Already at the beginning of the twentieth century

Yale had sponsored what was a university branch in China—Yale in China—and it brought active exchange of faculty and students. Many American universities and junior-year-abroad programs linked with specially selected foreign institutions. It was following a well-established pattern, therefore, for Brandeis to have many of its students leave the campus for a year abroad, and it was natural for large numbers to choose Israel. Brandeis was in a very literal sense one of the products of the reawakened pride in Jewish dignity and creativity; it came into being in May 1948, in the same month as Israel's Declaration of Independence. At the inaugural convocation in October, Israel was represented by its delegate to the United Nations, Eliahu Elath, who, though not yet a fully accredited ambassador, brought greetings for the newly established state of Israel. At virtually every convocation or commencement, Israeli statesmen and scholars were welcomed as special guests or as recipients of honorary degrees.

Many of the visiting Israelis could not resist the temptation to chide the students for not emigrating to Israel. At an early convocation, in June 1951, when thousands of students converged on the Brandeis campus from more than twenty-five New England colleges, Ben-Gurion scolded them affectionately for not being in Israel. "What are you doing here," he exclaimed, "when there is a *Maase B'reshet*, a work of creation, with so much exhilaration and pioneering adventure, waiting for you in a land that you can help build and fashion!" Some of the Israelis wondered why millions of dollars should be channeled to Brandeis when the American Jewish community was likely to be only a temporary doubtful refuge; surely the day would come when Jewish life in America would suffer the fate of other great Jewish settlements of the Diaspora! But these were only occasional voices, doubtless the reaction to the disappointment that the dreams of equality in the Diaspora had been so tragically betrayed by the Holocaust and so callously accepted by the Christian establishment. There was sober understanding that Israel needed a strong American Jewish life, and that American Jews could profit from a healthy continuing relationship with Israel. Dr. Rawidowicz had expressed the relationship graphically by the geometric symbol of the ellipse with two foci.

Cooperative projects, eagerly promoted by Israeli institutions and by Brandeis, were therefore established early. There was generous scholarship support available for Israeli students who came to Brandeis and encouragement was given to our students to spend some time in Israeli universities, with full credit assigned for satisfactory work done there. Indeed, the American Friends of the Hebrew University, who raised funds in the United States to provide scholarships for American students who wished to study there, noted that largest number from any one college always came from Brandeis.

In 1961 a special approach was worked out for the relationship with Israel by my son, Howard, who had earned his doctorate at Harvard in Middle Eastern studies. He began annual visits to Israel and concentrated most of his writing on the development of Israel and its relationship to the Middle East and the Diaspora. His proposal to Brandeis was to establish a traveling university, with its base in Jerusalem, where the teaching and study would be coordinated. This was to be no junket; the courses would be subjected to the usual standards that the Brandeis faculty maintained at home. They would relate to the social, economic, and political structure of Israel and to the history and politics of the Middle East. These would be supplemented by visits to the Knesset, the law courts, and to local and rural councils. Observation sessions would also be arranged, by special permission, at military training centers. Students would visit cooperative farm settlements, agricultural research stations, newly created industrial areas, irrigation and desalinization projects, and mineral drilling outposts in the Negev Desert. Under the guidance of the late Dr. Yohanan Aharoni, of the Hebrew University, the study of biblical history would be climaxed by watching the digs in the Byzantine ruins of Ramat Rachel. In an almost literal sense all Israel would become the classroom.

To acquire at least a working proficiency in the Hebrew language, it was planned that the students arrive early in the summer for an intensive eight-week *ulpan* training before the regular school term. By then it was expected that the enrollees would acquire at least tolerable conversational ability in order to communicate with the Israelis and to read the Israeli press. The enrollees were not to be limited to Brandeis students but would be drawn from universities across the country, with credit to be transferred for all work certified by the Brandeis Institute.

The complete funding for this ambitious program came from Jacob Hiatt of Worcester, Massachusetts, then a member of the Board of Trustees and later its chairman. Hiatt was a native of Lithuania who had completed his studies there at the national university and who had become an assistant district attorney and a circuit court judge. He immigrated to the United States in 1936 and quickly achieved industrial success as a paper box manufacturer, sharing his good fortune by complete involvement in Jewish and community causes. He became a generous patron of Clark University, where he received a master's degree in history, Holy Cross, Assumption, and the Hebrew Union College, and he was one of the earliest supporters of Brandeis.

The Hiatt students' experience in Israel was, of course, not confined to the Jewish population; every effort was made to bring the group into contact with Israel's Arab citizens, too. A three-day visit to Nazareth became part of the curriculum; this time was used to explore the special problems encountered by the Arab minority in the Jewish state. Hiatt students were the guests of Arab host families, and warm relationships often developed and were maintained. One prominent Arab citizen of Nazareth heaved a sigh when he commented to the Hiatt director: "If only the Jews of Israel were like these American Jews, there wouldn't be any problems!" What he forgot, of course, was that the American students who came to Israel for a relatively short period were not party to the intense political quarrels of the area, and that, once these political issues were solved, there would probably be few obstacles in the way for the same warm relationships between Israel's Arabs and Jews.

Fifteen years later, there were over five hundred alumni of the institute experience, many of whom indicated that the direction of their lives had been changed as a result of their exposure to Israel. Several entered the rabbinate or returned to settle in Israel, and there were at least a half-dozen marriages of fellow participants. In time, the institute was expanded into a two-semester program that included the humanities as well as the social sciences. It has become one of the strongest cultural exchange programs between Israel and Brandeis.

Meantime, there were other special responsibilities that Brandeis could assume because of its special position. In 1956 I was approached by Erwin Griswold, dean of Harvard Law School, who informed me that the State of Israel was eager to launch a major project for the codification of Israeli law, for the newly created state was plagued by the mixture of legal systems and practices that were hopelessly snarled. There was Talmudic law, British law, Arabic law, Turkish law, and the laws that had evolved in an ad hoc way in the successive occupations of the land and the influx of immigrants from nations around the world.

A commission was appointed to study the enormous social and cultural changes that had taken place in recent centuries and to evolve a modern system that could then be submitted for enactment to the Israeli legal authorities and to the Knesset. The project was as sweeping in its scope as the Justinian Code of ancient days and the Napoleonic Code of the last century. Harvard Law School was quite willing to cooperate with the State of Israel and to place its faculty resources at the disposal of the commission. What was needed was the seed money, an initial grant of $100,000, and Dean Griswold hoped that Brandeis, with its access to imaginative and generous supporters, could approach some of them in the interest of a Harvard-Brandeis-Israel legal codification project. It would become a significant contribution not only for the development of a consistent and efficient legal code for Israel; it could become the model for many of the developing countries.

I responded cordially to Dean Griswold's proposal, for it seemed especially appropriate for Brandeis to cooperate. The University was named for the justice who was a son of Harvard, one of the two or three most outstanding students ever produced by its law school, and whose Zionism had been rooted in reason and order and efficiency; therefore, the project was sentimentally as appealing as it was practical. I promised to approach some of our donors and then to remain in a consultant's role with whomever was appointed by the State of Israel to direct the research.

Within the next few months I obtained the ready cooperation of Judge Joseph Proskauer, one of our board members, who had been chief justice of the Supreme Court of New York, and James Rosenberg, who had had a long and successful career as a New York lawyer and was deeply interested in the University. They in turn brought into the project a number of their friends. The funding assured, a research director was appointed, Joseph Leifer, an Israeli with an excellent background in corporation law. By the end of three years, draft codes were ready in several areas. The data was sent on to the authorities in Israel, who assumed responsibility for its further use. The venture was a gratifying example of the special service to Israel that the University could perform.

Another instance of useful intercession came in 1960, after several years of strained relations between Israel and the U.S. State Department that grew out of the Suez War of 1956. It was deemed critical for Prime Minister Ben-Gurion to meet with President Eisenhower on a man-to-man basis to seek better understanding. But there was no initiative from the White House. The Israeli ambassador, Avraham Harman, approached me in the hope of using a ceremonial occasion at Brandeis to provide Ben-Gurion with an opportunity to visit the United States. Courtesy would then dictate that, as a visiting prime minister, he be received by the President. Using University occasions as the instrument for accomplishing diplomatic missions was not unprecedented; the Marshall Plan had been announced at a Harvard Commencement in 1947. Brandeis was a natural intermediary for Ben-Gurion's purpose, and its good offices were quickly made available. In March 1960 a special convocation was planned; the invitation from the White House was extended to Ben-Gurion as soon as it was announced that he was to receive an honorary degree. The meeting between Ben-Gurion and Eisenhower was cordial and effective.

Apparently Ben-Gurion also had confidence in the ability of the University to offer guidance in educational projects that were close to his heart. After he had completed his incumbency as prime minister, he became deeply interested in establishing a university in the Negev, building upon the nucleus that already existed in Beersheba. Early in 1967, he asked me to set up a conference with academicians and administrators to discuss some of the problems that a desert university would have to face and ways of coping with them. I welcomed the opportunity to have him return to the campus and suggested we might use the occasion to tape a television interview in which he could relate some of the dramatic turning points in his long career. We were then sponsoring a program called *Living Biography*, in which we recorded the remembrances of selected contemporaries. Ben-Gurion readily consented and the two purposes were happily combined.

During his stay on campus, in mid-March 1967, I asked some of the most knowledgeable men in the area to join the prime minister for lunch at the Faculty Center. There was our own trustee, Milton Katz, head of international legal studies at Harvard, Jerome Wiesner, provost and later president of MIT, and senior members of our faculty and administrative staff. It was fascinating to watch Ben-Gurion as he interpreted his dream of a university that would not only convert the Negev Desert into what the Bible had termed "a place of springs" but would also help to fructify the arid wastes of the world. Ben-Gurion hoped that when imaginative scientists applied themselves to such problems as the desalinization and purification of brackish water, the whole world would profit. The university would have access to nuclear power, since there was already a fully equipped reactor nearby at Dimona.

As the dreamer talked on, all practical problems seemed trivial. Milton Katz, one of the behind-the-scenes architects of the Marshall Plan, broke the spell. Gently he asked what table of organization Ben-Gurion had in mind, the scope of the university's faculty and research personnel, the necessary facilities, the source of funds—all practical questions. Ben-Gurion looked startled. What table of organization? What funds? What blueprint? "Do you think," he asked, "that there would have been an Israel if we had worried about such matters before moving into action!"

Yet miraculously, the University of the Negev came into being, although, it must be added, it required some hard-nosed administrators to give it shape and form. They were sensible enough, however, in their procedures, never to allow the dream to be eclipsed. They remembered that dreams often produce substantive support, but that support alone is never enough to sustain a dream. And they remembered, too, that when Ben-Gurion moved into the desert and settled with his Paula in the village of S'de Boker, his farewell speech was just one word: "Follow." It was such spirit that vindicated Ben-Gurion's working principle: Anyone who does not believe in miracles is not a realist. Thelma and I visited the university in 1969. Though the facilities for study and research were almost primitive, the esprit de corps of the pioneering faculty and the grim determination of the students were clear evidence that Ben-Gurion's spirit had enveloped the project. It was appropriate that, after Ben-Gurion's death in 1973, the university was renamed for him.

Sometimes, because of the symbolic respect that Brandeis evoked in the political as well as in the academic world, much more was expected of it than could possibly be delivered. Thus, in 1965, I was approached by Avraham Harman, still ambassador of Israel, who expressed grave concern at the increasing unfriendliness of the government of India toward Israel. India had never recognized the sovereignty of Israel and there were no diplomatic relations between the two countries. There was widespread admiration for Israel's democratic institutions, its service to the underdeveloped countries of Africa and Asia, but with eighty million Moslems in its population India's diplomatic dilemma was inevitable. In Nehru's last years and during the incumbency of his successor, Shastri, the diplomatic coolness had turned into outright hositility. Israelis were now continuously denied visas to attend international scientific and cultural conferences in India, even when they were specifically invited by their Indian colleagues.

Harman knew that Brandeis's contacts with Indian academic and political figures had been cordial. At the 1963 Commencement, Nehru's sister, Madame Pandit, had been the featured speaker. There had been a good opportunity to review with her not only the frustrating relations between Israel and India but also the growing anti-American influence there. When Nehru died in the fall of 1964, the memorial to him, in cooperation with the Indian Students' Association of Greater Boston, was planned at Brandeis, and Ambassador B. K. Gandhi of India flew in for it. With such excellent rapport, strengthened further by the continuous stream of Wien students from India, it seemed practical to explore ways in which the University could mitigate the alienation of India and Israel. I consulted with John Kenneth Galbraith, who had returned to Harvard after his post as American ambassador to India. He indicated that one of India's most influential diplomats, M. J. Desai, who had directed the Foreign Office under Nehru, had now retired and was eager to write a volume on the foreign policy of India during the first decades of Indian independence. He could do much of his research and writing if he were attached to a university, and Galbraith offered to be the intermediary if Brandeis invited Desai to accept a visiting professorship. This seemed like an excellent approach, and the invitation for a Ziskind Visiting Professorship was extended and promptly accepted.

Desai spent the 1965–1966 school year on the Brandeis campus, teaching several advanced courses in the history and politics of contemporary India and the Southeast Pacific and pursuing his own research. When Israeli officials visited the campus they conferred with Desai, who offered confidential advice. Unfortunately the times were not propitious for any diplomatic progress. The continued exacerbation of relations between Israel and the Arab states led to the Six-Day War in 1967 and ranged the entire Arab and Moslem world against Israel. Though the intellectual community of India and many of its leaders remained personally friendly, there was no diplomatic improvement with Israel.

But of course it was primarily in promoting academic exchange with Israeli institutions that Brandeis was most influential. A special fund was created by Joseph Foster of Leominster, a plastics manufacturer, who early in the history of the University established an endowed chair in Mediterranean studies, held by Cyrus Gordon. Upon urging by one of his dearest friends, Jack Hiatt, Foster agreed to set up a million-dollar trust whose income would provide an exchange so that our students and faculty could go to Israel to fulfill educational objectives, and their students and faculty could come to us. He died before the program was fully under way, but his wife, Esther, saw that his objectives were fulfilled and the program became one of the strongest links in the relationship between the University and Israel.

The strong emotional tie with Israel was demonstrated dramatically in 1967, when scores of Brandeis students volunteered for service in the war. This outpouring of concern was repeated in the Yom Kippur War of 1973. This response was in keeping with what happened in many colleges where there was a substantial Jewish enrollment. Those who were not accepted or who could not go made financial contributions from their earnings or their allowances, and they organized teams that spent long hours in solicitation of funds. Brandeis, too, demonstrated its concern. It was the first institution in the country to declare a moratorium on fund-raising, during the Israeli crisis, for new capital gifts and endowments and, when sorely pressed to meet its ongoing budget, it weathered its own crisis by concentrating on the collection of older pledges. Wherever possible Brandeis urged its supporters to make their contributions in the form of bonds of the State of Israel, expanding its long-established policy of placing substantial portions of its endowment funds in loans to Israel and in investments in its major industrial and commercial enterprises.

The pledge was given at the inaugural exercises in 1948 that Brandeis would always remain a school of opportunity, that there would never be any restrictions on the basis of creed or color or ethnic origin. This was meant as more than a commitment to avoid quotas in enrollment or employment. It was meant to emphasize that Brandeis was created for learning and scholarship, not for indoctrination. In reviewing the special emphasis and activities that gave the University its "Jewish character," I hope it is fair to conclude that the pledge was not in jeopardy. The Jewishness of Brandeis was in its climate, not its orientation. In the classrooms and laboratories it functioned in the highest tradition of other denominationally supported universities, which protected and encouraged the components that linked them with ancestral traditions without impinging on the completely nonsectarian quality of their academic contribution. It was by meticulously maintaining this sensitive balance that it was possible for Brandeis to earn a reputation for excellence in its studies and research while it also was sought out as an influential center of Jewish learning and communal responsibility.

Arabs and Jews
on the Campus

Jack J. Cohen

*B'nai B'rith Hillel Foundation
Hebrew University*

Shortly after I began my tenure in 1961 as Hillel Director at the Hebrew University in Jerusalem, I met with the leadership of various student groups—the general Students Union, the Orthodox Yavneh and the Arab Student Committee—in order to become acquainted with them, the needs of their constituencies, and their views on programming. I was warned by the Chairman of the Students Union to avoid the Arab Student Committee: "This is an out-and-out seditious group, seeking to undermine the foundations of the State. Have nothing to do with them."

I decided to ignore the advice, basing myself on the fact that Hillel had been requested, years before my assumption of duty, to provide housing for meetings of the Arab students. Since the Committee was their duly elected leadership, I did not see how I could avoid meeting with them and helping to plan their activities, most of which would inevitably take place under Hillel auspices.

Early in 1962, I had my first encounter with an organized group of Arab students. I was treated to a detailed and vigorously presented list of complaints—discrimination in housing and employment, social rejection, difficulties in gaining admission to the University, particularly in certain departments such as the physical sciences, limitations on freedom of expression and movement, and close supervision by the Security Service. The members of the Committee warmed to their task and expressed their concern about the problems of their villages—the lack of electricity and water, the prevalence of the *ḥamullah* (extended family) system and its exploitation by Israel's dominant political parties, the stumbling blocks in the way of Arab women who wish to acquire advanced education, and the "policy" of the Ministry of Education to deny teaching positions in Arab schools to leftists in order to prevent the improvement of Arab secondary education. They accused the Jewish Establishment of robbing them of their lands. They felt, in brief, that they were second class citizens.

And what of the Jewish side? The aforementioned opinion of the Students Union leadership was widely held among the rank and file of the Jewish student body. Furthermore, an atmosphere of cool co-existence prevailed on the campus. As far as the Jewish students were concerned, the fact that the University was open to Arabs was deemed a major concession. It was neither the responsibility nor the desire of the Jewish students to open their arms in comradeship to their Arab counterparts. It was sufficient that they be treated civilly. This attitude was readily understandable in view of the fact that many a Jewish student would return to his studies after engaging in armed conflict with Arab infiltrators or in retaliatory raids across the border. They were unprepared psychologically to distinguish between "friendly" and "enemy" Arabs. Here and there, Jewish students would rally behind the Arabs when they protested against the restrictions of the military government or the arrest of an Arab for alleged seditious activity. Such Jews were few in number and usually led by recognized leftists.

What role could Hillel play in such a situation? The response to this question, even after seventeen years of experience, requires dealing with a massive complex of moral, national, institutional, personal, and logistic factors that defy simple categorization. Yet, without such an effort, no understanding can be reached. The following ideas, while offered out of a background of rich experience, are nonetheless a tentative treatment of this difficult subject.

Problems of Identity and Existence

Arab and Jewish relationships in Israel are conditioned, of course, by the contending philosophies of nationalism which prevail among both peoples.

Both Arabs and Jews in Israel are hard put to define their national objectives to the extent that these impinge on the national aspirations of their respective sides. The Zionist dream for a national homeland never spelled out concretely the political and social terms that are essential to the proper accommodation to non-Jews in Israel. The whole concept of a "Jewish State" begs for clarification and for a consensus as to what can be legitimately protected as the preserve of the majority Jewish group and what cannot be subject to majority wishes and dictate. This clarification becomes increasingly important for Israel's deepening commitment and dedication to democratic statehood.

Israeli Arabs, on the other hand, have never been able to identify themselves clearly. The whole Arab world is convulsed by the questions of Arab identity. What is an Arab, and what obligations does the fact of Arabism impose on all Arabs? Does the present configuration of Arab states accord with the fulfilment of Arab destiny or is it a stumbling block in its way? Where do Islam and Christianity fit into Arab society and self-conceptions of Arab identity? How do increasing industrialization and the secularization of culture and education affect that identity? If these and other overwhelmingly complex issues perplex the Arab world as a whole, how much more difficult is the lot of the Israeli Arab, who has not only been thrust from the status of a majority to a minority but has been confronted with issues of loyalty and, since 1967, of identity, unmatched among his fellow Arabs?

All these questions receive sharp formulation and response on the campus. But the treatment of the problems on the part of the students, until after the Six Day War, did not emerge out of any profound understanding of the historical sweep of events or any effort at intellectual depth. Until about 1970, the Arab students responded eagerly largely to problems of their own status and experience.

In the early sixties the Arab students were just beginning to make their appearance on campus. In 1961 there were only sixty or so Arabs at the Hebrew University. Their concerns were very concrete, as noted above, and to the extent that they went beyond the campus, the problems were those of alleged discrimination by government and non-government institutions. The response of the Jews to Arab criticism also tended to be pragmatic. Arabs had to be kept in their place because they represented a security risk. The Jewish students reasoned—plausibly, from their vantage point—that Arabs, being subjected to daily barrages of propaganda on the radio, and subsequently on television, from Arab countries, could hardly be expected to be immune to appeals to their national loyalty. By and large, however, neither Arabs nor Jews were arguing about identity or national ideology.

The Arabs were articulating resentment against disabilities, and they went beyond the campus only to launch attacks against broad government policies. Military government, land confiscation, economic discrimination, limitation on village development, and housing were among the major items on the agenda of the active elements among Arab students.

Nor were Jewish students, to the extent that they responded to the concerns of their Arab colleagues, any more disposed to raise the debate beyond the level of the specific. They did not refer to such questions as the right to the land. They were satisfied with the vague understanding that Israel was a Jewish state and that there were also Arab citizens who really had no basis for complaints.

All this changed after the Six-Day War. Arab students at the Hebrew University now had East Jerusalem at their disposal, while those studying in Tel Aviv University, Haifa University, and Ben Gurion University (all of which had not yet existed when I took up my post) and at the Technion (where a few Arabs had begun to study) were brought into contact with their fellows from the conquered areas. Interestingly, the first contacts seemed to heighten the Israel Arab's sense of separate identity as an Israeli who had benefited from the cultural and economic advantages of Israel citizenship. I vividly recall conversations with Arab students who expressed their dislike of rooming with East Jerusalem families whose traditional Arab hospitality they found oppressive. The families made too many demands on their time and refused to recognize their need for privacy and for the opportunity to study.

Subsequently, however, as Arab students were exposed to the new Arabic newspapers, journals, and books that suddenly became available to them, as they took a new and deeper look at their brothers who had for almost twenty years experienced the benefits and responsibility of autonomy, as the Israeli occupation dragged on and Palestinian consciousness came to the fore, their thinking took on an increasingly ideological coloring. For the first time, I heard Arab students identifying themselves as Palestinians. The designation has often carried more emotional than ideological flavor, but the ideological implications have become clearer. Arab students are now more hesitant than ever in citing their identities as Israelis. They have not turned their backs on Israeli citizenship, but they make a point of stressing that they are Palestinians who happen also to be citizens of Israel—similar to Jewish Israelis who sometimes argue, as Ben-Gurion did, that they are Jews first and then Israelis. The articulation of such self-identification is, however, far different for the Arab than it is for the Jew. For the former, the distinction between Palestinian and Israeli carries political overtones that do not affect the Jew as Israeli. The former has to face up to his attitude toward the P.L.O. and to his aspirations for the future. Were a Palestinian state to be established, would he leave Israel to take up citizenship there? Would he want to acquire Palestinian citizenship and extra-territorial rights while remaining an Israeli?

This new state of mind came to the fore and, to some extent, was molded by and during the guard-duty crisis at the Hebrew University and Haifa University in 1975–76. This is not the place to record the details of that controversy. Suffice it to say, however, the Arab Student Committee used all of its influence to prevent Arab students from doing guard duty in the dormitories of the universities, arguing that the whole matter was a political issue. By doing guard duty, they would be violating their conscience.

Initially, right wing Jewish students took the view that any student who would not do his share for the common good should not be rewarded with a dormitory room. As the controversy continued, however, the real political polarization became apparent. Arab students were groping toward a Palestinian identity; Jewish students viewed this development as a threat to the existence of the state.

There were other, no less important, factors in the guard duty episode, but I have highlighted the political element as an indication of how Arab students respond to the Palestinian challenge to their identity. During the last three years, up to the writing of these observations, the process of radicalization among Arab students has been rapid, particularly on the part of their leadership. Whereas in the years prior to the Yom Kippur War the Arab Student Committee at the Hebrew University reflected the thinking of the Communist Rakah party, there has been a steady move in the Committee toward support for the P.L.O. Rakah candidates for office have been rejected, largely because Rakah, for all its own criticisms of Israel domestic and foreign policy, accepts the existence of Israel and is prepared to function reasonably within its political framework.

As I write this analysis, the picture is changing again. Even before the dramatic developments at Camp David, the Arab students were showing signs of dissatisfaction with their new style of leaders. They had discovered that the latter's rhetoric aroused strong opposition even among moderate Jews and that aside from expressing political opinions, the leaders did nothing to treat the ongoing problems which continue to plague the Arab student community. By the time this essay appears in print a new mood will undoubtedly prevail among Arab students.

It is remarkable, given the background depicted above (and it is only a small part of a vast panorama), that the confrontation of Arabs and Jews on campus has been virtually free of violence. In the period between 1961 and 1978, I can recall only one incident, at the height of the guard duty controversy, when violence broke out in the form of rock throwing. There have been incidents that would justify expectations of outright conflict (to cite just a few—the bomb blast in a student cafeteria at the Hebrew University, Arab student refusal to condemn terrorism, the increasing tension attendant upon border unrest), but to the credit of both Arab and Jewish students, the antagonism between them has been controlled and their disagreements expressed in verbal terms alone. This phenomenon is itself worthy of some study; it seems to be unparalleled. For our purposes, both the problems and the actors provide the setting within which Hillel has worked with the two groups of students.

The Hillel Involvement

Why should Hillel have been heavily involved in Arab-Jewish relations on campus? The simplest answer is that the Hebrew University, in the late fifties, discovered that the few Arab students then studying in Jerusalem had come under strong anti-Israel influences. They had no social outlet of their own, and Hillel was asked to provide it.

This answer, however, barely scratches the surface. Why should not the University itself have treated the needs of the Arab students? This is a problem far more weighty than the simple question seems to suggest. For the truth is that education has to be based on a philosophy and on clear objectives. Neither of these prerequisites seems to have been adequately conceived by any modern university. Beyond the dedication to truth and free inquiry, it is virtually impossible for a university to formulate a philosophy that would give unity and purpose to its curriculum and hold out to students a vision of life implicit in that philosophy.

The Hebrew University has always been forthright and proper in handling the academic problems of the Arab students. The only reservation to this remark would apply to the limitations placed upon Arabs in regard to acceptance to certain courses of study that have security overtones. But the most crucial problems that Arab and Jewish students have to overcome in regard to their common future as Israelis are to a great degree ideological and require decisions and commitments. They are problems that will be carried forward into an era of peace. What position is the University to take? Can it take any position? This is a matter of debate. Meanwhile, a forum has been needed in which Arab and Jewish students can conduct a continuous examination of their situations, learn how to articulate their questions, and grope for answers. Hillel, by virtue of its dedication to pluralism and fellowship between students, was and is the natural choice to undertake this venture.

Attempting to translate that dedication into concrete programming has been fascinating and difficult. Hillel was first forced to take a position in regard to the Arab Student Committee. By acceding to the request of the Chairman of the Students Union that we should eschew all contact with the Committee, we would have rendered all effective contact with the Arab students impossible. Such a step would have been a signal to the Arabs that Hillel, after all, is not an independent institution but simply a part of the "Establishment." On the other hand, by recognizing the Committee, Hillel risked the danger of being branded by Jewish students as outside the Zionist consensus.

Our decision to work with the Arab Student Committee was made in full awareness of this dilemma and also in full realization of the political motivations of the Committee. We were motivated in our decision by educational considerations alone, and we understood that we should have to steer a careful course if we were to maintain our independence of outside pressures and, at the same time, gain and preserve the confidence of both Jewish and Arab student leaders.

What were these educational considerations? First, the University wished us to foster good relations between Jews and Arabs on campus. That implied contact between the two groups, which would have been impossible had we rejected one set of leaders or another.

Second, as long as the rules of the academic game are adhered to, pluralism demands confrontation of ideas. Hillel had to fight for the creation of an environment in which opinions could be exchanged without acrimony, and that, in turn, required us to confront unflinchingly and fairly even the most extreme and antagonistic views.

Third, in a situation in which advantaged and disadvantaged are educated together, the latter require special encouragement. Preventing that encouragement from becoming paternalistic is essential to good education, and we have always been on our guard against this danger.

The strategy we employed was successful until the last three years. The Arab students did, indeed, look upon Hillel as their center, and we were trusted as a place where their interests were understood and their views given a fair hearing. The Arab Student Committee discovered that the Hillel staff insisted on programs that were varied, representative of the pluralism in the Arab student community, and pegged to a university standard of excellence. Many a planning session was heated; criticism on our part against one-sidedness or refusal to accept as a speaker a member of an outlawed group like Al-Ard was not always taken graciously. On the other hand, some of our policy decisions raised doubts in our own minds, such as the time we cancelled a program with an Al-Ard leader only to discover that the students came right back with a suggestion that we invite another Al-Ard personality who had written a book in Hebrew on Israel's Arabs that was being widely circulated in the country. Was he to be banned by Hillel while everyone was reading his research? The book was legal; its poison could be read by even the most naive. Was Hillel to refrain from inviting the author and to confront him with a serious critic so that students could at least hear two sides? After consulting a group of University teachers, we decided to let the barrier down and invite to the campus anyone wanted by the Arab students, provided that he was able, by general agreement, to give a college level presentation. To this day, I am not convinced that I was wrong in inviting the second one, despite the fact that he left Israel to become a prominent P.L.O. publicist. Sidney Hook's distinction between heresy and conspiracy is extremely relevant to Israel, but the preservation of free speech also assumes added significance in a setting in which every deviant opinion can be held up as a danger to national security.

In any case, programming with and for Arab students is a complicated matter, involving political alertness and astuteness, an awareness of the disparity between Jewish and Arab perceptions of reality, a capacity to be simultaneously firm and fair, and a willingness to take many risks.

Yet, despite my conviction that the method and the spirit of our approach are right, they did not prevent the deterioration of our relationship with the Arab student body as a whole and the Arab Student Committee in particular. A detailed account of the steps which led to a break between Hillel and the Arab Student Committee would be an interesting case study. In short, the new style leaders described above evidently decided that Hillel's brand of liberalism was too Jewishly nationalistic and that since the institution could not be used for their specific political purposes, the time had come to the place Hillel beyond the pale for loyal Palestinian Arabs. Contrived stories—all unfounded in fact—were circulated among the Arab students in order to prevent co-operation with Hillel. That the attack did not completely succeed is evident from the continued progress of the project in Arab-Jewish understanding, which Hillel has operated since 1968. However, it is true that large numbers of Arab students, scattered around the wide-flung campus of the Hebrew University, have had no opportunity to judge the validity of the "charges" and no longer turn to Hillel. There are other geographical considerations that help explain the present limitations of our work, but let no one be deluded into underrating the extent to which a handful of dedicated ideologists can twist truth and warp minds.

These observations should not be construed as an attempt at apologetics. I am certain, even as I write these lines, that we are about to open a new chapter in Hillel's role in Arab-Jewish understanding on campus. I wish, however, to make the point as strongly as I can that educators who work in this field have to arm themselves with the following understandings:

1. Arab-Jewish relations in Israel, for all that they share common elements of intergroup accommodation, are unique, by virtue of the uncertainties of identity in each community, the dilemma both peoples face in claiming title to the same soil, the wide disparity between their cultures, the demographic isolation of the Jewish community of Israel in an Arab world, and a wide variety of other factors.

2. Israel's campuses are also unique. Jewish students begin their university studies after army service, which affects not only their chronological relationship to Arab colleagues, who tend to be several years younger, but quite obviously their psychological preparedness or willingness to be open to the latter. In dealing with any of the issues between the two groups, which in themselves require intense and intensive intellectual exercise, the psychological barriers must be recognized and taken into account.

3. The volatile nature of the conditions surrounding the campus will frequently render useless carefully planned programming. Thus, the educators cannot afford to lose heart when well-laid plans are undermined by factors beyond their control. While it is well for them not to

overestimate the power of the educative process, it is equally important for them so to conceive their role as to recognize the long range impact of soundly conceived efforts. Seeming failures often prove to have a positive impact in years to come, when the student has had an opportunity to reflect on earlier experiences.

4. All education on campus is, after all, only a little chunk of the life experience of the student. Ours is not the obligation or the capacity to complete the educational task, but neither are we free to desist from it. With respect to Arab-Jewish relations, the educator has to ask what part of the job is his to perform. In this regard I shall list below a few conclusions at which I have arrived.

5. Israel's universities have not come to grips with many of the aspects of Arab-Jewish relations which require solid intellectual treatment. The universities ignore the psychic needs of Arab youths, a failure which also characterizes primary and secondary education in the Arab sector. There are, admittedly, courses in several departments on the history and the current status of the relations between the two peoples and the nature of the internal problems of each group. Even in this regard, however, the picture is far from satisfactory. For example, at the Hebrew University, Arab students cannot yet acquire adequate training in the special social work needs of the Arab village and the special skills required to meet these needs. Nor have the universities risen to the challenge presented by the unique position which Arabs occupy in Israeli society. If the universities are not to contribute to the growth of a disaffected and bitter Arab intellectual class, they must recognize that their academic obligation toward the Arab students is only part of their total educational responsibility. Were such a realization to be actualized, Hillel's role in Arab-Jewish student relations might be a lot easier and perhaps less important than it is at the present time.

The Future

Since Hillel's role cannot avoid being normative, our expectations regarding the future will condition our future programming. The following, based on our accumulated experience, seems to be the likely direction of our work for the foreseeable future:

1. Clearly, Arab-Jewish relations are determined by the vision both Arabs and Jews have of their own people and its destiny, and by the ability of both to achieve levels of commonality.

2. Hillel, therefore, has to try to help Jewish and Arab students, separately and across group lines, to work through their self-pereceptions and their conceptions of how the out-group fits into the common society of Israel. For the Arabs, there is the added problem of the extent to which they can ever feel—or want to feel—part of the culture of Israeli society and the political reality of the State of Israel. These considerations are, of course, not only matters of dialectic. A lot will depend on how interaction between Israeli Jews and Arabs proceeds in the decades ahead. If peace comes about, the problem will become even more complicated as a result of the inevitable contacts with a variety of Arab minds. Yet the situation holds out enormously interesting possibilities for study of the human condition. Hillel, as part of the University community, can anticipate many exciting sessions of soul-searching and historical and social analysis on the part of Jewish and Arab teachers and students.

3. How much interaction will take place between Arab and Jewish students in Israel? It is hard to predict, but, given peace, I hazard the guess that there will be three trends operating simultaneously. On the one hand, the search for identity and cultural roots on the part of both Jews and Arabs will intensify. These two trends will have the effect of encouraging a respectable coexistence on the part of two groups who recognize one another's rights to self-definition. But there will be a third trend in which Jews and Arabs who recognize the necessity of their creating a common, or at least an interactive, society in Israel will want to share experiences together. This trend will produce results that we cannot predict except in broad terms. Their vision may result in creating mixed neighborhoods, a degree of intermarriage, cultural departures, economic interaction, and political cooperation—in brief, a new kind of Israel society. The campus will undoubtedly become a focal point of such a development, with all the tensions and pain that accompany the shattering of old notions and the striking out in new directions. Hillel will have to contribute its share to interpreting what is happening and enabling the students to be aware of the dangers and opportunities for themselves individually and as members of these two proud peoples.

4. In brief, our work is likely to become less concerned with overcoming political difficulties and more involved in the very profound problems stemming from the national, cultural, and spiritual development of Israel's Arab and Jewish intellectuals.

The Uses of Jewish Values in Counseling Jewish Students

Eugene J. Lipman

Temple Sinai
Washington, D.C.

Dedication

Eva and Alfred Jospe have been affectionate and exciting friends for many years. The depth of feeling my wife and I have for them required my acceptance of the flattering invitation to participate in this Festschrift as a labor of love.

Preface

This paper is fundamentally a preachment based on training, observation, experience, some reading, and subjective notions. It explicates the ways a Jewishly committed counselor can use Judaism to help Jewish students with reality problems, to help them attain an increased consciousness of the Mitzvah/Averah dichotomony inherent in every decision, to help them acquire a greater capacity to make good decisions.

I

Religion-oriented counseling is not a fringe form of psychotherapy or a variation of it. To be sure, the counseling relationship and counseling sessions can have therapeutic value for the student. But so can a good cry on a friend's shoulder, or a session at a local *bierstube* with the gang, or any of a dozen other forms of positive human interaction. However, some formal distinctions need to be made between religious counseling and all forms of psychotherapy. These involve the nature of the counselor, the nature of the student, the nature of the relationship between them: assumptions, goals, approaches, boundaries, terms.

Who is the counselor to Jewish students? Whether rabbi or lay person, the counselor is, among other characteristics, a representative of Judaism and of the Jewish community. Prerequisites for such counselors should be a solid Jewish background and commitment, and specific training in interpersonal relationships and counseling techniques.

From case-books of religious counseling prepared by both Jewish and Christian experts, I have gotten the strong impression that Dr. Carl Rogers, in the non-directive phase of his professional evolution, stood at Mt. Sinai and received Torah-true, exclusive revelation regarding counseling by religious leaders. For example, Schnitzer (1956) and Perlman (1969) compiled case studies in rabbinical counseling—the former general in character, the latter concentrated on students. As one reads the counselor's contributions to dialogue with the counselee, two omissions are clear: at no time is it made manifest that the consultation takes place *because* the counselor is a Jew; at no time does a specific Jewish idea, principle, concept, or value receive explicit attention. "You feel that . . ." a la Rogers, is the constant. Insights out of the Jewish experience are not discussed or utilized in the counseling process.

Who, then is the Jewish counselor? One polarity of response is represented by the late Rabbi Henry Kagan. He believed deeply that the rabbi could and should be a soul healer, a therapist. He believed the rabbi could practice therapy, using all the tools and techniques of psychotherapy, including psychometric tests. (Kagan 1954)

Dr. Abraham Franzblau represents the other polarity. He argued for "a ministry of counseling" categorically different from psychotherapy. (Franzblau 1955) He listed nine ways in which the role and function of the religious counselor are and should be different from the role and function of the psychotherapist. They included, among others, the occasional giving of direct advice, the obligation to rebuke, the giving of solace and comfort, the performance of tasks which might help the counselee, the use of prayer when appropriate.

My view has been previously stated:

". . . the chief difference between pastoral counseling and forms of psychotherapy lies in the goal of the process. Pastoral counseling should not aim to change the personality structure of the counselee; that is the job of the psychotherapist. Pastoral counseling should aim to change either the behavior or the attitudes or both of people who are generally functional in their worlds. Certainly persons who come for pastoral counseling are under stress, but there need not be any psychopathology present as a prerequisite for counseling to be undertaken. I am not suggesting that only topical, immediate, problem-centered counseling is valid for the pastor. Spiritual counseling can cover a broader spectrum. But pastoral counseling begins with a problem and the pastor should be bound, in his/her own mind, to work at the present problem, expanding the field only when necessary." (Lipman 1978)

In sum, the Jewish counselor to Jewish students is not some sort of fringe psychotherapist. He/she is a person chosen by the student for consultation on problems, at the student's initiative, for the student's purposes. The Jewishness of the counselor is an aspect of the counselor's person. It should be a conscious factor in the counseling process.

II

What are some of the characteristics of the Jewish student who comes for counsel?

1. The student volunteers to see the counselor. The student does not pay the counselor, and consequently can invest only the need or needs which brought on the counseling request. When the student feels the need has been met, or cannot be met, by the counselor, no further sessions will be forthcoming. Student life being what it is, most counseling relationships are brief, regardless of the complexities of the problems involved. The students' calendars preclude a long-term relationship.

2. The student almost always comes about a specific problem. If, during their conversations, the counselor and the student agree that a more general process of personality change is indicated, the counselor may be asked for referral to an appropriate person or agency. Otherwise, the counselee must be considered a functioning student with a problem which is amenable to the knowledge and skills of a Jewish counselor.

3. The student has chosen to approach a Jewish religious counselor. Why? There may be several motivations:

a. Either the person of the student or the nature of the problem makes it desirable to bring the problem to a Jewish religious counselor.

b. The person of the counselor makes it desirable to bring the problem to him/her. This may be the result of previous, more "routine" contacts between counselor and student: religious services, lectures, classes, informal conversation. Or this may be the result of the title and office of the counselor. The contact may be undertaken because of the Jewishness of the counselor, or despite it. (see Noveck 1956 and Schnitzer 1952)

c. For the counselor, the motivations are not relevant. His/her own role-justification remains constant: Jewish counselor.

III

Webster's dictionary (3rd international, 1963) defines counseling as "a practice or professional service designed to guide an individual to a better understanding of his problems and potentialities . . ." This definition is valid for the counselor of students.

The practice is based fundamentally on mutual commitments by the counselor and by the student: the student must describe and discuss the problem truthfully; the counselor must listen concentratedly and attempt to help. (Segal 1959)

Katz (1963) emphasizes the primal significance of highly developed empathic capacities in the counselor. Quoting an anonymous English writer, he accepts this definition of empathy: "To see with the eyes of another, to hear with the ears of another, and to feel with the heart of another." Katz acknowledges that this principle is not acceptable to all schools of the helping professions. Practitioners belonging to what he characterizes as the "insight" group stress a minimum of active or direct participation and feeling on the part of therapist or counselor. Freud (1919) wrote of "abstinence" as the proper climate of psychoanalytic therapy. According to him, the diminution of anxiety resulting from empathy or affection between therapist and patient would slow down the analytic process.

On the other hand, there are schools of counseling theory which emphasize "relationship" between therapist or counselor and patient as essential to the therapeutic process. The person of the therapist, the feelings of the therapist, the attitudes of the therapist—all contribute to the expanding emotional capacities of the patient.

If my contention is correct, that deep personality change is not the goal of campus counseling, then there is no need to evaluate the two approaches. The religious counselor should belong to the second, the "relationship" group, no matter what. (Cf. Schnitzer 1950)

Of course, the counselor needs to exercise control to maintain some detachment.Too much identification with the student and the student's problem would have adverse effects on both the student and on the counselor. The student could become overly dependent and/or take on more guilt because of the counselor's suffering. The counselor could endanger his/her own privacy, or that of the student, and even establish a dependency on the student's needs. The counselor walks a rather narrow road, but it is clearly marked.

IV

Two kinds of principles should be in the consciousness of the Jewish counselor in responding to the stated needs of a student:

There are general principles of counseling which must be taken seriously.

There are general and specific values of Judaism which must be taken seriously.

The counselor to Jewish students should be trained in the general practice of counseling. Some of the principles have roots in Jewish thought as well as in psychological theory. Among them should be noted:

1. The counselor must be able to listen carefully and creatively, using more than ears alone. Words, nuances, physical affect—faces, eyes, hands, skin tension, body—all must be observed by the counselor to ascertain the maximum possible truth and reality of the student's situation or problem. It has been suggested (Kagan in Noveck 1956) that the contemporary rabbi has been conditioned so strongly to talking that real listening is difficult. To the extent that this suggestion is accurate, it jeopardizes good counseling by rabbis. Learning to listen creatively is a prerequisite to competent counseling.

2. The counselor must not serve as a judge. Hille's dictum is both appropriate and essential: אל תדין את חברך עד שתגיע למקומו "Do not judge another person until you find yourself in his situation." (Pirke Avot 2:5) That dictum is susceptible to two interpretations, one of which is not applicable here (In effect: do not judge another until you are as wise, as competent, or as prestigious). But the words also refer to moral judgments of other humans.

One of the frequent conflicts within the religious counselor is between the behavior of the student and the principles and values of the counselor's religion. However, any counselor, whether or not in a religious setting, should be conscious of the deep difference between agreement and acceptance. Schnitzer (1951) quotes Carroll A. Wise, one of the pioneer Protestant leaders in pastoral counseling:

"The pastor in accepting and understanding . . . is indicating his interest in the person, rather than the problem. He is not identifying his own role with that of God. He is performing a healing function within a much larger life process, not a judgmental function which is not his to perform any way. He is functioning in a way that binds together, rather than erecting more barriers."

To refrain from arguing about differences or condemning behavior viewed by the counselor as irreligious or immoral does not constitute agreement. Acceptance does keep doors open and make counseling possible. It does not follow, however, that the counselor may never rebuke or disagree with the student if such response appears appropriate to the goal of the counseling process. (Franzblau 1955 and in Noveck 1956, p. 190)

3. The counselor must not take over the decision-making from the student. The expansion of the will of the individual is certainly a major goal of counseling, as it is of all Jewish thought and practice. To make the student dependent on the counselor and subject to his/her authoritative will would be a violation of all canons of counseling and Jewish ethics. (See Schnitzer 1952) The counseling process should aim to help the student become a more independent, stronger, more self-reliant person. In Jewish terms, the student should come to know more firmly what a Mitzvah is and that he/she has the capacity to perform it.

4. Not only should the counselor avoid making decisions for the student; the counselor should consciously refrain from manipulating or pressing the student toward a decision desired by the counselor. The use of charm and other seductive techniques is a great temptation, to be eschewed at all times and at all costs. If the counselor is a rabbi, he/she must be especially careful not to influence students seeking vocational help in the direction of Jewish professional choices. The ego gratification for the counselor in producing disciples is both tempting and dangerous.

5. There is another danger in the authority status of the counselor: self-deification. The counselor is not all-wise. There are many other sources of wisdom available in the counseling process, and they should be used. Referral of the student for specific expert counsel—to special-

ists, to literature, to institutions—is frequently commanded and commendable.

6. *Derech eretz*—proper, courteous conduct—toward every human being is a cardinal principle of Judaism and of all counseling. There may well be no way for the counselor and the student to relate as peers, but there must be *derech eretz* between them, no trace of condescension or patronizing on the part of the counselor. In Va'Yikra Rabba, we are reminded that דרך ארץ קדמה לתורה *derech eretz* preceded Torah. But the phrase can be translated: *Derech eretz* takes precedence over Torah.

7. The absolute confidentiality of all conversations between counselor and student is essential. In the fourth century, Rabba, the great Babylonian Amora, expounded: "Whence do we know that if a man had said something to his neighbor the latter must not spread the words without the informant's telling him 'Go and say it?' From the Biblical text: 'The Lord spoke to him out of the tent of meeting saying . . .' (Leviticus 1:1)." The word "saying," said Rabba, meant: You have permission to repeat it. Without explicit permission, no word spoken may be repeated. Though there is no way for the counselor to enforce it, the student should know the desirability of mutual confidentiality. The counselor should no more be quoted without permission than should the student.

8. The basis of all counseling should be reality. The student should have no illusions about the counselor's capacities—or about anything else, for that matter. Youths have the right to see visions (Joel 3:1), but not to take fantasy into the real world or into real relationships. For the counselor to support illusion, let alone to foster it, cannot be useful. If Max Weber was correct about the young, that "experience has not yet hardened them to imperfection" (*Politics as a Vocation*), then the counseling experience should be one of the hardening forces.

V

There are specific Jewish concepts which are relevant to the counseling process. Those are not necessarily uniquely or exclusively Jewish either in origin or in their working out—but Jewish they are.

Over the ages the thinkers of Judaism have transmitted to us a most realistic view of the human person, of human relationships, human aspirations, human rights, human limitations.

Even though theology, philosophy, ideology are not "official" aspects of Jewish law and, consequently, differences of opinion regarding them are normal and acceptable, there is little disagreement with the concept that the human soul is unique, related to the Divine, and not tainted at birth. There is a deep consciousness among Judaism's thinkers that both the *yetser tov*—inclination to do good—and the *yetser ha'ra*—the inclination to do evil—are built into us. There is little disagreement with the concept that human beings have freedom of will, that they can deliberately decide to do that which is known to be good or known to be evil. Judgment, ultimately, is God's to render regarding human actions. But the God of Israel is merciful and forgiving, and no sin is beyond Divine forgiveness. Guilt is inevitable for any Jew who takes seriously the Covenant between God and Israel, who tries to live a life of Mitzvot as responses to Divine command, and who must recognize the gap between his/her performance and those commands. But confidence in the reality of forgiveness, following sincere repentance, should prevent guilt from festering into emotionally-crippling neurosis.

This approach of Judaism to the nature of the human has two values in the counseling process: it grounds the student's responses to other people and to life's experiences in a positive reality and it gives the student's own life a real sense of possibility, of hope. No situation need be hopeless.

In Kabbalah, Jewish mystical speculation, "oneness" is a key concept. Before there was any existence as we know it, there was En Sof—the Boundless, the Totality. By a mystical process of Zohar—radiation—En Sof became fragmentized within and existence came into being. But the ultimate aim of existence is to re-create total oneness: En Sof, the Boundless.

Whether or not this speculation is of significance to any individual, its emphasis on oneness is not without relevance. In our society there is much talk and much writing about the integration of the individual, about alienation from self as a deep and epidemic problem, about at-one-ness with the self as a great goal. In Judaism, the process of Tik-kun—of repairing broken fragments, of coming to oneness—is a real one, and the relating of the cosmic process to the individual is possible. This conviction of Jewish thinkers can be not only a comfort, but also a spur and a challenge to a student if it is properly introduced and used by the counselor.

Many students who come for counsel are beset with anger and hostility—directed against others, undirected and diffuse, or directed against self. Our society has taught from early childhood that all anger is bad. So many learn to suppress it, too often. When it cannot be suppressed, its expression brings on more guilt, and more suppression and/or depression.

The thinkers of Judaism wanted people to feel warmly and friendly toward one another. Impulsive anger, unnecessary hostility—these were condemned. But the qualifying adjectives are significant. There is proper anger; there is righteous hostility. In Leviticus (19:17) we read: "You shall not hate another person in your heart." The commentators underscore "in your heart." When it is necessary to be hostile, do not keep it in your heart; let it be open. Consequently, in the heart, inside, there should be no residual hate. It has been expressed when justified, used, all used up. For the counselor, this can be a usable insight.

In Leviticus (19:11) it is written: "You shall not steal; you shall not deal deceitfully or falsely with one another." And in Exodus (23:7) we read: "Keep far from falseness."

On those two verses the sages of Judaism built the principle of intellectual or emotional theft, *g'nevat da'at*. There are seven kinds of theft; "foremost among them is the one who would steal people's minds/hearts." (Tosefta Bava Kama 7:8) The implications of this principle range from the prohibition against lying to forms of dissembling, manipulation, hypocrisy. Hirsch (1962 ed.) devotes several pages of his *Horeb* to the destructive and sinful aspects of *g'nevat da'at*. Its implications for the counseling of Jewish students will be touched on here.

VI

The spectrum of problems which students may bring to a counselor is broad. In the only such survey available, Blakeman and Handley (1952) studied 126 colleges and universities and their religious counseling services. They found the following problems brought to religious counselors, in order of frequency: morals and religion; college adjustment; future education and vocational choice; finance, living conditions, employment; socio-psychological relations; social, recreational, religious activities; personal-psychological relations; home and family; health and physical development.

The list which follows is not the result of a survey. It consists of problems which I believe are brought by Jewish students to Jewish counselors with some frequency.

1. *Information-seeking: immediate need*

The student may be looking for source material for a term paper or other assignment, or for counsel about approaching such a project. The student may come seeking ideas about programs in Israel or a Jewish service project. The student may be seeking part-time employment, or need a reference from the Jewish counselor, or want help in getting an interview, or looking for ideas about job availability. The student may simply want to know the name of the best florist in town.

Not all information questions will necessarily tap into the Jewish knowledge or campus know-how of the counselor. Nor will all these requests for information involve conflicts within the student which require any kind of ongoing counseling. But some will—either in the student's mind or, eventually, as conversation ensues, in the minds of both parties.

The primary Jewish value which should be in the counselor's consciousness when dealing with this category of help-seeker is the prohibition against *g'nevat da'at*, intellectual or emotional theft.

The counselor should not bluff when he/she does not know about the school or about its surroundings. To bluff is to commit *g'nevat da'at.*

It would also be *g'nevat da'at* for the counselor to give the student less than full data for a course project because of the counselor's bias, religious or other. The counselor may not advocate Orthodox, Conservative, Reform, Reconstructionist, Humanist, or any other expression of Judaism as *the* truth in recommending readings or sources to the student.

It would be *g'nevat da'at* for the counselor to give the student illusions about his/her power to produce a job, or a positive response from the financial aid office, or acceptance into a summer program.

It would certainly be *g'nevat da'at* as well as extortion for the counselor to expect any form of *quid pro quo* for help rendered.

2. *Information-seeking: long term*

The student may come to discuss graduate schools. There may be aspects of conflict within the student or with parents, with fiancee or with spouse, with faculty adviser or with friends. The student may come to discuss vocational decisions which precede applications to graduate schools.

G'nevat da'at is a real temptation. The counselor can easily develop an ego investment in influencing the choice of graduate schools, in exercising power. The temptation becomes particularly sensitive with the expanding number of Jewish students who may be considering careers in Jewish communal service.

The Talmud properly urges: "Beware of one who gives counsel according to his own interests." (Sanhedrin 76b)

3. Information-seeking: specific Jewish data

The student may come to ask about some aspect of Jewish law, Jewish practice, Jewish theology or philosophy, the Jewish people—because he/she wants to know. The question may have come up in class, or in a Hillel seminar, or in informal conversation. Or the student may come to ask when the calendar would forbid a contemplated marriage, or when to stop saying Kaddish for a deceased parent, or where to go to Seder during the campus theater's spring tour.

The answers to these questions may or may not involve counseling. Whether they do or do not, the principles adduced above apply. If traditional Halachic data are sought, the counselor has no right either to deride or to distort the Halachah—only to cite it accurately or provide sources for finding accurate data.

4. Campus: institutional matters

The student may want to discuss some internal Hillel matter—from committee tasks to political tension among organizations or factions within the Jewish student community. Or the student may come to seek counsel about an intergroup problem on the campus. Does the counselor agree that antisemitism was involved in a recent Student Government controversy?

As always, the student may not have been aware of an internal conflict in connection with the presenting problem. If it isn't there, the counselor commits an act of *g'nevat da'at* in trying to induce one. If it is, the conflict must be dealt with.

An additional potential conflict with Jewish values must be in the counselor's consciousness. Whether or not the student requests it, is intervention or non-intervention the wiser course? It seems obvious in this regard that no generalization exists, except possibly: when in doubt, do not intervene. The temptation to counsel by taking over is real and pervasive. It should be resisted maximally. To take over a Mitzvah from another person is also a theft.

5. Campus: personal matters

The student may seek help in resolving a personal problem with a faculty member or an administrative official or another student. Roommates are frequently involved in such difficulties. Or the student may come to discuss pending changes in the financial aid situation. Or the student may request a written statement about the dates of a major Jewish festival in order to be excused from attending a class or taking a test.

There may well be no emotional conflicts about such requests. Straightforward data may be all the counselor is expected to provide. Whether or not to intervene with the faculty member or the dorm director of the aid office is determined by circumstances and by agreement with the student.

6. *Academic matters*

The student may want to discuss course selection, dropping a course, securing tutorial help.

Conflicts? Counsel? Intervention? The same questions apply.

7. *Sexual Relationships*

The student may seek guidance about the inevitable sexual pressures faced on campus. The student may come to discuss an inner conflict over dating a non-Jew or an open conflict with parents over the same subject. The student may be grieving over the breakup of a romantic relationship, or the student may be contemplating marriage and want counsel about the relationship or the ceremony. The intended spouse may or may not be involved in such pre-marital counseling. The student may be depressed or panicky over a general feeling of lack of success in intergender relationships, or the student may be homosexually involved—or afraid of becoming homosexually involved.

Every general principle of counseling appies to this complex arena— listening, acceptance, non-judgmentalism, avoidance of bias. Traditional Jewish principles about these matters exist and cannot be ignored. Nor can "traditional" Jewish violations of these principles be ignored either.

The counselor has an obligation to have studied carefully and asked such questions as: To what extent, if at all, has reality changed to make traditional Jewish principles more difficult or impossible of fulfillment? To what extent must we still invoke these specific Jewish principles? To what extent can we look to analogous Jewish principles to help us grope for norms and standards in today's realities, if indeed there are new realities?

This is not the place for a full study of historical background, the contemporary milieu, or possible approaches to the problems brought to the counselor in this broad area. Fortunately, serious people in the Jewish community are writing about the congeries of subjects and problems involved. The competent Jewish counselor will be acquainted with the literature, use its insights for counseling purposes, and provide relevant information and material for the student to read and ponder.

Homosexuality presents unique complexities as a counseling problem. The traditional Jewish attitude was clear to all: without exception, spermatic ejaculation anywhere but inside the female was forbidden. Female homosexuality received almost no attention in rabbinic literature, but was considered an obscenity to be punished. Maimonides suggested whipping as the proper penalty.

Today, the Jewish counselor faces a variety of problems and needs a variety of approaches to finding an appropriate response. The student who fears possible homosexual tendencies in himself/herself is different from the aggressively acting-out homosexual who demand's the counselor's agreement—Judaism's agreement, that is—that homosexuality is a legitimate "alternative life style." There may even be halachic justification for a distinction between deliberate and involunatry homosexuality. (Cf. Matt 1978)

The counselor must have a firm understanding of his/her own feelings about homosexuals, the level of comfort or discomfort dealing with them, and the level of acceptance of them.

8. Family problems

Married students may come for counsel about marital conflicts, or for guidance in some major decision. Married or single students may need to talk about parents, siblings, or family relationships. Or a student may face the serious illness or death of a close family member.

We need not rehearse the traditional significance of the family, family relationships, and family life in Judaism. Nor need we detail the radical changes which have taken place in the *de facto* living patterns of American Jewish families. But it can be stated with certainty that Judaism and its values are playing an insufficiently strong role in the conditioning both of parents and offspring in today's Jewish families. There are some serious efforts during the Jewish educational process to increase the consciousness of parents and children concerning the principles and practices of Jewish marriage and family. However, students who come for counsel about such matters may not have those values deeply imbedded. The counselor may have to represent those values, to express them, and to use them with flexibility and empathy.

At the same time, the counselor will have to deal with the conflicts and ambivalences which result from leaving home, the creation of adult distance between parents and offspring, and the new order of things as it engenders difficulties for both parents and students.

Perlman (1969) has catalogued thoroughly the kinds of parent-student conflicts which can come to the counselor. Some of them probably do not occur with the same frequency they did during the turbulent sixties and early seventies. But many are still with us and must be dealt with.

Perlman deals at length with serious illness and death in the family of the student. The reactions he describes are not unique to students, but they are certainly present when family tragedy strikes. The difficulty of accepting the reality, the anger, the relief and the inevitable guilt over that relief, the questioning of God's injustices—all these and more can come to the counselor.

I know of no area of Jewish experience in which our sages have served us more brilliantly than in the traditional sequence of responses to death. Even as he/she interacts with the individual student about all the feelings described, the counselor stands on firm, tested, effective ground in advocating the use of traditional Jewish mourning procedures as a significant way to recover from the death of a close relative.

9. *Other personal problems*

A student may be considering conversion to another religious system.

For the Jewishly-committed counselor, this student poses a potentially great emotional conflict. The Jewish people, that endangered species, cannot afford to lose members. For families, this blow strikes on a level exceeded only by death. A youngster who announces the intention to become a Christian or a devotee of Hare Krishna or the Mahara-ji induces an almost automatic panic. Such students are a keen test of the counselor's capacity to keep cool.

One major judgment will determine the counselor's approach: is the student emotionally healthy or emotionally ill? (The tendency to assume illness as an inevitable factor is foolhardy.) If the student is indeed ill, then referral is the counselor's task; this is unusually complex, since most frequently the student will not agree to this diagnosis until there is a major breakdown. But the student may not be ill. He/she may have failed to gain some significant emotional satisfaction or intellectual fulfillment in growing up as a Jew which, it is now being felt, some other system can fulfill.

Once again, the principles of good counseling must be utilized. The appearance of the student to discuss the matter may demonstrate that there is some conflict or concern; therefore, there may be a possible reorientation to Judaism as a maximally fulfilling way. If parents approach the counselor, dealing with them presents other challenges. If parents do not take the initiative, whether or not to communicate with them is a serious question, to be answered solely in terms of the well-being of the student.

A difficult but significant principle of Judaism which must be kept in mind by the counselor is the denial by our sages of the idea that Judaism possesses sole truth, and that somehow the eternal soul of the student will be irrevocably damned by involvement with another religious system.

The student may come to the counselor because of involvement in the "drug scene" and conflict about it. Or the student may have been "busted" and need help. Or the student may have developed a serious drinking problem and decided to bring it to the Jewish counselor.

The counselor should know as much as possible about the etiology of the use of drugs and alcohol by young people. The generalizations adduced by Preston Munter (in Farnsworth and Blaine 1970) appear to be accurate:

a. The self-image of the user is generally weak, accompanied by "distorted expectation."

b. The general mood of the user is depressed. The purpose of the artificial stimulant is to overcome the depression, apparently not possible without it.

c. The user has limited capacity for object relations.

The most hopeful sign for the Jewish counselor is the fact that the student has come to talk about the problem. It seems obvious that the counselor's decision to refer the student or deal with the person depends on the seriousness of the involvement. If the latter, several Jewish principles should be borne in mind:

In Judaism, the body is not the absolute possession of the individual. We are only the "stewards" of our bodies, and just as we are responsible to God for all our actions, we are responsible for our uses of our bodies. *Simcha shel mitzvah*—the joy inherent in performing Mitzvot—has a corollary in *mitzvah shel simcha*—it is a Mitzvah to be joyful at appropriate times and in appropriate ways. We are not a puritannical people. The "schneppsl" is preceded by the recitation of a b'rachah as appropriately as is the drinking of Kiddush wine or any other act we sanctify in the routines of life. But joys should be sought and accepted by Jews without dependence upon artificial stimuli.

In Jewish value terms, the chronic argumentation of the user that "soft" drugs and alcohol are not really harmful is fallacious. Physical and emotional dependence on any external and artificial source as the sole or major means of achieving serenity or joy is abuse of the human person. The separation of the physical and the emotional is contrary to Jewish ideation. It is on this solid ground that the Jewish counselor stands.

10. Ultimate crisis

Many of the previously discussed areas can be critical in the feelings of the student. But the ultimate crisis is the suicidal feeling or the attempted suicide. That suicides and attempted suicides are frequent on campuses is clear. (Farnsworth and Blaine 1970) That Jewish students are involved more than rarely is becoming clear, though warnings have been sounded for more than a decade.

It is important for the counselor to understand both the definiton of suicide under Jewish law and the traditional Jewish attitude toward it. Grollman (1966) has collected many of the source statements. They make it clear that, though suicide cannot be condoned Jewishly, the definition of suicide is such that the "penalties" suffered by the deceased can rarely if ever be invoked in our time.

For the counselor, several generalizations about students with suicidal feelings appear to be accurate:

a. It is a dangerous fallacy to believe that "if they talk about it they aren't going to do it." If a student talks about suicide, he/she must be taken seriously, immediately.

b. It is a deeply un-Jewish notion to conclude that an individual has the right to take his/her own life, some kind of an ultimate civil liberty. The Torah makes it clear that destructive or wrong intentions in others may not be ignored. (Leviticus 19:16–17) Certainly suicidal intentions must be included in that injunction.

c. It is clear that the depth of feeling which can lead a student to suicidal intent is not amenable to the kind of counseling we are discussing. Immediate referral for serious psychotherapeutic activity is indicated.

VII

This list of areas of student counseling is undoubtedly incomplete. But it seeks to demonstrate that both general principles of Judaism and specific Jewish concepts and values can be brought consciously to bear on the tasks of the Jew who serves as a counselor to Jewish students.

Bibliography

Blakeman, Edward and Handley, Mary Louise, "Campus Religious Counseling," *Christian Education*, Vol. 35: 212–228, 1952.

Borowitz, Eugene B. *Choosing a Sex Ethic*. Schocken Books, 1969.

Franzblau, A. N., "The Ministry of Counseling,"*The Journal of Pastoral Care*, Vol. IX, #3, 1955 (pp. 137–144)

Freud, Sigmund, "Lines of Advance in Psycho-analytic Therapy," 1919, in *The Standard Edition*, Vol. 17 (1955).

Grollman, Earl, ed. *Rabbinical Counseling*. Bloch Publishing Company, 1966.

Hirsch, Samson Raphael. *Horeb*. Soncino Press, 1962 (2 volumes).

Kagan, Henry E. "Role of the Rabbi as Counselor," *Pastoral Psychology*, Vol. V, October 1954, pages 17–23.

Katz, Robert L. *Empathy*. Free Press, 1963.

Lipman, Eugene J. "Pastoral Counseling and Psychotherapy: Comparison and Contrast," University of Maryland, 1978 (forthcoming).

Matt, Herschel J. "A Jewish Approach to Homosexuality," *Judaism*, Vol. 27, #1, 1978.

Noveck, Simon, ed. *Judaism and Psychiatry*. United Synagogue of America, 1956.

Perlman, Samuel, *Students Versus Parents*. Howard A. Doyle Publishing Company, 1969.

Porter, Jack Nusan, "Sexuality and Judaism," *Reconstructionist*, Vol., XLIV, #10, 1979.

Schnitzer, Jeshaia, "The Role of the Rabbi in Pastoral Counseling," *Bulletin of the Rabbinical Assembly of America*, Sept. 1950, October 1951, January 1952, April 1952, June 1952.

Schnitzer, Jeshaia, *New Horizons for the Synagogue*. Bloch Publishing Company, 1956.

Segal, Stanley J., "Role of the Religious Counselor's Values in Counseling, *Journal of Counseling and Psychology*, Vol. 6, pp. 270–274, 1959.

Vorspan, Albert and Lipman, Eugene J. *Justice and Judaism.* Union of American Hebrew Congregations, 1956.

Waskow, Arthur I. *Godwrestling.* Schocken Books, 1978.

Jewish Components in Campus Counseling

Norma F. Furst

Temple University
Philadelphia, Pennsylvania

and

Michael A. Monson

B'nai B'rith Hillel Foundation
University of Pennsylvania

That college years pose challenges and opportunities which are not always easily understood by students is a truism which needs no further explication. It is difficult to conceive of a truly outstanding teacher who has not shown the requisite skills for dealing with students' emotional and vocational needs as well as their cognitive requirements. Clearly, counseling in many forms existed in universities well before the process was institutionalized in centers staffed with professionally trained persons.

The phenomenon known as the university or college counseling center is fairly new; it came as a direct outgrowth of the need, after the second World War, to aid returning veterans make a smooth transition from G.I. Joe to Joe College. With aid from the federal government, universities established veterans centers to test, advise, and counsel returning servicemen. The specific population of these veterans subsequently diminished, but the centers had proved their efficacy, and more and more universities decided to continue them for the benefit of all students. Most of the resultant agencies would agree with the University of Houston's counseling center that they ". . . are designed to help persons evaluate and cope more effectively with their present situation and plan realistic goals for the future . . ."

At least twenty years before the first university veteran's counseling center was opened, Hillel opened its first foundation at the University of Illinois in Champaign-Urbana. It fulfilled a multi-faceted role on a college campus. Among the needs of the college population it served was the need to find help in coping with the environment. The first time that a student asked within the context of a Jewish setting on campus, "What should I do about . . ., I need help . . .," the Jewish university counseling center became a reality.

Despite the great expansion of university counseling centers, students are still coming to Hillel Foundations or Jewish student centers and asking the professional, "Can you help me? I have a problem." Students seeking answers come with certain expectations of which the professional must be cognizant. The assumption must be made that the client chose the Jewish setting because of a desire to arrive at a particular Jewish understanding of the immediate dilemma. The choice of a professional within the Jewish setting presupposes that Jewish answers are being sought.

The student comes to the center because there is a problem, or at least some uneasiness in anticipation of a problem. If the nature of the concern reflects a severe disorder or is of a pathological nature, then the counselor best serves a referral function, sending the student to a source more capable of handling the distress. Fortunately, the great majority of inquiries are of such a nature that the counselor can offer real service, comfort, and help. Most of the problems raised by the anxious student in a Jewish setting do have a Jewish dimension.

What types of people and what kinds of questions most often confront the counselor in the Hillel setting? Even if the problem appears to be of totally unrelated to a Jewish concern, involving grades and/or parent-child relationships, there is still a Jewish component in the individual's presence as a Jew in the Hillel setting. Rarely do we see students who, after some probling, are dealing with concerns that have no relationship to a Jewish question or no connection with their Jewishness.

The Jewish students we see tend to think about their Jewishness more than their non-Jewish counterparts think of their religious or ethnic backgrounds. This does not mean that every Jewish student we meet in the counseling situation is involved actively or even passively with Jewish commitments; on the contrary, many students may be running away from or indifferent to their Jewishness. However, the act of coming into the Hillel setting to discuss problems constitutes an act of Jewish involvement.

When students come to a counselor in a Jewish setting, there is often a great concern with moral issues. Although we cannot document it, we have the distinct impression that those Jewish students we see professionally have a great concern with questions of personal morality. This does not mean to say that they are either more ethical, or more moral, or more sensitive than their non-Jewish counterparts; it does imply that they have in mind a definite system of moral values that either guides them or, in its more negative aspects, plagues them.

Jewish students seem to carry around a 1:3 problem relationship, rather than the more common 1:2 relationships seen with other students. By this we mean to suggest that Jews relate to each other and to issues not only with the perspective of themselves, but also with the awareness of a tradition, or at least the visible symbol of a value-inculcating parent, that never leaves them. This may be expressed in terms of morality or of guilt, depending upon whether one sees the phenomenon as positive or plaguing. The problems of dealing with oneself in relation to another significant person or persons never seems to be isolated from group traditons and mores.

Many students approach the counseling situation with the assumed or implied task of dealing with their parents. The parent relationship becomes all-important to the student who is away from home for the first time and needs to deal with questions of personal responsibility while expressing individuality. Until these seemingly conflicting needs are brought into harmonious relation, they are often seen as competing forces, with the Jewish parent, more so than any other, perceived as a negative, guilt-producing agent. Discussion of a problem specifically focused on dating or even study habits often becomes intertwined with long-standing feelings about parents, about tradition, as well as about self; hence, the 1:3 relationship.

The Jewish student often comes to the Hillel counselor looking for a Jewish response, one that "can be lived with." As the students move away from their home environment they discover they may not be just one Jewish response to a problem, but a spectrum of Jewish responses. A troubled student can easily confuse the concept of alternatives with the concept of "anything goes." It is true that Orthodoxy, Conservatism, Reform, and Reconstructionism may offer differing positions on a variety of issues, and also that within each denomination there are a series of halakhic and other responses that may at times seem mutually contradictory. Yet there are boundaries and there are limitations. There is a point at which we can say "*not* anything goes." The Jewish student coming to a Hillel counselor must be told that there are responses that are not appropriately Jewish and are not consonant with the historical values of the Jewish tradition.

In this age of rapidly changing societal values and the concomitant need for "quick fixes," some Jewish students find themselves in a particularly difficult dilemma. There is much Christian proselytizing on college campuses, some of which promise easy solutions and instant salvation. Some Jewish students find that among their Christian counterparts the mood of the times demands fast answers to cosmic questions. Imagine the dilemma of the Jewish student who perceives Christianity as affording him the pleasure of answers, while his own tradition merely poses further questions to his already confused mind. Teaching students to sort out immediate solutions from long term effects is one of the counselor's main tasks.

Jewish professionals who work on the campus face constraints and discipline that may not affect their counterparts in other settings. Students entering a Jewish environment assume that the professional has a value commitment, whereas they would not expect to find any particular commitment on the part of a professional counselor in a neutral setting. Students expect Hillel counselors to have knowlege of Jewish content and to reflect Jewish values. Jewish counselors may not equivocate or compromise their own beliefs in Judaism. Helping students find Jewish alternatives to fit their needs is a primary goal.

It would be fair to infer from the discussion so far that the Jewish counselor has a great responsibility to be informed in depth and in breadth about Jewish responses to specific dilemmas. The counselor must have a deep base of Jewish knowledge and show a commitment to continue to itensify such learning. A basic knowledge of the history and practice of Judaism is essential. Seeing the counselor engaged in a quest for knowledge assures the student in the counseling situation that the search for appropriate responses is a mature and responsible act.

When students come to the Jewish setting, they often treat the counselor as the Rabbi, in a mythical, almost mystical sense, and not as a real rabbi. In the eyes of a troubled student the counselor often assumes the role of law giver, judge, and parent, as well as the source of Jewish and human response. These perceptions may occur even when the professional is not, in fact, a member of the rabbinate.

It is easy for the counselor to assume these attributes, and most professionals have to guard against behavior which suggests omniscience. The Jewish counselor must be on guard against behaving in ways which reinforce the innocent student's belief that the professional does, indeed, possess all-knowing and all-good characteristics. It is important for the counselor to be aware of limitations and not to promise more than can be delivered in the human encounter. The counselor is neither law-giver, judge, nor surrogate parent. The rabbi as counselor is particularly vulnerable, because the student frequently enters the situation with a host of pre-conceived and deeply imbedded expectations.

The Jewish counselor has the responsibility to express a value system while, at the same time, giving the client maximum freedom of personal choice. The counselor who has made peace with Judaism, has taken a position, and is willing to so confront the student gains more respect than the professional who equivocates.

Knowing that a student has specifically chosen a Jewish setting to air concerns means that the counselor must be aware of what it means to function as a Jewish presence. The counselor must be aware of this "special baggage" and be able to act upon it. This does not mean that a counselor must follow a predetermined and specific Jewish life style or display a certain degree of commitment. The demand simply is one of Jewish confidence, however defined. Put in other terms, we might say that the counselor is expected to have a Jewish agenda and should live up to the expectations that follow. The agenda should be readily conveyable to the student, and the counselor should feel free to share this agenda, not as a propaganda piece or a teaching tool but as evidence of a personal quest.

Within this context, the opportunity to question, to disagree, to challenge, and to rebel is the student's right as a Jew and as a human being. If the counselor does not approach the student with this sense of openness, the chance for a successful encounter is doomed from the start. When students visit counseling services, they do so in an effort to raise questions in an accepting setting. When they come to the Jewish counselor, they do not forfeit their right to raise their concerns in an atmosphere which allows them and their questions to be accepted as worthwhile and appropriate. As a matter of fact, it is questioning and facing ambiquities that convey Jewish interests.

On the other hand, students need to know that while all people are worthwhile and all questions deserve answers, some questions will receive Jewish answers. These may not always allow for the total freedom of the individual which some students think is of primary importance. Many of the cases brought to the counselor involve interreligious dating and intermarriage. The counselor does not have the right to indicate that intermarriage is fine and that parents will "just have to learn to live with it." Judaism imposes strictures which students need to know, just as they need to explore Jewish alternatives. An individual is responsible for his actions; these actions affect significant others, and consequences for both the individual and the collective need to be examined openly and honestly. A counselor needs to understand what boundaries exist within Judaism, what alternatives are possible, and what are the consequences when these boundaries are crossed.

This does not mean that the Jewish counselor necessarily imposes a personal value system. In counseling one needs to allow the client to make mistakes and to seek out the best path. The counselor needs to portray a positive Jewish stance and to provide resources for the client, so that the latter learns of alternatives and has a method of bouncing competing forces against a willing and participating "ear."

There is a significant role that was advocated by Rabbi David Mogilner ז״ל to hundreds of staff persons at Camp Ramah. He always taught that a counselor has to serve as an "honorable and accessible role model." The analysis we have made points to this objective. In dealing with the needs of Jewish students, counselors must be willing to share and expose their own lifestyle, to the extent that is required. They must also be individuals to whom the student turns because the counselor conveys the best that the Jewish value system has to teach.

Finally, we would add a word about the concept of community. One of the great blessings of the Jewish tradition is that one need not, in fact, cannot "be alone." Any student coming to the Jewish setting comes for the sense of community as well as for the sake of the individual. In essence, that individual represents all that exists in Judaism and all that has gone on in the past. The student comes to the Jewish setting out of a willingness, even if only subconscious, to explore alternatives within the context of that very tradition. Jewish tradition and community are a fine base from which the counselor may begin to help the student to help him/herself.

Part II
ללמד
*Jewish Education
in the Setting of the University*

Jewish Studies:
Their Scope and Meaning Today*

Alexander Altmann

Brandeis University
Waltham, Massachusetts

The subject I have chosen for my lecture seems to me of particular importance. Jewish studies comprise a field of scholarly research which may seem to have little relevance to the problems facing Jewry and Judaism today. They may appear to be of purely academic interest and the domain of specialists only. Yet I hope to show that they transcend by far the realm of academic pursuits, that the fundamental attitude underlying them represents the very spirit—for better or worse—of so-called modern Jewry, and that without the insights won by way of Jewish studies we could hardly orientate ourselves in the world in which we live. Perhaps we no longer fully share Lord Acton's optimistic belief that "knowledge of the past" is an "instrument of action and a power that goes to the making of the future." Too much knowledge, especially of the historical kind, can also be a "weariness of the flesh" and, as Nietzsche warned us, a hindrance rather than a spur to action. Yet, when all is said, Jews anxious to map out a future for our people cannot afford to be oblivious of our past. Nor can this past be understood and appreciated without an application of the methods of critical research. Whether scholarship can also give us the guidance we need for our religious edification is another matter. Theology, we shall have occasion to

*A Hillel Foundation Annual Lecture delivered at University College, London, on November 19, 1957, under the chairmanship of Sir Isaiah Berlin and published by the B nai B'rith Hillel Foundation, London, 1958.

observe, is not capable of replacement by philology and history. Personal faith which involves decision and surrender is even less so. But neither can theology and religion afford the pretense that modern scholarship does not matter. Where this attitude prevails, the result is either a blind type of orthodoxy unable to face the challenge of the modern age or a platitudinous kind of progressiveness out of touch with the realities of Jewish history.

What, then, is the scope and meaning of Jewish studies today? In trying to answer this question, I shall briefly survey the development of the concept of Jewish studies from their inception in the early part of the 19th century down to the present time. It is not my intention to give an account of the actual results achieved in the various branches of Jewish learning. Such a task would be beyond the compass of a single lecture. Nor is it my intention to re-traverse the ground already amply covered by previous treatments of the subject, especially by Max Wiener's very full and competent analysis and by Gershom Scholem's rapid, yet uncannily penetrating, sketch. What I hope to show is the character of present Jewish studies against the background of the 19th century approach.

I

The new type of Jewish studies, the so-called *Wissenschaft des Judentums*, which Leopold Zunz introduced in his little treatise *Something on Rabbinic Literature* in 1818, is a texture woven of several strands. How large the apologetic motive loomed in the mind of Zunz himself is apparent from repeated references to it in his writings. He had realized with dismay that the knowledge of Judaism in the non-Jewish world had hardly moved an inch from the position established by the notorious Eisenmenger 135 years earlier. Hence the fact noted by him that even estimable Christian authors assumed a "demonic nature" as it were whenever the subject of Judaism was broached, that all quotations from sources were copied from second-hand works of the 16th and 17th centuries, and that objections refuted long ago were being "dished up" again and again by consulting the "oracle of scoundrels." He felt that progress towards a greater tolerance and the granting of emancipation was held up by the deplorable absence of competent works by Jews on the nature and history of Judaism. Another no less compelling motive to which Zunz gave expression was the desire to halt the movement of ill-conceived reforms of the Jewish religion based on ignorance. "Hasty innovations", he wrote, "give to the old and—what is more calamitous—to the antiquated a higher value. In order, therefore, to know and discriminate between the old which is useful, the antiquated which is harmful, and the new which is desirable we have to set our hand in all seriousness to the study of the people and its history." Zacharias Frankel's approach was not essentially different, although more conservative in practice. Abraham Geiger, on the other hand, conceived of *Wissenschaft des Judentums* as a clear weapon of radical reform. Opposed as he was to what he called the "petrified legalism" (*Gesetzesstarre*) of traditional Judaism, he sought to justify far-reaching reforms by laying bare the historical processes which had led up to the present. He therefore defined the new science of Judaism as "historical research and criticism of post-Biblical theology," and proclaimed as its aim the establishment of a "refined Judaism." The new theologian whom he wanted to create with the help of modern Jewish studies is to be "a teacher of religion", not a mere expert in *halachic* matters. He must be able to "disentangle the chaotic material" of the tradition, obtain a clear view of the whole, and, in short, be guided by a "theology in the spirit of contemporary culture." In his *Introduction to the Study of Jewish Theology* (1849), he divides the history of his subject into three parts, viz., Biblical theology, post-Biblical theology, and "the new (*neuere*) theology," the last one commencing—with Geiger—in 1830. He praises Jost, Zunz and Rapoport as the pioneers of the new critical and historical approach, Solomon Munk, S. D. Luzzatto and Leopold Dukes for their learned contributions, and refers to himself as the one who went into the very depths of the problems and drew practical conclusions from his researches. He thus sees himself as the culminating point of the historical development of Judaism, as the Jewish Hegel as it were in whom the idea of Judaism had fully come into its own.

Whilst Geiger almost identifies *Wissenschaft des Judentums* with the theology of Reform, Zunz and, in particular, Moritz Steinschneider are anxious to develop Jewish studies as an unbiased, purely scholarly discipline. As Kurt Wilhelm has shown in a recent study, Steinschneider refused to see in them a mere propaedeutic to Jewish theology. "Jewish literature," he declared, "is as little purely theological as Arabic and Chinese literature are ... Nor is Jewish literature represented on the whole by Rabbis holding office." Research, he holds, is an activity for its own sake. He and, to a large extent, Zunz show a catholicity of scholarly interest which embraces all conceivable manifestations of the Jewish mind throughout the ages and in all lands and cultures. Zunz's treatise of 1818 gives an outline of the range of Jewish studies which includes not only such theological subjects as dogmatology, liturgy, jurisprudence and ethics but also such secular activities as Jewish participation in the physical sciences, mathematics, astronomy, geography, chronology, medicine, technology, industry, commerce, architecture, printing, calligraphy and music. We find an echo of this program in the essay of his friend, Immanuel Wolf, *On the Concept of a Science of Judaism* (1822), where the term "Judaism" is defined as "the essence of all the circumstances, characteristics and achievements of the Jews in respect of religion, philosophy, history, law, literature in general, civil life and all affairs of men, and not in the more limited sense in which it denotes the religion of the Jews only." Wolf hastens to add that in any event religion lies at the very root of Judaism and conditions all its ramifications. Precisely because religion plays such a fundamental role in Judaism can one detect its flavor in the totality of Jewish life. Wolf is obviously not prepared to recognize a secularized concept of Judaism and Jewish studies. Zunz's position is somewhat doubtful, whereas Steinschneider is quite unambiguous in his secularized outlook.

The foregoing account will have conveyed some idea of the variety of motives which went to the creation and pursuit of 19th century *Wissenschaft des Judentums*. Yet for all the complexity of the pattern it is not difficult to see the common element underlying it. This common feature is the fascination which historical thinking holds for all co-operating in the new science. Judaism is no longer viewed as a timeless entity. It is conceived as an essentially historical process. Its laws and doctrines, institutions and customs are seen as related to time and place and interpreted against their historical background. The element of Divine Revelation is not obliterated, though given a somewhat humanist shade of meaning. For Revelation itself is seen as a process in history. The doctrine of a succession of revelations was by no means foreign to the Jewish religious tradition, especially the mystical one. But whereas in the older tradition God revealed Himself spontaneously, it was now the *idea* of God or the *idea* of Judaism which realized itself in the course of history with the necessity of a Hegelian principle. Hence the endeavor to trace the historical development of Judaism and, to this end, "construct" Jewish history. The absolute truth of Judaism was not in doubt. Historicism had not yet developed into a crisis. History was held to bring out the truth of the Jewish idea of God. A Jewish Hegelianism was the instrument by which this reading of history was achieved. How this history was felt to approach its consummation in the modern age that had just dawned for the Jewish people we have noted in Geiger's view of his own historic role. Much of the secular eschatology of German Idealism is reflected in the Jewish "apocalyptic" mood which is so highly characteristic of the movement of Reform and the hopes connected with the Emancipation. Hence the stress on the alleged purely rational character of Judaism in contrast to Christianity. Moses Mendelssohn's verdict that Judaism was a dogma-less religion and completely in accord with the ideas of *Aufklärung* was re-adopted. It persisted throughout the liberal tradition down to Leo Baeck. Medieval Jewish *Aufklärung* was therefore regarded as typical of authentic Judaism. The loving care with which men like Jacob Guttmann and others devoted themselves to medieval Jewish philosophy as a field of study and research stems largely from this consideration. Jewish mysticism was rejected as an aberration from the true path, if not as outright stupidity and superstition. Only by suppressing the mystical tendencies in Jewish history was one able to uphold the image of a purely rational Judaism. Likewise, only by ignoring certain strata of *Halakhah* and *Haggadah* was it possible to picture Judaism as a faith essentially free from manifestations of intolerance. Where mystical or other undesirable features were encountered, they were explained as mere transitory stages in a dialectical process which tended inevitably towards a more enlightened fulfilment of the true idea. Zunz saw in the persecutions suffered by the Jewish people an excuse as it were for the "cabbalistic dissonances" which followed the sweeter melodies of an earlier age.

It was this rationalistic construction of Jewish history which enabled Jewish scholars and thinkers of the 19th century down to Hermann Cohen to feel a sense of superiority over the Christian religion. In his admirable essay, *The Science of Judaism and Historicism in Abraham Geiger*, H. Liebeschütz has pointed out the embarrassment which Jewish historians experienced vis-à-vis the Middle Ages, for which Christian historians had, if not Romantic sentiments, at least a sense of appreciation. He quotes Burckhardt's nostalgic reference to the medieval period as one of surpassing value: "All that ever makes life worth living is rooted there." To Zunz the Middle Ages are simply the "Age of barbarism." The modern world is seen as wholly and essentially opposed to the Middle Ages. Christianity is regarded as a spiritual force tinged with mysticism and Romanticism, in opposition to which the modern world has come into being. In Geiger's words, "Christianity is not modern, and what is modern is not Christian." Judaism, on the other hand, was considered to be in complete alignment with the new age. *Aufklärung*, not Romanticism, lies at the root of the interpretation of Jewish and world history offered by the scholars and philosophers of 19th century Jewry down to Hermann Cohen ("Romanticism is the greatest danger") and Leo Baeck who contrasted Judaism and Christianity as "classic" and "romantic" religion respectively.

The Jewish aversion to Romanticism as a historical perspective—due, no doubt, to political apprehensions as much as to the desire to paint Judaism in rational colors in contrast to Christianity—is, strangely enough, partly offset by the sway Romanticism held over the type of religiosity developed by German Jewry in the 19th century. Synagogal music completely reflects the Romantic mood, and the type of religion which Geiger had in mind when advocating a "refined" Judaism owes a great deal to Schleiermacher. He describes it in *Judaism and its History* (1865) as being "not a system of truths" but as the "rejoicing (*Jubel*) of the soul conscious of its elevation and, at the same time, the humble confession of its finitude." In another context he defines the "true essence of religion" as the innermost life of feeling which appreciates the unattainable high above us and is conscious of our smallness. In a letter written in 1843, the year in which the *Deutsche Jahrbücher*, the organ of the Young Hegelians, were declared illegal by the Government of the day, he wrote: "I detest this Young Hegelianism with its *hubris* of the subject; I detest that vulgar assailing of all humility in the human heart, of all consciousness of one's finitude." He adds that he recognizes the incomprehensible above us, and is conscious of man's dependence on the higher powers. All his Reform activity, he assures us, has its root in that feeling. In yet another letter he confesses that his belief in a personal Universal Spirit (*Allgeist*) or God is not a fully-grown and clear idea but more in the nature of poetic feeling. This Romantic attitude is not confined to Geiger. Its co-existence side by side with the rationalism of *Aufklärung* throws light not only on the emotional springs of the Reform movement, its stress on decorum and devotion (*Andacht*) in worship, but also on the lack of understanding for the *halachic* element in Judaism which is characteristic of Jewish studies in that period. Z. Frankel's grandiose plans for research in the Talmudic field could hardly be realized in the spiritual climate of 19th century German Jewry.

Much of the impulse for Jewish historical studies—and they include all the necessary paraphernalia of scholarship such as cataloguing of MSS, text editions, philological research, etc.—derives from the general interest in historiography which characterizes the age. The rise of the German Historical School which culminated in Leopold von Ranke (1795–1886) created a widespread concern for historical knowledge. In 1790, no less than 131 periodicals devoted to historical scholarship appeared in Germany alone. Many of the historians, including Ranke himself, had first been students of theology. Ranke's original motive in taking up the study of history was again theological. He wanted to understand history as the revelation of Divine Providence. In his Diaries of 1817, he betrays also the influence of Fichtean ideas. The task of the historian is described as that of tracing the divine *idea* at the root of things, so far as this lies within the scope of human understanding. But in the course of his work historical study for its own sake gains the upper hand. The Historical School severs its bonds with theology. Scholarship becomes an end in itself. The historians begin to discard the constructions imposed by both theology and philosophy. Ranke criticised Hegel's schematization of history. Essentially, the establishment of historical science as an independent discipline goes back to the Göttingen School in the second half of the 18th century, as Professor Herbert Butterfield has shown in his fascinating account of the history of historical scholarship. In 1818, Zunz and his contemporaries were certainly confronted with a fully-fledged secular type of historical research. On the Christian side, the influence of Historicism is pronounced in F. Chr. Baur's Tübingen School of Historical Theology, which in turn influenced Geiger's *Urschrift und Uebersetzungen der Bibel* (1857), as Liebeschütz has shown. Indeed, the most notable achievements of 19th century *Wissenschaft des Judentums* derive from the impact of the German Historical School and of the critical-philological method employed by Niebuhr. Outstanding amongst them are Zunz's stupendous works on Rabbinic literature, Steinschneider's catalogues, and—for all its faults—Graetz's monumental *History*.

II

The new phase of Jewish studies which may be dated from the end of the First World War is again the result of a combination of factors. Important changes were taking place in the historical outlook and philosophical thinking of the period. Sociology asserted itself as an important new science. In historiography, Friedrich Meinecke trod novel paths in his method of *Ideengeschichte* as the key to an understanding of political developments. In the study of religion a deeper understanding of the irrational and mystical element was gaining ground. Rudolf Otto's phenomenology of the "Holy" and Max Weber's discovery of the "charismatic leader" in religious society are instances of the new trend in research. Wilhelm Dilthey in particular had sharpened the historians' vision of the "meaning" (*Bedeutung*) of the literary expressions of the past. He taught them a more refined art of "re-living" and sympathetically understanding them. He showed how historical study can enable us to understand religious experiences of a depth and intensity such as in our own persons we are incapable of sharing. He stressed the need for imaginative understanding. And he underlined the necessity of seeing historical phenomena in terms of total configurations (*Gestalt*) rather than of isolated elements. Jewish scholars could hardly fail to take note of these advances in methodology and insight.

More important still, the Jewish attitude to the past was undergoing rapid changes. Zionism was in the ascendant, and it compelled a rethinking of the nature of Judaism and Jewish history. In 1907, Siegmund Maybaum could still declare with some pomposity: "The Messianic goal can be reached only by the intensive exercise of *Wissenschaft des Judentums*" which "ennobles the lives of its devotees" and "dispels prejudice about Jews and Judaism." But such sentiments had already begun to sound hollow and unreal. The recrudescence of antisemitism gave the lie to the sanguine hopes which from Zunz onward had inspired so much of Jewish scholarly work in the realm of apologetics. Zionism as conceived by Herzl was a Jewish answer of a different kind. It clearly perceived that *Wissenschaft des Judentums* could not "dispel prejudice" and secure Jewish existence in the Diaspora. One of the original motives of Jewish studies thus crumbled away as a result of bitter disappointment. Further, Geiger's dream that the new science would help to promote a "refined Judaism"—Maybaum's phrase about the "ennobling" of life is a clear echo if it—had been somewhat disproved by the inroads of assimilation in its more sinister and destructive aspects among the Jewries of the West. Ahad Ha-'Am was an unsparing critic of this particular phenomenon. The growing sense of de-judaization during the 19th century had alarmed many responsible leaders and led to an emphasis on Jewish studies as the panacea for all ills. Characteristic of this faith in

Wissenschaft des Judentums is the title of an essay by a certain Dr. W. Landau in the *Monatsschrift* of 1852: "*Wissenschaft,* the only means of regenerating Judaism." Jewish studies, it must be admitted, were then—and still are today—an indispensable means of Jewish revitalization. But the odds were heavily against the prospects of success on a large scale. Zionism visualized the regeneration of Judaism in a different and more realistic way. It certainly discarded Geiger's program of Reform as the only road to salvation. Thus another plank of 19th century faith in the function of Jewish studies was badly shaken.

Perhaps the severest rebuff which the 19th century concept of *Wissenschaft des Judentums* suffered was in the very approach to Jewish history. Zionism forced Jewish scholarship to view Jewish history not merely as a movement of ideas on the Hegelian pattern but as the complex reality of Jewish existence. There is symbolic significance in the fact that Martin Buber's famous journal founded in 1916 bears the name *Der Jude.* Though not devoted to scholarship in the technical sense, it indicates by its name the shift of emphasis which had occurred. It is no longer the "idea" or "essence" of Judaism which is regarded as the be-all and end-all of Jewish history. Attention is focused on the Jew and Jewish existence as the more immediate manifestation of Jewish historical reality. This means that historical construction of an abstract kind is no longer considered valid. Moreover, the Hegelian *hubris* which saw the past merely as a series of imperfect stages preparatory to the present is replaced by a more humble recognition that, in Ranke's phrase, "Every epoch stands in direct relation to God." Geiger and the 19th century Jewish philosophers (S. Formstecher, S. Hirsch) were very much imbued with the Hegelian devaluation of the past. Their reading of Jewish history was pre-determined by the foregone conclusion that it was only the present in which the truth of Judaism stood revealed. But the present as they saw it did not really issue out of the past. Its pale idealism was more or less suspended in mid-air, bereft of any vital link with the historical past. In spite of their professed "historical" orientation they did not, in fact, think in historical terms. They indulged in constructions intended to justify the present. To this extent, their historical studies had an "existential" motive. But they failed to find in the past a mirror of their own souls. The bygone ages were to them a dead object awaiting the historian's dissection, except for those periods—notably the "golden era" of Spanish Jewry—in which a kinship with the rationalism of the present could be detected. The breakdown of Hegelianism robbed this outlook of much of its attractiveness but it nevertheless persisted in the liberal tradition. It was Zionism which made it finally untenable. By introducing the category of Jewish nationhood and by stressing the need for a national renaissance it irresistibly swept away the cobwebs of a strained and artificial interpretation of Jewish history.

In 1919, Ismar Elbogen expressed the need for a revision of the entire program of Jewish studies in an article called *Neuorientierung unserer Wissenschaft* ("Re-orientation of our studies") which urged a more energetic quest for a Jewish theology as a focal point of the diverse strands of Jewish learning. A few years later, in 1922, he amplified and in some way revised this plea in his account, *Ein Jahrhundert Wissenschaft des Judentums.* His essay is the most instructive treatment of the century of Jewish studies which had elapsed by then, and clearly reflects the impact of Zionism. It surveys the entire field, evaluates the progress made, and describes the academic institutions devoted to Jewish learning. It poses the question as to the exact meaning of the term *Wissenschaft des Judentums*, and defends the legitimacy of speaking of Jewish studies as a distinct discipline. Why not relinquish, one might ask, the notion of *Wissenschaft des Judentums* altogether and deal with Jewish history within the conspectus of world history, with Jewish philosophy as part of world philosophy, with the development of the Jewish religion as part of the history of religion, with Talmudic literature as part of the history of law, religion and culture, etc.? Elbogen's answer is that all these segments composing Jewish studies can be and must be unified by a central viewpoint, i.e. the aim of promoting the understanding and further development of "living Judaism." He therefore defines Jewish studies as the "Science of living Judaism and its development as a sociological and historical unit." Philological research as initiated by Zunz is not enough. Our concern is not merely the resuscitation of past ages and their documents but the laying of the foundations upon which the Jewish present and future can be built. Elbogen mentions the plan of founding a Hebrew University in Jerusalem and expects a great deal of help for Jewish studies from its implementation.

The Hebrew University was indeed founded a year later, in 1923, and its first creation was the Institute of Jewish studies. Twenty years later, in 1943, G. Scholem wrote his *Reflections on Jewish Studies* in which he offered an analysis of the inner tensions and contradictions from which *Wissenschaft des Judentums* had suffered in the pre-Zionist period and expressed disappointment at the relative failure of Jewish scholarship in the new era. He depicted the 19th century as one secretly aiming at the liquidation of Judaism or—at best—at the reduction of its full stature. He rejoiced in the re-orientation brought about by the national spirit but felt that painstaking, rigorously precise and, at the same time, broadly conceived research was still a *desideratum*. The employment of the Hebrew language as a vehicle of expression had not caused a radical improvement in the quality of scholarship. But Scholem did not re-define the program of Jewish studies in any detail and his strictures are perhaps a trifle too severe. For it cannot be denied that *Wissenschaft des Judentums* had made considerable progress and grown into a multidimensional discipline served by outstanding scholars.

The position today, fourteen years after Scholem's plea, may be described as one of further consolidation. Many of the old guard have left us, but a fresh crop of well-qualified scholars has taken their place. Jewish studies, far from decreasing in range and intensity, have blossomed forth in many directions. They are today more free, less tied to ideologies and more objective than at any time in the past. We have gained a deeper insight into the social forces that have shaped our history. One of the fields which has largely benefited from the new approach is that of *Mishnah* and *Talmud*. The call for the application of the historical-philological method, developed and tested in Greek and Latin studies, to Rabbinic literature—a task already begun by Zacharias Frankel and Adolph Büchler—is no longer a cry in the wilderness. What it means successfully to tackle such a project will be apparent from a consideration of the qualifications necessary for this undertaking. A scholar dealing with the *Talmud* is now expected to master the literature and history of the Graeco-Roman period, Hellenistic papyrology, Greek and Latin epigraphy, Roman Law, New Testament and Patristic writings, apart from having a complete familiarity with rabbinic sources. Only in this way will he be able to understand the rabbinic texts historically, relate them to their background and see in them a mirror of actual Jewish life. As a result of such study Jewish history ceases to be a bundle of abstract constructions and assumes the flesh and blood of reality. The task implied demands boundless patience, deep historical insight and strict honesty. How much easier it is to indulge in homiletics or *pilpulim!* And how much the *talmid hakham* of the traditional school could learn for an understanding of Talmudic texts from some of the works of modern scholarship!

Another field which has come to the fore is that of Jewish mysticism.

As we have seen, 19th century Jewish scholars and philosophers fought shy of the mystical elements in the Jewish tradition which were in such sharp contrast to their cherished picture of a splendidly rational Judaism. Much has changed in this respect in the new spiritual climate of Jewish studies. We owe it to the brilliant efforts of one man—G. Scholem—that Jewish mysticism in all its aspects has been opened up as a field of critical research and historical interpretation. The significance of this study for an evaluation of Jewish spirituality and religious psychology cannot be overstated. The insights won are slowly percolating into our consciousness and dispel the idyllic notion of a placid and monolithic Judaism. We begin to see the strains and stresses in the Jewish soul, its antinomian and anarchic tendencies as well as its craving for holiness and order. Scholem's recent book on Sabbatai Zevi and the Sabbatian Movement gives added point to this insight. Modern Jewish history appears no longer as a sudden eruption of anti-traditional tendencies but merely as the last stage in a long process held in check as long as Jewish society was self-contained, but no longer effectively controlled in the age of Emancipation. How over-optimistic Franz Rosenzweig was in his assumption that there were no longer any spiritual conflicts to be solved in the inner history of the Jewish people, that it had already achieved its perfect form and stood, in this sense, "at the goal of history."

What has been said about studies in Talmudics and mysticism applies, as far as standards of research are concerned, to all other branches of Jewish learning as well. The aim is everywhere to see Judaism in the larger setting of world history, social patterns, political forces and cultural influences. Crises are bound to occur from time to time, but they are a sign of life because they indicate a healthy sense of self-criticism. On the other hand, the periodic recurrence of crises is also due to a difficulty inherent in the very nature of *Wissenschaft des Judentums*. It wants to be *Wissenschaft* des Judentums, and, at the same time, is not content to be mere historical science but aims at serving Judaism and offering an orientation to the Jew in the modern world; it wants to be Wissenschaft *des Judentums*. Jewish historical studies can and have been undertaken by non-Jews as well. But *Wissenschaft des Judentums* is a concern of Jews alone. It implies a personal involvement, the recognition that its students probe a past which, in R. C. Collingwood's telling phrase, is "incapsulated" and operative in their own present. In studying and recording the history of the Jewish people they are all the time aware that *tua res agitur.* In searching the past they are also searching for the abiding character, the normative essence, indeed, for the theology of Judaism. But can the historical and the theological approaches be reconciled with one another? Which of the various modes of Jewish thinking revealed by historical research can claim to be essential and normative? To the medieval mind it was possible to accept the different layers of Jewish spiritual history—Biblical, halachic, haggadic, philosophical, mystical—as so many ever-deepening aspects of one single revelation, diffracted as it were into its spectral colors. To modern historical thinking this blissful unification is no longer possible.

Perhaps the tension between the historical and the theological approach is fundamentally insoluble because the two attitudes stem from different types of civilization. René Guenon, that great critic of the modern world, sees our age as one of declining spirituality, as another Dark Age in which there is only "profane" philosophy and "profane" science, the empirical and analytical study of facts which are attached to no principle. The rise of Humanism, he declared, meant the reduction of everything to purely human proportions, the elimination of every principle of a higher order and the turning away from heaven under the pretext of conquering the earth. Historical science, in his view, is a powerful expression of this dissolution of the forces of tradition. Historical research takes its impulse from a desire to destroy tradition and to invalidate its impact upon the order of society. In our day, Arnold Toynbee made the interesting point that our forefathers who did not live in the age of historical research had in fact a profounder sense of the historical than we. In his *Civilisation on Trial* he says: "While our historical horizon has been expanding vastly . . . what we actually do see . . . has been contracting rapidly to the narrow field of what a horse sees between its blinkers." In the "contrast between our expanding historical horizon and our contracting historical vision" he sees one of the paradoxes of our age. Our medieval ancestors had "a broader and juster historical vision" than we have today. For them, "history did not mean the history of one's own parochial community; it meant the history of Israel, Greece and Rome . . . For our ancestors, Rome and Jerusalem meant much more than their hometowns."

These strictures are profoundly true, and one has to admit that in a sense our ancestors who derived their knowledge of history from religious sources had a larger vision of history and a more intimate affinity to it than we, their sophisticated, historically-trained progeny. To them, history was astir with meaning, unified and alive, stretching from the Creation to the Messianic age. They knew their definite place and purpose in that divinely-ordained process. On the other hand, it is hard to see how we can avoid thinking in the categories of the modern historical approach and refrain from employing the critical methods devised to meet its purpose. We know that we are paying a heavy price, but we cannot discard our very being, and modern man knows himself to be historically conditioned. This does not mean that he is constrained to shed his heritage, his traditions, and his quest for truth. But he must claim the right to put a distance between himself and his inherited traditions in order to view them as objectively as possible and to accept freely what is offered to him. Historical study should facilitate a sympathetic understanding and evaluation of the strata of the past which in some mysterious way are embedded in our own present. The analytical method is not an end in itself but a means to a new synthesis. The Jew who delves into the recesses of the Jewish past need not emerge bewildered and confused but should be able to form a more or less unified vision of Jewish reality in all its ramifications and with all its defeats as well as its triumphs. We simply cannot, without violence to ourselves, return to the pre-reflective level. We have to pass through the phase of historical orientation, but there is no warrant for stopping at that stage and losing ourselves in a non-committal historicism. Our religious needs will still require the guidance, solace and hope of religion and theology. Our metaphysical quest will still require the *lumen naturale* of philosophical Reason. Jewish historical studies will have fulfilled their purpose if they have made us understand our past, its currents and crosscurrents, its rational and irrational tendencies, its ethical and mythical trends, its sublime and sometimes less sublime aspects. Being connected with our past, at home in our literature, and in sympathy with ourselves as it were, we shall find it easier to approach the ultimate questions.

Until recently, *Wissenschaft des Judentums* was largely the domain and prerogative of rabbis. Rabbinical seminaries in Europe and America provided the main centers of Jewish historical research and no rabbi worth his salt would have dreamt of renouncing the privilege as well as the duty of engaging in research. This was true in particular of rabbis in Central and Western Europe. Their love of study and their ambition to enrich Jewish scholarship by publications of their own is a testimony to the scholarly spirit which pervaded the rabbinical seminaries at which they received their training. Unfortunately, more recent developments have somewhat spoiled this endearing picture. On the one hand, Jewish studies, as we have noted, have become a rather specialized affair, requiring much skill and expertise and depending to a very high degree on the availability of adequately stocked libraries. The increased tempo and vitality of Jewish communal life, on the other hand, has tended to make increased demands on the Rabbinate, with the result that rabbis no longer have either the expert knowledge or the leisure to devote themselves to Jewish studies on a level commensurate with modern requirements. The work of Jewish research has to some extent been taken over by Jewish academic institutions, the most prominent of which is the Hebrew University Institute of Jewish Studies. Fortunately, valuable work is still being carried on in the rabbinical seminaries both behind and this side of the Iron Curtain. The great revival of the *Yeshivah* type of education both in Israel and in the *Golah*, though welcome in itself, has not contributed towards a strengthening of the desire for Jewish research amongst the Rabbinate. Nor have many former students of *Yeshivot* ventured to join the ranks of Jewish scholarship, as it so often happened in the past. More than ever before *Yeshivot* tend to imbue their students with an aversion to the kind of study fostered by *Wissenschaft des Judentums*, and those who have overcome their inhibition and mustered the strength required for the transformation from a *Yeshivah* student into a scholar of the modern type are few and far between. Considering the vital importance of Jewish studies for a scholarly presentation of Judaism to the Jew of today, one must hope that spiritual leaders will in future show a greater alertness to scholarship. May I add that Jewish studies claim the allegiance and active participation of all sections into which, unhappily, Jewry is divided today. Scholarship should be regarded as common ground between them and this community of interest should be jealously guarded as a precious possession. In the unbiased search for historical truth scholars will find a bond of unity transcending synagogal affiliations.

I am grateful to the Hillel Foundation for having given me the opportunity of expressing the convictions I have uttered. I am particularly glad to have spoken from this platform because Jewish students in this country and all over the world are best suited to appreciate the need for Jewish studies. It is they who most yearn for an intelligent and scholarly presentation of our tradition. I hope that they will never have reason to complain that in this respect the community has failed them. The scope and meaning of Jewish studies today are of such tremendous importance that it dare not fail them. Equipped with a vision of historical truth, they will, we pray, take the further step and reach out for the eternal truths.

Postscript. The aforegoing observations were uttered more than twenty years ago in England, and they obviously reflect both the period and the locale in which they were conceived. They are republished here unchanged so as not to distort in any shape the specific situational quality they express and the philosophical mood as it were from which they sprang. The intervening years have witnessed an enormous expansion of Jewish Studies in the United States and in Israel which has affected the very fiber and self-awareness of this discipline, calling for a fresh appraisal. In the light of this fact the essay published here anew is offered as a "documentary" rather than an up-to-date statement. It may serve as the formulation of the intellectual creed of a Jew reared in the German-Jewish tradition of *Wissenschaft des Judentums* who endeavored to carry his heritage with him to England (and later to America). As such it is dedicated in friendship and admiration to Alfred Jospe, a fellow-participant in the same inheritance, who drew on its inspiration to the immeasurable enrichment of the Jewish student body of American universities over a long span of dedicated leadership.

Modes of Academic Advocacy:
The Case of Judaism

Jacob Neusner

*Brown University
Providence, Rhode Island*

Hillel rabbis and directors know full well that theirs is a career fundamentally different from that of their colleagues in pulpits. It demands different ranges of competence. It values different human gifts. It may not be wholly fair to the pulpits and the congregations to say that, in a university, traits of intellect and character bear greater promise than political skills. But it is so. If that is the case, then we have to concur on the essential discontinuity between the rabbinate of the university and the rabbinate of the synagogue. It was Alfred Jospe's early recognition that Hillel rabbis and directors require different foci and should concentrate on different activities which gave the Hillel leadership of our own day its clear understanding of its distinctive task.

Now the same is to be said for Jewish learning, but, until now, it has not been said with sufficient clarity.

When Jewish studies take place in synagogues and schools, they take up one set of quite legitimate and socially relevant tasks. When these same studies take place in a college or university, because of the utterly different setting, they take up a totally different set of quite legitimate and socially relevant tasks. What that means—and must mean—is that in no way are Jewish studies in universities continuous with Jewish studies in synagogue schools, high schools, yeshivot, youth programs, programs of study in the State of Israel, and the many other excellent modes in which Jewish learning is carried on under Jewish auspices and for Jewish purposes. Jewish studies in universities not only are not continuous with Jewish studies in parochial settings, but they are continuous with humanistic studies in universities. Students who pass from a course in philosophy or classics, history or literature, to a course in some aspect of Jewish learning do not move from the twentieth century to the tenth, and they also do not pass from neutral to holy territory. They are in the same university. They see the same faces. Professors talk with them in the same way, in the same language of thought and discourse, and, in a university worthy of the name, the range of issues of analysis and argument is essentially cogent and harmonious. That is what makes a university education distinctive.

When Jewish studies are pursued under parochial, Jewish auspices, whether they take place in a synagogue kindergarten or in a rabbinical seminary or yeshiva, their goal is to verify, validate, and vindicate the life and beliefs of the Jewish people. The paramount apologetic task of education is carried out in the right way, which is to say, not through apologetics but through technology which *assumes* the validity and veracity of that for which apology is required. Everyone knows what is commonly accepted. The propositions of the faith need no defense because they are spelled out within a closed system of society and mind. Since that is the case, the intellectual substance will be composed of three elements. First comes technology, as I said, the knowledge of how to read and write the given language of meaning. That is why stress is laid upon instruction in the Hebrew language, as though it were functional to American Jews. Second comes exegesis of texts. Here the apologetic is much clearer. "We all know" that the texts which are read are holy. "We all know" that there is reward in "learning" them. It follows that "we all know" that what is important is to say the words and explain the words. Why these texts and no others, why what is learned is self-evidently valid, and what these texts mean when put together with many other texts into a large and cogent picture of the whole—these are not useful questions, and they are not asked. The Jewish class room, continuous with the Jewish pulpit, normally consists in the reading of a few lines of a text, followed by a few lines of commentary upon it, whether philological or homiletical. For it is only philology, on the one side, and homiletics, on the other, which serve. Third comes homiletics, divorced from exegesis of texts. Here the overwhelming power of the accepted ideology of Jewishness—that frame of "history-and-peoplehood" which are supposed to make sense of all and explain everything—is brought to bear. In this context scholarship is a tool of sanctification, and that which is to be sanctified is the student and the teacher, the congregation and the rabbi, the listener and the speaker.

This relationship of mutual validation and verification produces an agreed exchange. The people listen with awe and respect to the teacher, whether rabbi or professor or melamed. The teacher then praises the student and tells the listener what the student and listener are expected to hear: pretty much what they already know. The role of the teacher is not to surprise but to reassure, not to question but to answer questions, above all, not to bring about the turning of the wheels of thought, but to make sure that, instead of turning, they merely spin.

It remains to observe that, for a people small in numbers and subject to intense pressures of disintegration, this system of education and mode of instruction are a natural remedy. The work of learning is indoctrination. In this instance, that which is to be indoctrinated is irrelevant to learning. It is loyalty, devotion, commitment, to something worthy of the same. And that is, to begin with, to the figure of authority—rabbi, teacher, melamed—who bestows, in exchange for loyalty, devotion, and commitment, a sense of self-worth and importance. It is a system of status conferred, and a world in which value is determined by consensus of sentiment. That is how a tradition preserves itself against change, and that is how, in its diverse settings, the Jewish group has determined to struggle for its life.

The reason that Jewish studies in universities are discontinuous with Jewish studies in Jewish settings in particular is that universities are different from all other institutions of learning in our society in general. While they follow upon high school, in point of fact few university subjects are even taught in high school. I should guess that at least half of the departments of a liberal arts curriculum have no counterpart in the high school curriculum, or, at best, have so little place in the pre-collegiate program of studies as to be essentially absent, for instance, philosophy, economics, sociology, religious studies, engineering, and the like. Some subjects are carried through, for example, English, history, mathematics, foreign languages. But to that group are added many new ones, and, it goes without saying, there prevails a quite different attitude toward the whole.

Our task as teachers is different as well. In high schools the successful teacher wins the attention of his or her students to the subject at hand and teaches that subject. The work is to impart information, and success is measurable on college board exams. No one should under-

estimate the difficulties and challenge, since we have no natural constituency, in ordinary life, for the work of learning, beyond certain
required skills of communication. Most of what children study in junior
high school has no bearing upon the realities with which they cope; perhaps we thereby try to solve their problems by distraction. Most of what
high school students study has no immediate application, and is not
meant to, so that, just as before, it is no small work to win students'
attention to the work and help them develop the will to learn. And the
generality of high school teacher succeeds in that task.

In universities the successful teacher takes for granted the attention
of the students because the students are present, while in most instances
they are not required to be present, in a given course. Consequently the
work is not to interest the students. Nor is it solely to impart information, though that is an important part of the work. The center of the task
is to begin the work of analysis, by which I mean, to help the student
realize that knowledge is there to be taken apart and put back together,
to be understood as system, process, or construction, and to make sense
of the working of the system and the process, and the coherence of the
construction. When the students' minds begin to move and to work,
when important questions come to mind and can be distinguished from
unimportant or irrelevant ones, when students learn how to listen to a
lecture and intelligently to read and assess a book, and when they take
on their task as participants in learning, then the work of the university
has succeeded. Clearly, this work of analysis is meant to prepare students for important tasks, if not for specific jobs. University education
insists that modes of critical thought and capacities for accurate perception and clear expression make a difference. They serve both to prepare
for useful work and to make possible an interesting life. Learning is not
"for its own sake," nor am I clear what "its own sake" consists of. Learning is for the accomplishment of certain concrete, socially relevant tasks.
But these tasks are to be achieved in those particular ways in which
universities have learned to do their work. If universities are not permitted to work in the ways they know how, then they cannot be useful to
the society or to the social class which sponsors them. Academic freedom
is more than a slogan. It speaks to more than the situation of a holder of
unpopular opinions (indeed, unfortunately, it seldom speaks to that
one's situation at all). And the inner structures of peer review, faculty
governance, collegiality, tenure, and those other dimly perceived and
seldom understood institutions of university life hold up a widely per-

ceived and generally understood world for learning. It all fits together. It all makes sense only when it fits together.

Enough has been said about these two utterly diverse, mutually unperceiving, worlds of Jewish schools and universities so that the obvious may now be stated very briefly. Jewish schools for Jewish learning and university programs in Jewish studies have nothing in common in their context, and therefore have nothing in common in anything but subject-matter—if that. The theories of learning in these two distinct worlds are different, because the works of learning and its tasks are unrelated. I think the very theory of what learning is and how it works must be different, given the rather didactic and authoritarian character of the pulpit and its class-room equivalents in synagogues and yeshivot. Surely a system of learning garbed in theological splendor, in which one's very presence assures this-worldly esteem and other-worldly reward, cannot be compared to that other world in which learning is, at best, its own reward.

It must follow, in my view, that Jewish studies in university are simply not continuous with Jewish learning under Jewish auspices. The cognitive frames are distinct from one another, the social settings diverse, the constituencies utterly dissimilar, and the purpose of the one has no relationship to the purpose of the other. People have tended to argue that the difference between a professor in a theological seminary or yeshiva and one in a university is that the latter is not free to advocate, and the former is; or the former is not objective and the latter is. The categories are irrelevant to real life. We always advocate, and we never are objective: free of values. University professors of Jewish studies care very deeply. Theologians who claim to teach something not laden with values are valueless to their students and to the world.

More important: the curriculum and methods of Jewish studies in university require formation in response to the particular educational tasks of the departmental setting and of the university's intellectual and social context. Precisely what response is to be recommended of course cannot be stated, since the contexts and purposes vary. In one setting emphasis may be upon the study of language and literature; in a second, upon the study of history, religion, culture, or philosophy; in a third, upon social traits and problems. What is forbidden is the essential replication of the curriculum of the Jewish schools, with their stress upon rote-learning of language and the technology of Jewish observance, on the one side, and the apologetic of "history-and-peoplehood," on the other. The former is not relevant, the latter, not respectable, to this other context. When Jewish studies, in all their diversity and promise, find their place, in a university's taxonomy, under "exotic languages," then Jewish studies are effected in an impoverished way. When our principal concern is to impress our colleagues in the State of Israel or rabbis in pulpits with the continuity of our work with theirs, as is the case in many of the Hebrew programs and departments, then, again, Jewish studies are effected in a way which is awry. When nearly all the students in nearly all the courses are of Jewish origin, then Jewish studies have not yet found their way into the center of the humanistic or social scientific curriculum. The catalogue of deadly sins is not a long one, but the death is nonetheless as real. Nor is there a poison to the field more effective than to treat the Jewish studies professor as interchangeable with the local rabbi, or to have the rabbi serve to begin with as a professor, or to have the professor pretend to be a rabbi—or a Hillel director. None of this will do, and those who do not know why do not know the territory of universities. To be sure, they may know full well and not care.

When these things are understood and the tasks of teaching about Judaism or Jewish history, Hebrew, philosophy, sociology, and the other works of the Jewish humanities and social sciences are adequately defined, then, of course, the work of the Hillel rabbi or director becomes vastly more important. For, so far as the professor advocates what professors should and do advocate, the Hillel rabbi or director takes on the task of advocating Judaism. How he or she does that work is a separate and equally important set of issues. I think it is to Alfred Jospe's credit that he understood both the distinctiveness and the importance of the tasks before the Hillel rabbi or director. And this was so, specifically, because he grasped and respected that distinctive context and that difficult work framed by universities and entrusted to them by society and culture.

Teaching the Bible

Arnold Jacob Wolf

B'nai B'rith Hillel Foundation
Yale University

In 1927 Franz Rosenzweig wrote a letter to Jacob Rosenheim, leader of separatist Orthodox Judaism (Agudat Yisrael), in which he set forth his views of the Bible. Two years earlier he and his co-worker, Martin Buber, had begun their translation of Scripture, and he was vigorously conscious that they were trying to do something unprecedented and of surpassing difficulty. He wanted to assure Rosenheim that his views had nothing in common with the neo-Orthodoxy of his time, yet were "faithful" in every real sense of the word.

Buber and Rosenzweig constantly walked the "narrow ridge" between a liberalism which regarded the Bible as a document for human history of particular interest to Jews but revelatory in no way distinct from any other great literature, and an Orthodoxy that made the Torah so utterly different that it almost became a sacred irrelevance. Thus, Rosenzweig writes Rosenheim that for him belief in the holiness of the Torah has nothing to do with the question of its origin, presumed or authentic. For the Bible to be sacred it need not have come to us in any special way. Rosenzweig believes in *Torah min Hashamayim* while suspending any question of *Torah l'Moshe miSinai*. In the final analysis, the two questions have nothing to do with one another; the crucial question is: what do we have? The secondary one is: how did we get it?

Franz Rosenzweig reads the Torah as we have it, as one great document, bracketing any question of how the canon came to be what it is. Not the "original" authors, inaccessible and mysterious as they must remain, but the redactor, the editor of last resort, whoever and whenever he was, is, for us, the mediator of the Word. Using scientific terminology, Rosenzweig calls him "R," but that signifies not (only) Redactor, but Rabbenu, our master Teacher. The Bible is finally one book, and translation or interpretation turn on reading it in its own powerful context. Fifty years later Brevard Childs, in his commentary on Exodus, has begun to use this technique for the post-modern Christian reader. He, too, sees the Bible precisely in its "canonical" form, behind which we often cannot penetrate and never need to go. Documentary notions are in great doubt now, but even in Rosenzweig's lifetime the work of Benno Jacob and Umberto Cassuto had begun to rock the Jewish scholarly world, at least, and render nugatory some of Wellhausen's hypotheses on the origins of Hebrew faith. Still, Rosenzweig took no sides in the scholarly debates. He had another task: to recover the depth and power of the "Torah now in our hands," as Maimonides called it.

Accordingly, the Bible must be read dialectically: written word against oral tradition; what we have against what Jews have understood it to mean during all the various centuries of our study of Scripture. Our Bible is indeed, as Jakob Petuchowski insists, the Bible of the Synagogue. We have no other Bible and we never did. The *p'shat* (straightforward meaning) always came freighted with interpretation. Eisegesis is the inevitable other side of the gold coin of exegesis that some claim alone is genuine. The Jew reads his Bible as a Jew; he cannot and should not pretend that he is innocent of any pre-history. He does not come to it new-born, but instructed and chastened by generations of earlier readers, commentators and "learners" like himself. He will not permit the old prophetic voices to be wholly swallowed up in later rabbinic modalities, but neither can he falsely pretend that biblical voices have no echo, no ambiance, no horizon.

Scholarship, *Wissenschaft*, is not the enemy of commitment. Even Ranke, the first, most critical of historians, was a believer. On the contrary, we cannot emphathize with our biblical predecessors until and unless we also meet them faithfully. God as well as history speaks through a learning which knows its own limits and shares those insights that only commitment can lend to learning. We do not wish to go back to any pre-scientific way of looking at biblical texts. We want, rather, to be beyond *Wissenschaft*, to sublate *Wissneschaft*, so that we may know more than any formal knowledge teaches. We have no quarrel with the scientific study of Judaism so long as it knows that Judaism is much more than science. We have no quarrel with traditional believers so long as they do not identify their own beliefs with the history of Israel's faith.

The Bible, of course, is a book. When we read it, as we must, like any other book, we learn that it is also strangely unlike any other book. The word of man is also precisely the Word of God, and only it is. As Buber later wrote in his *Eclipse of God,* "Human substance is melted by the spiritual fire which visits it and there now breaks forth from it a word, a statement which is human in its meaning and form, human conception and human speech, and yet witnesses to Him who stimulated it and to His will. We are revealed to ourselves, and cannot express it otherwise than as something revealed."

A traditional Jew can only confront the Bible honestly by foregoing his own preconceptions, by nakedly opening himself to the wholly un-expected. He must not force Scripture to affirm what he already holds, merely to authenticate his present conviction. He must not be guilty of pious anachronism or dogmatic presupposition. A liberal Jew, any modern, critical person, must, however, forego his doubts, suspend his disbeliefs and hold himself open to the infinitely self-renewing power of the word. Neither task is easy. Both are just possible.

Teaching Bible to university students is both necessary and possible. Necessary, because they do not know the book, possible because it can be learned. At Yale, the American Studies Department found that their students' knowledge of Scripture was inadequate for the study of American literature, and instituted remedial sections to prepare students to approach their own literary history, one which consistently refers to biblical themes. The Department of Religious Studies, confronted with enormous new enrollments in their courses on the Bible, discovered that most of the students (like many in Yale Divinity School as well) simply had never read most books of the Bible and were registered to do what they might have done long before in religious schools, but somehow never did. Jewish students, of all varieties and denominations, betray sketchy acquaintance with biblical texts even if they happen to know somewhat more about Jewish holidays and Israeli history, or even if they can make out the Hebrew language. Some have heard the Torah read (not, usually, carefully translated, and almost never interpreted and dis-cussed) during the Sabbath service, but they have rarely even turned the pages of most of the rest of the *Tanach.* Hence a study of Scripture is necessary.

It is also possible. Unlike the vast talmudic literature, for example, it is of manageable length. A good semester course can cover a major book (like Deuteronomy) or a small one (Song of Songs) with additional comparative materials of many kinds. For those who cannot read Hebrew there are now excellent English translations, as well as important ones in other modern languages. A weekly informal course can complete the two Books of Samuel in a year or the Five Books of Moses in about three. Everyone senses that Biblical material is absolutely basic; they soon learn it is also striking in its concern with living issues. It is as available in some respects to the neophyte as to the Talmudist, to the student of comparative literature as to the theologian. It is ancient and elusive and profound, but it is also straightforward and quintessential. No text could possibly be more than that.

The real question is not whether but how to teach the Bible to modern university students. First of all, I believe, we must teach them *p'shat* and not *d'rash*. *P'shat* does not quite mean the plain sense or simple meaning of the text, as several recent studies have proved. It is a far more flexible and rich methodology than that. But there still is a difference between reading what is there and using what is there for what is not. There is an irremovable distinction between going out to meet the Bible (to be sure, with all we have to bring) and forcing the text into our own, necessarily narrower categories. Teaching Bible means disclosure, confrontation, even careful extrapolation; it should not mean sermonics, manipulation or historicism. However much we want to use the text to prove something (even something true), the text must remain more sacred than anything we ever could prove. The simple meaning of Scripture is of course, not so simple, but it is far more precise and instructive than any interpretation, even and especially our own.

The method of choice is discussion and not lecture. When I work over Jewish texts with students in an open discussion, I feel myself back not only at the University of Chicago Great Books seminars where, sixteen years old, I painfully worked through the *Republic* and *Paradise Lost* with gifted teachers who could both listen and respond, but also back in a most traditional *Bet Midrash* where any Jewish scholar proved his learning not by displaying it in a fine discourse, but by leading his students carefully into the intricacies and depths of the sacred word. Jewish learning is not hearing someone talk about a book; it is studying a book, under expert teachers who are also themselves "students of the wise." Rabbi Solomon Goldman once said to me that Jews do not read books, they only study them. If a book is not worth studying, he said, it is not even worth perusing. But study classically means study *b'havruta*, in a community, with a leader. The words may be read alone or together, but meanings can be disclosed only to a community of learners.

The leader's role is, therefore, delicate. He or she cannot and should not pretend to know less than he does, though, of course, not more either. He is *primus inter pares*, not master of all he surveys. He, or she, must, as Maimonides tells us in the *Hilchot Talmud Torah*, sit equally with his students and not above them, perhaps preferably in a circle of chairs. He may neither dominate nor absent himself; he must listen fully as carefully as he speaks. He must steer the discussion's tone between levity and over-seriousness. The Bible is important but our own views are somewhat less than final.

It also follows that group size is crucial. Three people are too few, fifty too many. Within those limits, various numbers are possible. While I prefer a group of fifteen (that is the number set for Yale College seminars by the administration), I have found that five or thirty are both feasible. The room must be big enough to hold the participants but not too big so that it intimidates them. The same could be said for the teacher. His or her task is not self-presentation nor pontificating. It is precisely *explication de texte*. The group teaches each other and the teacher is the teacher of them all who is taught by them all. Ideally, the student remembers less about the teacher than about the text; a good teacher is translucent to what he is teaching, and this is never more true than with biblical material. Many years ago a fine teacher introduced me to the Book of Exodus. I remember much about him, more about what he said about the book, but most about the book itself; I have often merged the teacher into the book.

The leader is present more to raise questions than to provide answers. The text is, itself, a kind of answer, though one that, like all profound answers, raises ever new questions. The Bible is a mystery to be confronted, not a problem to be solved. Over and over again, in teaching Bible commentary, my teacher, Abraham Joshua Heschel, would ask: "What is Rashi's problem?" What is the question which gives rise to the interpreter's "answer," and what questions are raised by that answer itself? Questions should proceed from the relatively minor to the most general and profound. We might begin the study of the Flood with a trivial question about why the raven preceded the dove, since it did not in the earlier comparative Near Eastern material. Then, or another time, we might think about the deeper problem of a good person in a bad generation. Finally, we must sometime talk about the meaning of the world-covenant and the promise of unending human history.

In thinking about the Creation story, we might begin with the special formulation of the creation of mankind which differs subtly from those that frame the earlier of God's creations. God does not (cannot?) produce a person, like a world, by fiat. Perhaps the fact that God cannot bring himself to call human creation "good" (although the sixth day as a whole is "very good") shows a certain ambivalence about His final creature. He would have good reason for that. Nehama Leibowitz is often brilliant at raising small questions that open out to vast concerns. My only objection to her method is that it leaves the questions only partly open, and "solves" problems that are too mysterious for solution.

Questions that are posed should not be left vague nor completely open-ended, but they must not be seen as gimmicks or entering-wedges for a preconceived solution. The truth is that we do not know the truth: the Bible asks unanswerable questions, and we must not claim more than to have posed them carefully and looked hard for explanations. The end of each session should not leave the class with a sense of closure, however much they might enjoy the sense of having solved a venerable riddle. Their mood should rather be one of being driven back to the text to look again at what seemed at first to be an answer but turned out to be a deeper and harder question. It is good for us Jews to have to read the Five Books over and over again, year after year. The mere act of repetition says that the meanings elude us as we go out to grasp them. A class should reflect something of that infinite longing which is beyond both failure and success.

The kinds of questions posed should not, in most settings, be only scientific or aesthetic. It is a help to know source-criticism if only to discover that it, too, is no answer but a series of insoluble puzzles; still, criticism is not our final task. Nor are we to see the beauties of the Bible as literature unless, as seems to me increasingly the case, literature itself is swallowed up in a much larger category. If I am forced to give a name to the kind of questions I think are posed by Scripture, it would have to be "existential," but that word, too, says considerably less that I mean.

The Bible is not only a book about what happened. It is also about what happens; not only what was, but what we are; not only about ancestors but also, since what happened to them is "a sign" to us, about ourselves. The themes of family, law, power, lust, faith and faithlessness, nationalism and war, suffering and death are the great themes not only of world literature but of human life. Thus our questions must not be of the kind: in Scripture who is said to have lived the longest life? Rather: how can a holy land be promised and how rightfully taken by force? No one is more subtle in this kind of ethical-personal query than the French savant, Emanuel Levinas, who goes to the heart of Scripture and rabbinic texts not with the equipment and concerns of the specialist, but with a philosopher's questioning passion and a Jew's conviction that there is more in the Bible than is dreamt of in any person's philosophy. The Bible is not so much a book as a world, and our study of it must be not the study of literary forms only, but of life. Technical questions can often lead beyond themselves: our task is not to find out only what is said but also what is meant. We are not critics of the Bible but its co-conspirators.

Scientific questions are, of course, not excluded in principle: they remain, however, inevitably propadeutic. We are, as we said, not going back to a pre-scientific dogmatism of any kind, but nineteenth-century *wissenschaftliche* concerns are no longer our own. Scholarship is always welcome, certainly in biblical studies, but it is preliminary to the concerns, not only of faith but of life. The Bible must, of course, be read against its own environmental background, but the latter includes not only Ras Shamra and Gilgamesh but also myself. I am, we are, the skein on which Scripture is continually woven. I do not read Wellhausen or Cassuto to find out where they are wrong, not even where they are "right," but to read the Bible over their shoulders with my own eyes. It is a great accomplishment to be a biblical scholar, a still greater one to be the addressee of the biblical message. And that each of us can be.

Our method of study must be dialectical not apodictic. The text is always, as Heschel says about all God-statements, an understatement. It is always more than we say it is, never less. So we must use the Socratic method more honorably than Plato did, not to prove what we already really know, but to sharpen our sensibilities in order to know and feel more. The text eludes our pursuit, so we must redouble our pace. It is beyond our reach, so we reach ever higher. We can never specify it in some final fashion, only point to it and use it to point to where it points. Everyone can read the Bible except one who thinks he already has.

It is very useful to use the Bible to interpret itself. There are in it apparent contradictions. I believe there are also real contradictions. Good! Use the contradictions dialectically: what is the truth in each? how does one limit or refute the other? why are both necessary? Some truth, not the least important, can only be stated paradoxically; much can only be understood by a method of query and response and query. Solutions stifle, but deep questions drive inevitably deeper into our souls. A good Bible class is very confusing, though not obfuscating. A good teacher teaches the Bible's wisdom and his or her own ignorance.

The class, therefore, will be full of controversy. It will not conform. There will be no consensus. Each view of each student, especially the teacher-student, will be resolutely attacked. Nothing will be admitted without debate. We must each be humble enough to see our own pet ideas demolished, and proud enough to war against other people's interpretations. The class will sound more like a bazaar or a courtroom than like a Quaker meeting. Class members will be on their toes, not on their best behavior, because we honor Scripture best by taking it seriously enough to argue about it, not for the sake of argument, but for the sake of Scripture. Something important is at stake. We are not debating fine points of scholarship, except as those show us that we are the subject of our own debate. The adversary proceeding is crucial to our innocence or guilt, as in a courtroom. It is essential to our method that anyone may speak and no one may be ignored. But no view is final, and no agreement is sought. Each debate ends in a Talmudic *teku:* inconclusive, unfinished, everlasting.

Tradition is a more valuable tool than mere innovativeness. A good word from an old interpreter often helps us more than an ingenious speculation by our contemporary. No interpretation or interpreter is privileged, not Rashi, not Buber, not the teacher of our class. We are all in it together, the dead we well as the living, the medieval as well as the post-modern. Times rejoin each other. Nothing seems more old fashioned than the day before yesterday. Nothing is more radical than naked tradition. No scholar but has his day, no idea whose time will never come around. We are not in the business of thinking up a new thought, certainly not of deconstructing an old one, so much as in discovering our past, imagining the present, and remembering what many before us have already forgotten.

Apologetics has its place, but not in the kind of biblical study here envisioned. Our present task is not to defend the Bible against its detractors ("primitive, bloody, tasteless") or its people against their enemies ("why did Abraham lie, Moses kill, the Israelites commit genocide, the prophets exaggerate, Ezra legislate ethnocentrism?") We must assume that the Bible can withstand relentless criticism. It does not need any of our ineffectual apologies. We owe the text honesty, which means confronting jarring as well as comfortable passages. I have personally found far more significance in passages that offend me than in those that soothe, though the latter also have their time and place.

The Bible is not the Boy Scout Manual. It is not above the fray; it *is* the fray. It does not condescend to our moral dilemmas; it makes them dramatically vivid and often heartbreaking. Its God is not Olympian and will not conform to our image of Him. Its Torah does not mandate the ethics of Mill or Rawls. Its central characters are always ambivalent and sometimes doomed. Its holiness is a holiness of expectation, not one of accomplished fact. We should not try to smooth out its wrinkles nor hide its warts. We need not judge it in order for it to judge us.

A Bible class should not be manipulated but opened wide up. Data must be fully and precisely put. It is important how many times and where a specific Hebrew word is used. It is important what is said and left unsaid, who is described by whom, and how the Commandments in Exodus differ from those in Deuteronomy. Biblical material is as precise as a sonnet, more careful than a formula. Accuracy in interpretation is essential. We must be attentive to detail if we are to encompass signification. The Bible is not a book for speed readers. Revelation cannot be skimmed. Erich Auerbach has taught us that, unlike a much more explicit Greek literature, the Hebrew writer alludes and refers, speaks in silence, subtly. No one can teach the *Tanach* who does not believe God is in the details, especially in the most boring ones.

We teach carefully but never completely. We teach parts of the Book, never all of it. We grasp some of its meaning, never the whole of it. What we are presently studying is not all there is; things may seem lopsided if we forget there is more—and different—wisdom elsewhere in the Book. We need not assume previous knowledge to begin to teach the Scripture, but we must emphasize that learning some of it may be not only incomplete but also misleading. A little revelation is a very dangerous thing.

"Turn it and turn it, for everything is in it." Everything! More than we expect. More than we want. More than we can understand. More than we can teach. More than appears on the surface. More than moves in the depths. More, perhaps, than anything human beings have ever, unaided, themselves produced.

Teaching Modern Jewish Thought

Eva Jospe

Georgetown University
and
The George Washington University
Washington, D.C.

Having always regarded the establishment of a Jewish studies program on the American campus as desirable, I happily accepted some five or six years ago the invitation to become part of this—then still fairly new—venture. But partly because the rationale and objective of such a program seemed to me so self-evident, and partly because the experience of teaching at both The George Washington University and Georgetown University has been such an entirely positive one, I never stopped to theorize about something I considered a perfect "natural," a sort of "given." The following remarks will, subsequently, not attempt to contribute any learned theories to or scholarly analyses of the topic of Jewish education in the setting of the university. They are meant only to offer some personal reflections, observations based on pragmatic classroom situations in teaching modern Jewish thought, as well as on frequent less formal contacts with college students.

Still, even a mere practitioner of the art of teaching must proceed according to certain principles. Without them, one's choice of subject matter and methodology could hardly be determined, to say nothing of the educational goals one hopes to achieve or at least to approach. Actually, it is a somewhat artificial undertaking to describe these three—subject matter, methodology and educational goals—as distinct entities. They are, it seems to me, correlated, both functionally and substantively. One is the concomitant of the other, and all depend to a considerable degree on the teacher's personal inclinations, gifts, and aspirations.

My own field of concentration, for instance, was chosen because of my fascination with what modern Jewish thought has distilled out of classical Jewish thought. Judaism's religio-cultural tradition and its modern interpretation can, I am convinced, say much that is urgently needed to an age ("age" in the double sense of an era and of a stage in an individual's life) undergoing the stress and strain of transvaluing all values. Believing in the abiding validity of Judaism's central teachings, and touched to the core by its existential insights, I fully appreciate the various and widely varying attempts to restate these teachings and insights in an idiom apt to make them newly significant to the "new," the nineteenth and twentieth century, Jew. To be sure, not all of these attempts are ideologically acceptable or even logically compelling, and some of them, dated by their very "modernity," appear already outdated to the post-modern mind. Nevertheless, I consider their study indispensable, both as *Ding an sich* and because they build a two-way bridge between Judaism's past and future.

It is for this reason that my courses, cutting across all denominational lines without blurring any denominational distinctions, deal with the work of men (to cite only the most outstanding among numerous others) like Moses Mendelssohn, Abraham Geiger, Samson Raphael Hirsch, Leopold Zunz and Zacharias Frankel, Hermann Cohen, Leo Baeck, Franz Rosenzweig, Martin Buber, Abraham J. Heschel, and Mordecai M. Kaplan. What these and more recent representatives of modern Jewish thought have to say about certain questions with which students have either already grappled on their own, or with which they are confronted for the first time, is bound to have a direct impact upon them. I am referring to concepts (again to select but a few) such as creation, revelation, and redemption; man's freedom of will and subsequent moral responsibility; the individual's self-worth and task within society; to issues concerning the centrality of *halakha* in Jewish life; to the tensions between faith and reason or between universalism and particularism; and to problems related to social injustice or any other kind of suffering of the innocent. A discussion of these questions can, and frequently does, reach students where they really are, so that occasionally the hoped-for happens: a mind-boggling perplexity is turned into a mind-stretching learning experience, and someone's groping progress from where he/she is to where they would like to be is helped along.

A teacher can provide another assist in that progress by showing the student how to make constructive use of the data being conveyed; that is, how to weigh and compare these frequently confusing if not contradictory nuggets of knowledge so as to integrate them into a cogently interlocking whole. Only as they learn to "see how all the pieces fall into place, how everything suddenly comes together" (as one of my seniors recently put it), will students be adequately prepared for any future academic work. The development of a faculty of intellectual discernment seems to me one of the most essential educational desiderata. The undergraduate in particular, often overwhelmed by an embarrassment of riches in the form of lectures, books, and trendy campus ideologies, needs to acquire a sense of discrimination. Without it, the student will be ill equipped to cope with any number of academic, practical, and psychological problems—among the latter those arising from exposure to the enticements of pseudo-religious cults and life-styles euphemistically named "alternative." A student who can distinguish between open-mindedness and gullibility should be less likely to buy junk-food to satisfy what is usually referred to as "spiritual hunger," but what in reality may more often than not be merely a vague sense of disorientation and discontent.

We also discuss, of course, the historical, ideological, and psychological factors whose interaction created the *Zeitgeist* that gave rise to and fructified modern Jewish thought. Though the need for such background exploration is obvious in any case, it seems particularly urgent in the case of college students. Living almost exclusively in the present, hence existentially related only to the Now, they must be given an understanding of, and with it the possibility of relating to, the Then. To find out that and how the Now and the Then hang together in the world of ideas, and that this world did not start with anyone of us—though in a very real sense it does begin with each one of us anew—can be an at once sobering and exciting discovery.

The intellectual excitement that, fortunately, can sometimes be generated in the classroom has something to do with a notion I consider of signal importance for any kind of teaching: relevance. It is a notion currently not much touted about. The hue and cry for it, raised only so recently (and often so absurdly) in the halls of academe, has subsided. It has gone the way of all slogans, from deafening noise to silent discard. Yet, though my students may no longer insist on relevance, I still do. That is, I try my best to make the subject matter we are dealing with meaningful to them, to make it their personal concern, to give them a sense of *tua res agitur*. For if I succeed in making an idea come alive for them, this idea—whether disturbing or confirming some of their own notions—may give them the impetus to develop a "value-stance" (a term I borrow from Arthur Lelyveld). And this, I believe, is or ought to be the goal of any teaching which aims at being more than mere instruction, which is not satisfied merely to inform the student *of* certain values but seeks to in-form him/her *with* them.

Admittedly, I do hope to contribute to the in-forming of my students. Yet I definitely do not wish to serve as their "role-model," a function assigned to the teacher of Judaica by some writers on the subject. To assume that one does or ought to occupy a paradigmatic position is, I am afraid, conducive to assuming a pose. True, I do let my students know, in so many words or without, where I stand and what I stand for. But this stand of mine has evolved and is being maintained unalloyed by any intent to make it exemplary. In fact, the near-equation of teaching with modelling makes me acutely uncomfortable. Nevertheless, and despite my rejection of any kind of role-playing, I am far from ruling out the possibility or even likelihood that the teacher's personal convictions might exert an influence upon his/her students. I realize, moreover, that convictions and beliefs have a way of transmitting themselves, without any conscious effort on the part of those who hold them, almost osmotically—in the classroom, during personal conferences, and even over coffee and cookies in one's home, whose library or art and ceremonial objects give tangible evidence of their owner's "self-respecting rootedness in Jewish values."[1]

It is, however, precisely because I am aware of a teacher's potential for influencing students that I agree with all who consider it improper if not illegitimate to attempt any "proselytizing" in the classroom. And when that classroom is located, respectively, in a Department of Religion and a Department of Theology (as mine is), and when the courses offered stress the religio-philosophical aspect of modern Jewish thought (as mine do), this consideration is of paramount importance. There is no doubt in my mind that academic freedom, that cherished prerogative of the teacher, must extend also to the taught. My endeavour to deepen my students' understanding of modern Jewish thought is, hence, free of any conversional intent. And that goes alike for Jews and non-Jews in my "constituency"—undergraduates, here or there interspersed with a graduate or post-graduate—whose background and diversity may (among the non-Jews) range from Muslim through American Indian to

Mormon, and (among both Jews and non-Jews) from a studious religious affiliation to a studied a-religious non-affiliation.

There is, of course, no necessary connection between grasping the meaning of Judaism and embracing its faith. But even if such a connection were to exist or could be established by the teacher, the latter would be duty-bound to refrain from even the most subliminal ideological missionizing. Religious commitment, or lack thereof, must remain the student's private affair.

And yet is is not entirely correct to say that I have no conversional intent. There is a certain way in which I do wish to convert my students, though neither to Judaism if they are not Jews, nor to any of its branches if they are. I do wish to convert them in the literal sense of turning them around: from indifference to matters of the mind toward a concern with them; from a complacent acceptance of hand-me-down, preconceived notions toward investigating them; from the self-centeredness of today's "me-generation" toward a sympathetic outreach to the world. In short, I hope that their exposure to modern Jewish thought will arouse in my students an interest in thought-as-such, or that it will at least induce in them the latter's preliminary stage, thoughtfulness.

This hope of mine does not in any way contradict my just stated conviction that proselytizing and academic teaching are mutually exclusive activities. In fact, I have made this conviction a guiding principle both in presenting the various denominational approaches to Judaism to my students, and in monitoring their (actively encouraged) discussions. As for the latter, I think it mandatory that their give and take, no matter how animated, be kept free of animosity. I am trying to impress all participants—preferably by implication only, but if necessary also by explication—with the need to distinguish between convictional fervor and personal rancor, between holding an opinion and being opinionated. More than that, I should like to instill in my students respect for what Buber has called "the other's otherness." At the moment, this is actually not particularly difficult. Ever since "doing one's own thing" (or, in a more updated version, "being into" some private, esoteric pursuit) became the dominant campus ideal, tolerance and an attitude of *laissez faire* have been the order of the day. Whether this attitude will carry over into "real" life—and in the process become a bit more selective— remains to be seen. In any event, if my students, launched on or settled in their respective careers, were to shun that internecine aggressiveness which characterizes so much of the public debate among today's professionals and scholars, one of my educational goals would be realized.

But there are other, more substantive goals to be attained, and to do so, one has to come to terms with an old pedagogical problem: the question of objectivity vs. subjectivity. Reflecting on that question (though with reference to "philosophizing" rather than teaching), Franz Rosenzweig wrote in 1927: "The obligation to be objective demands only that we look really at the entire horizon; it does not ask that we see it from a point of view other than our own, or from no particular point of view at all. Admittedly, our eyes are our eyes only; but to believe that we must pluck them out so as to see properly would bespeak a Chelmite mentality (*waere schildbuergerhaft*)."[2]

Yet it takes a wide-angle lense, an all-encompassing perspective to see the entire horizon. And the objective/subjective dilemma can become especially acute where religious convictions are involved, or in connection with so potentially loaded a question as that of early Zionist theory vs. the demands of today's *Realpolitik*, or that most haunting of subjects, the Holocaust. How evenhanded can one be in the former case, how dispassionate in the latter? Even pertaining to less soul-searing issues, one may occasionally have to tread a precariously thin line as one tries to strike a balance between objectivity and subjectivity. There is a certain ambivalence about affirming the need for academic objectivity, and at the same time feeling strongly that a teacher's job is not merely to transmit but also to evaluate data of knowledge, especially when those data have been gleaned from the fields of ideology.

The tension between objectivity and subjectivity is apparently built into the entire educational process, from the selection of one's material to its presentation, from one's methodology to its objective. And the fact that all of these are, inevitably, the products of a personal pre-judgment gives rise to a dual question: how much objectivity does one owe to one's subject matter, how much subjectivity to one's students? In an effort to resolve the conflict between academic neutrality and personal value-judgment, I therefore proceed by observing the one in exploring any given issue, while expressing the other in answering any "convictional" questions put to me. In this way, I hope to do equal justice to the postulates of academic integrity and the needs of searching young minds.

The attainment of this dual objective remains an ongoing challenge. But another goal, substantively quite different and envisaged by those who originally asked that Judaica become part of the university curriculum, has by now been realized: academe's acknowledgment of Judaism's intellectual respectability. That Jewish studies have academically "arrived" is palpably noticeable in the very atmosphere in which they are pursued. There is no longer any need to engage in apologetics, nor in efforts comparable to, say, those of a Hermann Cohen, who still had to labor mightily to demonstrate that Judaism is conceptually equal to the best in Western thought. Such efforts would actually strike as undignified if not ludicrous a campus population (both faculty and students) of second and third generation American Jews—and the more so the less they realize that their own self-assurance and self-acceptance are in no small measure due to the fact that they never had to justify their own existence, nor to defend the worth and validity of their spiritual heritage.

The term spiritual heritage has become such a cliché that I am embarrassed to use it. Yet I know of no better word to describe the sum-total of that set of values, derived from the matrix of Judaism's classical sources, which modern Jewish thought examines, elucidates, or redefines. To paraphrase what I have said before: I see this examination, elucidation, or redefinition of Judaism's ethos and of its way to deal with ultimate questions not as a propagation of faith but a propagation of thought. And if the classroom is decidedly out-of-bounds for the former, it must just as decidedly become the arena for the latter. To my amazement and dismay, I often find that even seniors with their three or more years of college experience need to be coaxed to think and to question. But I also and almost invariably find that once the initial hesitation or even bewilderment have been overcome, class participation is eagerly sought and openly enjoyed.

Another source of amazement (though not of dismay) is the great difference of intellectual endowment and educational background among even a small group of students. This difference makes teaching at once harder and more of a personal challenge. I accept that challenge in something close to a fighting spirit; that is, I bend every effort to get even the less bright and least knowledgeable first interested in, and then really conversant with, our current subject, without making things tedious for the class as a whole. As for the occasional Mr. or Ms. Know-it-all—they can rather easily be shown how far they are from knowing it all. This exigency, however, arises very rarely. The great majority of my students seem genuinely receptive to what modern Jewish thought can teach them. And sometimes—joy of a teacher's joys—there are even a few who ask to be given more than the merely required reading.

Even so, I do realize that it is the need to fulfill certain degree requirements rather than an overpowering yearning for knowledge that
determines most students' choice of courses. Among Jewish students,
moreover (and the next few paragraphs refer to Jewish students only),
there may quite possibly be some who are motivated to take a Jewish
studies course by the hope that it will be a "snap." I suspect that the
well-known business practice of "ethnic buying" has a campus
counterpart: ethnic registering, with the negligible difference that the
former is undertaken in anticipation of easy terms, and the latter in
anticipation of an easy term. Should my suspicion be justified, and
should among the new registrants in any course of mine really be any
"ethnic" ones, they would soon find themselves disabused of the naive
notion that I, by dint of being their fellow-Jew, might compromise my
professional standards. Whoever enrolls in my classes is bound to realize
during our first meeting that I look upon modern Jewish thought as an
academic (though certainly value-oriented) discipline, and that I expect
the same attitude of my students.

But there is also another, and a more acceptable, motivation for any
"ethnic" course enrollment: the by now almost obligatory "search for
roots" which, in turn, has something to do with the wish to establish
one's self-image so as to prevent or overcome an "identity crisis." It is a
motivation welcomed by some and decried by others who are concerned
with these matters. I myself see nothing wrong with choosing Jewish
studies as an instrumentality for finding out as much as possible about
one's cultural antecedents, though I do not disregard the scholars'
postulate that Judaica be studied for their own sake, as it were *by* "pure"
rather than *for* any practical reason.

As for any identity crisis actually or potentially threatening our
students—this malady, so rampant among their parents who still felt
torn by the particularist/universalist conflict, seems no longer to afflict
the present college generation. At least those of its members with whom
I come into personal contact show no evidence of it. In fact, I see much
evidence to the contrary, unless I misread the meaning of such ubiqui-
tous badges of identification as the *kipah* on male heads (no longer worn
by orthodox Jews alone) or "Jewish" ornaments around both male and
female necks. Observing the campus-scene—or that minuscule and not
quite typical segment of it open to my view—I gain the impression that
its current Jewish residents feel entirely at ease with their Jewishness,
and that somewhere along the line of succession there has been a com-

plete transformation from Jewish self-consciousness to Jewish self-awareness. (I should add, though, that such ease need not always be a sign of affirmation. Total indifference to the fact of having been born a Jew can also make for an absence of tensions. But since those who dwell in this comfortable state for negative reasons are no likely candidates for a Jewish studies program, they are of no, or at least of no immediate, concern to our present considerations).

Strangely enough, if not paradoxically, it is the very ease with which Judaism (or, to be more precise, Jewishness) is largely accepted today which makes me somewhat uneasy. I do appreciate and indeed can enjoy the lifestyle of "doing Judaism" currently chosen by many young adults. It has a sort of folk appeal, an engaging naturalness and lively directness—all vastly preferable to the routine observance or performance of some of their elders; moreover, it is obviously emotionally satisfying to those who participate in its variegated activities. Yet spirited as these activities are, they often seem to lack a certain spirit. I mean that spirit of intellectual inquiry, indeed of soul-searching, which has at least the potential of transposing a "doing" into a "doable" Judaism, its "sancta" into its sanctification, and thus of giving to Judaism a depth dimension "doing" alone cannot bestow upon it.

A folk Judaism is doubtlessly legitimate as a cultural phenomenon, and I do not wish to derogate any of its constitutive elements. Nor do I belittle the importance of the "mood and food" factor in experiencing Judaism as a way of life. Still, a folk Judaism is, to me, not yet a full, a conceptually grasped Judaism. One can surely bake a delicious ḥallah, weave a beautiful tallit, build a sukkah and even light candles without engaging in "spiritual," let alone torturously theological, premeditations. Still, if one wishes to teach one's students that "we are responsible not for what we learn or fail to learn, but for what we think or fail to think,"[3] or if one feels that an unexamined Judaism is not worth "doing" (with due apologies to Socrates), one is happy to rediscover, and feels reassured by what Hermann Cohen, advocating "higher Jewish learning," said already in 1907: "All cultural life, including the religious, must involve the mind as well as the heart. It is not enough that our soul be satisfied and exalted by our old customs and ancient spiritual treasures. These treasures must be acquired ever anew."[4]

I am sure that the acquisition of these "treasures," along with an appreciation of the spirit which created them, remains one of the principal goals of "higher Jewish learning." I am not so sure how "high" this learning will take most of us, teachers and students alike. The plateau reached may lie all too often below the desired altitude. But as long as I am able to ascertain that my students know at the end of each semester more than they did at its start, and that they have made some small progress not only in knowledge but also in understanding, I feel that both modern Jewish thought and I, its transmitter, have fulfilled an eminently worthwhile task. For though, as I have said before, I have no wish to serve as anybody's "role-model," I do cherish the opportunity to introduce my students to that world of mind and heart and "meaning" called Judaism. It is a world of whose intrinsic value I am profoundly convinced, and to whose comprehension and perpetuation I should like to contribute my modest bit.

In conclusion, and inasmuch as these pages are written for the *Festschrift* in Alfred's honor, I want to state publicly and gratefully that it was he who originally initiated me into that world, who continues to be my personal Director of Program and Resources, though he long ago stopped being Hillel's, and without whose mentorship I might quite possibly neither have made my spiritual home in modern Jewish thought, nor have learned how to teach it.

NOTES

1. Irving Greenberg, "Scholarship and Continuity: Dilemma and Dialectic"; *The Teaching of Judaica in American Universities*, p. 128.

2. Letter to Rudolf Stahl, 6/2/1927; *Briefe*, p. 597 (my transl.).

3. Franz Rosenzweig, *On Jewish Learning*, Schocken Books, Inc., 1955, p. 116.

4. *Reason and Hope*, Selections from the Jewish Writings of Hermann Cohen, N.Y. 1971, p. 51.

The Role of Philosophy in Jewish Studies

Marvin Fox

Brandeis University
Waltham, Massachusetts

In this essay I shall argue that without close attention to philosophic issues and methods, work in almost every area of Jewish Studies is deficient, although it is certainly the case that western culture has exhibited ambivalent attitudes toward philosophy and philosophers. In praise of philosophy it is claimed that it is the supreme architectonic science, the model of true wisdom, the fulfillment of the highest human aspirations. Plato is the classic source for this conception of philosophy, and his ideal man is conceived on the model of the philosopher. Plato's Socrates is presented as the best possible realization of the human ideal, which is to say, the true philosopher. Detractors of philosophy, on the other hand, have seen it as concerned with trivia and as threatening sound belief and even public order. This view, expressed by the accusers of Socrates in Plato's *Apology*, recurs throughout the history of western culture. Cicero makes the acerbic comment that, "There is nothing so absurd that it has not been said by some philosopher."[1] Aristophanes in the *Clouds* pictures Socrates as a somewhat dangerous buffoon. While Thales is admired by some for his astute use of meteorological knowledge for personal profit, another tradition pictures him as so impractical that he fell into a well while gazing at the stars.[2] And Shakespeare's Romeo finds scant comfort in "Adversity's sweet milk, Philosophy." In his agony he asserts that, "Unless philosophy can make a Juliet, Displant a town, reverse a prince's doom, It helps not, it prevails not."[3]

There is a similar ambivalence toward philosophy in the history of

Judaism. Some medieval Jewish thinkers give to philosophic knowledge the highest place in their system of values, but their views can hardly be considered normative for all of Judaism. As is well known, there is a tradition of anti-philosophy within Judaism, which ranges from relative indifference to active hostility. The few direct references to philosophers in the rabbinic literature are on the whole uncomplimentary.[4] Philosophers are generally represented in Talmud and Midrash as heretics or as posers of rather foolish questions. There is little evidence that Greek philosophy had any significant influence on classical rabbinic thought. Professor Harry A. Wolfson said that he was "not able to discover any Greek philosophic term in Rabbinic literature," and Professor Saul Lieberman eliminates all doubt on this point when he adds, "I want to state more positively: Greek philosophic terms are absent from the entire ancient Rabbinic literature."[5]

Contempt for philosophy as a dangerous and misleading effort to substitute human wisdom for divine wisdom also occurs frequently in early Christianity. In a characteristic passage, Paul warns the Collosians against the dangers of "philosophy and empty deceit" which are mere human teachings and thus utterly unreliable.[6] The early church fathers considered certain Christian heresies to have their origins in "erroneous doctrines of the philosophers."[7] Tertullian expresses fierce opposition to philosophy as he depicts with delight the pleasures that await the faithful, when they will view, from a front row seat in heaven, the agonies of philosophers burning in Hell.[8]

Later periods in Jewish history exhibited some of the ferocity of the early Christian attacks on philosophy. The anti-Maimonidean controversy may have been the most extreme and extended case of such an attack, but it was by no means the only one. Suspicion of philosophy continued to manifest itself throughout the Jewish middle ages, and in certain circles the phenomenon continued in modern times. In some of the very yeshivot in which the study of Maimonides' *Mishne Torah* was mandatory, the study of his *Guide of the Perplexed* was frequently prohibited, or, at least, very actively discouraged. There are contemporary Jewish circles, as well, in which the rejection of philosophy continues to be considered as one mark of religious and intellectual virtue.

It is natural, therefore, to ask whether philosophy has any role in the study of Judaism. One immediate and easy justification is that there is, after all, a large literature of Jewish philosophic works, beginning with Saadia (if not with Philo) and continuing unbroken to the present.

Surely, these are worthy of study, and they do constitute an appropriate segment of any curriculum of Jewish studies. While it seems pointless to argue against this claim, we can hardly ignore the argument made by some major scholars of our time. Leo Strauss held that the *Guide of the Perplexed* "is not a philosophic book."[9] Isaac Husik acknowledged that there was Jewish philosophy in the middle ages, but he was convinced that this discipline did not persist in the contemporary world. He ends his *History of Medieval Jewish Philosophy* with the melancholy observation that, "There are Jews now and there are philosophers, but there are no Jewish philosophers and there is no Jewish philosophy." Of course, neither Husik nor Strauss would exclude from our courses of study works which seek to interpret Judaism philosophically. They only want to argue that they are not works of philosophy.

Despite the existence of such extreme views, I doubt that any reasonable student of these matters will wish to assert seriously that there is no literature of Jewish philosophy. It exists and it is worthy of study. Without question such study constitutes one part of the role of philosophy in the Jewish Studies curriculum. In considering our topic, however, we must recognize how severely and needlessly we limit philosophy if we restrict it to the study of the history of Jewish philosophy. The thesis which I present here does not address itself to the question of the place of philosophy in Judaism. It does, however, argue that we are urgently in need of serious philosophic study and analysis of the whole range of textual materials which are the subject-matter of Jewish Studies, not only of acknowledged Jewish philosophic works, but also of every type of Jewish literature from antiquity to the present.

The very nature of philosophic thinking is such that it can and should be applied without exception to the entire corpus of Jewish literature. Bible, Talmud, and other major Jewish works are not systematic philosophic treatises, but they will never be fully understood if we do not approach them with the concerns and the techniques of philosophy. Opposition to philosophy at various times and places in Jewish history does not invalidate the propriety and usefulness of a philosophic study even of the very works in which such opposition is expressed. On the contrary, the texts which seem least philosophical are often the ones which most demand philosophical analysis.

I shall not attempt to offer here a definition of philosophy. Anyone familiar with the literature knows the range and complexity of the definitions that have been attempted. Yet we can set forth certain general

characteristics of the philosophical approach to texts which is advocated
in this essay. I suggest that in the study of any Jewish texts we must
engage in philosophic work on two levels, substantive and methodological. Substantively, the texts are almost certain to contain specifically philosophical subject-matter. In one way or another, directly or by implication, serious works take some stand with respect to some of the "ultimate questions" which are usually considered the subject-matter of philosophy. Even non-philosophical Jewish books contain both explicit
and implicit metaphysical theses, fundamental claims about the ethical,
philosophical or theological anthropologies, views about knowledge and
truth, systems of logic, and other types of specifically philosophical
teachings.

A proper philosophic study of these works will be concerned not
only with subject-matter but also with method. Perhaps the least limiting characterization of philosophic method is that it is critical thinking
about the theoretical foundations of whatever subject or text is being
analyzed. A philosophic study of Jewish texts will thus be concerned
with careful analyses of the foundations on which the doctrines set forth
rest. It will give critical consideration to the arguments which are set
forth and will uncover the premises of those arguments. Beginning with
the assumption that the texts before us are the work of men who were
both intelligent and serious, philosophical analysis will seek to provide a
coherent and intelligible account of what was in the mind of each author.

Philosophical thinking stands at the center of all serious intellectual
work. Any field of scholarship which ignores its own philosophical subject-matter and rejects any method of critical philosophical analysis,
condemns itself to a certain narrowness of vision and extracts from its
subject matter far less than it is capable of yielding. For philosophy is a
universal and inescapable human activity. It is not the exclusive domain
of the professional philosophers, but an ongoing task of every man. It is
this which led G. K. Chesterton to assert that

> The most practical and important thing about a man is . . . his view of the
> universe. We think that for a landlady considering a lodger, it is important
> to know his income, but still more important to know his philosophy. We
> think that for a general about to fight an enemy, it is important to know the
> enemy's numbers, but still more important to know the enemy's philos-
> ophy. We think the question is not whether the theory of the cosmos affects
> matters, but whether, in the long run, anything else affects them.[10]

Our task is to uncover and explicate the philosophy, implicit or explicit, in the Jewish texts which are the subject of our study. If they are works which are relatively unsophisticated, they still have an important philosophical dimension which forms their foundation in thought. If they are highly sophisticated, but non-philosophical texts, they demand most careful philosophical study. And if they are genuinely philosophical texts, we need to learn to read them philosophically, not just as pieces to be moved around on the grid of the history of terms, arguments, and ideas.

Philosophic study of a body of materials is not a substitute for rigorous and specialized scholarship. Each field of Jewish Studies requires its own modes of scholarship and uses those tools of learning and those methods which are appropriate to it. Philosophic analysis and construction depends on that scholarship and can only be meaningful if it works with reliable texts, if it is fully informed about the cultural ambience of those texts and their authors, if it is aware of the relevant social, economic and political data, and if it has access to as much as can be known of the inner life of the authors and the modes of thought which underlie the texts. Philosophic work is not done in a vacuum. Since it is unlikely that any one individual will have the whole range of learning that is required, the task of philosophy in Jewish Studies must result from cooperative scholarly efforts. Yet, having said this, we can proceed here to outline and illustrate some of the main features of the specifically philosophic enterprise within the various fields of Jewish Studies.

For anyone engaged in a philosophic study of the literary sources of Judaism, a first requisite is a highly sophisticated understanding of theories of interpretation. We are dealing with a literature much of which is, or claims to be, an interpretation of earlier works. We record differing interpretations of a text; we compare and contrast them; but we almost never ask the philosophic questions: What is the theory of interpretation which is being employed in each case? How do the interpreters understand their own activity? What are the principles which guide them? To take a typical case, the *Encyclopaedia Judaica* articles on "Hermeneutics" and "Interpretation" set forth certain general principles and discuss the details of various types and rules of interpretation, but never once do they raise the critical philosophic questions. In the discussion of rabbinic modes of biblical exegesis, the thirteen hermeneutical rules of R. Ishmael are classified into two groups, "Elucidative Interpretation" and "Analogical Interpretation." There is then added to the thirteen principles a category named "Logical Interpretation." Shall we infer from this that the principles of R. Ishmael are not logical? If so, must we not try to understand the nature of the non-logical thinking that goes into their formulation and use? What shall we make, for example, of the rule of *gezerah shavah?* It is not enough to know that versions of this mode of interpretation, which in many cases seems to defy all logic, were used by Greek and Roman rhetoricians.[11] Neither does it solve our problem to be informed that the rabbinic authorities tried to limit the danger of abuses of this method. We need to enter into the minds of those who proposed what seem like far-fetched conclusions based on *gezerah shavah.* What was behind their thinking? What theory of interpretation were they following? How did they conceive their task as exegetes? What is needed is philosophical analysis. We may not be successful in every case, but we can surely hope to illuminate much that is now obscure and to emerge with some sense of a coherent systematic structure which informs particular modes of interpretation.

A philosophic mode of study and analysis has an important role to play in our understanding of each of the various types of Jewish literature. Whether it be Halakha or Aggadah, Mishnah or Midrash, there is a philosophic task to be done, but any study of the existing literature will show that the philosophic work has hardly begun. Let us consider a sample case. It is generally acknowledged that the Aggadah is a major source for Jewish religious thought. The point was made in tannaitic times in the well known statement that if one wants to know the Creator, he should study Aggadah, since this is the way to know God and to cleave to His ways.[12]

We see that Aggadah was thought of by some teachers as one important way to the knowledge of God. This certainly should make aggadic literature a major focus of philosophic interest, and one would expect students of Aggadah to treat the texts philosophically. However, the major works on the subject deal with everything but the philosophical dimension.

Yizhak Heinemann's דרכי האגדה is an indispensable handbook for the study of this form of Jewish literature. It has the seeming advantage of having been written by one whose primary work was in philosophy. Yet the book deals with almost every aspect of the study of Aggadah, but pays no attention to the philosophical analysis of aggadic texts. The bulk of the discussion in Heinemann's book comes under the headings "Methods of Creative Historiography and "Methods of Creative Philology." He discusses in one place what he calls הזנחת הלוגוס מהקיף in the Aggadah, but even here he does not confront the philosophic issues. It is hardly enough to list examples of the apparent lack of rational order and structure in the Aggadah, as he does. To take one case, Heinemann informs us that: חז"ל פירשו אמנם את שיר השירים כולו דרך משל, אבל בנוגע לנמשל בולטת בפירושיהם אי עקביות גמורה.[13] He then goes on to list instances of this "total inconcsistency." This should be the beginning, not the end, of the investigation. If we take the Aggadah seriously, then we must subject it to searching philosophical analysis. A pattern of thinking which appears to be patently irrational, but which is pursued by intelligent and serious men, must engage all our philosophic acumen. We need to penetrate beneath the surface to the intellectual foundations of their thought and to their conceptions of textual interpretation. Our task is to find the way to bring order out of the apparent chaos, to understand the seemingly incoherent texts in ways which penetrate philosophically to their depths and discover their inner principles of order and structure. Glib slogan-like solutions are insufficient. Heinemann does little to illuminate the obscurity when he gives us a capsule explanation to the effect that aggadic writers see the contradictions in Scripture as a reflection of the paradoxes of life. Just how do they conceive these paradoxes? Are they saying that the world is irrational and lacking inherent principles of order? Or is it human life which is irrational? If all is paradoxical, what role does God play in the world? And what is their conception of God? These are only a few of the philosophic questions which must occupy any student of this aspect of the Aggadah. If Heinemann wants to argue that certain literary forms are deliberate instances of art imitating reality, then we must have some clear and coherent notion of the view of reality which underlies these literary texts.

The achievement of a philosophic understanding of the Halakhah is an equally great and urgent requirement. Here philosophy has a major task in a field where hardly any serious work has been done. Although the centrality of Halakhah in Judaism is not subject to debate, little effort has been made to explicate the philosophic foundations of the law or to search out its philosophic meanings. The study of Halakhah with philosophical insight is perhaps the most important work that is required for any genuinely philosophical study of Judaism. In the limited context of the present discussion, I shall not attempt to show how this applies to the great and overarching questions. Before we are ready to deal with the most fundamental and comprehensive issues in the philosophical exposition of the Halakhah, we shall have to do much intensive work on the smaller questions. To illustrate the point, let us consider in a limited context some problems about ethics and Halakhah. This is a subject on which there is considerable literature, much of it apologetic and most of the rest selectively descriptive, which is only a subtler form of apologetics.

A mishnah reads as follows: "If one paid money for produce, but did not draw the produce into his possession (לא משך), he can nullify the purchase. But they (i.e. the Sages) said: He who punished the generation of the flood and the generation of the dispersion will punish whoever does not keep His word."[14] We have here a puzzling situation. The law is clear. There is no consummation of the sale without the act of drawing (משיכה). Payment of money does not constitute legal purchase. Therefore, even if money has been paid, the purchaser has full legal right to change his mind and to nullify the purchase. Nevertheless, the very mishnah which sets forth the law condemns anyone who take advantage of his legal rights. Neither the classical nor the modern commentators seem to be troubled by this paradox. They simply record the case, explain the main terms, and state that the sages invoked a curse on one who behaves this way. In the standard literature a number of specialized versions of this type of case are discussed, but no attention is paid to the curious logic of the situation. This is the point at which philosophical analysis must enter.

Certain basic questions present themselves for consideration. Does the invocation of the curse, with its stress on the importance of keeping one's word, imply that there are non-halakhic moral principles which are superior to the law? If so, how are such principles known and what is their source? Since the law is Torah and, from its own inner perspective, an expression of God's teaching, how can it be morally imperfect? Does not the suggestion of moral imperfection in this law open up the possibility of questioning the moral soundness of any other halakhah?

Investigation of the Halakhah as an ethical system forces us to deal with these and similar questions. These basic philosophic issues cannot be resolved (if they are in fact open to solution) if we restrict ourselves only to one specific case. What is required is a careful study of the whole group of parallel cases which occur in the Mishnah, Tosefta, etc. Each case needs to be examined in its individual setting, and then we must determine whether there is some pattern that emerges. The various expressions which are used to convey similar ideas need to be considered individually and in their interrelationships. For example, in a Tosefta which is parallel to our Mishnah, we find an additional statement,[15] אבל אמרו הכמים כל המבטל את דיבורו אין רוח חכמים נוחה הימנו. Does this have identical force to "He who punished," or is it less intense? When all such matters have been considered, there remains the major philosophic work. Until we determine whether there is an extra-halakhic criterion of the morality of the Halakhah, we shall not understand the Halakhah itself fully. By failing to clarify the ruling in the law itself that it is wicked to abide by the law, we leave the law without a meaningful foundation. It is not my task here to deal with the substantive issues, but only to cite a sample case in which philosophic analysis is required in order to illuminate the Halakhah.[16]

The ethics of the Halakhah is only one area in which philosophy has a contribution to make. The field is far wider than this. Once we recognize the Halakhah as a major source (and in the view of many *the* major source) of Jewish doctrine, we shall be moved to develop not only the ethics, but the metaphysics, epistemology and logic of the Jewish legal system.[17] Here we are in a field that is little explored and demands massive effort. We don't know for certain how to begin, what methodology to employ, or even exactly what we are expecting to find. Nevertheless, it is time to put to the test the classic Jewish emphasis on Halakhah as the core of Judaism. The pious often assert that there is more religious depth in שור שנגח את הפרה than in the great works of theology. It is a long way, however, from such folk piety to sophisticated and systematic philosophic explication of this thesis. We need to fashion appropriate philosophic instruments and then to approach the study of the law with a combination of the learning of the classical *talmid hakham* and the critical thinking of the philosopher.

One point which should be stressed is that we are far from ready to produce a comprehensive account of the philosophy of the Halakhah. It is not even clear that there is a single body of philosophic thought which is the basis of the Halakhah. We should be initially suspicious of any work which purports to reduce rabbinic thought to a single, neat, and orderly structure. So many strands need to be disentangled, so many specific issues need to be analyzed, that it will be a very long time before we can hope to be ready to develop a complete philosophical picture of halakhic literature.

The problem is many times more complicated if we want to address ourselves also to the Aggadah. What we can do, however, is to take up one by one smaller and more limited topics. Some examples were given above in the area of the ethics of the Halakhah. Other studies in this area might include philosophic examinations of such topics as freedom, personal responsibility, the individual and society, divine law and the political state, ideas of justice, hierarchies of values, and similar subjects within the Halakhah. Such studies, properly done, might give us the ground for a comprehensive account of ethical theory in the Halakhah. In a similar way we need to pursue a series of individual studies which could result in a sound account of the metaphysics and epistemology of the Halakhah. If these studies were also extended to the Aggadah, we might finally be able to speak responsibly and with insight about what we so glibly today call rabbinic thought.

While the Halakhah and Aggadah may constitute the first priority for serious philosophical analysis, the study of the Bible is no less in need of a sophisticated philosophical dimension. There are many books and chapters in books which purport to offer a philosophical account of biblical thought. We encounter such comprehensive titles as "The Philosophy of the Old Testament," "The Basic Ideas of Biblical Religion," "Philosophy and the Bible," or "Prophetic Philosophy." In almost every case these turn out to be collections of vague and undefended generalizations or highly selective concentrations on a few themes chosen arbitrarily. Frequently they fail to take into account the best available biblical scholarship on each particular point, and they tend to substitute preaching for sober philosophical reflection. For example, one writer construes the קול דממה דקה of Elijah's experience to mean that "the voice of God is heard in the inner recesses of the soul." According to Bible scholars the expression קול דממה דקה is obscure, but there is no ground whatsoever for identifying it with the familiar modern definition of conscience as "the voice of God in the soul of man." A passage such as this can only be interpreted soundly if we first take account of all that we can learn about its meaning from biblical philology, comparative studies of ancient Near Eastern religions, and similar disciplines. To these may then be added the special insights and analysis of philosophical study. If the passage is an important biblical instance of a theophany, then it deserves and demands both sound biblical scholarship and meticulous philosophical analysis. Comparison is required with the immediately preceding episodes in which the divine power is manifested in public actions as well as with similar episodes elsewhere in the Bible. We must consider a number of philosophic questions. What conceptions of God are expressed in the various episodes in I Kings 18 and 19? How are these conceptions related? Do they form a systematic whole or are they separate and even contradictory? What shall we make of the God who shows his power publicly through the אש ה' which consumes the sacrifice and who proclaims only a few verses later לא באש ה'? Is there a difference in theological meaning between the expressions אש ה' and לא באש ה'? Careful comparative studies are required to understand the religious meaning of these terms and of the episodes they portray. For, in addition to the questions arising directly out of the manifestations of God in the fire or His failure to be known through the fire, there are other more general problems that have to be worked through. For example, what is the status of the kind of empirical test which Elijah proposed?[18] How shall we understand in this episode the role and power of the prophet? Does God respond to his prayer as a free agent or is the prophetic force that of צדיק גוזר והקב"ה מקיים? These are some of the philosophic questions which would occupy us in any serious analysis of this biblical passage. Similar philosophic questions confront us in the study of almost any biblical passage chosen at random.

What is called for, within the framework of sound biblical scholarship, is serious philosophical work. As Nahum M. Sarna, a distinguished Bible scholar, puts it, "No study of biblical literature can possibly claim to do justice to the subject if it fails to take account of the world-view of the biblical writers, or if it ignores their ideas about God and man and pays no regard to their deep sense of human destiny."[19] Sarna goes on to take note of the tendency, in the enthusiasm for parallels, to draw easy and imperceptive comparisons. "Scholarly integrity," he says, "demands that the conclusions drawn from the utilization of the comparative method to be recognized for what they are—generalizations of limited value. One has to be sure that one is not dealing with mere superficial resemblances . . . There always remains the possibility that we have touched upon purely external characteristics . . . Further, we may have torn a motif right out of its cultural or living context and so have distorted the total picture." We must move with great care in this field and with an acute sense of the integrity of cultures and the central role which philosophic ideas play in these cultures.[20] This requires us to overcome the temptation to premature and unfounded generalizations. Instead, we must be prepared to work carefully on individual passages, particular themes, or special and limited topics. Out of these studies we may hope, at least, for philosophic insight into the small subjects to which we address ourselves. As in the case of rabbinic literature, we must leave open the question as to whether we may be able to achieve that grand synthesis which could legitimately be represented as biblical philosophy. So much more limited work must first be done that it is pointless to speculate on the final outcome. Unless we proceed more or less in this way, we shall simply be multiplying the arbitrariness and the intellectual irresponsibility which is typical of so much of the existing literature in this field.

Even careful and philosophically sophisticated scholars seem to lose control of their material when they generalize about biblical thought. In a major book by one of the greatest students of Jewish philosophy of the last generation, there is a discussion of basic ideas in the Bible which includes the following statement:

> Jewish thought is not oriented towards metaphysical questions. The slough-ing off of mythological cosmogonies eliminated all potential starting points for the growth of metaphysics. The notion of a Creator provides no occa-sion for a theoretical interpretation of the world. This may well be the answer to the question: Why did Judaism not develop its own philosophic system?[21]

I find it impossible to offer an intelligible explication of this passage and am utterly perplexed by its claim to represent biblical thought. What can it mean to say that "the notion of a Creator provides no occasion for a theoretical interpretation of the world?" That notion *is* a theoretical interpretation of the world, just as is the notion that the world is eternal and uncreated, or the notion that the world came into being when eternal matter was given form by the demiurge or the notion that that world came into existence as the result of a "big bang." Can we accept a read-ing of the first chapter of Genesis that concludes that biblical thought has no concern with metaphysics? The first verse of Genesis makes a metaphysical claim, no less than the first verse of the Gospel of John. Both verses leave much unsaid, but what they say is more than enough to generate intense philosophical reflection.

In the study of the Bible, as in other Jewish literature, we must free ourselves of easy generalization, romanticization, and homileticization. To know the bible in its full depth and importance, we must reflect on its philosophical dimension. To begin with the familiar, biblical ideas of creation, revelation, and redemption await sober analysis. We are lacking serious philosophical analyses of the main aspects of biblical ethics, of the relationship of ethics to law, and of both to divine commandment. We need to determine whether the Bible anywhere recognizes a natural moral law which is not derived from divine commandment. These questions are typical of the work that remains to be done in a philosophic study of the Bible. As in the case of rabbinic literature, the work can only be done initially in small segments. From these studies we may expect a considerable degree of philosophical illumination which will raise our understanding of the Bible to new levels of sophistication.

Another area which awaits serious philosophical study is medieval and modern biblical commentaries. With some exceptions, the vast literature of *Parshanut* has been treated as if it were of little or no philosophical interest. It is usually thought that only commentaries by philosophers contain philosophic elements, while others stand beyond the boundaries of philosophy. In his admirable little book, *Parshanut ha-Mikra*, M. Z. Segal has one section entitled "Philosophical Commentaries" and another headed "Modern Philosophical Commentaries." The implication is that the figures discussed in these sections are the only ones who offer commentary which is philosophically interesting. Thus, he tells us with respect to Rashi that,[22] אין אצלו כלום מהפרשנות הפילוסופית. אמנם ... השאלות שהטרידו את חכמי ישראל בארצות הערביות ... לא העסיקו כלל את רש"י ... הוא ידע שאין לקחת את דיבורי ההגשמה כפשוטם ... והוא משתמש הרבה בדיבור "כביכול" ... אבל בכלל הוא מפרש דברי ההגשמה כפשוטם, ואינו מרגיש בתמימותו להתקשות בהבנת הדברים כהוייתם. Or, speaking of R. Yoseph Bekhor Shor, he says:[23] למרות חירות הדעות שלו, נשאר ר"י בכור שור נאמן למסורת של האסכולה הצרפתית ולתמימותה באמונות ודעות. הרציונליות שלו היא מיוסדת על השכל הישר, ולא על שום השקפה פילוסופית כדרך הפרשנים הספרדיים.

There are certainly important distinctions to be drawn between the French and Spanish schools of commentators, among them the fact that the latter dealt directly and explicitly with philosophical issues while the former did not. But it is precisely at this point that we see the important and unfulfilled role of philosophy in the study of this literature. Philosophy is not contained only in packages that are explicitly labeled; every instance of human thought has a philosophical dimension. The commentaries of Rashi and Rashbam may not be discussed in histories of Jewish philosophy, while Kaspi and Gersonides claim their rightful place there. However, a proper understanding of the "non-philosophical" commentators demands no less philosophical insight and sophistication than is required for the study of the "philosophic" commentators.

Consider the hidden implications in the observations of Segal that were just quoted. First, there is a theory of textual interpretation implicit in Rashi's method. This is a philosophical issue and can be fully exposed and explicated only by methods of philosophical analysis. Second, if, as Segal says, Rashi does not take anthropomorphisms literally, then he has a philosophic stance on this point. Third, if he has no hesitation, nevertheless, about using anthropomorphic language, we must try to grasp the principles that are the basis for his method. When Segal tells us (in the passage cited above) that שעוררים תמיהה לא עלה על דעתו במקומות . . . שצריך לעקם את הכתוב כדי לקרב אותו אל מושגינו, he has presented us with a question, not an answer. Perhaps it is a question which can be answered by cultural historians who will help us to see why in Rashi's setting this way of speaking about God posed no problem. Even then we shall still need the perceptions of the philosopher to clarify just what Rashi is doing and how it differs from the way of other commentators. Fourth, if "temimut" is a proper characterization of Rashi and his disciples, that too is a philosophic stance. I confess that I do not know with certainty what it means, but I do know that philosophical innocence is also a form of philosophy. Fifth, if Bekhor Shor is both loyal to the "temimut" of the French school and also a "rationalist" (as Segal seems to say), then we surely need a philosophical account of this interesting combination of rationalistic simple-mindedness. Sixth, we need a philosophical exposition of a rationalism "which is based on common sense and not on any philosophical perspective." These are some philosophical issues which arise from a cursory reading of a few lines in a major secondary work on the biblical commentators. How much more is likely to emerge from a close and sensitive reading of the commentators themselves!

As examples, I shall mention only two types of commentary which in every case demand philosophic study. One is the treatment of contradictions in Scripture. Most, if not all, commentators deal with this problem at some point, the philosophically "innocent" Rashi no less than the philosophically "sophisticated" Abraham ibn Ezra. Contradictions are an offense to human reason, and methods for their resolution are always of interest to the philosopher in his role as logician. However the resolution is achieved, it presupposes some logical theory which may be implicit rather than explicit, but which is the controlling intellectual force. A comparative study of the ways in which individual commentators deal with contradictions would be extremely valuable. Do they all follow some standard version of Aristotelian logic, whether they know it as such or not? Are there different logics at work? Do we have adumbrations of multi-valued logics? Is contradiction always held to be inadmissible, or do we have commentators who glory in paradox? In the latter case, on what metaphysical-logical ground do they rest? There is much philosophic work to be done here, even in the study of supposedly non-philosophical commentators.

A second example may be found in the problem which is posed by the multiplicity of interpretations of a single passage, interpretations which differ widely and frequently contradict each other. The critical philosophical issues which this phenomenon raises stand at the heart of the whole commentarial enterprise. How is the biblical text understood by each commentator? Does he suppose that it has one and only one true meaning, or that it is laden with many layers of meaning? When a commentator openly rejects midrashic explanations in favor of his own version of the *peshat*, what theory motivates him? Is he affirming the authority of his own intellect against that of the official literature of the tradition, and if so on what ground? What of the cases in which midrashim which soften extreme anthropomorphism are rejected in favor of a crudely literal interpretation; as, e.g., Rashi to Genesis 3:8? Is he moved by a theory of literal meaning even at the price of questionable theological consequences? Why in this case are "helpful" midrashim rejected while in other cases, e.g., the previous verse, rather fantastic midrashim are accepted? Answers to these questions will not come from purely philological studies. They are, at their depth, philosophic questions and they demand philosophic answers.

The cases we have cited to illustrate the role of philosophy in the study of various types of Jewish literature and subject matter are by no means an exhaustive account. There is no area of Jewish learning that does not have need for this kind of philosophical analysis. One more area, however, does require our explicit attention, and that is the relationship of philosophy to the study of Jewish philosophic literature. Put this way the matter sounds either absurd or paradoxical, but it is neither. At the beginning of this discussion, we indicated that our main concern was to show the extent to which philosophy has a productive role in the study of various non-philosophical types of Jewish literature. Now we must reflect briefly on the role of philosophy in the study of the literature of Jewish philosophy itself.

The reason that this is neither absurd nor paradoxical is the fact that there are many non-philosophical ways of studying philosophic texts.

At their best these are valuable propaedeutics to genuinely philosophical studies. We must know the uses and meanings of the key technical terms employed in a philosophic work. We need to know all that we can about the historical-cultural setting in which the work was written and about the audience for whom it was intended. We need to know what the main influences were on an author, and to what extent he is reproducing the ideas and arguments of his predecessors. Scholars who provide us with this information have performed an invaluable service. Without their work no responsible study of these texts is possible. But we must stress again that such studies are (in addition to their intrinsic interest) a necessary but not a sufficient condition for the philosophic study of philosophic texts.

The required work of preliminary scholarship has been so massive that it has occupied most of the energies of the available specialists in Jewish philosophy. And that work must continue. It will be a long time before we have a complete set of thoroughly reliable scientific texts, which we lack for many important works in medieval Jewish philosophy. However, as scholars continue to pursue these and similar studies, they should not lose sight of the philosophic purpose of the enterprise. The immense and remarkably productive scholarly effort in this field is intrinsically valuable and needs no further justification. Nevertheless, from the perspective of true philosophical interest, this work matters most because it provides us with the accurate learning without which no philosophical understanding of these philosophical works is possible.

In our enthusiasm for philological and historical research, we sometimes forget that we are dealing with works of philosophy. It is at least as important to read a philosophic argument critically as it is to know its history. The great Jewish philosophers, from Saadia to our contemporaries, have offered us profound philosophical interpretations of Judaism. Their works contain rich philosophic treasures. Read analytically, they include theories of textual interpretation, cosmologies, theologies (in the literal sense of the term), ethical theories, theories of knowledge, theories of prophecy, accounts of the nature and purpose of the *mitzvot*, eschatologies, and more. Read synthetically, they integrate these disparate elements into coherent and systematic philosophies of Judaism.

One of our greatest needs is genuinely philosophical study of these great works. With sound knowledge of the meanings of terms and with a thorough grasp of the intellectual background of each work, we are in a position to devote ourselves to the kind of philosophic reading which is rarely done. We need critical philosophical analyses (not only historical accounts) of the doctrines which are advanced and of the arguments by which they are supported. It is our philosophic responsibility to ask if these doctrines are true and if the arguments are sound. It is equally our responsibility to determine whether the teachings of the philosophers, even if they should be sound, are authentic versions of Judaism. We must first decide, of course, whether the notion of an "authentic version of Judaism" is itself tenable and meaningful. A decision in its favor requires us to produce criteria of authenticity. A decision against forces us to ask whether "Judaism" stands for anything at all.

Much profound and subtle philosophic work has to be done in order to gain a perceptive philosophic understanding of the Jewish philosophers. Each had his own vision which informed his work, giving it structure, unity, and direction. The kind of philosophic approach which we take for granted when we study Plato or Aristotle, Descartes or Spinoza, Whitehead or Wittgenstein, should be adopted in our studies of Jewish philosophy. To do anything less is to transform great philosophic works into textbooks for linguistic and historical studies. We can only claim to understand a serious Jewish philosopher when we are able to provide a systematic formulation of his philosophy of Judaism. That important goal is yet to be achieved for most of the major figures in the history of Jewish philosophy. It is a goal which should be the culmination of our philosophic efforts, following on the philosophic reading of the non-philosophic Jewish materials.

There is no area of Jewish studies, just as there is no area of human endeavor, to which philosophy is irrelevant. Philosophical ideas abound and must be identified and comprehended if we are to have an intellectually sound grasp of any Jewish text which we study. Furthermore, the philosophic methods of critical analysis are an indispensable tool in all serious reflection on the great achievements of the human spirit which abound in the Jewish tradition. The role of philosophy is central here as it is in the study of the human achievement embodied in every culture and in every literature.

NOTES

1. Cicero, *De Divinatione*, II, 58.
2. Plato, *Theaetetus*, 174A.
3. *Romeo and Juliet*, III, 3, 55–60.
4. See, for example: *BT*, Abodah Zarah, 54b, Shabbat, 116a; *PT* Shabbat, III, 6a; Gen. R. 1:9, and similar references.
5. Saul Lieberman, "How Much Greek in Jewish Palestine?," *Biblical and other Studies*, ed. A. Altmann, (Cambridge, Mass., 1962), p. 130. Lieberman notes that, "Whereas we have no Greek philosophic terminology in Rabbinic literature, the situation is quite different with regard to Greek and Latin legal terms." (*Ibid.*, p. 132).
6. Collosians, 2:8.
7. Harry A. Wolfson, *The Philosophy of the Church Fathers*, Cambridge, Mass., 1956), p. 16.
8. Tertullian, *De Spectaculis*, Chs. 29f. See the comments on this passage by Nietzsche in *Zur Genealogie der Moral*, Sec. 15.
9. Leo Strauss, *Persecution and the Art of Writing*, (Glencoe, Ill., 1952) pp. 42–43.
10. G. K. Chesterton, *Heretics*, (New York, 1927), pp. 15–16, as cited by Lewis White Beck, *Philosophic Inquiry*, (New York, 1952), p. 6.
11. On this point see the discussion in Saul Lieberman, *Hellenism in Jewish Palestine*.
12. *Sifre Debarim*, 49, ed. Finkelstein, p. 115: דורשי אגדות אומרים, רצונך להכיר את מי שאמר
והיה העולם למוד הגדה שמתוך כך אתה מכיר את מי שאמר והיה העולם ומדבק בדרכיו.
Some texts read דורשי רשומות. For our purposes there is no need to deal with the problem of the differing terminology. The main point is unaffected.
13. P. 137.
14. M. Baba Meẓia, IV, 2.
15. T. Baba Meẓia, III, 14.
16. For some useful discussions of the general problem in recent literature see: Aharon Lichtenstein, "Does Jewish Tradition Recognize an Ethic Independent of Halakhah?" in *Modern Jewish Ethics: Theory and Practice*, ed. M. Fox (Ohio State University Press, 1975); Shmuel Shilo, "On One Aspect of Law and Morals in Jewish Law: *Lifnim Mishurat Hadin*," *Israel Law Review*, 13, No. 3 (1978); Saul J. Berman, "Lifnim Mishurat Hadin," *Journal of Jewish Studies*, 26 (1975) and 28 (1977); Moshe Silberg, "Law and Morality," Ch. VI of his *Talmudic Law and the Modern State*, (New York, 1971).
17. For a study of some aspects of the logic of the law, see Louis Jacobs, *Studies in Talmudic Logic*, (London, 1961).
18. This problem is discussed by Emil L. Fackenheim in *Encounters between Judaism and Modern Philosophy*, (New York, 1973), Ch. I.
19. Nahum M. Sarna, *Understanding Genesis*, (New York, 1966), p. xxiv.
20. *Ibid*, p. xxvii.
21. Julius Guttmann, *Philosophies of Judaism*, (New York, 1964), p. 15.
22. M. Z. Segal, *Parshanut ha-Mikra*, (Jerusalem, 1952), p. 66.
23. *Ibid.*, p. 76.

Not a Mirror but a Window: Some Comments on the Study of Rabbinic Literature

Lou H. Silberman

Vanderbilt University
Nashville, Tenessee

There are, to be sure, more ways than one along which to approach the teaching of rabbinic literature so that its values, its concepts, its ideas are apprehended and comprehended by students. Yet it has seemed to me at the outset of study, at its very beginning, the manner in which the teacher perceives his task must be manifest. How to do that, too, may vary, so that what I shall do is not to pretend a normative statement but offer a personal account and that not by describing what I have, over the years, done but by doing it.

George Foot Moore, in Volume I of his work *Judaism*, presents on pages 125–216 the sources on which that work is based. Yet, before describing them, he offers a discussion of the critical principles governing the choice and use of these sources. This is a methodological question of the greatest importance and one that at the outset commands our immediate attention.

On what shall we base our description of the origins and emergence of rabbinic Judaism in the last two pre-Christian and first several Christian centuries? That question is more complex that at first blush it seems—because of its context and connotations—for the principles on which the choice of materials is made may not be and have not always been "objective." Much polemic and much apologetic have been mixed in with what may at the beginning have seemed to be no more than a question of collecting as large a number of materials as is available, judging them on the basis of internal and external evidence as to their general and specific reliability, and constructing them into a scholarly edifice. One recognizes at once that, unfortunately, no such uncomplicated situation exists anywhere in the field of scholarship. One need only attend to the remark of Aptowitzer to recognize how very quickly complications arise:

> "The antiquity of a tradition is no more guarantee of the antiquity of the source in which it occurs than is the lateness of a source proof of the lateness of a tradition."

But we have to face up to the situation, uncomfortable or not.

In the first instance we are confronted by a vast mass of writings that represent or claim to represent the authentic and authoritative texts of rabbinic Judaism. This is the self-conscious tradition: these are we! In a real sense this is so. But if we are at all troubled by a critical mind, then we are forced to examine it in order to discover—if we can— its genesis, its development, its flowering, and its decline. We become aware of its positive and its negative features, its virtues and its faults. We try to date the material and find ourselves confronting a terrifying task. It becomes apparent that this body of literature has come into existence over a long period, that it has a literary history as well as a content. Its final redaction, it becomes evident, was preceeded by one or more earlier redactions. Its contents were transmitted along several parallel chains of tradition and on occasion much of the chain is not available or is fragmentary. When, we find ourselves asking, is a statement that of the person uttering it? When are we to assume he is the most recent in a long series of transmitters, his name being attached at a point where the tradition is being codified? How well does the tradition understand itself at any point? May not changes in social, political, and economic structures cause shifts in emphasis so that a later generation is either unaware of the circumstances that gave rise to a particular point of view or is consciously suppressing the original meaning and providing a new meaning? In other words, the material itself shows us that it has not only a literary but a tradition history as well.

Now this would be in and of itself a sufficient problem for our methodological considerations, but it is not all there is. Paralleling this gathering of sources, there is another body of materials created with the Jewish world but representing a point of view or a content that does not always coincide with that represented by those who collected, transmitted, and received the first collection. These writings, many of them apocalypses, that is, disclosures of secret matters, of that which is yet to come, are not included within the body of rabbinic literature. They have had their separate histories. Indeed, Foot Moore wrote: "Inasmuch as these writings have never been recognized by Judaism, it is a fallacy of method for the historian to make them a primary source for the eschatology of Judaism—much more to contaminate its theology with them." Yet, when one attends to what some of them are saying, a content or attitude that may be called apocalyptic, one is far less convinced that Moore's radical exclusion is justified. These documents were created within the community broadly viewed; they represent the point of view of some part of the community at some time. If we say the existence of this point of view was ignored by a larger part of the community, we will want to know how this was possible. If we hold that it was rejected, then we will want to know why, and by whom and when? At any rate, it was at one time a part of the thinking of the community taken as a whole, so that we shall have to make certain whether or not there is any "contamination" from this source in the included, the accepted literature, and whether it is indeed "contamination." Here, too, we must be careful to retain our sense of proportion, to recognize the nexus of ideas. It would be as faulty to over-emphasize this aspect as to refuse to find a place for it. Sound scholarship demands sober judgment.

Within the last generation a whole new and complicating set of factors has been introduced. We have been faced with that growing body of recent discoveries subsumed under the heading "The Dead Sea Scrolls." These discoveries tended, at the beginning of the discussion, to throw out of balance our methodology for, to quote Foot Moore in another context, there is "the elation of discovery by which the just proportion of things is dislocated . . ." For about thirty years we have been attempting to determine, with varying degrees of success, who the creators of this literature were and what place they may have in our portrait. What is unmistakably clear is that what ultimately emerged as rabbinic Judaism did so out of a situation of struggle far more complicated than seemed the case to earlier generations of scholars.

There is still another complicating factor—the existence of yet another literature that has its roots in the Jewish community but whose growth and flowering were outside it. The New Testament is, in is literary form, earlier than much of rabbinic literature in its literary form. It is, as well, a judgment upon ideas that hold a significant place in rabbinic thought. It is, indeed, a witness to such ideas, but it is a partisan witness, one that cannot be used uncritically but must take its place in the box, there to be cross-examined. We must know how these documents came into existence, what their point(s) of view is (are), before we make any statement—on their basis—as to what Judaism was or was not.

To all of this we must yet add the evidence of such classical writers as Philo and Josephus and carefully sift patristic materials. In other words, unlike Moore, nothing—it would seem to me—may be excluded *a priori*. All should be brought together, weighed judiciously, and understood thoughtfully. We cannot view a previously drawn portrait but must ourselves gather the materials for our own. It is out of such an interplay that the ideas, the concepts, the values of rabbinic literature begin to emerge. One does not begin with formal structures borrowed from other disciplines and force the ideas, concepts, values—predetermined by those structures—into them. It makes no difference whether the structures are those of orthodox or liberal Christianity or those of traditional or liberal Judaism. The ideas must be allowed to make their appearance within their own situation, their own *Sitz im Leben*. Before one may even begin to wonder how such ideas may inform contemporary thought, one is duty-bound to learn how they functioned in the lives of those who inherited, developed, and thought them in their own time. The past is not a plaything of the present; it is its parent. The New Testament scholar Henry Cadbury wrote of the two dangers scholarship faces, that of contemporizing the past and of archaizing the present. To these I would add a third, the danger of ignoring the past. If it is rightly summoned up—and it has here been suggested how that summoning may take place—its deposit, its literature, may become transparent and its own life shine into ours, with unanticipated results. It is only when a teacher is willing to be vulnerable—in this context: to let students understand what the search for the ideas, the concepts, the values is—that these step forth in their aliveness to engage mind and heart.

Part III
לשמור ולעשות ולקיים
The Shaping of
Contemporary Jewish Identity

Liberal Judaism's Effort to Invalidate Relativism Without Mandating Orthodoxy

Eugene B. Borowitz

*Hebrew Union College—
Jewish Institute of Religion
New York, N.Y.*

The search for an Absolute goes back to ancient times. Much of Hindu religion centers on attachment to Brahman, the one, unconditioned ground of all existence, and a major strand of Greek philosophy, initiated by Parmenides, concentrates on the nature of what truly exists and must therefore be beyond change or impermanence.

The search for an Absolute, then, is not specifically a Jewish problem. Rather, we may say, translating the issue now into Jewish terminology: because this matter concerns God as God relates to all humanity, it is part of the universal teaching of Judaism. Yet, as often happens in Judaism with a univeralistic doctrine, the peculiar religious experience of the People of Israel gives the general teaching a particular slant. By contrast to the monistic concerns of Hindus or Greeks, ancient Israel has no search and a different sort of Absolute. As to the quest, the reality and continuity of God's revelation so dominate biblical experience that the Absolute is regularly pictured as forcing itself upon resisting individuals or the community. Moreover, the Hebrew Absolute, in its most primary manifestations, is relational. God creates a fully real, independent world and puts people in it fully free to accept or reject God's will. This God makes covenants with mankind, thus limiting God's own options for the future—as in promising Noah there will be no more floods—and providing people with grounds for standing up to God and disputing certain divine actions—as Abraham did in calling for justice for the righteous gentiles of Sodom and Gomorrah. This God makes a Covenant with a single people, thus linking God's own destiny in history with the Jews. And by giving them the Torah, God is now bound by certain of its provisions—such as accepting the earthly court's determination on just which day God's own festivals will be held.

The Hebrew God is an Absolute, for biblical and rabbinic Judaism know no reality or rule equal to, much less greater than, that of God's. Yet this is no distant, uninvolved, steady-state Absolute but a God of history. We can best capture this special Jewish sense of God's absoluteness by utilizing a common device of modern philosophy and calling it an Absolute in a weak sense of the term though not in a strong sense. In Judaism we can speak properly only of a weak Absolute and this somewhat paradoxical sense of the Absolute is nicely captured in the most common Jewish practice relating to God. God has a personal name and we Jews know it; but we may never say it. *Adonai* stands for the Absolute we know intimately but can only express in the limited ways made available to humankind.

This distinction between the strong Absolute of certain philosophical and mystical systems and the weak Absolute of Jewish revelation lies at the heart of many erroneous judgments about biblical religion and numerous efforts to improve upon it. Thus Richard Rubenstein does not understand that Judaism has a God of history who is not the author of all its acts, even as, outside the community, Calvin argues that if the sovereignty of God is properly to be acknowledged for the first time in Judaism or Christianity, a belief in predestination must be accepted.

The modern Jewish search for an Absolute and, what succeeds it, the contemporary one, to be considered in turn, receive their characteristic form from their rejection of the traditional doctrine of revelation: *Torah Mi-Sinai*, the self-disclosure of God's will, once and for all, in the Oral and the Written Law. Liberal Judaism comes into being under the impact of a seismic social change and by the irresistible attraction of the liberal, rationalist culture associated with it. What kept these post-ghetto converts to liberalism Jewish was their intuition that the Torah can change in ways not traditionally permitted but whose results are, somehow, authentically Jewish. Adapting Jewish existence to modern culture might require revolutionary self-assertion, yet it would not result in heresy or sectarian withdrawal. This rebellion was carried out in the name of the freedom of a given generation of Jews to define what God required of them perhaps against what past generations thought mandatory or by creating new forms of observance or expressions of Jewish faith. Though the revolt was directed at the authority of the Torah, broadly conceived, on a deeper level it struck at the old absoluteness of God, weakly understood though it may have been. For the God of Sinai, though allowing significant place to human initiative, also restricted it within the limits of the *halakhic* process. To an emancipated Jewry these severe limits to the right to change and innovate seemed—and indeed still seem—religiously inadequate. The liberal Jews wanted more rights for the human partners in the Covenant relationship between God and the Jews. In this demand they were not only responding to their new social situation but also to the surrounding confidence in humanity's capacity for self-legislation that was to be found in late 18th century culture and became so prominent a feature of 19th century life.

With all this concern for freedom, it did not occur to any of them who did not assimilate but identified themselves with some variety of liberal Judaism to make an Absolute of freedom itself. It has taken until our own time for someone who remains within our community to suggest that the logical implication of adopting liberalism is that Judaism has no independent claim upon us. No liberal Jewish spokesman ever saw his affirmation of freedom except in dialectic tension with the Jewish tradition. Even for Samuel Holdheim, the leading radical of liberal Judaism, the Torah has more place in our lives than as a mere resource which those who need it or are still emotional drawn by it might perhaps want to utilize. And Holdheim's God stands over against modern Jews, laying demands and judgment upon them. Having been raised in the Jewish sense of the Absolute, liberal Jews may simply not have seen the virtue of replacing God, the weak Absolute of their past, with a dogmatic assertion of the rights of the self, the strong Absolute of modern freedom. These historical observations and interpretations do not prove this modern interpretation of liberal Judaism false. They only demonstrate what an extraordinary burden of proof it takes upon itself to validate calling itself an authentic form of liberal Judaism, much less its sole consistent exposition.

The liberal Jewish search for an Absolute retains the classic dialectic form of traditional Judaism; the Absolute, God, is understood as self-conditioned by creation and Covenant; but in the modern situation the technical "weakness" of this Absolute is increased by strengthening the rights of the Covenant partner. Note liberal Judaism's two critical rejections, in which its basic affirmations, besides freedom, are decisively revealed. For all its love affair with agnosticism, it never passes over into a full-scale humanism, though the possibility was open to it as, for example, in Ethical Culture. And though the Torah no longer had unquestioned authority over liberal Jews, they knew that because of their affirmation of the continuing validity of Torah for them, they were decisively different from the Unitarians.

On the intellectual level, then, this new, intense affirmation of human freedom as a significant Jewish religious reality (and therefore exercised within the Covenant) is the root of the modern search for an Absolute. It was not essentially expressed, however, in discussions about the nature of the sort of God who could afford such rights to the Covenant partner. Rather, because Torah was classically the means through which the reality of God was mediated, affirmed, and celebrated, most of their quest for a new Absolute was sublimated to their effort to create a modern understanding of what authorized and determined Torah, the liberal Jewish way of life.

Through the 19th century and down to our own time, the weak absolute as the counterpoise to modern Jewish autonomy was easily found. For the intellectuals it was reason. The term may have had different connotations for the neo-Kantian Hermann Cohen and the naturalist Mordecai Kaplan, yet both show the typically covenantal, dialectical operation of autonomy. In the case of Cohen human freedom is understood to be fulfilled in and therefore constrained by the laws reason discloses. In Kaplan's case, despite his commitment to the primacy of the social, a people's normally unquestioned right to create its own civilizational forms cannot violate the imperatives of universal ethics. The same sort of rational counterpoise to human autonomy may be found in the less tidy thinkers, such as Kaufmann Kohler, whose rationality is essentially historically manifested, and Leo Baeck, who enlarges the notion to include the consciousness of mystery. Jews not so philosophically inclined proposed to live out their freedom in terms of modern culture, specifically, the university, the arts, good manners, and socially concerned politics. They knew, with all reasonable certainty, that this was how modern Jews ought to go about ordering their lives. The "best of the modern mind" set the context for the exercise of their freedom and the expression of their Judaism. Rationalty/culture was the modern Jewish Absolute. This was symbolized in the unique curriculum Isaac Mayer Wise created at the Hebrew Union College, which was the first rabbinical school to require a college degree as a pre-requisite for rabbinic ordination. And, symbolically enough, the HUC student devoted the better part of his day to such study, first at Hughes High School and then at the University of Cincinnati. The Jewish courses were taken supplementally. The Absolute was seen less in the old Torah than in the new culture.

The path European philosophy was pursuing during these years is worthy of some comment. Historically, the term "the Absolute" and the search for an appropriate Absolute do not become significant in Western philosophy until the early 19th century. This development is commonly traced back to the effect of Immanuel Kant's work. Kant found he could overcome Hume's skepticism about our knowing what was real in the world itself only by positing that there were necessary structures to our thinking and these were thoroughly reliable. But once he had introduced this distinction between the way the mind works and the way the world, in fact, is, the intellectual doors were opened to the possibility that our ideas about the world are always, perhaps only, subjective. Kant unwittingly gave rise to the possibility that our conceptions are only relative. It is this threat of radical relativity—in liberal Judaism the replacement of Torah with autonomy—which engenders the subsequent philosophic quest for the Absolute. The most notable solution to the problem remains that of Hegel. He dissolved the distinction between mind and nature, and his ingenious reinterpretation of the rational as a dynamic force enabled him to give an incredibly rich and comprehensive account of its operation in persons, society, and history. But having linked the mind of the creative thinker to the ultimate mind which orders all reality, Hegel advocated a strong Absolute. As the philosopher brings the notion of Absolute mind to full self-consciousness, he and the Absolute are, in significant measure, one. Hegel's refusal to acknowledge each individual's necessary finitude was exposed to parody and scorn by Kierkegaard with a devastating effect. More significant to us is the social level. In ways Hegel could never have accepted, his hopes for the Prussian State became in rightist and leftist transformation the absolutist model for the Nazi government of Germany and the communist regimes of Lenin and Stalin. In assuring us that our ideas about the world are reliable, mind has become so strong an Absolute that human individuality can no longer have an independent ground over against it and the state can claim absolute rights over its citizens.

In F. H. Bradley, the famous British absolute idealist, the contrast between a strong Absolute and the biblical God is made quite explicit. For Bradley, true reality must be utterly unconditioned, that is, not dependent on anything other than itself. Such reality is the Absolute. Two significant consequences flow from this assertion. First, the idea of the Absolute is inconsistent with any sort of change and therefore with any sort of involvement. Hence the Absolute has no relations with anything else. Bradley thus rules that the God of the Bible is, philosophically speaking, not true reality, the Absolute, but only an appearance. *Adonai* is too weak an Absolute to be Bradley's sort of reality. But second, Bradley's Absolute is so unrelated to anything else that we can say very little indeed about it. The cost of being so consistent about the absoluteness of reality is that we are left with an empty category, the sort of utter transcendence that the Jewish mystics could create because, in typical Jewish convenantal dialectic, they balanced the *En Sof* by their extravagantly anthropomorphic doctrine of the *Sefirot*.

The loss of individuality in such strong absolutisms is so great a violation of the spirit of enlightenment that one may see Nietzsche seeking to become the great antagonist of all sacrifice of self. In his work the individual, instead of being sublimated to a universal, cosmic Absolute, is rather itself exalted to the status of an Absolute. That is, for Nietzsche, the single self, freely expressing the full range of human power, is the only creative, authoritative power in history. Nothing can stand against the superior single self. By such standards, even the weak Absolute of the Bible is far too strong and the expression of the full personhood of humanity demands, no less, that God die so people can take on the absoluteness to which they now know they are entitled.

Modern Jewish religious thinkers found both Hegel's Absolute Mind and what I have pointed to here as Nietzsche's Absolute Self uncongenial to their search for an Absolute. As to the former, the only effort known to me to create a Hegelian interpretation of Judaism, that of Samuel Hirsch, significantly breaks with the master on the issue of the independent, autonomous stance of the individual. Without the benefit of Kierkegaard, and presaging the Jewish thinkers who were to follow him, Hirsch, though he takes his major intellectual categories from Hegel, refuses to sacrifice the ethical dignity of persons and swal-

low up their self-legislating power in the body of the state or in identification with absolute mind. Thus, for the sake of humanity, Hirsch can
affirm only a weak Absolute. I see it as no accident, then, but the culmination of a philosophic and Jewish search that the greatest Jewish
philosopher, Hermann Cohen, makes his intellectual mark as one of the
creators of Neo-Kantianism, a position in which human autonomy is
properly lived out within the transcendent realm of reason. In Cohen's
system this includes and is climaxed by the rational idea of God. In such
a philosophy the tension between the transcendent and the individual
produces the high ethical tone associated with Cohen. No wonder
Jewish thought for several generations has, in one fashion or another,
been derivative from him. Against much other modern philosophy he
gave us the sort of weak Absolute we were seeking. So too, when Rosenzweig in the opening pages of *The Star of Redemption* seeks to go
beyond rationalism (and thus anticipates the later, contemporary search
for an Absolute), he does so by first positing the independent reality of
Man and, against him, the world. Only then does he posit the reality of
God. Rosenzweig takes this stance in conscious opposition to the strong
Absolutes of Hegel, Nietzsche, and other thinkers in the stream of
German idealistic philosophy. And the result of this tri-partite starting
point for his thought is that neither the individual, nor science, nor God,
nor any sort of reason (which could not explain their brute givenness—
existence here preceding essence), can now lay claim to be a strong
absolute. The fundamental realities are all in relation to one another.
Hence even God, the most significant of them, can only lay claim to be a
weak Absolute.

I think it fair to say then that though modern Jewish thinkers
changed the balance of power in the traditional Jewish sense of the relationship between God and God's Covenant-partners, they did not
change its essential form. As a weak Absolute dominates the biblical and
rabbinic writings, so too, against the strong Absolutes of modern philosophy and its own strong emphasis on human autonomy, modern
Jewish thought also centered around a weak Absolute. If in the name of
freedom it can only speak figuratively of the One who came down at
Sinai, it still considers itself covenanted to the One who undergirds
modern culture.

The contemporary search for an Absolute began as it became clear
we could no longer trust even the weak Absolute of liberal culture, in
our case of liberal Judaism. The certainties of the enlightenment—educa-

tion and culture, the university and the democratic process, the innate goodness of humanity, the nobility of rationality, the characterological effects of esthetics—all have betrayed our trust. In the face of our increasing realism—now almost become cynicism—they have little to say. Modernity is at its best dealing with technical issues, a skill which partially creates and then cannot deal with the questions: why bother being skillful? or for what purposes? whence come our hope and confidence? Liberalism has foundered on the question of the ground of our values, and this is no mere "failure of nerve" but the collapse of the Absolute on which we moderns had based our lives. To be sure, not everyone accepts this reading of our situation. The doctrinaire liberals insist that all we need is reinvigoration of the democratic process. Most people, however, prefer withdrawal. The complexity of our problems is so overwhelming that they prefer to devote themselves to the enjoyment of life: good food, good wine, good sex, and good times—the estheticization of existence, captured in our use of the term "beautiful" for what was once a moral judgment.

The greatest benefactors of this disarray have been our various orthodoxies and fundamentalisms. Having by now picked up much of the liberal style—sophistication in ideas and less up-tightness in personal matters—they can present themselves as the saviors of our civilization. It will help to distinguish between the two main appeals of the intellectual right. One is directed to our emotions and our fundamental personality need for order. Now that our culture seems to permit everything, the threat of inner anarchy panics us. When even incest and suicide become options, there is no right. Worse, every choice of this over that confers guilt, for we have obviously turned our back on certain other alternatives. We cannot bear such awful freedom. Any system, as long as it is reasonably clear cut, is preferable to the emptiness of pervasive permissibility. So we save our sanity by adopting an orthodoxy. Freud thought this was religion's customary neurotic function. More popularly, it was Herman Wouk's epilogal justification of Captain Queeg against the mutineers on the S. S. Caine, and the basis of Wouk's turn to Orthodox Judaism. Humanly, the argument has much power. Intellectually, it only identifies what may be terrifying us. If we still retain the nerve to face our potential panic, to give it its due but not therefore immediately surrender our hard-won autonomy, this appeal to our neuroticism will not move us to orthodoxy.

There is a much better reason for seeking a new Absolute. It is the

quiet confidence that the universe and its creatures are not utterly abandoned. We are confused and foolish and not infrequently perverse. But
that is not all we are. For we know that what we have done is evil and
that it is not that which we ought to do. In this recognition of sin and
guilt, or, more positively, of righteousness and redemption, we people of
faith know we deal not with our needs or conditioning or illusions or
class consciousness, or, better put, not exclusively with these. We know
values inhere in the universe itself and they are so basic to it that they
are worthy of our lives. Some years ago, responding from this sensitivity, we identified culture with revelation. Now that this claim has shown
itself to be spurious, orthodoxy can make heard its message that God,
through revelation, has given the creatures reliable guidance.

I think that liberals largely concur in this stance. Though their Absolute may be weaker than that of the Orthodox, it is not non-existent. It is
real enough to be the standard of the right use of human freedom. And
for them too—to use traditional language—to believe in God's goodness
implies the availability of God's instruction. The only difference here
between the Orthodox and the liberal is the nature of the balance one
sets between revelation and autonomy. Against the pagans and the nihil-
ists of every kind, believing orthodox and liberal religionists join in fundamental alliance. They share a common view of the cosmos as value-
full and of humanity as having been instructed on this score. I can therefore understand that orthodoxy today is an option to the liberal mind in
a way that was once unthinkable. Then one asserted one's autonomy
against tradition on the basis of the self-evident power of culture. Now,
with little confidence in the value-creating and value-sustaining power
of enlightenment, one may well feel that the weak Absolute of much
Judeo-Christian orthodoxy is weak enough to give adequate scope to
human autonomy. I personally cannot share this turn to orthodoxy. In .
the face of the many failures of traditional religion to give adequate
recognition to our proper personhood—for example, the rights of
women—I do not see that traditional religion gives adequate dignity to
human freedom and the virtue of self-determination. But sharing with
the Orthodox a basic view of reality, as I do, I can warmly sympathize
with those who now see it, rather than a discredited liberalism or a per-
missive paganism, as the most adequate view of our situation.

Where today may liberal Jews find an Absolute strong enough to
ground their values yet weak enough to make human autonomy possible
and even the hallmark of our being created in the divine image?

Some years ago my answer would have been Buberian, that the most promising way of pointing people to the reality of God was to make them aware of the difference between I-it and I-thou encounters. They might then, in their daily experience, recover the dimension of transcendence which is available in all genuine interpersonal relationships and particularly in the most transforming I-thou situations. That was a very helpful approach in a time when people were becoming aware of what it meant to be treated like a person rather than as an object. Giving God the benefit of the same sort of un-analytic, non-manipulated approach we wished to have from others made the possibility of faith in God, even something of the "nature" of God, available to us in ways we had not previously anticipated. And since this was a personal route to God, one whose validity we could explore and renew in our own experience, it was a most effective form of apologetics.

In many ways, I still think that is a useful strategy. Yet a shift in our cultural concerns has suggested a more direct response to our situation. The central human experience of our time is the failure of liberal culture and, for all those who cannot now turn to an orthodoxy or ignore the problem, the loss of any ground for values. For many Jews, the rejection of the new nihilism has become more spiritually decisive than the absence of God felt in the horror of the Holocaust. If this observation is correct, the best apologetic tactic would be to help them recognize the implications of their response to the suggestion that the universe is a moral void. If faith is understood in Tillich's terms as ultimate concern, such Jews might now best find what they actually believe by analyzing their most basic values. Why do we still often devote ourselves to creating faithful marriages, concerned families, cultured individuals, a caring society, and high human excellence generally? These demanding concerns are no longer self-evident, or rational, or socially commended, or commonly expected. When, then, we recoil from unbridled permissiveness and reject the social pressure to paganize, when we stake our lives on these values, attesting that they are not our arbitrary choice but fundamental to the universe itself, we are acknowledging a reality that transcends us yet impinges upon us and rightly lays a claim upon us and our freedom.

Peter Berger terms these ordinary experiences of religious significance "signals of transcendence." They do not compel our consent but they do explain why, though we must respond to them in faith, we do not feel unreasonable in doing so. Berger does not list the rejection of nihilism as a contemporary signal of transcendence, but this testifies to the difference between his Lutheran and my Jewish sensibility. We Jews remain fixated on *halakhah*, existentially transformed for liberals into ethics or, more comprehensively today, values that humanize and sanctify.

I believe this apologetic approach is universal enough to count in our culture yet Jewish enough to speak authentically of our particular style of existence. And the reason many Jews today have identified *Yiddishkeit*, or the State of Israel, or the Holocaust, as our Absolute is that they are signals of transcendence for us though, I would argue, they should not be identified with the transcendent itself. Positively, we may not find it easy to talk about the Other we discover calling us to live by standards of uncommon quality. Surely we cannot explain why Reality operates in so odd a fashion. Yet what we shall now know, often to our own surprise, is that as we live in loyal Jewishness, we are in our own fashion people of faith and partners of God.

Perhaps the reality I have pointed to seems so weak that it cannot serve as an Absolute, even for liberals. That may be true. But I suggest that we must evaluate our Absolute in terms of our situation. A decade or so ago we were confident that science and philosophy would teach us the truth and that conventional ethics and liberal politics would bring the Messiah. In that time of high human self-assurance, suggesting so tentative and hidden a God as worthy of our belief would have been ludicrously inappropriate. But today, there is nothing left we can ultimately believe in: not democracy, or pleasure, or psychiatry, or human nature—not even ourselves, the biggest problem of all. In a day when R. D. Laing can be taken seriously when he suggests that schizophrenia is a rational response to reality, to have anything at all to believe in is an accomplishment indeed. To do so not out of fright or panic, but continuing the old Jewish experience that despair is false and value real and lasting, is a redemptive act in a dismal time.

Our primary liberal Jewish task then is to help our people gain access to God. Since I see traditional observance and *Yiddishkeit* and the People of Israel and the State of Israel and the struggle for Soviet Jewry as intimately related to this God, I do not hear myself calling for less ethnicity, only for a proper Jewish hierarchy of values. We need to create a new sense of Jewish piety, so that *berakhah* by *berakhah*, in ethical act or communal service, in study or rite, we will so link our lives to God that we will survive in Jewish and human integrity a vile and venomous age. Once we have achieved a measure of effective Jewish spirituality, it will be time to discuss concepts of God and the sort of ontologies into which they can fit. In a post-liberal age the creation of a coherent, rational philosophy cannot be made the prerequisite of our being believing Jews. Trusting Judaism more and rationality less than liberal Jews once did, we should first try to make our shaky Jewish faith more personally secure and then proceed to the task of seeking to understand it.

A Bibliographical Addendum

I have tried to set this theme in its Jewish historic context in my article, "The Changing Forms of Jewish Spirituality," *America*, vol. 140, no. 16, April 28, 1979. The effort to use the State of Israel or the Holocaust as an Absolute is dealt with by me in "Liberal Jews in Search of an 'Absolute'," *Cross Currents*, Spring, 1979. The relationship of this topic to the contemporary search for transcendence is analyzed in my paper, "Beyond Immanence; how shall liberal Jews educate for spirituality?", *Religious Education*, vol. 75, no. 4, July–August 1980.

Jewish Peoplehood:
Implications for Reform Judaism

Richard G. Hirsch

World Union for Progressive Judaism
Jerusalem, Israel

In his introduction to the book *The Jewish State*, Theodor Herzl declared: "We are a people—one people". That definition became the premise on which the Zionist movement was founded, just as the rejection of Jewish peoplehood became the leitmotif of 19th century Reform Judaism. But not only Reform Judaism: the 1897 Declaration by the Protestrabbiner, the Executive Committee of the German Rabbinical Association, was signed by two Orthodox as well as three liberal rabbis. Stating that "Judaism obligates its adherents to serve with all devotion the Fatherland to which they belong and to further its national interests with all their heart and with all their strength," they opposed the convening of the First Zionist Congress. Their protest was responsible for the transfer of the Congress, originally scheduled for Munich, to Basle. Seventy years after the publication of the Protestrabbiner, an article in *Maariv* (July 16, 1968) recorded the amazing discovery that almost all the living descendants of the five protest rabbis were living in the Jewish state.

The protest is no more. No more do we hear the question: What are the Jews—nation, people, religion, race? We have found a definition which fits us. History and destiny have reinforced the conviction: The Jews "are a people—one people".

We have by now overwhelmingly agreed. Throughout the world there is a *Jewish People*, who in the *Land of Israel* are organized into a *Jewish State. Am Yisrael, Eretz Yisrael, Medinat Yisrael.* Three related but clearly distinct, separate, and definable terms. However, it is my contention that though we have agreed on the terminology, we have not yet come to terms with the full implications of peoplehood. I believe that most of the controversies within Reform Judaism, as well as within American Jewry in general, are contemporary reflections, adapted to the changed conditions of Jewish life, of the old controversy over definition. Though we use different words than the previous generations, the religion versus peoplehood conflict is still an activating force. However, whereas in the past the debate was between opposite poles, in this generation it is between degrees of emphasis. It is accordingly more subtle, complex, and muted. Yet, if we are to refine alternative courses of belief and action, we need a continuing maḥloket le-shem Shamayim ("controversy for the sake of Heaven"), which will bring the issues to the fore rather than submerge them.

I have selected three areas of conflict within Reform Judaism— theology, Halakhic practice, and Zionism—wherein the debate between the religion versus peoplehood emphases continues. I make no effort to be comprehensive, but deal with one issue in each area, presenting in each instance a perspective which stresses the peoplehood dimension.

1. Toward a Theology of Peoplehood

Classical Reform presistently distorted the component parts of the triad God, Torah, and Israel. It elevated the elements of faith and theology, minimized Halakha, and tried to expunge the significance of the land, language, and people of Israel. Messianism was de-nationalized and the mission denuded of particularism. The prophets were ejected from the earth of their historical milieu and projected into universal space, like a science fiction time capsule. The very phrase Prophetic Judaism became synonymous with a de-Judaized, de-Torahized, de-nationalized universalism.

Though contemporary Reform Judaism has presumably rejected classical Reform and restored the particularist dimension, it is still tied to the linguistic and conceptual premises of classical Reform. Many if not most of our statements still bespeak a theology which perceives universalism and particularism as two forces in constant tension. This view is reflected in some of the papers delivered at the symposium sponsored by the Central Conference of American Rabbis in 1976 on the theme of universalism and particularism. One participant defined universalism as "that category of thought which tends to subordinate the distinctiveness of the Jewish people to the greater good of the general society, to minimize the distinctiveness of the Jewish people, to maximize that which it shares with other groups in society, or to put the survival of the Jewish people second to the survival of the general society." (*CCAR Journal*, Summer 1977, page 39). In the Centenary Perspective adopted in 1976, the CCAR identified universalism as a "concern for humanity" and the "messianic hope (is) that humanity will be redeemed"—without reference at that point to the traditional messianic hope, the precondition of which is that the Jewish people will be redeemed. The document also states: "The State of Israel and the Diaspora, in fruitful dialogue, can show how a people *transcends* (italics mine) nationalism even as it affirms it." In these and other expressions, universalism is translated as cooncern for humanity, ethics, and social justice in society at large. Particularism is translated as concern for the Jewish people and the Jewish community, cultural distinctiveness, ritual, Zionism, and the Jewish State. Whereas both are deemed essential, the universal is interpreted as being on a higher plane, selfless, ultimate, and transcendent, whereas the particular is parochial, nationalistic, penultimate, and a necessity for survival—but of lesser value in the scales of eternity.

This continuing effort to separate the inseparable is a corrosive vestige of classical Reform. It has been my privilege to serve the Reform movement on the cutting edge of both dimensions. When I was Director of the Religious Action Center in Washington, D.C., I functioned ostensibly in the arena of universalism, articulating Jewish concerns and positions on issues of civil rights, civil liberties, social welfare, and war and peace. In many if not most of our efforts, no Jewish vested interests were involved. I remember once receiving a call from a group that was convening a public hearing on the problems of migrant workers. The man in charge told me that they wanted testimony from a Protestant, a Catholic, and a Jewish migrant worker. He asked me to find a Jewish migrant for the hearing. We scoured the country—to no avail. Finally, I called him back and asked if I could testify, on grounds that, with all my peregrinations around the country, I was the closest thing we could find to a Jewish migrant. Throughout all the years in Washington, laboring in behalf of universal causes, I was always motivated by my Jewish particlarism and always cognizant of the impact of our actions on the status and well-being of Jews. I never offered testimony before Congress or gave a speech which was not rooted in Jewish tradition. I considered it my task not only to speak for Jews, but to speak for Judaism as the 4000-year-old heritage of commitment to the pursuit of justice and the advancement of the human condition.

And now that I am working in the State of Israel, supposedly the arena of Jewish particularism, I find manifold opportunities for expression of the universal impulse. In serving on the board of an international center for youth which sponsors community centers for Jewish and Arab children, or in working in behalf of civil liberties causes, or in behalf of new olim, we respond to the divine imperative of *Tikkun Olam* (perfecting society). In fact, if I were to be asked where in our entire world Progressive movement is the interdependence of the universal and particular impulses most manifest and relevant, I would say that it is in our new small community in the Arava called Kibbutz Yahel. For there young Jews from Israel and the Diaspora are putting down roots literally in the soil of Eretz Yisrael, building an outpost for the defense of the Jewish people, planting the seeds of a new Jewish society, seeking creative forms of Jewish religious observance, implementing in their own lives, not once a weekend or once a month but twenty-four hours every day, the Jewish values of communal responsibility, economic and social justice. I challenge anyone to point to any Reform group or congregation which is more universalistic or more particularistic.

How misguided and unfounded is the trepidation expressed in some quarters that too intensive a Zionism in Reform Judaism is upsetting the classic balance between universalism and particularism. The genius of the Jew is to be found not in the *balance* but in the *blend* between universalism and particularism. Zionism is not only Jewish particularism; it is the epitome of Jewish universalism. The Jew instinctively understands that the ethical imperatives of religion cannot be applied or tested in the abstract. The striving for a just society must be undertaken in a specific place and a specific time. Our tradition holds that the return to Zion will provide the framework, the testing grounds, within which the Jewish people as a collective, fulfilling Jewish values, will create the good society, and that society in turn will light the way for humankind. אור חדש על ציון תאיר ונזכה כולנו מהרה לאורו ("Cause a new light to shine on Zion, and may we all benefit speedily from its brightness."). The secular Zionist may not phrase his aspirations in the same way, but we as religious Jews should be committed to the national restoration as a means toward the fulfillment of the Messianic vision. In the words of the Zohar, quoted by Martin Buber, "The world can be redeemed only by the redemption of Israel, and Israel can be redeemed only by reunion with its land." (Martin Buber, *On Zion: The History of an Idea*, p. 77)

A theology for peoplehood will have to revise the facile delineations of previous generations. The true function of prophetic Judaism was to transmit the divine command: דרשו טוב ואל רע למען תחיו. "Seek good and not evil that ye may live." (Amos 5:14) That is a command which Jews can and should fulfill in every society, Jewish as well as non-Jewish, and for the benefit of humankind, which includes fellow Jews as well as fellow human beings. Leo Baeck summarized what should be our position when he wrote "This people . . . has life . . . only when it holds to itself for the sake of humanity and to humanity for the sake of itself." (*This People Israel*, p. 387)

2. Toward an Halakhic Orientation of Peoplehood

The refusal to acknowledge the peoplehood of Israel molded early Reform Judaism's ritual character and its relation to Halakhah. To be sure, other factors, such as the demands of reason and aesthetics, were at work. But, to use Kaufmann Kohler's phrase, to "transform the national Jew into a religious Jew" was a prime motivation. Abraham Geiger, foremost liturgist of early Reform, boldly proclaimed the rationale for his revision of the Siddur:

"The people of Israel no longer lives. . . . It has been transformed into a community of faith."

"Hebrew no longer lives. . . . If Hebrew were to be represented as an essential element of Judaism, then Judaism would be pictured as a national religion. A distinctive language is a characteristic of a distinctive peoplehood."

"The present heap of ruins, Jerusalem, is for us, at best, a poetic and melancholy memory, but no nourishment for the spirit. No exaltation and no hope are associated with it. Jerusalem is a thought for us, not a spatially limited place. But where the literal meaning of the prayers could,lead to the misunderstanding that we direct our adoration to that place, the words will have to be eliminated." (Jakob J. Petuchowski, *Abraham Geiger, the Reform Jewish Liturgist*, HUC-JIR Symposium, 1975, p. 44,45)

Recent generations of Reform leaders have rejected these premises of Geiger. No sanctity reposes in misconceptions of the past. But rejection must be followed by affirmation. New truths demand new consequences. If anti-peoplehood was a motivation for radical change in liturgy and practice in the past, then why should not peoplehood serve as a motivation for liturgical and ritual changes in our day? Shall not peoplehood be our "Geiger counter"?

Take the issue of *Ishut* (personal status). Whether we like it or not, the composition and character of world Jewry today will not permit us to ignore forever the ramifications of our actions on the Jewish people as a whole.

Reform Judaism is a response to the Jewish confrontation with modernity. I predict that the confrontation with Israel as the focus of Jewish peoplehood will have no less impact on future generations than did modernity on previous generations.

Given the unique character of Israel as the state of the Jewish people, given the coalition politics (which have traditionally allowed the religious parties political influence far beyond their numerical weight), given the reciprocal influence of *Dat U-Medinah* (religion-state) issues on Israel-Diaspora relations, questions of *Ishut* will continue to be high on the agenda of Israel and world Jewry for generations to come. It is no coincidence that these issues come to the fore during the Israel election process and assume such significance that an airplane landing at the onset of Shabbat or a conversion performed by a Reform rabbi can jeopardize the existence of the government. We cannot wish these circumstances away; they are a reality to which we must relate if we are concerned about the unity and well-being of world Jewry.

Years ago, a delegation of leaders of the World Union for Progressive Judaism met with the Minister of Religious Affairs to complain about the discrimination against the Reform movement in Israel. He offered to give Reform Jews full rights in Israel on one simple condition—that they register as a distinctive sect, like the Karaites, who receive full government support and have full autonomy over their religious affairs. But the Karaites cannot intermarry with other Jews, and their *de facto* status is that of a separate and separated religious community. We told our would-be godfather that his offer was one we had to refuse. We have no intention of separating ourselves or of permitting others to separate us from membership in the house of Israel. We are in Israel by right, and not by privilege. We do not ask for any special status, but for equal status as full participants in the upbuilding of Zion.

But if that is so, then we cannot have it both ways. Rights entail responsibilities. Either Reform rabbis are agents of a separate American sect, in which case we establish our own rules, oblivious of or indifferent to their impact on other Jews, or else we are the representatives of the Jewish people, in which case we must be sensitive to the traditions and practices which determine Jewish status. I do not refer to Jewish tradition in the narrow connotation of Halakhah as interpreted by the Orthodox establishment. I do refer to Jewish tradition in a broad sense as interpreted by Jews some of whom are classified as secular, including the vast majority of the Jews of Israel, who, though themselves non-observant, have some knowledge and appreciation of tradition.

In 1974, at the time of the "Who is a Jew?" controversy, we met with the leadership of the left-wing Mapam party. The meeting started with a ringing endorsement by the secretary of the party in defense of our position that the Law of Return should not be amended to exclude the State's recognition of non-Orthodox conversions performed abroad. And then, after we had already won their support, some of their Knesset members began to ask questions about the Reform Movement and its conversion procedures. When it became clear to them that our rabbis in America do not require *Berit Milah* (circumcision) or *Tevilah* (ritual immersion), we sensed a retreat. The secretary of the party bluntly told us: "Our membership is by-and-large irreligious, some even anti-religious. We are still in favor of rights for your movement, but it is hard for us to understand how any Jewish group would not require *Berit Milah* and *Tevilah*. They put the *Hekhsher* (Kosher) stamp on the conversion. How can you expect other Jews to recognize your acts as authentic?"

That is the very question that many of us have begun to ask. And here I confess that my own perspective has altered as a result of living in the more intense peoplehood setting of Israel. There are certain fundamental religious acts which are so ingrained in world Jewry, including secular Jewry, that they assume a *national* character and function. When the High Court of Israel ruled that Brother Daniel, a Catholic convert from Judaism, could not become a citizen under the Law of Return, they rendered a decision that was contrary to Halakhah. According to Halakhah, Brother Daniel was still a Jew, but according to the secular, national understanding, a person who converts to another religion is no longer a Jew. The *national* understanding prevailed. When not one car in Israel moves on Yom Kippur, that is an act of *national* self-discipline. When we officiate at a conversion ceremony, we are the agents of Klal

Yisrael. We assume responsibility for accepting a person not into membership in a Reform congregation, but into an enduring commitment to spend the rest of his life as a member of the Jewish people. The religious act serves a *national* purpose. That is an awesome responsibility which affects the status of converts and their progeny for generations. We are the officials commissioned to issue the passport to travel in the Jewish world. Of course, the Orthodox rabbinate will not authorize us to serve this function. For them it is not the act of conversion which counts, but who officiates at the act, and in their eyes we are not authorized. However, the issue is not a clear-cut conflict between autonomy and authority, between the right of the Reform rabbi or movement on one side and the Orthodox interpretation of Halakhah on the other side. The conflict is between autonomy and that vague, indefinable, intangible, but nevertheless very real perception of Klal Yisrael.

The question is not will the Orthodox rabbinate recognize us, but will the rest of the Jewish world recognize us? Will the secular Jew consider us authentic? And most important of all, will we, in this new era of peoplehood, consider ourselves authentic? That is the ultimate question. I take seriously the counsel of the distinguished elder statesman who urges us "to be ourselves." But what are we, and what do we want to be? I submit that what we want to be is not what we were. The movement which proclaimed itself a religion can with comparative ease lop off whole sections of ritual and liturgy, abrogate *mitzvot*, promote Sunday as the Sabbath, and oppose the reconstitution of Am Yisrael. But if we are a people, then let us "be ourselves." Let us act as a people. Let us be willing to explore the distinctive "way" of the people called Halakhah, knowing full well that the Orthodox definition ascribing divine origin to the Halakhah will continue to separate us, and that we are talking about *a Halakhic orientation* rather than *the Halakhah*.

Let us respond to the thrust of Jewish peoplehood which has prevented abstract reason from taking precedence over tradition, which has reinstated the Kol Nidre, retained Hebrew as our essential language of prayer, and refused to let convenience set the Jewish calendar. Let us not be ashamed of asking the question "*Mah Yomru HaYehudim*," as we are now in retrospect ashamed of having so often asked the question "*Mah Yomru HaGoyim*." Let us "be ourselves," a reforming, progressing movement within Klal Yisrael, which can respond to the challenges of the changing circumstances and perceptions of Jewish peoplehood.

3. *Toward a Zionism for Peoplehood*

As a movement, Reform has demonstrated ambivalent feelings toward Zionism. Even though the *Gates of Prayer* has reintroduced most of the peoplehood components of the traditional Siddur, it has systematically excluded even a modified reference to *Kibbutz Galuyot* (ingathering of the exiles). The Amidah prayer תקע בשופר גדול לחרותנו which reinstitutes a modified particularist element in the Hebrew, translates חרותנו ("*our* freedom") and עשוקנו ("*our* oppressed") by petitioning for the "liberation of (all) the oppressed" and "liberty in the four corners of the earth." This is a noble thought, but one which appears elsewhere in our liturgy and which alongside the Hebrew text reflects, to say the least, an intellectual inconsistency. The original draft of the Centennial Perspective contained no mention of the word Aliyah, and when, on behalf of our colleagues in Israel, I proposed a sentence to include Aliyah, the Chairman of the drafting committee informed me that the committee had voted overwhelmingly against its inclusion. The reason? The subject of Aliyah would inject divisiveness into a statement whose purpose was to find the common denominators which bind us together. It was only when an amendment was presented from the floor that the word Aliyah was finally inserted.

In order to stimulate discussion on the significance of Zionism, I find it helpful to differentiate between pro-Israelism and Zionism. What distinguishes the two is not formal identification with the Zionist movement. A person can be an active leader of a Zionist organization and still be a pro-Israeli rather than a Zionist. I have devised a test for determining the intensity of an individual's Zionism. The test is not ideological as such. It does not enter into the debate over "centrality of Israel" or *Shelilat HaGalut* ("negation of the Diaspora") or the *Bavel-Yerushalayim* (Babylon-Jerusalem) controversy. The test relates to an individual's personal beliefs and actions. A Zionist should be able to say:

1. I believe that the Jewish state is indispensable to my existence as a Jew, to the survival of the Jewish people, and to the fulfillment of the Jewish vision.

2. I do everything possible to educate myself Jewishly and to provide an intensive Jewish education for my children, including knowledge of Hebrew as a second language.

3. I would be pleased if one of my children or grandchildren made
Aliyah.

The test is simple, but when put to American Jews, very few answer
all the statements affirmatively. Not all agree on the criteria. I hope they
will agree that it is essential to sharpen the discussion in terms of placing
before Jews *personal* obligations which go beyond financial and political
support. I speak about children and grandchildren because we project
our highest values in terms of aspirations for our progeny.

The real test which confronts American Jewry in general and our
movement in particular is whether Zionism can be incorporated into our
Weltanschauung as an essential element of our own lives. To this day,
the average American Jew still relates to Israel as an object of philanthropy and as a refuge for homeless Jews, as if to say, "Israel is for
others, not for us". Our task, therefore, is to demonstrate the interde-
pendent relationship between the Jewish state, the Jewish people, and
the individual Jew.

The State of Israel is an instrument created by the collective will of
the Jewish people. But even as the people has established the state, so the
state has re-established the people. Only *Am Yisrael* could have
redeemed *Eretz Yisrael*, and only *Medinat Yisrael* could have reconsti-
tuted *Am Yisrael*. Martin Buber wrote, "In other respects, the people of
Israel may be regarded as one of many peoples on earth, and the land of
Israel as one among other lands, but in their mutual relationship and in
their common task, they are unique and incomparable." (*Writings of
Buber*, ed. Herberg, p. 303). Zionism and Jewish peoplehood are inter-
dependent. The uniqueness of the people will be nourished through contact and identification with the land, and the state will retain its incomparable character only through contact with the people.

That is the primary ideology inherent in traditional Judaism which
Zionism has made an operative principle in our day. In contrast to early
Reform, which mistakenly believed that the individual Jew could be preserved without the people, we have now come to realize that it is the
preservation of the people which gives the individual his *raison d'etre* as
a Jew. Therefore, the highest priority of the Jew as an individual is to
keep the people alive. In turn, the *sine qua non* for the creative survival
of the Jewish people at this juncture in our history is to secure and
develop the Jewish State. This State offers the first opportunity in 2,000
years for the Jews as a people to have some control over their destiny

and to create an indigenous Jewish culture in an environment identified as Jewish. There will not be another opportunity. It is this state or none, this time in history or never. Our commitment to the state should, therefore, not be affected negatively by the conditions or the quality of life in the State. I am troubled, even aggrieved, by many aspects of Israeli life: the deficient application of Jewish values, the socio-economic-cultural gap, the inadequacies of government, the exacerbation of problems relating to the Arab minority, the all-pervasive bureaucracy, the *Yeridah*, the failures in *Aliyah* and *Kelitah*, the intensifying militancy within a coalition of right-wing politics and right-wing religionists, the politicization of religion and the religionization of politics, the obstacles to religious pluralism, etc.

Each of us could compile a similar list on the character of American society or of the American Jewish community or of the institution called the synagogue. But those who presume to be leaders would betray their trust if they permitted the frustrations to deter them from pursuing the vision which propelled the original establishment of the society or institution, or if they permitted the shortcomings to serve as a pretext for less than full support and participation.

Here is where we as individuals and as a movement have been deficient and shortsighted. Those among us for whom the peoplehood dimension is of lesser significance do not accord the status of indispensability to the State of Israel. They are prepared to "think the unthinkable." But I assume that most of us would subscribe to the definition in II Samuel (7:22) מי כעמך כישראל גוי אחד בארץ ("Who is like your people, like Israel, a unique nation on earth."). If we are indeed a גוי אחד, then the way to retain our uniqueness is בארץ, "through the land of Israel." Eretz Yisrael is not just another land and the Jews who live there not just another Jewish community. Israel is the setting where the Jewish character was forged and where Jewish destiny will be determined. A movement which is content to sit in the bleachers watching the gladiators battle for survival in the international arenas of the Jewish people fails to assume its responsibility and has no right to demand accountability. A movement which is not integrated and integral in Israel can have no integrity and will neither have influence nor be influenced, neither count nor be counted.

Our unique peoplehood imposes obligations on Reform Jews as individuals and as a movement.

No less crucial to Jewish survival than the struggle to achieve peace with the Arabs is the struggle to define the Jewish character of the Jewish state. Reform Judaism has a stake and a say in that struggle. Our message is universal: the revivification of tradition in response to modernity, the application of tradition to social concerns, the affirmation of the viability of the Diaspora, the equality of women. The principles we advocate and the *Orah Hayyim* (way of life) we espouse are relevant in Israel as in America.

The demographic pattern and socio-economic conditions of Israel are such that the state will not remain Jewish unless the Jewish population is bigger and better; and it will not be bigger unless it is better, nor better unless it is bigger. We have an obligation to foster Aliyah, not because there is no future for Diaspora Jewry, but precisely because the way to assure the future is to fortify the state which is a major instrument for the survival of Diaspora Jewry.

Cultivation of the Hebrew language is as essential to unique peoplehood as is cultivation of the land. An American child struggling to spit out a Hebrew sentence may in that very process develop a more intense Jewish consciousness than his Israeli counterpart chattering away fluently. We have an obligation to strengthen American Jewish consciousness by establishing the educational programs, schools, and camps, both in Israel and the Diaspora, which will encourage the use of modern Hebrew as a second language for American Jews. We have the obligation to provide adults and youth with the extended learning experiences in Israel which represent continuing booster injections of unique peoplehood.

The implications of peoplehood for Reform Judaism can be summarized in the Shaharit prayer:

"For the Lord has chosen Zion, He has desired it for His habitation,

For the Lord has chosen Jacob unto Himself, Israel for His own treasure,

For the Lord will not cast off His people, neither will He forsake His inheritance."

Profane Religion and Sacred Law

Milton R. Konvitz

Cornell University
Ithaca, New York

Towards the end of the seventh century B.C.E. there reigned in Judah a king, who, following the ways of the Egyptian pharaoh, his contemporary, built himself palaces by forced labor. In the book which bears his name, Jeremiah wrote: "Thus says the Lord: 'Go down to the house of the king of Judah, and speak there this word, and say, . . .

Woe to him who builds his house by unrighteousness,
  and his upper rooms by injustice;
  who makes his neighbor serve him for nothing,
  and does not give him his wages; . . .
Do you think you are a king because you compete in cedar?
Did not your father eat and drink and do justice and
  righteousness?
Then it was well with him.
He judged the case of the poor and needy;
  then it was well.
Is not this to know me?
  says the Lord."[1]

Now let us assume something most improbable: that the President of the United States would find a way of conscripting men to build for him a private mansion. What would happen? A team of courageous investigative reporters would uncover the facts and the story would be published in leading newspapers and would be reported on television and radio, so that, within a matter of days or hours there would be a great public scandal, and the president would face court actions and impeachment proceedings, and editorials would call for his resignation, indictment, and removal.

In the kingdom of Judah twenty-six hundred years ago there were no newspapers, there were no investigative reporters, there were no congressional investigative committees, there was no radio or television. The technology was different, the institutions were different. Jeremiah stood before the king and, in the name of the Lord, condemned him for injustices and cruelties. We call Jeremiah a prophet, and we think of his words as part of our great religious heritage. No one, however, would think of referring to Sam Ervin as anything but a senator, or to Bob Woodward and Carl Bernstein as anything but journalists, or to Archibald Cox as anything but the Watergate special prosecutor, or to John Sirica as anything but a federal district court judge.

Or take the book of Jonah. It relates that the word of the Lord came to Jonah, and instructed him to go to Nineveh, and proclaim judgment upon it, for, said the Lord, "their wickedness has come before Me."[2] Now Nineveh was a great city in Assyria. Whatever wickedness the Lord had seen in Nineveh, it had nothing to do with the people of Judah. The wickedness of Nineveh was purely, as Brezhnev would say today, an internal, a domestic affair. What the king of Nineveh did to his people, or what the inhabitants of that city did to one another, need not have distressed the people of Jerusalem. Yet the book relates that the word of the Lord came to Jonah, son of Amittai, and told him to leave his home and go to Nineveh and uncover the wickedness of the place and tell the people there how the Lord judges them.

Soon after taking office, President Carter took actions which clearly showed that the American government and people were very much concerned with the cruel, inhuman ways in which the government of the U.S.S.R. was treating its own dissidents, and on March 17, 1977, when he appeared before the United Nations, President Carter gave special emphasis to the American concern with human rights in other countries as well as at home. The President knew, of course, that the Soviet government would strongly resent what it termed interference into internal affairs—matters which did not threaten the peace or security of the United States (just as the wickedness of Nineveh was no threat to the peace or security of Judah). But President Carter answered this criticism by saying that all the states which have signed the U.N. Charter have pledged themselves to observe and respect human rights, and by referring to the U.N.'s Universal Declaration of Human Rights and the Helsinki accords; and he concluded by saying, "Thus, no member of the United Nations can claim that mistreatment of its citizens is solely its own business."[3]

When Jonah appeared in Nineveh,[4] he could not speak of the United Nations documents and the Helsinki Declaration; he could speak only of the Lord. Jimmy Carter, on the other hand, no matter what his private feelings and thoughts may have been at the moment, could not speak in the name of the Lord, but he could speak of the international commitments and agreements, which bind all nations, the U.S.S.R. no less than the U.S.A. We know of Jonah as a prophet, and his book as part of our Sacred Scriptures, as part of our religious heritage; but we idenfity Jimmy Carter as head of our state and government, and think of his speech as a political action. Jeremiah and Jonah each spoke in the name of the Lord; President Carter, speaking to repesentatives of nearly 150 member states of the U.N., spoke in the name of American ideals, which he said, "we are determined fully to maintain as the backbone of our foreign policy."

There are obviously good reasons why the President of the United States cannot say that he speaks in the name of the Lord, and why we must continue to distinguish in our language between the religious and the secular, between the sacred and the profane; but we must also be prepared to penetrate through words to the relatives behind them; and where do we do that, then, I submit, we would find that there is more similarity than difference between Jonah addressing the king of Nineveh and Carter addressing the United Nations; between Jeremiah addressing the king of Judah and Judge John Sirica issuing an order against the President of the United States.[5]

We make a sharp distinction between the things that are God's and the things that are Caesar's, and for many purposes this is wise and even necessary; but often this language misleads; it cloaks a reality and keeps us from seeing the substance; it prevents us from penetrating to what goes on under the mask of convention, tradition, and habit. Seeing the representation and not the substance, we fail to see that Jeremiah and Jonah acted out their prophetic role as politicians. When we look at the realities and not at what Francis Bacon called Idols of the Theatre,[6] we see that often words are interchangeable but we nonetheless, for pruden- tial reasons, stick to the convention. But it is important to bear in mind that there is a deeper wisdom than that which prudence offers.

II

"Whence this worship of the past?" Emerson asked. "The centur- ies," he went on to say, "are conspirators against the sanity and author- ity of the soul. . . . Yet see what strong intellects dare not hear God him- self unless he speak the phaseology of I know not what David, or Jeremiah, or Paul."[7] Emerson expressed the hope that the time will come when man will see that "the world is the perennial miracle;" "he will learn that there is no profane history; that all history is sacred."[8]

When Ahab, king of Samaria, and his wife Jezebel contrived the judicial murder of their neighbor Naboth, so that they could add his vineyard to their property, and Elijah the prophet appeared before the king and asked, "Have you killed, and also taken possession?"[9]—we think of the events as sacred history, as we should. But when the case of President Nixon came before the Supreme Court in 1974,[10] and the Court unanimously ruled that the President must turn over 64 tapes of his White House conversations—a decision which precipitated Nixon's resignation about a fortnight later—we do not think of these events as part of sacred history. But why? When Ahab saw Elijah, he cried out: "Have you found me, O my enemy?" The prophet replied: "I have found you, because you have sold yourself to do what is evil in the sight of the Lord. . . ."[11] The institutions are different, the style of address is different, but the essence is the same: in each instance the Rule of Law was affirmed, the principle was vindicated that the head of government, called king or president, is subject to the law and is not above or beyond it. Nixon, too, could have cried out: "Have you found me, O my enemy?" And the Court could have replied: "Yes, we have found you, because you have sold yourself to do what is evil in the sight of the Con- stitution." With Emerson we could say, there is no profane history, all history is sacred.

The plain fact is that we get out of our thoughts what we put into them. If we think of religion as only that which goes on in our churches and synagogues and only that which is found in certain books that we call sacred, then it follows that our schools and colleges, our libraries, art museums and concert halls, our offices, shops, mills and factories, our legislatures and courts, our parks and forests, even our homes—then it follows, I say, that all the furniture of earth, that everything but the choir of heaven, falls into the domain of Caesar, from which God is shut out. To my mind, there can be no greater blasphemy.

Nor, I think, can there be a greater perversion of thought. For what we have done is this: We have taken the principle of separation of church and state, which is of transcendent importance for our political organization and civil life, and made it applicable to all phases of our personal and social life. We have carried it over from the political sphere, wherein its usefulness can hardly be exaggerated, and have applied it to our culture generally, including our ethics and metaphysics. This may be an instance of the logical fallacy of composition, which arises when we affirm something to be true of a whole when it is true only of a part. The result has been a trivialization of religion into a part-time leisure interest—a process that has left much of life absurd, shallow, and inane.

The whole purport and drive of biblical religion was to exclude nothing—absolutely nothing—from the rule and judgment of God. The religious tradition rooted in biblical categories took its stand to repudiate, plainly and forcefully, any dualism which would relegate or confine God to a restricted jurisdiction. Marcionism, Gnosticism, and Manichaeism, which taught that a substantial part of the world and of man was ruled, not by God, but by Satan or evil archons, inspired some of their votaries toward extreme asceticism and others toward extreme licentiousness, and each of these sects offered a certain logic that sounded convincing. But the main streams of Judaism and Christianity denied the premises of these dualistic religions, and refused to turn over the world as we know it to the power of Satan.

It is no longer fashionable to avow a belief in Satan or his entourage of evil archons. But the fact is, nonetheless, that we are dualists. We have divided the world between God and ourselves. Part of what we consider our own, we are willing to turn over to Caesar, but believing in civil liberties, part we retain as our private domain. Some are willing to share a part of this domain with God, but some are very jealous of their privacy and exclude Him from it; they divide the world only between themselves and Caesar. The dualist is either a total or partial atheist. If he totally excludes God, then obviously he is an atheist. If he excludes God from a substantial part of the world, then to that degree he is an atheist.

The foundation on which modern man in the West builds his world is not God, not Satan, nor Caesar, but himself. This individualism is the

inheritance from the Cartesian philosophy, which starts with oneself—
Cogito, *ergo sum;* from the Protestant Reformation, and especially the
notion of the duty of the private judgment—*Hier steh'ich, ich kann richt
anders;* and from the Renaissance, which glorified the integrity and dignity of the individual mind. It is man, then, who assigns a place to everything, even to God. It is just as it is related in Genesis. Every creature
passes before Adam, and he gives to everything a name; but there is a
significant difference, for even God, too, passes before him, and it is not
God who names man, but man who names God.

While many good and some even sublime values can be attributed to
this development, it is necessary to say that some consequences have
been highly detrimental and even odious because of the tendency to
absolutize the individual and to make individualism into an all-encompassing ideology—like the tendency to make the scientific method and
the spirit of science into scientism, or to make the secularizing process
into secularism. Individualism was carried to the extreme where it was
forgotten that the self is always the social self; to the extreme where it
was forgotten that, as Professor John Macmurray wrote, "The self is one
term in a relation between two selves. . . . The self exists only in the
communion of selves."[12] The individual man may have all the grandeur
and greatness that was spoken of him by Giannozzo Manetti in his treatise *On the Excellency and Dignity of Man* and by Pico della Mirandola
in his *Oration on the Dignity of Man,* and that is assigned to him by the
Bible when it says that God made man in His own image, and that He
made him only a little less than Himself.[13] But this can be true only if we
recognize the fact that man is not man if he exists in isolation, alone.
"Imagine yourself alone in the midst of nothingness," said A. S. Edding-
ton, "and then you try to tell me how large you are." We tend constantly
to forget that God did not create the solitary man but man-in-relation,
or mankind.

> Then God said, "Let us make man in our image, after our likeness; and let
> *them* have dominion over the fish of the sea, and over the birds of the air,
> and over the cattle, and over all the earth, and over every creeping thing that
> creeps upon the earth." So God created man in his own image, in the image
> of God he created him; male and female he created *them.*[14]

Before there were two there was no one, for there is no male when there
is no female; and when there are male and female, then, and only then, is

there the genus man, which the Hebrew word *Adam* means, and only then is there mankind. The self, as Professor Macmurray has said, can exist only in relation to the other; he exists as a person only as he is in relation to others.[15]

In biblical contemplation, a man fulfills himself as person chiefly in so far as he fulfills his role as neighbor; in other words, he realizes himself mainly in his relations with others, or as and when he sees *himself* as *the other*.

III

This, I think, is the way it was intended that the Parable of the Good Samaritan be understood. The lawyer who stood up to test Jesus asked, in effect, the following question: "The Torah commands me, as you say, to love my neighbor as myself. What I want to know is who is my neighbor?" In answer Jesus told of a man who was robbed and beaten while on the highway. A priest and a Levite saw the helpless man but looked the other way. Then along came a Samaritan, who stopped and took care of him. Now, asked Jesus. "Which of these three, do you think, proved neighbor to the man who fell among the robbers?" The lawyer said, "The one who showed mercy on him." And Jesus said to him, "Go and do likewise."[16] One of the two significant elements in the parable is the way Jesus handled the word "neighbor." We ordinarily think of the other man being the neighbor. Jesus turned the relationship around. "Which of the three, do you think, proved *neighbor to the man who fell among the robbers?*" That is, it was only the Samaritan, himself a stranger,, who showed *himself to be a neighbor* to the man in need of a neighbor.

The essence of man is to be a neighbor. Each of us is born a neighbor. "To be a man," Leo Baeck wrote in *The Essence of Judaism*, "means to be a fellow man."[17] Kierkegaard, in *Works of Love*, commenting on the Parable of the Good Samaritan, wrote:

> He towards whom I have a duty is my neighbor, and when I fulfill my duty I prove that I am a neighbor. Christ does not speak about recognizing one's neighbor but about being a neighbor oneself, about proving oneself to be a neighbor, something the Samaritan showed by his compassion. By this he did not prove that the assaulted man was his neighbor but that he was a neighbor of the one assaulted.[18]

The Neo-Kantian philosopher Hermann Cohen, in his *Religion of Reason Out of the Sources of Judaism*, has argued, and I believe convincingly, that before one can think of man, one must think, first of all, of *fellowman*—not *Mensch*, but *Mitmensch*.[19]

This is so not only for psychological, sociological, and philosophical reasons, but even more for religious, ethical, and even metaphysical reasons. Ethics and religion depend, Hermann Cohen has argued, on the concept of fellowman.[20] For if, he wrote, "The correlation between God and man is the fundamental equation of religion, then *man* in this correlation must first of all be thought of as fellowman."[21]

That the correlation between God and man is the fundamental equation of religion—at least of the biblical religions—we can readily see as we go back to the Parable of the Good Samaritan. The Gospel according to Luke relates that a lawyer stood up and asked Jesus, "Teacher [Rabbi], what shall I do to inherit eternal life?" Jesus said to him: "What is written in the law [Torah]?" The lawyer answered: "You shall love the Lord your God with all your heart, and with all your soul, and with all your strength, and with all your mind; and your neighbor as yourself." And Jesus said to him, "You have answered right; do this, and you will live [i.e. inherit eternal life]."[22] Then the lawyer, feeling a bit argumentative , went on to ask Jesus, "And who is my neighbor?"—a question which provoked the exegesis so wonderfully concretized in the Parable of the Good Samaritan.

In the version given in Matthew, it is not the lawyer but Jesus himself who combines the sayings from Deuteronomy and Leviticus. "Teacher," said the lawyer, "which is the great commandment in the law?" And Jesus answered with the texts from the Torah: "You shall love the Lord your God with all your heart, and with all your soul, and with all your mind. This is the great and first commandment. And a second is like it. You shall love your neighbor as yourself. On these two commandments depend all the law and the prophets."[23]

But how does one love God? Judaism and Christianity never left one in doubt on the answer to this question; for one can love God chiefly through the love of man, by being a neighbor, by being a fellowman. They are, indeed, not two commandments but only one: *You shall love the Lord your God by loving your neighbor as yourself.*

I shall not go so far as to say that this love commandment exhausts the nature of Judaism or Christianity. The religions rooted in the Bible have been conditioned by history, culture, and the nature of man, and they reflect and express men's frustrations and aspirations. As the late Professor Hocking wrote:

> Religion has fostered everything valuable to man and has obstructed everything: it has welded states and disintegrated them; it has rescued races and it has oppressed them, destroyed them, condemned them to perpetual wandering and outlawry. It has raised the value of human life, and it has depressed the esteem of that life almost to the point of vanishing; it has honored womanhood, it has slandered marriage. Here is an energy of huge potency but of ambiguous character.[24]

It was precisely because religions have so much potentiality for evil as well as for good, for enslavement as well as for liberation of the human spirit, it was because of their ambiguous character, that Theodore Parker drew a distinction between their transient and permanent qualities.[25] What, then, is fundamental or permanent in Judaism and Christianity if it is not the love commandment?

The prophets drew a distinction between the transient and the permanent, between the essential and the accidental. Jeremiah, for example, has God saying to Israel:

> . . . in the day that I brought them out of the land of Egypt, I did not speak to your fathers or command them concerning burnt offerings and sacrifices. But this command I gave them, "Obey my voice, and I will be your God, and you shall be my people; and walk in the way that I command you . . ."[26]

And what is the way that God commanded? Jeremiah left no doubt as to its meaning:

> Thus says the Lord: "Let not the wise man glory in his wisdom, let not the mighty man glory in his might, let not the rich man glory in his riches; but let him who glories glory in this, that he understands and knows me, that I am the Lord who practices steadfast love, justice, and righteousness in the earth; for in these things I delight, says the Lord."[27]

Walking in His ways means to live a life in imitation of God, that is, life that manifests the practice of steadfast love, justice, and righteousness. "You shall be holy, for I the Lord your God am holy."[28] "You, therefore, must be perfect, as your heavenly Father is perfect."[29] Examine, said Theodore Parker, the duties enjoined by a life in the imitation of God, and what do we find?—"humility, reverence, sobriety, gentleness, charity, forgiveness, fortitude, resignation, faith, and active love;" and all these duties are summed up in the command, "Thou shalt love the Lord thy God, . . . thou shalt love thy neighbor as thyself."[30]

The true love of God, said William Ellery Channing, "perfectly coincides, and is in fact the same thing, with the love of virtue, rectitude, and goodness." We esteem only him a pious man, wrote Channing.

> who practically conforms to God's moral perfections and government; who shows his delight in God's benevolence, by loving and serving his neighbor; his delight in God's justice by being resolutely unright; . . .[31]

To say that this is the whole of religion, that Judaism and Christianity teach only this, would be to overlook, at one's peril, a great deal that is of vital importance and to falsify the record. But first things should come first, and one has a moral, as well as an intellectual, duty to distinguish between the permanent and the transient, between the fundamental or intrinsic and the accessory, derivative, adventitious, and historically-conditioned aspects of religions. When we look for this differentiation in Judaism and Christianity, there can be no doubt as to what we will uncover. Let me cite but one other instance out of many. It is the stirring passage in which Job portrays the model biblical man of righteousnesss and loving-kindness:

> because I delivered the poor who cried,
>   and the fatherless who had none to help him.
> The blessing of him who was about to perish came upon me,
>   and I caused the widow's heart to sing for joy.
> I put on righteousness, and it clothed me;
>   my justice was like a robe and a turban.
> I was eyes to the blind,
>   and feet to the lame.
> I was a father to the poor,
>   and I searched out the cause of him whom I did not know.
> I broke the fangs of the unrighteous,
>   and made him drop his prey from his teeth.[32]

The difference between the essential and the accessory or adventitious is put in a dramatic and paradoxical way in *Lamentations Rabbah*, where God is made to exclaim: "If only they were to forsake Me but observe My teachings!" The rabbis felt safe in saying this because they knew that the evil man consciously or impliedly denies, forsakes, or forgets God, but that the man who observes God's teachings, whether he knows it or not, has faith in God, for he hates what God hates and he loves what God loves. With Jeremiah we can ask, "Is this not to know Him?"[33]

IV

If we are correct in this analysis, then it follows that the sharp differentiation that we make between this-worldly and the other-worldly, between the immanent and the transcendent, between the profane or secular and the religious or sacred, falls away—because these polarities come together in the nature of God and in the nature of man. God, being infinite, is found in all spheres and all levels of existence. Since God is the Creator and His essence is definable in ethical terms, inadequate as such terms may be, and since man is made in His image, it follows that—except for some specific purposes, in order to achieve certain ends—there is no separate realm that can be denoted as the "religious," and that to exclude God from the realm of Caesar is a supreme blasphemy and heresy. It is easy enough to find God in the hushed, awesome, candle-light of the temple or church, or in the stillness of the forest, or in a storm on the high seas; but our great need is to look for Him where Caesar wields his power, to look for Him in the marketplace, in our teeming cities and towns, in our shops and factories: to find Him in our sciences and technologies, in our clinics and hospitals, in our constitutions and bills of rights.

It is only a perverse blindness that makes it possible for us to see God's law in the Bible, but only the law of Caesar in the statutes enacted by Congress or the state legislatures or in the decisions and opinions of our courts.

There can be no question but that this-worldliness opens the door to staggering corruptions, but who that knows the history of religions will care to say that other-worldliness is totally exempt from its own kinds of perversion and corruption?

The Bible provides: "Thou shalt not have in thy bag divers weights, a great and a small. . . . A perfect and just weight shalt thou have; a perfect and just measure shalt thou have."[34] When we read this in Deuteronomy, we think of it as an example of what God ordained as a moral

principle of honest, fair, and just dealing; but why do we consider our
legislative enactments on just weights and measures as something of
lesser worth and dignity? Why does one belong in the realm of God,
another in the realm of Caesar? A law in Deuteronomy provides that
when a war is waged against a city, its trees—at least its fruit-bearing
trees—shall not be cut down—"Are the trees in the field men that they
should be besieged by you?"[35] From this passage the ancient rabbis
derived the general principle that no natural or man-made object may be
wasted or needlessly destroyed.[36] We think of these laws as divinely
ordained, for they are based on the principle that "The earth is the
Lord's and the fullness thereof,"[37] and that man is only a temporary
tenant and a steward. But Congress and our state legislatures have
enacted laws for the protection of the environment and the conservation
of resources that seek to achieve the same ends. In 1964, for example,
Congress set up a National Wilderness Preservation System. The statute
defines a wilderness as "an area where the earth and its community of
life are untrammeled by man, where man himself is a visitor who does
not remain," and which offers "outstanding opportunities for soli-
tude."[38] I submit that it is only dullness of sensibility and a perverse kind
of spirituality that refuses or fails to see that our own enactments are no
less religious nor less sacred. The religious man who has not turned over
governance of this world to Satan must see in man's intelligence a manifestation of God's governance of the world, for how shall God govern
this nation but through the intelligence of its citizens and the officers of
government whom they have chosen?

If there is any principle that is distinctively biblical it is the bias of
righteousness in favor of the poor and helpless. Time and again the Bible
singles them our for special concern. But if God is so deeply concerned
with the poor, why does He not save them? Why do the prophets call
upon us to practice righteousness toward the poor and needy?

Martin Buber relates that Rabbi Moshe Leib of Sasov taught his disciples no human quality or power was created by God to no purpose,
and that even base qualities can be uplifted to serve God. A disciple
asked him what purpose can atheism serve in God's world. This, too,
said the rabbi, can be uplifted. For if someone should come to you and
ask your help—someone who needs bread to eat, or shelter, or clothing—
you might be inclined to say to the poor man, "You believe in God as I
do. Well, take your needs to God and pray that He may help you." Only
an evil man, said the rabbi, can give this response. For when the poor

man comes to you, you must act as *if there were no God*, and as if there were only one person in the whole world who could help him—only yourself.[39]

Heaven knows how far short of perfection are the anti-poverty programs that we have evolved since President Johnson in 1964 declared "unconditional war on poverty." In his State of the Union Message, President Johnson said that the goal of the war on poverty was "total victory." We know how far we are from this goal. But no personal or social ideal is ever fully realized. What is important is that we have committed ourselves to an ideal which had never before been so fully articulated and projected by a nation and its government. No one who knows the record can accuse us of being callous, indifferent, or miserly. Why is the biblical law on leaving gleanings, for the poor to gather, a sacred text, but the Economic Opportunity Act of 1964 a mere profane piece of congressional legislation? "Bread for myself," wrote Berdyaev, "is a material question: bread for my neighbor is a spiritual question."[40] In so far as we devote our time, thought, and resources to the question of bread for our neighbors, we concern ourselves with a central religious duty, and it is a gross corruption of thought and language to assign our efforts a place in the realm of Caesar as if the light of God does not penetrate that place of total spiritual darkness. We continually forget that it is in His light that we see light; that it is only through His infinite wisdom that we have ideals, thoughts, and plans.[41]

It is, I believe, important for us never for a moment to forget that there is no word for "religion" in the whole of the Hebrew Scriptures, and that the word appears only very few times—five times, to be exact—in the New Testament.[42] Judaism and Christianity were conceived of as "teachings" or as "ways of life." To be a Jew or a Christian did not mean to be "religious" only on certain days of the week or year or to perform only certain acts. It meant to spiritualize, to sanctify everything that one does, to elevate all that one touches. It meant that religion must pervade all of one's work, that it should blend into all one's actions, so that there would be no separation between the sacred and the secular, but only between the sacred and the sacred.

The way, however, our lives and our society are organized, we feel compelled to fragmentize and compartmentize our thoughts and our actions. In the interest of a greater liberty, we must believe that the United States Constitution provides for a strict separation between Church and State and that the realm of God and the realm of Caesar must not be allowed to intermingle. But we must recognize the fact that these terms are arbitrary signs, constructed and imposed for practical and concrete purposes, and were intended to contribute to the safeguarding of our lives and liberties. They are, however, semantic and institutional inventions. Used appropriately, they are superb conventions. But these concepts have no legitimate place outside the political arena. Our innermost thoughts and our lives as we live them ought to know no such artificial divisions which we have arbitrarily yet rationally imposed upon ourselves and our institutions.

Maimonides, commenting on the statement in the Talmud, "Let all thy deeds be for the sake of God,"[43] wrote that a man must seek his physical health and vigor, for he cannot pursue intellectual work and think properly if he is hungry, or sick, or in pain, Whoever, he wrote,

> throughout his life follows this course will be continually serving God, even while engaged in business, and even during cohabitation, because his purpose in all that he does will be to . . . serve God. Even when he sleeps and seeks repose, to calm his mind and rest his body, so as not to fall sick and be incapacitated . . ., his sleep is service of the Almighty.[44]

How ridiculous, he thought, is the veil which men have imposed between the transcendent and the immanent, and between themselves and God. All natural forces, he wrote, are so-to-speak "angels."

> How great is the blindness of ignorance and how harmful. If you told a man who is one of those who deemed themselves "the Sages of Israel" that the Deity sends an angel, who enters the womb of a woman and forms the fetus there, he would be pleased with this assertion and would accept it and would regard it as a manifestation of greatness and power on the part of the Deity. . . . But if you tell him that God has placed in the sperm a formative force shaping the limbs and giving them their configuration and that this force is the "angel," . . . the man would shrink from this opinion. For he does not understand the notion of the true greatness and power that consists in the bringing into existence of forces active in a thing . . .[45]

When, in 1962, the Supreme Court held that the prayer formulated by the Board of Regents and authorized by them to be recited in the public schools of the State of New York was unconstitutional,[46] there was a great outcry that the Court had taken God out of the schools and had "deconsecrated the nation."[47] What a shocking corruption of religion these charges were! God is in a school, and that school is consecrated, when the teachers—supported by the parents in their homes—feel themselves dedicated to a high and noble vocation and bring to bear on their work and in all their relations with their students the best of their thoughts and energies. Whether the children do or do not hurry through the mumbo-jumbo of a 22-word officially-drafted so-called prayer, if the teachers, administrators, and parents perform their services with purity of motives and singleness of heart, that school will be no less sacred than any synagogue or church. "Would that all the Lord's people were prophets, that the Lord would put His spirit upon them!"[48]

We must remember, wrote Jeremy Taylor in the seventeenth century,

> that the life of every man may be so ordered (and indeed must) that it may be a perpetual serving of God: the greatest trouble and most busy trade and worldly encumbrances, when they are necessary, or charitable, or profitable in order to any of those ends which we are bound to serve, whether public or private, being a doing [of] God's work. For God provides the good things of the world to serve the need of nature, by the labors of the ploughman, the skill and pains of the artisan, and the dangers and traffic of the merchant; these men are, in their calling, the ministers of the Divine Providence, and the stewards of the creation, and servants of a great family of God, . . . So that no man can complain that his calling takes him off from religion; his calling itself, and his very worldly employment . . . is a serving of God . . .[49] Blessed be that goodness and grace of God, which, out of infinite desire to glorify and save mankind, would make the very works of nature capable of becoming acts of virtue, that all our lifetime we may do Him service.[50]

NOTES

1. Jeremiah 22:1, 13–16.
2. Jonah, 1,2.
3. *New York Times*, March 18, 1977, p. 10A. Cf. Leonid I. Brezhnev, *New York Times*, March 22, 1977, p. 14.
4. The book may have been written in the fourth century B.C.E. It would therefore have been written in Judah, centuries after the destruction of Nineveh in 612.
5. Archibald Cox was dismissed on October 20, 1973, after he threatened to secure a judicial ruling that Nixon was violating a court order to turn over the tapes to Judge Sirica.

6. Francis Bacon, *Novum Organum*, Book I. Aphorisms 39 and 44.

7. Emerson, essay on "Self-Reliance."

8. Emerson, essay, "The Over-Soul."

9. 1 Kings ch. 21.

10. U.S. v. Nixon, 418 U.S. 683 (1974).

11. 1 Kings 21:20.

12. John Macmurray, *Interpreting the Universe* (London), 137.

13. Genesis 1:26; Psalm 8:5 (Revised Standard Version).

14. Genesis 1:26,27. Italics supplied.

15. John Macmurray, *Persons in Relation* (London, 1961).

16. Luke 10:25–37.

17. Leo Baeck, *The Essence of Judaism* (New York, 1948), 193.

18. Kierkegaard, *Works of Love* (London, 1962), 38.

19. Hermann Cohen, *Religion of Reason out of the Sources of Judaism* (New York, 1972), 114.

20. *Ibid.*, at p. 115.

21. *Ibid.*, at p. 114.

22. Luke 10:25–28.

23. Deuteronomy 6:5; Leviticus 19:18.

24. William Ernest Hocking, *The Meaning of God in Human Experience* (New Haven, 1912), 11.

25. Theodore Parker, "The Transient and Permanent in Christianity," sermon delivered in Hawes Place Church, Boston, May 11, 1841.

26. Jeremiah 7:22–23.

27. Jeremiah 9:23–24.

28. Leviticus 19:2.

29. Matthew 5:48.

30. Theodore Parker, "The Transient and the Permanent in Christianity," in *Three Prophets of Religious Liberalism: Channing-Emerson-Parker* (Boston, 1961), 140.

31. William Ellery Channing, "Unitarian Christianity," sermon delivered in Baltimore on May 5, 1918, in *op. cit. supra*, note 30, at p. 81.

32. Job 29: 12–17.

33. Jeremiah 22:16.

34. Deuteronomy 25:13–16; cf. Leviticus 19:35–36.

35. Deuteronomy 20:19.

36. See Milton R. Konvitz, ed., *Judaism and Human Rights* (New York, 1972), 247 ff.

37. Psalm 24:1–2.

38. United Stated Code, Title 16, secs. 1131 ff.

39. Martin Buber, *Tales of the Hasidim* (New York, 1948), Vol. II, 89.

40. Nicolas Berdyaev, *The Fate of Man in the Modern World* (Ann Arbor, Mich., 1935), 124.

41. Psalm 36:9.

42. Acts 26:5; Gal. 1:13; Gal. 1:14; James 1:26; James 1:27.

43. Avot 2:17.

44. Maimonides, *Mishne Torah*, quoted in David Hartman, *Maimonides, Torah and Philosophic Quest* (Philadelphia, 1976), 231.

45. Maimonides, *Guide of the Perplexed*, translated by Shlomo Pines (Chicago, 1963), 263–264.

46. Engel v. Vitale, 370 U.S. 421 (1962).

47. See Konvitz, *Expanding Liberties* (New York, 1966), 44 ff.

48. Numbers 11:29.

49. Jeremy Taylor, *Holy Living* (1650) in *Holy Living and Dying* (Bohn's Standard Library, London, 1883), 4.

50. *Ibid.*, at p. 12.

Some Implications of Middle East Peace for Relations Between Israel and the Diaspora

Seymour Martin Lipset

Stanford University
Palo Alto, California

What will be the effect of peace on Israel and the Diaspora? In order to deal with this question, it is necessary to first discuss some consequences of the creation and existence of the State of Israel on the Diaspora, for a prediction is essentially an extrapolation of the past.

The Background

The two key events which have affected the consciousness and organization of Jewry in recent times are the Holocaust and the creation of the State of Israel. Both had the effect of returning Jews to their group. The first, of course, challenged religious people; how could God permit this to happen; what in the nature of Judaism is worth preserving at such horrible cost; what about the Jews could elicit such a reaction by Gentiles? If the Holocaust had occurred without any immediate subsequent positive outcome, it is possible, even likely, that the Holocaust would have enhanced assimilation, the desire to escape being Jewish.

But the events of Holocaust were intimately related to the creation of Israel, much as Pharaoh's persecution of the Jews in Egypt led to the Exodus and the formation of the First Commonwealth. The Gentile world exhibited guilt and either helped the creation of the new state or dropped their former opposition to Zionism. Most Jews in Diaspora, feeling guilt at their passivity in the 1930s and during the war, became visibly pro-Zionist. Various events, in particular the problem of refugees and the existence of DP camps, and military action by the Jews in Palestine, resulted in the UN's voting for partition and a Jewish state. The U.S. and the Soviet Union joined to support it.

It is interesting to note that the immediate impact of the creation of Israel was not to unify all Jews behind Israel. The anti-Zionist groups, e.g., the American Council for Judaism, intensified their disidentification efforts; the more numerous non-Zionists were supportive of Israel, especially of DP migration, but they held off from identifying as Zionists.

During the early years of the new state, the Diaspora did not mobilize intensively behind Israel. Zionism was stronger than before, but Israel was not the center of American Jewry; perhaps because they took its existence for granted, they did not fear for it. The 1956 Suez War created a dilemma for the liberal-left oriented Jews, as Israel joined the "imperialist powers," Britain and France, in invading Egypt. American public opinion was not behind Israel's action, nor were the Jews. Most supported Israel, but they were deeply divided about the wisdom of the invasion; some were affected by the negative feelings of many of their non-Jewish neighbors and the president of the United States.

Nineteen sixty-seven was the turning point in the position of Israel among both Jews and non-Jews. The concern emerged that she would be destroyed by an Arab invasion. Suddenly a passion swept through the Jewish world to protect Israel. Victory in the Six-Day War produced exhiliration. From then on, Israel became the "religion" of American Jews and of much of the western Diaspora. The war, however, also had the effect of isolating Jews from their neighbors. They discovered that non-Jews, though generally sympathetic to Israel, lacked the Jews' sense of concern. As a result, Jews heightened their interactions with each other. This has been true among intellectuals, as well as among other Jews. The American Professors for Peace in the Middle East, for example, formed only in 1967. Collections for the UJA went up and stayed up. Travel to Israel increased greatly. Organized Jewish life mobilized around Israeli political concerns, reacting sharply to U.S. pressures to make Israel give up the land she had gained in 1967.

The political left, including the Jewish left, however, increasingly turned against Israel after 1967. This occurred because the Communist

world saw more to gain from twenty Arab states, because of the identification of Arab states with the Third World, and because of Israel's
appearance as a powerful, increasingly more well-to-do state, as a
"have" power, allied with western imperialism. This development resulted in some division among Jews, as younger radical western Jews
turned against Israel; but it also led many radical Jews out of the Left, as
they discovered that the Gentile Left had little sympathy for Jewish
causes. Anti-Jewish behavior by the Soviets and western leftist groups
also helped to deepen Jewish consciousness generally, and to give to
western Jewry a new cause, that of the persecuted Soviet Jews.

It is necessary to differentiate between the situation in the United
States and that of western Europe. Most liberal-left political groups in
the U.S. did not turn openly against Israel. The largest such segment, the
New Politics element, led by George McGovern and the Kennedys,
clearly did not, perhaps in large part because Jews have been such a large
part of their constituency. Many in the American radical left even
played down their anti-Israeli position; their papers often have ignored
the Middle East. In Europe, however, where Jews are less numerous and
less important, while Arab and Third World students are more significant, the left, particularly the young left, has turned aggressively anti-
Israel, although it should be noted that older Social Democrats have not.
Hence, young left-oriented European Jews have been pressured to dis-
identify with Israel. Basically, however, the European Jewish communities have expressed their solidarity with Israel both in financial and political terms.

The Yom Kippur War reinforced the feelings of 1967, as have most
post-1973 political events. Diaspora Jewry remains Israel-centered. The
greatest source of Jewish identification and participation by far is fund-
raising for Israel. Many Jews who do not belong to any other Jewish
group are involved in the UJA or its equivalent. And such participation
has led some people to memberships in temples, synagogues, and other
Jewish groups.

Israel-centeredness, the current religion of Jews, has been a source of
anxiety, of concern, as well as of pride. But as we know, it has not led to
much *aliya* (immigration to Israel), or to an acceptance of the traditional
Zionist ideology that the Diaspora is Galut (exile), or to the belief that
history teaches that massive anti-Semitism is inevitable in the future of
any given prosperous Jewish community. Membership in *aliya*-oriented

Zionist groups (*Habonim, Betar, Hashomer Hatzair*) has declined considerably. Whatever *aliya* from the west occurs has come largely from the ranks of Orthodox Jews.

Ironically, however, it must be reported that Israel and Soviet Jewry have become sources of population growth for western Jewry. Israel estimates that there are altogether 300,000 *yordim* (emigrants from Israel), but American authorities indicate that there are 300,000 here alone, with many more in Canada, Britain, South Africa, France, and even Germany. Not only has Israel been unable to attract western Jews; she has increasingly failed to appeal to Soviet emigres, the great majority of whom now opt for the west, particularly the U.S., as well as to most of those leaving Argentina, Iran, and South Africa; and she has problems keeping a significant minority of her own young. A sizeable minority of young Sabras tell Israeli pollsters that they would like to go abroad to live.

The Diaspora Today

If we turn to the general situation of the Jews in the Diaspora, we find that the post-1945 era has probably been the best, most free, least anti-Semitic period ever experienced by Jews in their long history. This has been true as a result of reactions to Holocaust, but also because the period has largely been one of economic prosperity, in which people with skills, education, and ambition could succeed within the bureaucracies of business and government, in the professions, and in self-employment. There have been fewer formal or informal barriers to Jewish economic, social, and political mobility than ever before. The external walls that forced Jews to be together, to support each other, have broken down, although the memory of anti-Semitism has continued to provide a strong self-segregating force for the generations who knew the Holocaust either directly or through their parents' discussions. The Jewish penchant for education could be satisfied, with close to ninety percent of American Jewish youth going to college and with majorities doing the same in other countries. Jews could become intellectual and even political leaders in various countries far beyond previous experience. In the United States, close to one-third of the faculty at major universities are Jewish.

The breakdown of the walls, of course, has meant a challenge to group solidarity and membership. Jews, almost everywhere, were associated with post-Enlightenment liberal orientations, which meant among non-Jews a disdain for religion and ethnic particularism, a belief in secularism and universalism. The liberal-left world, particularly its intellectual and university segments, has favored the assimilation of all forms of particularism into the universalistic whole.

Since Jews are part of this integrationist world and, as noted, send almost all of their offspring to its ideological center, the university, Jews have found it difficult to maintain the barriers, to prevent dating and mating. Intermarriage rates for young Jews (under 30) in the United States are close to 40 percent. In countries with much smaller populations, they are even higher. As Jews disperse from the Jewish neighborhoods of the central city to integrated suburbs or to parts of the country or colleges with small proportions of Jews, the intermarriage rates inevitably grow.

Some have suggested that increasing numbers of intermarriages offer an opportunity to the Jewish community, since studies of religiously mixed couples indicate that, in the United States at least, many non-Jewish partners identify themselves or their families as Jewish; hence, the Jewish community gains many non-Jews. But though this area is still a relatively unknown field with respect to research knowledge, it seems evident that only a small minority of the Gentile mates of Jews actually go through a conversion ceremony and, more importantly, that such families are much less likely to be involved in any Jewish communal activity, including contributing to the UJA or providing their children with any form of Jewish education, than are families in which the spouses are both born Jews. Hence, even though most intermarried couples report to pollsters that they are Jewish, many, probably most, are going through a two-generational process of defection from the Jewish community.

The high and growing rate of intermarriage in the Diaspora, combined with the suggestion that Judaism has some sort of positive appeal to many non-Jews, implied in the fact that many, if not most non-Jewish spouses, identify as Jews, could mean that such developments may turn out to be a blessing in disguise for western Jewry. Rabbi Alexander Schindler and others have proposed that Judaism return to the role of a proselytizing religion that external forces forced it to give up over 1,500 years ago for reasons of physical safety and survival. Discussion, research, communal, and financial resources should be devoted to an evaluation of this suggestion. The Diaspora can not survive under conditions of freedom, secular education, prosperity, high intermarriage rates, and low birth rates as a highly particularistic birth-right religious group, composed of the most universalistically oriented people on earth. We must seriously consider ways of introducing that universalism into the religion, and to make it, or part of it, wide open to all who are attracted by its message, including particularly but not exclusively, those who marry its members.

It may be noted, however, that any commitment to converting others runs counter to the objections raised by some Jews to Christian pro-selytizing efforts both in the Diaspora and in Israel. Jews can not have it both ways. If they seek to recruit, they can not deny the same right to others. And in any case, legal obstacles to missionary activities in Israel constitute violations of the right of free speech and advocacy.

The increasing educational attainments of Diaspora Jews appear to have adverse consequences on communal strength other than those which flow from a higher rate of intermarriage. They also make for a lesser commitment to the community and a reduction in Jewish partici-pation in the kind of economic pursuits which have made possible the incredible levels of contributions to the UJA and other institutions. As noted earlier, higher education in the West is associated, increasingly so in recent years, with universalistic liberal to left non- or anti-religious values. Although there appears to be an increase in the number of Jewish college students participating in Hillel and other Jewish activities, it must be noted that the majority do not. Although we have no reliable trend data on the subject (research on this and other subjects is desper-ately needed), there is no reason to deny the frequently asserted general-ization that young western-educated Jews socialized in a free environ-ment are little oriented to the Jewish community. Hence, it may be anticipated that any decline in concern for Israel, in tandem with these trends, will produce a further reduction in the proportion involved in the community.

Furthermore, increased education appears to result in fewer Jews fol-lowing the traditional pursuits of self-employment, occupations which have resulted in many attaining a considerable degree of wealth. The bulk of young Jews who go on to graduate schools have preferred var-ious forms of professional and intellectual occupations which carry with them a sense of creative accomplishment beyond that associated with the accumulation of money. Thus, the proportion of Jews in academe, in the media, in the creative arts, in politics and government, in the healing and other professions, in research and development activities, has increased greatly. Many of the scions of business families have refused to continue in their parents' firms. Such developments, of course, have had the effect of increasing the influence of Jews in informing the ideas and values of the larger population and in setting the public agenda. Many in a position to do so, of course, do not act as Jews when playing such roles. In addition, however, it must be noted that the shift among Jews from business to these largely salaried occupations means that fewer Jews will have or create large personal estates, a fact which should result in a decline in contributions. The importance of this development may be seen in the fact that five percent of all those who contribute to the UJA have been responsible for eighty percent of the monies received. The change in the occupational structure, of course, is a long-range trend, which will not show up in the immediate future. Still, it is one which the community should be cognizant of in any effort to anticipate and plan its future.

The ultimate size and strength of Diaspora communities are, of course, also affected adversely by the low Jewish birthrate. Stephen Cohen has posed the magnitude of the problem dramatically by noting that the median age of Jews in the United States is 35, while for all Americans it is only 27. A number of circumstances have combined to place Diaspora Jews in those social conditions which everywhere correlate with a low birthrate—high education, secularist outlook, middle-class status, metropolitan-urban residence, strong feminist orientations. The Jewish birth rate is highest among groups which are a minority—the Orthodox and the poor.

Conversely, however, it may be reiterated that emigration to the West from Israel, the Middle East, the Soviet Union, and parts of Latin America has led to increases in the Jewish population, particularly in France (North Africans), South Africa (Israelis), Canada (Israelis and Middle Easterners) and the United States (Israelis, Soviets, Iranians, South Africans, and Latin Americans). The implications of such population movements for the receiving communities have largely been ignored, in part because of the embarrassment for Israel seemingly implied by Israeli emigration, or by the fact Soviet and other refugee populations, e.g., the Argentine and Iranian, prefer the West to Israel. It should be obvious that whatever dysfunctional implications these developments have for Israel, they strengthen the Diaspora numerically, and, in part, culturally, since the presence of many Israelis produces a group whose Hebrew culture enhances the Diaspora host communities. Unfortunately, we know very little about the cultural life of the *yordim*, the education of their children, and their relationship with the larger Jewish communities. Some limited data gathered by Dov Elizur suggest that they are intensely pro-Israel, Jewishly identified, and that many of their children strongly support and want to go to Israel.

Any effort to predict the future of Diaspora communities, as well as the prospects for *aliya* to Israel, must evaluate the potential relations between Jews and their host communities, specifically the possibilities for the revival of political, social, and economic anti-Semitism. That adverse changes can still occur may be seen in the renewed threats to the physical and communal safety of Jews in Argentina and Iran. Beyond the potentials for religious anti-Semitism stemming from renewal of fundamentalist sentiments in parts of the Christian and Moslem worlds, leftist groups in countries varying from Iran and Turkey to Argentina, Uruguay, Quebec, Britain, Italy, France, and Germany have emerged in open criticism of Jews, usually couched in anti-Zionist language, but sometimes voiced directly as attacks on Jewish economic and cultural power. Although reactions to the Holocaust seemingly created a situation in which overt expressions of anti-Semitism were banned in polite society, anti-Israeli feeling, which increasingly has found expression in religious and political circles, has once more legitimated attacks on Jews. In Britain, for example, leftist student organizations succeeded for a time in efforts to deny Jewish student organizations the right to use facilities controlled by student governments, on the grounds that these groups were supporting a racist regime, Israel.

Opinion polls seeking to estimate sentiments towards Jews generally agree that there was a considerable decline in anti-Semitic attitudes after World War II, as compared to the 1930s. Still the results of recent surveys suggest that a sizable minority continue to harbor such views in many western nations. In the United States, national polls taken in late 1974, 1976, and 1978 by the Louis Harris organization indicate that between a quarter and a third of the population voice agreement with various anti-Jewish stereotypes dealing with Jewish business practices, cliquishness, and power. For example, in both 1974 and 1978, 34 percent agreed with the statement: "When it comes to choosing between people and money, Jews will choose money." One third in 1974 and 29 percent in 1978 felt that "Jews are more loyal to Israel than they are to America." Such attitudes are to be most found among poorer and less educated parts of the population, most strikingly among other minorities, Blacks, and Hispanics. Although there is no evidence that these negative attitudes are growing, they are not declining either. It should be noted that "philo-Semitic" sentiments, agreement with positive statements about Jewish characteristics, voiced by majorities of those interviewed in surveys, are declining. The late 1978 Harris poll reported much less support for such sentiments than had earlier studies. The proportion of the Gentile public who feel that Jews "are discriminated against" has also fallen, from 22 percent in 1974 to 7 percent in 1978. This change is in line with the attitudes of Jews themselves, for the percent of Jews interviewed by Harris who believe that Jews face discrimination declined sharply from 49 percent in 1974 to 18 in 1978.

The greater willingness of various non-Jewish leaders to voice open antagonism to Jews, particularly with respect to their support for Israel, but also with regard to the positions which leaders of American Jewry have taken on issues of special preference for other minorities, could have the effect of pressing non-affiliated Jews to return to the fold. It must be noted, however, that the Harris surveys do not suggest that American Jews have an increased sense of rising anti-Semitism. When asked whether "anti-Jewish feeling is on the rise around here today, is diminishing, or is about the same as it has ever been," the percentage of Jews replying "on the rise" fell from 43 in 1974 to 21 in 1978. It would appear that the bulk of American Jewry has been unaware of the extent to which "Jewish issues," emerging around Israel, Soviet Jewry, and minority rights, have given rise to increased criticism of Jews among a number of key political, business, and minority groups. In any case, the Jews interviewed are correct in their belief that anti-Jewish feeling has not risen among the public at large.

It is impossible to make any definitive prediction about the stability of the Jewish position in other western communities with large communities. Developments in Argentina and Quebec indicate that political crises can foster attacks on visible minorities of "outsiders." Anti-Semitism, "the socialism of fools" as August Bebel once described it, can find a home among the left. The pressures stemming from the Jewish communities to have their nations and business communities follow policies supportive of Israel or Soviet Jewry which may be economically and politically costly have already aroused antagonism within political and economic elites. The presence of the large reservoir of popular anti-Semitism documented by the opinion polls can form the base for anti-

Semitic movements, should the western world ever again witness a major economic crisis along the lines of that of the 1930s. It should be obvious that no Jewish community can ignore the possibility of a revival of anti-Semitism as a major force. Jews must be vigilent in monitering relevant indicators. Increased anti-Semitism will, of course, strengthen commitment both to the community and to Israel, including the potential for *aliya*. But it will also weaken external support for Jewish causes and for Israel.

The Consequences of Peace

This discussion is preliminary to any effort to analyze the possible effects of a real peace between Israel and the Arab states, one which, except for Egypt, still looks like a dream. It is obviously impossible to anticipate the parameters of Israel's relations with all her neighbors. Clearly, even with the signing of the peace treaty between Egypt and Israel, Israel remains in a state of war with her other neighbors. P.L.O. terrorism is likely to increase, possibly aided by the Iranians. Much of the Moslem world, reacting both to reviving religious fundamentalism and leftist agitation, will probably intensify anti-Israeli activity. It should be clear that no stable peace is possible without finding a solution to the Palestinean problem. The presence of over three million people, probably the most able group in the Arab world, who look upon themselves as a nation in exile, within a number of Arab states, constitutes a standing *casus belli* for the Arabs. Still, both Israeli and Diaspora Jewry have welcomed the Israeli-Egyptian peace treaty as a beginning of the end of the conflict. If the most populous and militarily strongest Arab state is no longer a threat to Israel; if real social and economic interactions occur between them; if, in addition, some moderate states, particularly Saudi Arabia, show real support for Egypt's action, even while publicly rejecting it, then most Jews everywhere are likely to believe that the state of siege has been lifted, that a new war is unlikely, and that Israel has finally attained legitimacy and security. They will probably come to view the continued opposition of the P.L.O., the Syrians, and the Iraqis as largely irrelevant noise which will not undermine Israel's fundamental security.

While these anticipations bear little relationship to what has happened since the treaty was signed, it still may be worthwhile to try to trace the implications of a real peace. It may be suggested that a greater sense of Israel's security and the lesser possibility of a new Arab-Israeli war will both increase the attractiveness of *aliya* for Soviet and western Jews and reduce the pressures for emigration among Israelis. There is evidence that some Diaspora Jews, including Russians, have hesitated to go to Israel because of concern about the possibility that they or their children will have to spend years in the military, face reserve duty and repeated call-ups, and experience the risks of actual war. Similarly, many young Israelis have also been disturbed by the same factors, by the effect of military service on career and family planning. Such concerns are held by some to drive young Israelis abroad and to reduce the possibilities of their returning home.

Peace also may result in economic and social improvements. While Egypt is a very poor, non-industrialized country, the very fact that it has close to 40 million people means that its small middle class can constitute a sizable market for Israeli products. Israel can offer Egypt technical assistance. Joint Israeli-Egyptian-Diaspora enterprises may develop. A sense of peace and Israel's new political legitimacy may open doors and markets in various Third World countries, some of which now do business with Israel covertly, and possibly even with the People's Republic of China and the Soviet Union. Investors generally may feel that an Israel at peace is a better capital risk than in the past. And such developments may in turn make the country more attractive for *aliya* and enhance its capacity to retain its population.

Yet, as with almost all events, it is possible to anticipate alternative scenarios which are at least as probable. A decline in Israel's insecurity may also reduce the feelings among Israelis that emigration is akin to treason, to defection from a beleaguered fortress. Rates of emigration are not affected solely, or even mainly, by "push" factors; they also are a product of "pull" variables. Many Israelis who leave, as well as Soviet or Argentinian emigrés who go to countries other than Israel, do so because they see America or other western countries as offering higher standards of living and better professional or cultural opportunities than exist for people like themselves in Israel. Given the size of the country, the low number of academic, cultural, and research institutions, the small size of her industrial establishment, and the limited audience for intellectual products, it is not surprising that many young Israelis go west for greater opportunity. Some who would like to go abroad (surveys taken by the Israeli Institute of Applied Social Research have indicated that at times since 1973 as many as 25 percent of young Sabras would like to emigrate) have been inhibited by the fact that such behavior has been regarded as betrayal, as desertion of a nation which has viewed herself as at war. Presumably, however, once Israel is seen as at peace with the Arabs, inhibitions against leaving will be reduced.

If one looks over the history of emigration from pre-state Palestine and Israel, it is clear that adverse economic and political circumstances have precipitated leaving, as occurred during the post-World War I period and in the aftermath of the Hebron massacre of 1929, the 1965–66 recession, and immediately following the Yom Kippur War. But the largest stimulus to emigration since the state was proclaimed followed on the Six-Day War, when renewed prosperity gave many the resources to travel or to give their children support to study abroad. More significantly, the then widely felt sense that Israel was militarily secure seemingly gave rise to the feeling that people could leave without betraying a weak homeland.

"Peace" may also have other adverse consequences on the domestic social and economic situations. Some observers of the Israeli social scene have accounted for the lack of student and youth protest during the turbulent 1960s, which witnessed such conflict in almost every other free country, or the absence of severe ethnic protest, in spite of the wide social gap among Israel's ethnic communities, to the siege mentality. If such analyses are valid, peace should be followed by increased social turmoil, as has often occurred in various post-war societies elsewhere. The pressure to do something immediately for the poorer strata, to increase opportunities for youth, may grow. The currently critical economic situation will probably not be improved by peace, especially in the short run. Continuing to fear the consequences of a future war with Arab nations, Israeli authorities cannot afford to let their defenses down because of the Egyptian-Israeli treaty. Peace has not resulted in decreased defense expenditures, since Israel has to erect various security barriers to replace those lost in the Sinai. External economic help and contributions and personal technical assistance from the Diaspora communities may decline if the latter come to feel that Israel is no longer in danger. The increased assistance provided by the United States and other western countries to back up the Egyptian-Israeli peace treaty may also not last very long if the treaty actually results in a visible drop in Arab-Israeli intransigence.

A significant improvement in Israel's security position and international legitimacy may reduce the pressure on Diaspora Jews to concern themselves with Israel as a place of investment, philanthropy, political concern, or *aliya*. If Israel is viewed as politically and militarily secure, then Jews with little commitment to Judaism as a religion will probably cut down their involvement with the Jewish state. The decline in the image of Israel as a "utopian" society, linked to the weakened position of the *kibbutzim* and labor or socialist Zionism, has severely reduced the interest in *aliya* for politically liberal, non-Orthodox Jews.

Although Israel's economic situation will clearly remain bad for some time after a peace treaty with Israel's other neighbors is signed, a fact which may also continue to discourage *aliya* and encourage emigration, it is likely that the belief that Israel has finally attained security will reduce the number and average of financial contributions. In the past, such donations have risen or fallen in tandem with threats to Israel's security. Hence, peace should reduce them.

These analyses and prognostications imply a continued bleak economic and demographic future for Israel if there will be signs that peace is really possible. The possible effects on the Diaspora are also more likely to be negative than positive. If an embattled Israel had become the religion of the Jews, a perception of Israel as secure, and as a normal, non-utopian state, like other states, may result in a more secularized Diaspora, one less emotionally involved with the Jewish state. The sense, also, that Judaism is likely to be assured permanent survival in a legitimate Jewish nation may help validate Arthur Koestler's annoying argument that the creation of Israel would mean the ultimate disappearance of the Diaspora, for secularized Diaspora Jews, knowing that Judaism was guaranteed survival in its own state, would no longer feel the multi-millenia-old pressure on Jews to act so as to assure the continuation of Judaism in a hostile Gentile world. Much as some contend that ambitious or cosmopolitan Israelis will feel less inhibited about leaving a secure Israel, it is also argued that Diaspora Jews with a relatively weak commitment to the Jewish religion will feel less inhibited about inter-marrying or non-participation in the community as a result of the improvement in Israel's position.

In viewing the possible consequences of peace on Israel and the Diaspora, I have been deliberately pessimistic. All nations and groups concerned with their own security and survival must draw up possible scenarios that are pessimistic and then seek to devise strategies which will prevent their occurrence. The question which arises, therefore, is what can the Diaspora and/or Israel do to prevent the worst from occurring? Clearly what is most desirable and necessary is to create a prosperous Israel whose people will enjoy a high and cultured standard of living, much as other small countries, which currently experience little emigration, e.g., Scandinavia and Switzerland. Optimally, also, such a prosperous Israel will be seen as socially attractive in terms of the way in which her ethnically and religiously diverse population lives together while retaining special religious and cultural attributes.

Israel's academic and intellectual eminence should strengthen her ability to keep and attract intellectually oriented Jews. In the past, many foreign scholars and artists have worked closely with Israelis in joint projects, e.g., interchanges between the German Max Planck Institute and the Weizmann Institute. In absolute terms, tiny Israel receives the fifth largest number of American scholars going abroad for study and research. Shalheveth Freir has reminded us that, during the 1960s, the Greek government encouraged its students to pursue graduate work in Israel, both because doing so would reduce the potential that study abroad would precipitate a brain drain and because geographical proximity would permit continued cooperation between Greek students and their Israeli teachers after their studies were completed. This important case of a Middle Eastern country treating Israeli intellectual strength as a regional resource offers an obvious example of the way in which a real Israeli-Arab peace can lead to significant close cooperation between Israel and her neighbors. Israel clearly should endeavor to create a variety of culturally creative institutions and think-tanks which serve other countries as well as itself, both within and outside the region. The fact that Jews form such a large part of the intellectual and artistic world in the West (60,000 American professors are Jewish) should facilitate such endeavors.

The Diaspora, in turn, should use some of the financial resources it has been sending to Israel to foster Jewish intellectual and cultural life at home. Philip Klutznick once told Golda Meir that her concern about trends which indicated that American Jewry might disappear through assimilation could be reversed if Israel would allow the American community to use the cost of two Phantoms for Jewish education here. Golda, Klutznick reported, then abruptly changed the subject, but he had a good point. At a moment when ninety percent of all American Jewish youth spend one or more years on college campuses, Hillel is vastly under-funded. There are few, if any, universities where Hillel can afford to engage enough professional workers to satisfy the expressed desire of Jewish students for organized activities, let alone reach out to marginal and unaffiliated ones. As we all know, most other forms of Jewish education, both for young people and adults, are also under-funded and many use traditional, but outmoded, techniques. More money, alone, is never the whole answer for educating people, but it is almost always part of the answer.

Assuming peace, it is necessary to think about strengthening the links between Israel and the Diaspora. The jet plane has made possible a degree of personal interaction between the communities such as was inconceivable to Herzl, Weizmann, or the young Ben Gurion, Meir, or Begin. Haifa and Jerusalem are closer in time to London, Paris, or New York than they once were to each other. Families divided between Israel and the Diaspora are no more separated than those with members in New York, Miami, and Los Angeles. We see a new breed of Jews who spend time in Tel Aviv and Montreal, Haifa and San Francisco. Jewish academics teach and carry out research in Jerusalem, Oxford, and Berkeley. Musicians and dancers based in Tel Aviv perform in Toronto, Paris, and San Francisco.

Such developments are not to be deplored. They are to be welcomed and encouraged. If Diaspora Jewry is to remain vital, it must have strong, positive links to Israel. Such ties may be forged by relating individuals, businesses, groups, and communities in the Diaspora with their peers in Israel. While the creation of Israeli-Diaspora institutions will be difficult, efforts should be made to develop more of them, e.g., businesses, policy research, technological development, pure scholarship think-tank educational institutions, cultural organizations, etc. Diaspora institutions should seek out settings in Israel to which they can send their young people for periods of work and education. And, conversely, they should host Israelis who come to work with or visit them. Language is and will be a problem. Hence, Diaspora communities should seek to foster a speaking knowledge of Hebrew, while Israel should stress knowledge of Diaspora languages, particularly English and French, as well as, of course, Arabic.

One difficulty with winning the enthusiasm of Diaspora Jews, particularly the youth, for further involvement with Israel is that she and her institutions are established. To emigrate to a functioning society, to take a job in a going institution, is not an inspirational goal; one does it generally for personal gain. In the past, settlers in Israel could take pride in helping to establish new *kibbutzim*, communities, universities, medical systems, businesses, and the like. The decline in socialist ideology and practice lost for Israel the appeal endemic to the objective of helping to create a new ideal society. The founding and ideological era is ended. It may be possible, however, to think of creating partial functional equivalents by encouraging western Jews to come to Israel to help found new institutions. New settlers from economically more privileged societies might be encouraged to plan new "pioneering" endeavors, activities, which they can identify with as their own, institutions which they create from nothing.

Finally, I come to a topic which as a Diaspora Jew I find most distasteful, or perhaps the right word is *chutzpadic*, to raise: what Israel can do to make herself more attractive to outsiders. It is clear that from a practical standpoint the least desirable aspects of life in Israel from the perspective of western Jews stem from her lower standard of living and the strains and obligations imposed on residents by military insecurity. Still, it must be reported that many who have thought of migrating or who have done so and then returned home have complained about the low level of the civic culture, of politeness, of concern for the feelings of others, the bureaucratic rigidities, and the like. Fortunately, it is possible to cite an Israeli on this point. Nathan Telnir, the General Secretary of the Society for the Prevention of Accidents, has recently stressed that the major factor involved in the abysmally high rate of road accidents in Israel is the human one. As he notes: "Interpersonal relations are at a very low level in all facets of life in the country. Look how impatiently we queue and push past people on the pavement. Such behavior on the roads means that courtesy is a word that many of our drivers have never even considered."

Western Jews coming from more affluent and more secure societies, in which the institutions and customs of a civic culture have developed over the countries, are accustomed to a higher degree of politeness, of courteous treatment by others, including government officials, than they find in Israel. Women, including Israelis who have lived abroad, complain about an intolerable degree of sexism, of assumptions men make about their rights and privileges, including direct sexual exploitation. Directing such complaints to a nation which has both suffered and accomplished so much may seem like insignificant carping. Yet, if we are to discuss frankly the factors which affect relations between Israel and the Diaspora, particularly in terms of those factors which influence the potential for *aliya*, they must be mentioned. Can Israel do anything to improve her civic culture? If peace really comes, if the sense of insecurity which undoubtedly contributed to the anxious conduct of many Israelis is reduced, some of these behavior patterns may change naturally in the course of time. But a campaign to make Israelis more conscious of these problems may help a bit. Road signs and media campaigns as well as government directives to civil servants, which stress the importance of politeness, even the value of forming and respecting a queue, may speed up the process. It is important to think how a country looks to outsiders if one seeks to attract them. Israel obviously has had to solve too many other important problems to think of these minor ones. Perhaps peace will permit her leaders to devote some time to these, including, to raise another petty point, a serious upgrading of the appearance and surroundings of Ben Gurion Airport, the first sight visitors and prospective *olim* have of the country.

These suggestions, some major, some minor, may appear to be "Utopian," i.e., impractical, visionary. But as Weizmann once said: "Those who do not believe in miracles are poor planners." No one has ever explained to my satisfaction, at least, the miracle of Jewish survival, as a remnant of a remnant, for over close to six thousand years. No one has adequately explained the disproportionate, to say the least, Jewish contribution to innovative and creative activities of all kinds, cultural, political, and economic. No one would have predicted the particular constellation of factors which made possible the restoration of a Jewish state in our lifetime. Rational scholarly analysis based on realistic projections from available evidence would have had to conclude from the start of the Common Era to literally yesterday that much of what has happened to and by Jews was highly unlikely, if not impossible. This past is the glory of the community, but the despair of those who would plan policy. How can we plan, how can we anticipate, when we have no way to find out for what we have been or will be chosen?

Zionism as Idea
and American Reality

Stanley A. Ringler

B'nai B'rith Hillel Foundations
Washington, D.C.

The birth of political Zionism among the Jewish populace of Europe was a direct consequence of anti-Semitism. Zionism aś an ideology was derived from an analysis of the precarious nature of Jewish life on the European continent. In Eastern Europe, particularly, virulent anti-Semitism compromised the physical security of an already miserable people. And in the Western European countries, where Jews realized that the Enlightenment and Emancipation were ultimately limited and disingenuous, Zionism provided a conceptual framework in which western Jews could effectuate their own psychological rehabilitation and re-identification with the Jewish people. Indeed, it was from this very group that advocacy of the political solution to the Jewish problem was first articulated. Ironically, it was precisely the double-edged character of their emancipation which propelled them into the political arena. On the one hand, these western Jews had been able to acquire skills and knowledge available only under the conditions of a relatively open society. On the other hand, their own assimilation was restricted by a subtle anti-Semitism which demanded the renunciation of Jewish ethnic and national identity, while qualifying the potential of acceptability within restricted bounds of social and economic marginality. Thus, in the words of one historian, it became clear "that accommodation to Gentile standards, whether of the *ancien régime*, the bourgeois, or the classless society, was not a satisfactory basis for solving the Jewish problem; and, in particular, that anti-Semitism must be taken seriously, that it would persist and dog the footsteps of the Jews wherever they went, seeking toleration. Only the 'auto-Emancipation' of the Jews in an independent society of their own could make possible a rational solution to the Jewish problem.[1]

The World Zionist Organization with its various ideological manifestations was created as the instrument designed to forge idea into reality. The goal was the territorial and political concentration of the Jews in a land of their own. On this matter there was always widespread consensus. Only on questions of the state's structure and character do opinions diverge and positions contract.

There are two primary schools of Zionist thought regarding the nature of the Jewish state. There are those who with Theodor Herzl have advocated the notion of normalization. And, there are those who with Nachman Syrkin have propagated the idea of uniqueness and exceptionality. Herzl's aim was the creation of a Jewish national home where it would be possible for Jews to "live as free men on their own soil, to die peacefully in their own homes." His conception of the Jewish state was a mirror image of the 19th century European industrial democracy. In his novel *Altneuland*, Herzl described his vision of the reborn state. It differs from its European archetype only with respect to its social and political character, which are to be fundamentally democratic and based on a harmonious class structure. What distinguishes the state is not its Jewishness or its political structure, but the harmonious nature of the social and political relationships among the various ethnic and religious groups constituting its citizenry. Herzl assumed that territorial concentration and political sovereignty would suffice, under such conditions, to ensure Jewish security and survival.

At the other end of the spectrum stood Nachman Syrkin and those who insisted that the state must be distinguished from all others by virtue of its Jewish and social character. Indeed, they argued, to fail to create a unique society and state would be to ignore the imperatives of the Jewish tradition of prophetic social idealism. Furthermore, the creation of a state like any other would simply result in the transfer of many of the problems indigenous to European society. A socially and economically stratified society would necessarily preclude the resolution of the social dimension of the Jewish problem as it is linked to the class conflict. The genuine resolution of the Jewish problem, Syrkin argued, would depend upon the authenticity of the revolutionary image assumed by the Jewish state. It is interesting to note in this regard that both socialist revolutionaires and religious idealists found a commonality of purpose and coincidence of vision. Both groups readily acknowledged their social ideals and ethical imperatives as expressions of the Jewish heritage. Without these elements it was understood that the state would lose its *raison d'etre* in terms of the essential Jewishness of its purpose and meaning.

Regardless of its ultimate form, the vision of the Jewish state presupposed the negation of the Diaspora. According to classical Zionist ideology, Jewish life everywhere was seen as subject to conditions over which Jews have little or no control. Perceived as an "alien class," the Jews were condemned to a position of social marginality and economic insecurity. As outsiders, they were subject to the forces of both class and national discrimination. As such, the Jews became dependent on the will of the native majority for the privilege of exercising what for others are natural rights. In sum, Diaspora life is characterized by its unremitting condition of alienation, isolation, and insecurity. The possibility that one's place of residence in the Diaspora might at a given moment result in less severe circumstances was of little ultimate consequence. Even where Jews are able to realize high social positions or significant levels of economic achievement, the native population will continue to view them as aliens. It is therefore impossible for the Jew to realize a condition of normality in a society where Jews and the characteristics of Jewishness are by definition incompatible with those of the majority. Under such conditions Jews cannot lead a full Jewish life and certainly not a life of their own making. In this sense the Jews of the Diaspora were thought to be condemned to a condition of psychological and cultural homelessness as well as social and economic exclusion. From this perspective it was accurate to describe life in the Diaspora as living in *Galut*.[2]

Throughout the Diaspora experience, the Jews have been largely on the economic periphery of society. Relegated to an interstitial position in the economic structure, the Jewish contribution to the economic life of the native community, while frequently useful, was nearly always of marginal consequence. Of course, in large measure the Jews had been restricted in this regard. The native national class, in fear of competition or out of pure racism, traditionally sought to isolate the Jews in positions of vulnerability subject to forces of hostility and dispossession. Taken together, these factors determined of necessity the desire to create a Jewish state. Social and psychological alienation, cultural and religious dependency, impoverishment, economic marginality, exclusion and the

resulting essential condition of perpetual insecurity, and frequent suffering were all factors contributing to the development of the Zionist
movement. Under such conditions it was natural enough for Zionism to
co-opt the classical Jewish principles of exile and redemption.

Zionism proclaimed that only by means of a process of national self-
emancipation and the establishment of a sovereign Jewish national home
would the Jewish problem find resolution. In this way the classical myth
of redemption was politicized by secular Zionist idealists and religious
visionaries. In point of fact, one could hardly gainsay the reality that
modern European Jewry, by and for whom the Zionist idea was conceived, neatly fit the analysis of the Jewish condition. The concept of
sh'lilat ha'galut was therefore the logical extension of the redemption
myth. At the time it appeared to be an inordinately reasonable conclusion. Jewish security, authenticity, and creative survival appeared to be
subject, exclusively, to the conditions of national self-determination and
territorial sovereignty. It is ironic and tragic that the people for whom
Zionism was conceived as the urgent response to their situation were the
very ones to be largely eradicated by the scourge of Nazism.

With the post-war absorption of the surviving European remnant,
along with the ingathering of Jews from the North African and Middle
Eastern countries, Zionist ideological principles ceased to have universal
applicability. One could no longer speak out of an ideological context of
negation when the condition of the majority of the Jewish people
appeared on both objective and subjective grounds to be radically different from that which obtained in the generations which came before. This
is the case particularly with the Jews in the "free world" countries of the
West.

The largest and most important Diaspora community is in America.
On the surface, American Jewish life is rich, unbounded, and flourishing. From this perspective it is clear that the analytical basis for classic
Zionist thought has changed. Today it would be most difficult to make a
credible argument about the imperative of Zionist self-realization
because of the "condition of distress" of American Jewry. And even
though one could use traditional Zionist ideological categories to
develop a theoretical case portending the ultimate displacement and dissolution of Jewish life in the American diaspora, *it would not be very
convincing to those most in need of understanding*. One can, for
example, point to the over-concentration of Jews in non-essential areas
of the economy. One could describe the Jewish condition as ultimately

insecure because of its social and economic vulnerability. The marginality of Jewish life and its still somewhat restricted nature could be a credible theoretical basis for arguing the potential for virulent anti-Semitism in America. These could be the basis for making a classic Zionist case about the American diaspora.[3] However, the test of the relevance for ideological principles lies in the appropriateness of their application in a given historical time frame. In the case of America, conditions are simply not conducive to the logic and applicability of classical Zionist theory. American Jewry is too successful, too comfortable, too productive, and too well accepted by the majority group to believe that Zionist principles need be applied to American Jewish life. The myth of American freedom, opportunity, and security, linked, as it were, to the tradition of the Emancipation movement, is much too persuasive to be contradicted on either objective or subjective grounds. The few restrictions and forms of discrimination which do exist are not sufficient to create among Jews a feeling of unease in or with America. Furthermore, there is adequate opportunity and latitude in American life to compensate psychologically and materially for the narrow-minded and elitist attitudes which prevail within certain classes and ethnic groups. In short, the Jews of America are happy captives of the American Dream!

It is therefore meaningless and counter-productive to employ the concept of *Galut* in the context of a discussion of American Jewish life, at least so far as American Jews are concerned. The question is not whether appearances are deceptive. For the American Jew life is basically good, rooted in conditions which appear to be normal and healthy. American Jews neither feel nor think of themselves as living in exile. There is no palpable sense of alienation. Indeed, it should not be forgotten that the American Jew's presence in what *he* will allow to be called the Diaspora is voluntary. Although there are contemporary Zionist thinkers who ask whether *Galut* can exist in the absence of a consciousness of *Galut*,[4] it really doesn't matter. What does count is the profound and pervasive quality of the American myth. There is sufficient evidence to support its reality and to sustain its positive and attractive power in the foreseeable future. It is this reality and its consequence, i.e. widespread assimilation, with which Zionism must come to terms. The Zionist analysis of Jewish life in the emancipated Western world must be radically revised if Zionism is to have any contemporary relevance or meaning.[5]

The process of redefinition must being with a new understanding of

American Jewish life, for which the analytical premises of the nineteenth and early twentieth century European experience are not useful. American Jewry is not, like its European antecedent, bound together by real or symbolic ghetto walls. Nor are America's Jews subject to a condition of collective discrimination and alienation. To the contrary, American Jewry constitutes what is perhaps the first Diaspora Jewish community in history to believe itself to have been *successfully* emancipated. The relative openness of American society, its absorptive and productive capacity, its mobility, and the achievement orientation of its populace— all these are elements contributing to the American Jew's conviction that the quality of life in the American Diaspora is distinctive. As far as they are concerned, America *is* different; this is the considered conclusion of those Jews who still possess a Jewish memory and are moved to think about the matter. Most American Jews, however, don't bother to think about it; they act out their attitudes in their style of living and in the manner in which they treat the circumstance of their Jewish identity. The same seductive elements which have enabled the Jews "to make it" in America have simultaneously initiated a process of almost blissful assimilation. The consciousness of being a collectivity in matters of community and even in the idea of value-relatedness has, in the course of two generations, dissipated along with the myth of consanguinity.

With each generation the increasingly dispersed American Jewish citizenry assumes more and more similarity to the Gentile mainstream. It is a law of nature which an emancipated Jewry could hardly resist. Unlike the experience in Europe, America has established few and distant limits to her capacity to absorb "alien" minority groups. The material benefits and opportunities proferred those who accede to the implicit demand for national or racial self-denial are alluring and persuasive. Assimilation is in any event an inevitable process to which all minority groups are, by sociological norms, fated. Striking testimony to this reality may be noted in the general tendency of American Jewish college youth to deny the notion that Jewish identity is an ascribed status.[6] Rather, they consider Jewish identity to be an achieved state. One must opt for it and give it a manifest form of expression if Jewishness is to have any relationship to one's life. In spite of this contention, fewer and fewer Jewish youth choose to make Jewish commitments. They appear to lack both the motivation and the capacity to do so.

This has tended to accentuate the feeling of psychological ambivalence in American Jewish circles because the emancipated character of

American Jewish life confines one's choice to the religious realm. In America it is religion which is the recognized and accepted category of differentiation. Since the "Hebrew" religion is a primary source of the Puritan tradition, it is accorded a degree of legitimation unequaled in the European experience. Nonetheless, the Jewish religious tradition is foreign to an ever growing majority of American Jews, especially among the young. The most optimistic studies have found that in most communities fewer than fifty percent of the Jewish populace affiliate with a synagogue. Among the youth fewer still, around 30%, are exposed to even a nominal Jewish education. Inasmuch as this is the way in which America both permits and actually encourages Jews to identify, these data are of great consequence. Historically it has been the religious institution which has legitimized not only Jewish religious life but the whole panoply of cultural, national, and political activities which Jews conduct in the context of the religious community's life and responsibilities. A survey of the activities at the typical American synagogue would confirm that two-thirds of the program for its members has little or no objective religious purpose. There is nothing inherently incorrect about using the religious institution for "secular" purposes; to the contrary, it has been recognized as a logical and necessary practice if Jewish life is to flourish within the normative boundaries of American acceptability. The consequences of this pattern, however, have been antithetical to the intent. In quantifiable terms Jewish life has declined; it has been sacrificed on the altar of privatism and secularism.

The American constitutional principle of separation of church and state has insured the viability of this process. Religion is by law a private affair. Within one's home or in the confines of the religious community there is freedom to celebrate and identify with a faith system. In the public domain, however, religion is not an integrative force or organic element. By definition, therefore, America is a secular society which tolerates religious life within distinct boundaries. It is hardly surprising that the achievement of a normative identity in America implies a process of secularization. This is the way one integrates into the American mainstream. Furthermore, since the values and norms of society are determined by the majority cultural group, the myth of cultural pluralism collapses. The majority group is White Anglo-Saxon Protestant; therefore, the American mainstream is the reflection of WASP American normality.

In Protestant America the Jew is frequently subject to pressures which set achievement and success as primary goals. These, in turn, are usually identified by the symbols of materialism. Thus, domestic migration patterns for the American Jew, like his gentile counterpart, are usually determined by opportunities for economic advancement. This has affected the traditional cohesive nature of Jewish religious and communal life and resulted in its growing dissolution. For the individual, the pattern has meant isolation and alienation from Jewish life. There is, after all, little opportunity for the Jew who is isolated from the centers of Jewish communal life to identity, even superficially, with the community and its concerns. The exception is the Jew who belongs to the diminishing minority of the religiously observant who are capable of sustaining their faith and practice wherever they find themselves. More typical, however, is the countervailing reality—distance from Jewish life, in both physical and psychological terms, is producing a community of voluntarily alienated, and consequently assimilating, Jews. The forces of American secularism have propelled American Jews into a state of subjective vertigo. The consequence for most is a falling away from Jewish life. A significant majority of today's American Jews make merely a token financial contribution to any Jewish cause. Otherwise, these Jews are neither involved, affiliated, or interested in things Jewish.[7]

Perhaps the most dramtic expression of the successful emancipation of American Jewry may be seen in the absence of an identity crisis among American Jewish youth. Unlike their parents and grandparents, generations of the Holocaust and the great migration from the Russian Pale, Jewish youth today are not compelled to confront the philosophical challenges of the "new world." The cultural and religious baggage brought by parents and grandparents has been buried in the attic of the past or, literally, sold in a garage sale to curio seekers.

In the beginning it was necessary to sort things out. Being Jewish in traditional "old world" terms meant being in tension with America. Conversely, becoming American meant coming into conflict with the way one had been accustomed to being Jewish. The resolution of the identity question was of fundamental and universal importance to the immigrant and second generations. For these Jews there was a tension inherent in the process of development and absorption into the American milieu. It naturally revolved around the identity question. The benefits of American life would not accrue to those who contradicted the analytical basis of social and political emancipation. Remaining Jewish and becoming American were not compatible if the intent was merely to transfer ones locus from Vilna to New York. Emancipation, by definition, presupposed social and cultural integration.

There was also a political corollary. Consider, for example, secularist Jews who identified exclusively in political and cultural terms. Their identity was distinctively Jewish. The socialist Bund was committed to Yiddish as the language of discourse and to Yiddish culture as the manifestation of an indigenous Jewish heritage. For such Jews, as for any Jew who wished to implant his cultural or religious traditions in America, there were consequences of conflict and unresolved tension. This issue may have been a factor leading to the passage of highly restrictive immigration legislation after World War I. One of the articulated reasons for support of these new laws by some members of the American Congress was a concern about the Jewish "problem," i.e., political radicalism in America!

The consequence of severly limited immigration was the choking off of what had heretofore served as a nourishing inflow of Jews committed to the preservation of religious tradition and political activism. In time, many of the first generation immigrants, along with most of their children, made their accommodation to America. Religious life and Jewish cultural norms were modified and isolated within the private sector. Political integration took the form of a rapid dissolution of distinctively Jewish political movements and the more gradual transvaluation of Jewish principles into the categories of American liberal ideologies. Another result of this process has been the depolitization of the American Zionist movement in terms of its focus on domestic concerns.

By the time of the fourth generation, few American Jews remain in tension over their identity. For the most part, American Jewish youth are comfortable, quiescent, and inured to the American secular mainstream. They are American in the fullest sense of the term. Jewishness is an accident of birth of little consequence and diminishing interest. Relatively few Jews in contemporary America can still be classified as members of an organic Jewish community, whether the community is defined in cultural, political, or religious terms. What remains is a Jewry identified at best by declining levels of religious commitment or by increasingly superficial forms of association.

In its response to this American reality, Zionism has failed. It continues to apply ideological principles rooted in European concepts of racism and nationalism. The Zionism of catastrophe has no reality in an American framework. To continue to speak in such terms is to perpetuate a ludicrous fantasy of little interest or relevance to American Jews. Even among Jews of the Holocaust generation, Zionism and the centrality of Israel have become little more than extensions of the American Jewish tradition of philanthropy for homeless and persecuted Jews. As one Israeli thinker has put it, the quality of Jewish devotion to Israel is such, that it "soothes their consciences rather than arousing the problem of their Jewishness."[8] Among American Jewish youth even this vestige of guilt is hardly felt.

The truth is that in American Jewish circles the content of Zionism was never much more. For the vast majority it did not imply *aliyah*, a fact which Ben Gurion understood quite well. With the establishment of the state, he concluded, Zionism no longer had any real meaning in the Diaspora; he insisted that the authentic Zionist must be committed to *aliyah*. Otherwise, he believed, there would be little to distinguish Zionists from other American Jews who demonstrated good will, financial support, and political backing for Israel. The present spectacle of the Zionist Organization speaking of *aliyah* as a preeminent goal is little more than an exercise in hypocrisy. Even worse is the argument that *aliyah* is needed for demographic reasons to insure a Jewish majority in Israel. To make this the case for *aliyah*, particularly among Jews for whom Zionist ideology has no meaning, is to indulge in intellectual brinkmanship. Consciously or not, the American Jew has categorically rejected the analytical premises of classical Zionist thought. It is unlikely that he could be motivated to make *aliyah* based on an argument about Jewish demography. If such reasoning has little meaning for the Zionist believer, how much less will it appeal to the Diaspora Jew who is more effectively motivated to travel the easy road to assimilation than to ascend the high road to Jerusalem. Zionist thought today is trapped by its own polemical tradition in an intellectually wasted Levantine desert.

The only present link between history and ideology exists in the connection between contemporary Israeli reality and the pre-Holocaust situation of European Jewry. The Zionist expectation then was that the creation of a Jewish state would bring about the normalization of the Jewish people. The state was envisioned as standing apart, a model of peaceful revolution for all humanity. In fact, however, it has failed at both normalization and humane revolution. The tragic cycle of war and terrorism which has plagued Israel since its creation has served only to dramatize the national texture of Jewish suffering. The historical continuity of Jewish distress has not been relieved by the creation of the state. Rather, the state has served as an instrument for the legitimization of hostility against the Jewish collectivity under the guise of anti-Zionism.[9] The result of this process has been the creation of a siege mentality. Rooted in the historic consciousness of Jewish isolation and despair, the Israeli has sought to identify himself with the heroic tradition of the condemned. Today, the Masada epic speaks to the Israeli in visceral terms of negation. It is, nonetheless, difficult to find very much Zionist or Jewish content in the rallying cry "Masada will not fall again."

What, after all, does Masada represent? The Zealots took their stand after Jerusalem had fallen. The Romans had already conquered the sovereign Jewish state; even if the Zealot community had survived, it would have made little difference. It was Yohanan ben Zakkai who insured the survival of the Jewish idea and people. The establishment of Yavneh on the broken foundation of the Jewish State served as the sustenance of Jewish life and faith for two millenia. The Zealots, by contrast, overturned the basic Jewish principle of *pikuah nefesh* in their fanatical act of mass suicide. The cry "Masada will not fall again" merely suggests that Israel is determined not to allow itself to be placed ever again in such an ultimate situation. Instead, it appears that Israel is determined to become an unconquerable fortress, even at the cost of her Jewish identity. But the survival of this modern Masada will not be able to speak to the Jewishness of its residents any more than it will be able to communicate with the Diaspora. Gershom Scholem addressed this dilemma when he said ". . . we are first and foremost Jews, and we are Israelis as a manifestation of our Judaism. The State of Israel and its construction is an enterprise meant to serve the Jewish people, and if one deprives it of this goal, it loses its meaning and will not prevail long in the stormy course of these times."[10]

As an enterprise committed exclusively to survival, without recognition of the equally binding Jewish obligations to sanctify life, the Zionist state is bound to fail. In the end it may become "a state like other states," but lacking even the harmonious character envisioned by Herzl. If this be the case, if Israel comes to be simply a distorted realization of the ieal of normalization, it will signify the end of the Jewish people. Today, the Jew who comes to the Zionist state in search of renewal frequently finds himself morally and spiritually assaulted. One is confronted, for example, by the degenerate quality of religious life: its obscurantism, reactionary social attitudes, pervasive hypocrisy, ethical bankruptcy, and spiritual impoverishment.

In Israel today social and economic stratification has resulted in tremendous inequities within the population. This is ironic, for the social foundations of the state were, after all, based on principles of social justice and economic equity. Since the establishment of the State, however, Israeli leadership has consistently dismissed the urgency of gnawing social problems in favor of a preoccupation with foreign affairs. The result is a host of festering and potentially explosive social problems—poverty, crime, delinquency, alcoholism, slum housing, discrimination, and environmental pollution. A careful look at the Israeli Arab sector shows an even more disturbing picture.

Anyone who embraces the Zionist vision, at least in its social and ethical dimensions, finds his values blunted by the harshness of Israeli reality. It is a fantastic self-delusion to think that such an image can speak to the assimilating Jews of the Diaspora. Paradoxically, the present Zionist dilemma is as much a problem of reality as of idea. If Zionism cannot speak to its own mundane existence, it surely cannot be expected to speak authentically to the Diaspora.

Zionist renewal must be stimulated in the land as well as without. If the State of Israel is, as Zionism proclaims, the state of the entire Jewish people, then it must express the spirit and aspirations of all the people. A renaissance of Jewish life will not be brought about through proficiency in the use of armaments and celebration of Jewish power. Let us not forget that it was by the force of faith in the idea of messianic redemption that the Jewish people has been sustained. Jews have always understood this to be a process of both particular and universal consequence. Jews committed to the traditions of social idealism, including Zionists, have understood that their responsibility was to engage in efforts which would advance the Jewish people and, by example, all mankind toward realization of the messianic idea. In Jewish tradition, as in Zionist ideology, the Jewish State (Zion) is perceived as an instrument in the larger Jewish and human drama of redemption, *not as an end in itself.*

American Jewish youth, Jewishly ignorant, socially distant, and psychologically dulled by the culture of materialism will not be moved by calls for Jewish identity and solidarity. Least of all will this youth be motivated to make *aliyah* because of a presumed sense of obligation or

Jewish responsibility. It is possible, however, that the same generation would respond to a revived spirit of Jewish social idealism. The challenge of participating in a dynamic collective national effort at social and political reform may yet attract bright and thoughtful Jewish youth. The opportunity to join in a creative process of cultural and spiritual renaissance may represent the last hope of raising the level of Jewish interest in this otherwise rapidly assimilating Diaspora population. But the necessary first step in this process is the authentic renewal of the Zionist idea among its advocates at home. The regeneration of Jewish life and Zionism in our time will occur when Israel brings the Zionist vision back into focus.

NOTES

1. *The Idea of the Jewish State*, by Ben Halpern, p. 80.
2. David Ben Gurion, in his work *Rebirth and Destiny of Israel*, made the case as follows: "Exile is complete dependence—in material things, in politics, in culture, in ethics, and in intellect . . . They are dependent who constitute an alien minority, who have no Homeland and are separated from their origins, from the soil, from labor and from economic activity. So we must become the captains of our fortunes . . . We must become independent . . ."
3. For two examples see the author's "Borochov For Today" in *Jewish Frontier*, March 1972, and *Socialist Zionism* by Allon Gal, Schenkman Publishing Co., Cambridge, Mass. 1973.
4. See Nathan Rotenstreich's "Israel's Exile in American Jewish Thought" in *Forum*. Winter 1978.
5. There are many who make the case that America is different, and not only in appearances. Melvin Urofsky, in an article in *Forum* #28-29, "The Vision Disrupted" sums up these views as follows: "America is different. It lacks the historic conditions that created European anti-Semitism (Oscar Handlin, Ben Halpern); life in the Diaspora could be Jewishly creative and fulfilling (Salo Baron)' American Jews felt at home in the United States, and did not even begin to understand the concept of *galut* (C. Bezalel Sherman, Abraham Duker); American Jews had faith and hope in the future of the United States and in their own future in that country (Marie Syrkin); there had to be a partnership between Israel and the Diaspora (Mordecai Kaplan) . . ."
6. See "American Jewish College Youth" by Chaim I. Waxman and William B. Helmreich in *Forum* #27.
7. See Daniel Elazar's descriptive analysis of the American Jewish community "Deci-

sion-Making in the American Jewish Community" in *The Jew in American Society*, Ed. by M. Sklare, N.Y. 1975.

8. "Jewish Identity and Israeli Silence" by Yeshayahu Leibowitz in *Unease in Zion*, ed. by Ehud Ben Ezer, p. 187.

9. See Shmuel Ettinger's "Zionism and Its Significance Today" in *Forum*, Winter 1978, p. 14, and *A History of Zionism* by Walter Laqueur, p. 599.

10. "Israel and the Diaspora" in *On Jews and Judaism in Crisis*, by Gershom Scholem, Schocken Books, N.Y. 1976.

The Fall of Jerusalem
and the Birth of
Holocaust Theology

Richard L. Rubenstein

Florida State University
Tallahassee, Florida

The passing of time normally serves to diminish memory and personal involvement. Most of us are less agitated by unpleasant events that happened to us a decade ago than a week ago. Yet, there are exceptions. There is, for example, far more concern with the long-range implications of the Holocaust today than there was in the immediate aftermath of World War II. At the time, the trauma was simply too severe to permit disciplined reflection.

To the best of my knowledge, no book on Jewish theology published between 1945 and 1966 regarded the Holocaust as in any sense a challenge to Jewish religious belief. As we know, since 1966 there has been a fundamental change. It is now generally conceded that the Holocaust is *the* central issue for contemporary Jewish theology. Moreover, many who have devoted careers to disciplined reflection on the meaning of the Holocaust have long been convinced that it raises moral and religious issues that do not concern Jews alone but are, in fact, of the greatest significance for all of western religion and civilization.[1]

One obvious indication of the intensifying involvement of thoughtful men and women in the moral and religious questions arising from the

Holocaust has been the very wide interest in the literary achievement of Elie Wiesel. Although this writer has reservations about Wiesel's intellectual perspectives, as well as the ways in which his work has been used, he nevertheless recognizes its very great significance. It sometimes happens that literary exploration of a problem precedes and makes possible other modes of reflection. Wiesel's *Night* comes as close as any work to taking the mammoth, inhuman Kingdom of Death out of the realm of statistics and bringing it into the realm of individual experience. At his best, Wiesel is a witness of supreme importance to his time.

Nevertheless, there is a very important difference between the *individual* witness who offers the testimony of his own experience and disciplined reflection on the *structures* that created the Kingdom of Death. Because the witness focuses on personal experience, he is usually handicapped in comprehending the larger structures that entrapped and destroyed his world. If we recall that one of the strategies of those in command in wartime Germany was to manipulate the perceptions and indeed the modes of consciousness of the victims, it becomes apparent that, in addition to the indispensable testimony of witnesses, other types of reflection are also indispensable.

Regretably, the conclusions of those who reflect on the structures which made genocide possible often arouse the anger of those who seek to comprehend what took place primarily from the perspective of individual experience. Thus, Wiesel has stated that, while the Holocaust is an appropriate subject for religious questions, he rejects the possibility that the questions can be given adequate answers.[2] He also vehemently rejects the appropriateness of the analysis of the phenomenon by historians, sociologists, political theorists, and theologians who did not share his experience.[3] This writer cannot concur in Wiesel's rejection of disciplined reflection on the Holocaust for reasons that will become apparent in this essay.

The most obvious challenge to accepted notions presented by the Holocaust is, of course, the theological issue. Unlike philosophy, which knows nothing of the doctrine of covenant and election, Holocaust theology begins by taking with the utmost seriousness the biblical-rabbinic belief in the God-who-chooses-Israel. Its starting point is not speculation about a philosophically defined First Cause, but careful reflection on what the Bible, the rabbis and, in the case of Christianity, the earliest Christians said about God and Israel. On the basis of such reflection, it would seem that only two conclusions are possible concerning the nature of God as understood within the biblical tradition. If such a sovereign Lord exists, the Holocaust must be seen as ultimately an expression of his purposes. Such a conclusion can only be justified within the biblical-rabbinic tradition, if, like the Flood, Auschwitz is interpreted as punishment visited by a just and righteous God upon a sinful people.

Alternatively, one could conclude that no crime of fallible mortals could have justified so drastic a punishment of an entire people. Hence, the kind of God affirmed within the biblical-rabbinic system, one who is both just and faithful to his covenant with Israel, could not possibly exist. An infinitely sadistic or capricious God might exist; a less-than-omnipotent God might exist; a God who is indifferent to the actors in human history might exist, but the just, righteous, and all-powerful God as understood within Jewish tradition could not possibly exist. Thus, while the Holocaust would not serve as empirical disconfirmation of all belief in God, one would have to conclude that the experience of Auschwitz presents a most serious disconfirming challenge to the understanding of both God's nature and his relationship to Israel.

Nevertheless, while this writer is perhaps best known for having argued that it is impossible to maintain the normative-biblical-rabbinic belief in God in the light of Auschwitz, it is his conviction that the Holocaust presents a grave religious challenge to normative Jewish institutions for reasons *other* than the question of God's involvement in that event.

As is well known, normative rabbinic Judaism did not become dominant within the Jewish world until after the Holocaust of ancient times, the fall of Jerusalem in 70 C.E. Before the Judeo-Roman War, the Pharisees, the party of rabbinic Judaism, were but one of a number of competing religious sects within the nation.[4] Control of the officially sanctioned "media of redemption" was not in their hands but in the hands of the party of the priestly upper class in Jerusalem.[5] In the aftermath of the defeat of the Jews by the Romans, control of the media of redemption passed for the first time to the Yavnean Pharisees.

At Yavneh, Rabbi Yohanan ben Zakkai and his successors created new religious and communal institutions to take the place of the destroyed Jerusalem cult. As in our time, so too in the aftermath of the Holocaust of ancient times, the question of the theological meaning of the debacle was a matter of overwhelming concern to the Jewish religious community. Yohanan met the crisis of meaning by affirming that Israel's God had been the ultimate author of the catastrophe and that the event was truly a heaven-sent chastisement for Israel's sin.[6] He further specified that the most important offense for which Israel had been afflicted was her failure to obey God's commandments, *as they had been interpreted by the Pharisees.* It followed from Yohanan's interpretation of the catastrophe that Israel's sole hope for redemption lay in turning wholeheartedly to obedience to the Torah as taught and expounded by the Pharisees.

The achievement of Yohanan and his circle in meeting the new situation was extraordinary. These men were responsible for a sociological as well as a religious revolution which involved the rise to primacy of a new class of leaders, a new set of institutions, and a new hierarchy of values. We need not review that transformation here, but it is worthwhile to recall that the political and religious revolution that attended the shift of power from those whose power was based upon the Jerusalem Temple and its related institutions to the Yavnean institutions of the rabbinic party was more a consequence of deliberate Roman imperial policy than the power of the Pharisees.

According to Jacob Neusner, in the aftermath of 70 it was Roman policy "to reconstitute limited self-government among the Jewish population through loyal and non-seditious agents."[7] In plain language, Rome initiated a political process which turned control of the Jewish people over to those who were her willing collaborators. Without Roman support, the religious opinions of the men of Yavneh and their successors would have been at best a sectarian curiosity. With Roman support, the rulings of the Pharisees came to possess the force of law. Rabbinic Judaism is, thus, in large measure the sacralized expression of a political decision made by Imperial Rome as a means of controlling one of its most important ethnic minorities.

And, in choosing the Pharisees, Rome chose wisely. As Neusner has asserted, the Romans wanted to avoid an ethnic revolt.[8] The rabbis were eventually able to assure Rome that under their leadership the hitherto warlike Jews could be transformed into docile and submissive subjects. There were, of course, flare-ups under Trajan and under Hadrian, but after the Bar Kokhba War, neither the Romans nor their European successors ever again had to fear a Jewish rebellion until the Warsaw Ghetto uprising of 1943. Every Diaspora rabbi for almost two thousand years has been the heir of Yohanan and his bargain with the Romans. More important, every rabbi has encouraged his people to develop those traits of inner discipline that would enable them to foreswear acts of aggression in their dealings with overlords, no matter how grave the provocation.

In effect, Yohanan gambled that the only remaining defense available to his community was the credibility of its utter defenselessness. It was, of course, a good gamble. Any other course of action could easily have resulted in the annihilation of the community and its traditions. Nevertheless, the gamble did have profound risks which were clearly understood by both Yohanan and his Jewish contemporaries. It is doubtful that Josephus had any way of knowing exactly what Eleazar ben Yair said to his followers on Masada before they took their own lives rather than surrender to the Romans in 73 C.E., but the speech ascribed to Eleazar by Josephus does present accurately the issues at stake in the decision of the men of Masada:

> Let us take pity on ourselves, our children, and our wives while it is still in our power to show pity. For we were born to die . . . and this even the fortunate cannot escape. But insult and servitude and the sight of our wives being led to infamy with their children, these among men are not natural or necessary evils, though *those who do not prefer death, when death is in their power, must suffer even these because of their cowardice.*[9]

The words ascribed to Eleazar by Josephus make it clear why Eleazar could have accepted neither the authority nor the institutions of Yohanan ben Zakkai. Both Eleazar and Yohanan understood the risks of powerlessness, but Eleazar was not prepared to take them. The conditions Yohanan accepted and upon which he built a religious civilization made the question of Jewish survival totally dependent upon the good will of the conquerer and his heirs. Eleazar was not prepared to place his trust in the good will of Caesar.

In the language of contemporary sociology and political theory, Eleazar understood intuitively that Yohanan's program involved the transformation of Jews into a people of servile consciousness, in the technical philosophical sense that such a consciousness has been understood in the thought of both Hegel and Nietzsche. As Hegel observed, while the slave submits, he nevertheless works for the day when the power relationships will be reversed.[10] As Nietzsche understood, the slave's act of submission is an expression of his will to power.[11] Above all, the servile consciousness is only tenable as long as it is sustained by a hopeful vision of the future, by the conviction that the day will surely come when the present degradation will be reversed. Diaspora Jewish messianism must thus be seen as an expression of a servile consciousness. Only the slave, never the master, yearns for the day when *another* will redeem him.[12] When in need of redemption, the lordly consciousness redeems itself.

Yohanan felt the risks of defenselessness had to be taken, and it must be conceded that the survival of both the people and the religion of Israel were thereby assured. There was no other viable choice at the time. Nevertheless, the bargain struck by those who surrendered and the conqueror, as well as its religious legitimation, only made sense as long as the conqueror and his heirs kept their part of the bargain, namely, by allowing the Jewish people sufficient cultural and religious autonomy to maintain a dignified existence. When the conqueror sought seriously to tamper with the spiritual integrity of the community, as happened at the time of the Bar Kokhba War of 132–135, even the heirs of Yohanan felt that the bargain was not worth keeping.

The bargain between the Caesars and the Pharisees was more or less kept by every European ruler until Adolf Hitler. Even those European rulers who expelled the Jews from their realms were acting within the limits of Vespasian's bargain. When rulers such as Ferdinand and Isabella of Spain decided that they could no longer permit a religiously autonomous Jewish enclave within their realm, they gave their Jewish subjects the options of conversion or forced emigration. Harsh as they were, these were options predicated upon the humanity of the Jews. The Jews had some choice in their future. By contrast, the Nazi Final Solution was predicated upon a total rejection of Jewish humanity.

Thus, until the twentieth century, the strategies adopted by the rabbis for Jewish survival were both adaptive and functional. *The sacralized culture of submisssion made sense as long as the bargain with Vespasian's political heirs retained its credibility.* However, as soon as a successor of Vespasian determined to take advantage of Jewish powerlessness for the purpose of a policy of unremitting extermination, the culture of submission no longer made sense. This was understood by the Nazis long before it was understood by their victims.

It was for that reason that the Nazis consistently sought to disguise their real intentions in their dealings with European Jewish communities even in the midst of the war. For their part, the *Judenräte* that cooperated with the Nazis reacted according to characteristic patterns of response the rabbis had fostered for two millenia. These patterns of response had become a predominant element in their pre-theoretical consciousness as a result of two thousand years of religio-cultural conditioning. Regretably but understandably, in their dealings with their oppressors, the *Judenräte* were less dependent upon realistic perceptions concernings the enemy's intentions than upon inherited assumptions concerning what Jews might expect in their dealings with a gentile ruler. Admittedly, Jews were not alone in responding according to predetermined patterns, but such responses proved to be a luxury the Jews could ill afford. It was not until the Warsaw Ghetto uprising that there was a large-scale transformation in Jewish patterns of response. By that time, all that was available was a choice between an Auschwitz and a Masada-type death. The Warsaw rebels chose Masada as their model.

As soon as World War II was over, the vast majority of the Holocaust's survivors attempted to flee the European continent. Understandably, they could no longer trust their neighbors and had no desire to attempt to start life again in a graveyard. As we know, a goodly part of the survivors made their way to Palestine, where it was by no means certain that they would gain their safety. That, however, was not the fundamental issue. It was clear that the patterns of response fostered by rabbinic tradition could no longer meet the needs of Europe's Jews. The survivors rejected them in the most dramatic way they could, by a primordial movement of return to their nation's place of origin, where survival depended upon a very different pattern of response.

Yohanan had counselled submission and a strategy of non-violence. He had built his religious culture on that basis. Without reflection the survivors understood that once a ruler used his power over the Jews as had Hitler, Europe's Jews had little choice but to gather themselves at a location and under circumstances in which Jewish survival was no longer solely dependent upon the unilateral decision of strangers. As was the case with Yohanan's bargain, so with the return to Israel after Auschwitz, a gamble was taken, but this time the gamble involved the rejection of the strategies and the culture of the rabbis and a partial return to the strategies of the men and women of the ancient Jewish resistance against Rome. Such a gamble might someday result in another Masada; it could never result in a second Auschwitz.

As we know, the Holocaust was followed by the birth of the state of Israel after a hiatus of almost two thousand years. It is possible that the significance of this revolutionary transformation was understood with least ambiguity by that sector of the extreme Orthodox wing of contem-

porary Judaism which refused to give the State of Israel wholehearted
allegiance and which minimized the spiritual, as contrasted with the
political and social, significance of the Holocaust. The extreme Orthodox
understood instinctively that the kind of men and women the new state
would bring forth would be moved by a radically different hierarchy of
values than theirs and would, in fact, be radically different people than
those who had been loyal to the traditions of rabbinic Judaism.

It is interesting to note the convergence between the views of the
extreme Orthodox and that of the French sociologist Georges Friedmann, who sees the establishment of the state of Israel as marking the
"end of the Jewish people."[13] To the extent that it survives as a predominant religious and cultural force within the Jewish community,
rabbinic Judaism survives with greatest vitality not in Israel but the
United States. (By "rabbinic Judaism," I mean all variants of Judaism
which receive their fundamental perspectives from the religious world of
the Pharisees. I include all three branches of mainstream American
Judaism.) Rabbinic Judaism is fundamentally a diaspora phenomenon. It
survives best where Yohanan's bargain remains socially and politically
relevant, as it does in North America.

Rabbinic Judaism was not the only modern religion that was formed
in response to the fall of Jerusalem, the Holocaust of ancient times. In
addition to its reflections on the religious situation of contemporary
Jewry, Holocaust theology lends its own distinctive perspectives to our
understanding of the birth of Christianity. Christianity was born at a
time when the Jewish people were rapidly approaching the most overwhelming disaster they were to experience until the Nazi Holocaust. If
the Gospel accounts are accurate, not only did Jesus foretell the destruction of the Temple and Jerusalem's ancient Holocaust, he also proclaimed the catastrophe to be a fitting expression of God's righteous
judgment against the Jews.[14] Today, many critical New Testament
scholars question whether Jesus actually pronounced the prophecies of
Israel's doom in the form ascribed to him.[15] It is the consensus of many,
though by no means all, critical scholars that the four Gospels were written in the aftermath of the fall of Jerusalem.

It is also the opinion of many critical scholars, an opinion I share,
that the Gospels contain extensive evidence of the Christian response to
that event.[16] Even those scholars who date Mark before 70 seldom date it
before the outbreak of the war in 66. All four Gospels are at one in their

interpretation of the Holocaust of ancient times, but none expresses it with the bitter emotional intensity of the most Jewish of the Gospels, Matthew. The classical Christian response to the fall of Jerusalem is expressed in the parable of the Wicked Tenants, the tale of the householder who planted a vineyard and "let it out to tenants and went into another country." (Mark 12:1) When the land rents fell due, the landlord sent three servants, one after another, to collect from the tenants. The wicked tenants assaulted the first and murdered the second and third servants. Finally, the landowner sent his own son to collect the rents. Matthew records what is then said to have transpired:

> But when the tenants saw the son, they said to themselves, "This is the heir; come, let us kill him and have his inheritance." And they took and cast him out of the vineyard, and killed him. (Matthew 21:38,39)

Matthew then depicts Jesus as describing the householder's angry response:

> When therefore the owner of the vineyard comes, what will he do to those tenants? . . . He will put those miserable wretches to death and let out the vineyard to other tenants. (Matthew 21:40,41)

In their versions of the parable, Mark and Luke depict Jesus as saying that the landlord will destroy "the tenants." Matthew adds an element of emotional intensity by substituting "miserable wretches" (Greek, *kakous kakos*) for the older, more original reading.

In Matthew the parable of the Wicked Tenants is immediately followed by the parable of the Marriage Feast. In this parable Jesus is depicted as likening the kingdom of heaven to a marriage feast given by a king for his son. Twice the king sent forth his servants to invite the guests. On both occasions those invited refused to come. Some even dared to abuse and kill the messengers. Jesus is then depicted as saying:

> The king was angry and he sent his troops and destroyed those murderers and burned their city. (Matthew 22:7)

According to Bultmann and other critics, this is a clear reference to the fall of Jerusalem and was composed, not as a prophecy of, but as a response to that event.[17]

The most savage expression of Matthew's response to the fall of Jerusalem occurs in the terrible scene found only in his Gospel in which Pontius Pilate, finding no fault in Jesus, nevertheless condemns him to appease the Jewish mob, washes his hands before the crowd, and proclaims,

> And *all* the people answered, "His blood be upon us and our children."
> (Matthew 27:25, italics added)

The moral is clear. It is constantly reiterated. No difference of opinion on the issue separates the Jewish Christianity of Matthew from the Gentile Christianity of Mark and Luke. *The Temple was destroyed, Jerusalem ruined, and the Jewish nation slaughtered, not by the profane strength of the Roman empire, but by a just, all-powerful, avenging God who was determined to teach the Jews the true cost of rejecting his Son.*

It is sometimes said that Holocaust theology was born in the nineteen-sixties when, after a generation of silence, theologians finally turned to the extermination of Europe's Jews and began to seek for religious meaning in the most devastating catastrophe to befall the Jewish people since the fall of Jerusalem. In actuality, Holocaust theology was by no means solely a product of the sixties. *Holocaust theology is at least as old as the fall of Jerusalem. Moreover, the four Gospels are the oldest classical expression of Christian Holocaust theology.*

In the aftermath of the Judeo-Roman war, Christians had no doubt that Jesus himself had pronounced the dire judgement against Jerusalem ascribed to him in the Gospels. The fall of the city was taken by Christians to be the fulfillment of his prophecies and the confirmation of his divinity. Whoever may have been the actual author of the prophecies—and it is impossible to rule out Jesus—all that was sacred to Christians moved them to interpret the Jewish catastrophe as incontrovertible evidence of God's rejection of the Jews and their religious institutions. This view was reinforced by the fact that the misery of the defeated Jews seemed to confirm the Church's claim to be the successor of Judaism.

Consider the situation of thoughtful Gentile Christians in Rome about the year 75. Even those who did not have direct contact with the Jews knew that they actively rejected such distinctively Christian beliefs as Jesus' messianic status, his atoning death, his resurrection, and his heavenly lordship. Christians regarded these beliefs as decisive for their eternal salvation. Jewish opposition was no small matter because it came from the people who were of the same nation as Jesus and shared with Christians a common faith in the authority of Scripture.

Moreover, because of their superior numbers, Jews could and often did express their rejection with harsh and undiplomatic arguments, as well as with outright persecution of those Christians who had not broken completely with the Jewish community. Such conduct was bound to anger believing Christians. Today, as a result of the work of social psychologists in the field of cognitive dissonance, we are able to understand the way a group is likely to respond to those who present disconfirming evidence or who seek to discredit beliefs in which the group has a very strong emotional investment.[18] One of the most frequent responses is to discredit the integrity and even the humanity of those who question the group's beliefs. Apart from all considerations of class, ethnic, or economic conflict, there has always been a built-in element making for mutual hostility between believing Jews and Christians in the profound challenge the faith of each poses for some of the most deeply held beliefs of the other.

Since both traditions affirm the existence of the God-who-acts-in-history, it was inevitable that Christians living in the year 75 would regard the fall of Jerusalem as an expression of divine judgement. If events had demonstrated that the unbelieving Jews had been rejected by God, there was no reason to be concerned with Jewish arguments against Christian faith. Thus, *the supreme Jewish disaster of ancient times was quite logically seen as a confirmation of the truth of the very faith the Jews had rejected.*

The more one studies the history of the first Christian century, the more one realizes how important the ancient Holocaust was for the development of early Christianity.[19] Furthermore, if one enters the thought-world of both Christianity and biblical Judaism with their shared belief in God's purposeful intervention in Israel's history, it becomes apparent that the Christian interpretation of the significance of the fall of Jerusalem is altogether plausible from a theological perspective. Jesus is portrayed as having predicted the catastrophe; his prophecies appeared to have been speedily fulfilled. When the Pharisees offered their own equally plausible explanation of the reasons why Jerusalem fell, they did not deny that the event was an expression of God's punishment of Israel. The Pharisees only differed with the Christians concerning the nature of the sins that had moved God to act.

Moreover, if one applies the categories of the Christian thought-

world to the Nazi Holocaust, that event can be interpreted as further
punishment of the Jews for having rejected Jesus. As a matter of fact, no
other interpretation of the Holocaust is consistent with the classical
Christian theology of history as it is expressed in the Gospels.[20] Yet,
when one turns to the writings of Christian theologians and New Testament scholars writing between 1945 and 1965, one finds that the Nazi
Holocaust is passed over in almost total silence, as if there were no connection between the disaster Jesus is said to have predicted and the
Jewish misfortunes of the twentieth century.[21] This does not mean that
Christian scholars are necessarily indifferent to the Nazi Holocaust.
Some are; many are not.

One evidence of Christian concern is to be found in some, though by
no means all, of the more recent Christian commentaries on the books of
the New Testament. Post-war commentaries often attempt to mitigate
the harshness of the anti-Jewish prophecies ascribed to Jesus.[22] The tendency is by no means uniform or consistent even in the same work, but
when Jesus' dire predictions about the fate that awaits the Jews begin to
resemble descriptions of the Nazi Holocaust, some recent commentators
tend to argue that Jesus' words were not meant to be taken as a blanket
condemnation of all Jews. Nevertheless, when Christianity is understood on its own terms, as a religion that proclaims the deeds of the
God-who-acts-in-history, no Christian interpretation of Jewish disaster is theologically more plausible than that which is ascribed in the
Gospels to Jesus.

Furthermore, no group of scholars has contributed more to the
study of the Bible in modern times than the Germans. Taken as a group,
German scholars have been the world's most innovative and authoritative interpreters of the New Testament for generations. Most of the
senior professors of New Testament in German universities today were
adults during the Second World War. Many served in the German
armed forces on the Eastern Front where the slaughter of the Jews took
place. As citizens of the Third Reich, the professors could not avoid
some measure of involvement in the most violent assault on Jews since
the birth of Christianity. Yet, we find a studied silence in their works on
the theological significance of the Holocaust and their own personal
involvement in it.

No matter how much a German might have been privately opposed
to Nazism, it was impossible for any adult living in the Third Reich not
to have been *structurally* involved in the destruction of Europe's Jews.

The Holocaust was not carried out by a band of criminal adventurers but by the legally constituted government of Germany, a government which commanded the loyalty of the overwhelming majority of its citizens until almost the very end of the war. In 1942, for example, to be a patriotic adult German male meant to serve in the war effort. Every victory of *any* branch of the German armed forces, the Wehrmacht as well as the SS, sealed the doom of yet more communities of Jews. Even if one were a member of one of the church groups opposed to the Nazis, as were a number of New Testament scholars, to be a German Christian at the time meant to be objectively involved in the massacre of Europe's Jews.[23] Those who had been trained in the world's foremost institutions for the study of the Bible had a more informed conception of what Jesus was depicted as having said about the Jews than any other group within Germany, if not the rest of the world. They also knew how important the physical destruction of ancient Israel had been for the rise of Christianity. Yet when we turn to their writings, we look in vain for any indication that the assault, which took place often before their very eyes, has any relevance to their theological enterprise.

This writer cannot pretend to fathom the motives for their silence. Perhaps they are silent because, like the first Christians, they see the Holocaust of their era as a further chastisement visited by God against the Jews for their unbelief but find it inexpedient to say so explicitly. Immediately after World War II, some very respectable German theologians were less reticent. They assembled at a nation-wide conference, bade the Jews to learn well the lesson of the death camps, repent, and confess Jesus Christ as their Savior.[24] In so doing, of course, the Germans were no different than those Christian theologians elsewhere who interpret the Holocaust in triumphalist categories.

Perhaps some scholars find such a theology humanly unacceptable but know of no acceptable alternative within their own tradition. Perhaps they simply regard the fate of the Jews as of too little relevance to their religious and scientific concerns to warrant special attention. They may regard the years of the Third Reich as a parenthetical moment during which they were involuntarily distracted from their real concerns. Still, the silence is puzzling in view of the Gospels' accounts of Jesus' prophecies and the extraordinary importance the fall of Jerusalem is known to have had for the emerging Christian Church. Whatever the motives for the silence, it is this writer's conviction that no one can ignore the contemporary Holocaust and arrive at an understanding of

Jesus of Nazereth or the birth of Christianity that is relevant to our time. If nothing else, can there be any doubt concerning Jesus' fate had he quietly reappeared and rejoined his people in wartime Europe?

In conclusion, it is this writer's conviction that the theological issues raised by the Holocaust are of decisive significance for both contemporary Judaism and Christianity. The normative forms of both faiths, Rabbinic Judaism and emergent Gentile Christianity, were born in the aftermath of and were very largely responses to the Holocaust of ancient times. Before the Judeo-Roman War, it is likely that none of the Gospels had been written, and Christianity was a Jewish movement in leadership if not in total membership. Before the war the Jewish-Christian Mother Church enjoyed unchallenged prestige and authority among the churches of Christendom. Afterwards, Christianity ceased to be a movement within Judaism and became instead a predominantly Gentile rival over against it. In all likelihood, it was to foster the irreversibility of this development that the earliest Gospel, Mark, was written.

In all likelihood the Pharisees were one of several competing Jewish sects, including the Jewish Christians and the Essenes at Qumran, each of which claimed that theirs was the true religion of the Jewish people. By 75 the Pharisees were well on their way to becoming the unquestioned spiritual masters of the household of Israel. In both Judaism and Christianity, those who enjoyed the greatest prestige and authority before 70 did so no longer afterward. Both Rabbinic Judaism and Christianity as we know them were born in the wake of the greatest catastrophe experienced by the Jewish people until the Holocaust of the twentieth century. Both the Judaism and the Christianity that arose in the aftermath of the fall of Jerusalem utilized a theology of history which, when applied to the Nazi Holocaust, must interpret that event as God's chastisement of a sinful Israel.

Admittedly, there is little public evidence of satisfaction with such an interpretation by either religious Jews or Christians. Yet, it must be admitted that the Nazi Holocaust can be utilized to confirm the plausibility of an uncompromising Christian theology of history. Only one crime could conceivably justify God to act so drastically against an entire people and that crime would be deicide: a deicidal people would by definition be a satanic people, and, as such, deserving of no mercy whatsoever. Such enemies of God could only be dealt with by being exterminated root and branch. This kind of legitimation of uncompromising violence against Israel is implicit in the following remarks the author of the Fourth Gospel depicts Jesus as having said to the Jews:

> If God were your Father you would love me, for I proceeded forth from God; I came not of my own accord but he sent me. Why do you not understand what I say? It is because you cannot bear to hear my word. You are of your father the devil, and your will is to do your father's desire. He was a murderer from the beginning and has nothing to do with the truth because there is no truth in him. When he lies, he speaks according to his own nature, for he is a liar and the father of lies. But because I tell the truth you do not believe me. (John 8:42–45)

The ascription of a satanic nature to Jews had the effect of legitimating even the basest violence perpetrated against them. Furthermore, this condemnation was not uttered by a man, but, from a Christian perspective, by God himself. It is therefore far more resistant to critical scrutiny than a condemnation uttered by even a saintly human being would have been.

Thus, a literal reading of the Gospels presents us with a perfectly plausible theological legitimation of the Holocaust, a fact that was clearly understood by the Nazi leaders who claimed that, in eliminating the Jews, they were doing the Lord's work.[25] The literal reading becomes entirely consistent with faith in an all-righteous God who acts in history, if, as in the Gospels, a satanic identity is ascribed to the Jews. More than any event since the birth of Christianity, the Holocaust can be used as confirming evidence that Jesus was the Messiah whom Israel rejected and crucified and for which they were rightly and justly punished.

Yet, we seldom hear this kind of argument publicly expressed even among conservative, believing Christians, although one wonders what is sometimes stated in private. Nevertheless, few Christians want to draw the obvious parallel between the way their faith interpreted the fall of Jerusalem and the way their faith logically might interpret the Holocaust today. Perhaps this reticence is not without a measure of wisdom, for no matter what the alleged offense, decent people shrink from associating the just and righteous God, to whom they have committed their ultimate fate and destiny, with anything so pervasively obscene as Auschwitz. Perhaps that is why one Christian thinker, Professor John Roth of Claremont College, has argued that the Holocaust is a time bomb ticking away in the midst of Christianity.[26] Christian faith can no more reject the God who acts in history nor deny the special concern of that God for Israel's fate than can rabbinic Judaism. Yet, there is no way it can can affirm such a God without regarding Auschwitz as one of his most decisive historical acts. This issue is yet to be dealt with openly and frankly by theologians of the two faiths that emerged out of the Jewish Holocaust of ancient times.

NOTES

1. This view is expressed by John T. Roth in his *A Consuming Fire: Encounters with Elie Wiesel and the Holocaust* (Atlanta: 1979), pp. 37–57. See also Alan T. Davies, *Anti-Semitism and the Christian Mind: The Crisis of Conscience After Auschwitz* (New York: 1969) pp. 35ff.

2. See Elie Wiesel, "Trivializing the Holocaust: Semi-Fact and Semi-Fiction," *New York Times*, Sunday April 17, 1970, Arts and Leisure Section.

3. Wiesel, *loc. cit.*

4. See Morton Smith, "Palestinian Judaism in the First Century" in *Israel: Its Role in Civilization*, ed. Moshe Davis (New York: 1956), pp. 67–81.

5. See Shelly Isenberg, "Millenarism in Greco-Roman Palestine" in *Religion*, 4:26–46, Spring 1974; Shelly Isenberg, "Power Through Temple and Torah in Greco-Roman Palestine" in *Morton Smith Festschrift*, ed. Jacob Neusner (Leiden: 1975), pp. 25–52. On the conception of "media of redemption," see Kennelm Burridge, *New Heaven New Earth: A Study of Millenarian Activities* (New York: 1969), pp. 6–7.

6. See *Mekhilta de R. Ishmael*, trans. Jacob Z. Lauterbach (Philadelphia: 1933), *Bahodesh* I, Vol. II, pp. 193–4; *The Fathers According to R. Nathan* ed. Judah Goldin (New Haven: 1955), Chapter 4, esp. p. 34, and Chapter 17, pp. 88–9. For a succinct discussion of R. Yohanan ben Zakkai's theological and religious response to the Fall of Jerusalem, see Jacob Neusner, *First Century Judaism in Crisis* (Nashville: 1975), pp. 156–175.

7. Jacob Neusner, *From Politics to Piety: The Emergence of Pharisaic Judaism* (Englewood Cliffs, N.J.: 1973), p. 148.

8. Neusner, *op. cit.*, p. 147.

9. Josephus, *The Jewish War*, trans. H. St. J. Thackeray (London: 1928), Vol. VII, 381–383, p. 613.

10. It should, however, be understood that Hegel sees the Slave as transcending his situation through *labor* rather than through a renewal of the original combat. See G.W.F.

Hegel, *Phenomenology of Spirit*, trans. A.V. Miller (Oxford: 1977), pp. 117 ff. This interpretation is dependent upon Alexandre Kojève's reading of the *Phenomenology*. See Kojève, *Introduction to the Reading of Hegel*, ed. Allan Bloom, trans. James H. Nichols Jr. (New York: 1969), pp. 42–70.

11. Friedrich Nietzsche, *Genealogy of Morals*, trans. Walter Kaufmann and R. J. Hollingdale (New York: 1967), First Essay, Sections 10 and 14.

12. It is surely no accident that Nietzsche's aristocratic ethic is linked with his doctrine of eternal recurrence. Eternal recurrence is the polar opposite of the idea of a messianic redemption at the end of history. For an informed discussion of eternal recurrence see Ivan Soll, "Reflections on Recurrence: A Reexamination of Nietzsche's Doctrine *Die Ewige Wieder-Kehr des Gleichens*" in *Nietzsche*, ed. Robert Solomon, (Garden City: 1973), pp. 322–342.

13. See Georges Friedmann, *The End of the Jewish People?*, trans. Eric Mosbacher (Garden City: 1967)

14. Matt. 22:7.

15. See S.G.F. Brandon, *The Fall of Jerusalem and the Christian Church* (London: 1968), pp. 231; W.D. Davies, *The Setting of the Sermon on the Mount* (Cambridge: 1966), pp. 298 ff.

16. Davies, *loc. cit.*; Brandon, *loc. cit.*; see Norman Perrin, The New Testament: *An Introduction; Proclamation and Paranesis, Myth and History* (New York: 1974), pp. 40–1.

17. See Norman Perrin, *Rediscovering the Teaching of Jesus* (New York: 1976), pp. 110 ff.

18. See Leon Festinger, Henry W. Rieken, and Stanley Schachter, *When Prophecy Fails* (Minneapolis: 1956); Elliot Aronson and Gardner Lindzey, eds., *The Handbook of Social Psychology* (Reading, Mass.: 1968–70); Elliot Aronson, *The Social Animal* (New York: 1972); Elliot Aronson, "The Rationalizing Animal" in *Psychology Today*, May, 1973.

19. "The destruction of Jerusalem and the Temple by the Gentiles sent a shock wave through the Judaeo-Christian world whose importance it is impossible to exaggerate. Indeed, much of the subsequent literature both of Judaism and Christianity took the form it did precisely in an attempt to come to terms with the catastrophe of 70 A.D." Norman Perrin, *op. cit.*, pp. 40–1.

20. See Richard L. Rubenstein, "The Dean and the Chosen People" in *After Auschwitz* (Indianapolis: 1966) pp. 47–60. In that essay the author relates an incident that took place in Berlin in 1961 in which Dean Heinrich Grüber's statement was that it was *not* uttered out of malice but was consistent with the classical Christian theology of history.

21. One important exception is Jurgen Moltmann who is a theologian rather than a New Testament scholar. However, Jewish readers may come away from Moltmann's discussion with the feeling that they have been exposed to an expression of Christian triumphalism. Moltmann contends that "God in Auschwitz and Auschwitz in the crucified God . . . is the basis for a real hope which both embraces and overcomes the world and the ground for a love which is stronger than death and can sustain death." Jurgen Moltmann, *The Crucified God* (New York: 1978), pp. 278.

22. Commenting on the Parable of the Vineyard (Matt. 21:33–46) in which the wicked tenants kill the owner's "son" and in which Jesus is depicted as saying that the owner will "put these wretches to death" and on the Parable of the Wedding Feast (Matt. 22:1–1–10), W.F. Albright observes, "It is necessary here to add that nothing which has been said above is meant to imply a permanent rejection by God of his ancient people. Still less that the judgments pronounced by Jesus . . . are to be taken as they have unhappily in the past as

valid judgments against the entire institution of Judaism . . ." W.F. Albright in *Matthew: A New Translation and Commentary by W.F. Albright and C.S. Mann* (Garden City: 1971), p. cxxxiii. For yet another example of the tendency to mitigate the harshness see Raymond Brown's comments on John 8:31–59 in *The Gospel According to John*, Introduction, translation and notes by Raymond Brown, S.S. (Garden City: 1966), pp. 361–368. For a commentary which is unmitigated in its harshness after the Holocaust, see John Marsh's comments on John 8:31–59 in John Marsh, *The Pelican Gospel Commentaries Saint John* (Harmondsworth, Middlesex: 1968), pp. 365–6. For Marsh nothing has changed.

23. Among the New Testament scholars who were at least passively anti-Nazi were Hans von Soden, Heinrich Schlier, Julius Schniewind, Günter Bornkamm, Ernst Käsemann, and Rudolf Bultmann. I am indebted to Professor David Lenson of Florida State University and Professor Dieter Georgi of Harvard for this information.

24. "Ein Wort zur Judenfrage" Der Reichsbruderrat der Evangelischen Kirche in Deutschland, Darmstadt, April 8, 1948 in *Der Ungekundigte Bund: Neue Begegnung von Juden und christlicher Gemeinde*, Hrsg. von Dietrich Goldschmidt und Hans-Joachim Kraus, Stuttgart, Berlin 2. Auflage, 1963, pp. 251–54. I am indebted to Prof. Eva Fleischner for this reference.

25. See Raul Hilberg, *The Destruction of the European Jews* (Chicago: 1961), p. 12.

26. See John K. Roth, *op. cit.*, pp. 37–57.

Part IV
תורה לשמה
Essays in Jewish Scholarship

Paradox in Religion:
Judaism and the Sense of Wonder

David A. Altshuler

The George Washington University
Washington, D.C.

I treasure Alfred Jospe as a teacher and a friend, and it is a great privilege for me to contribute to this volume in his honor.[1] His writings on the teaching of Judaic Studies and on aspects of modern Jewish thought have stimulated and sharpened many of my own interests. In this essay I shall discuss some lessons from the field of the "History of Religions" and indicate their possible applicability to Judaic Studies.[2] Specifically, I want to suggest how students of Judaism may benefit from considering the paradoxical nature of both history and religion.

Modern university studies of religion began little more than a century ago. Typically, the first investigators sought the origins of religious life, often believing religion to derive from "faulty thinking." Another early phase consisted of social science approaches, which commonly attempted to explain religions as reflecting patterns in individual and societal needs and behavioral responses. A third tendency in the nascent academic field was to compare types and structures of diverse religious traditions, and this phenomenological study often was combined with historical interpretation. Arguments in behalf of the "History of Religions" school often claim that other methods err by reducing religion to something else.[3]

History of religions has enjoyed increasing popularity in recent decades because it is empirical rather than normative, allowing and indeed requiring investigators to empathize with their data. However, while early proponents confidently saw history as a way to unravel "what really happened" in the past, writers recently have recognized some important limits of historical "science."[4] In presuming uniformity in nature and regularity in causal connection, the modern critical historian becomes, in a sense, a "believer." "The past is available to us only as a dimension of the present," Whitehead observed.[5] Thus, writing history is an "act of faith," lacking the possibilities of experimentation and lawmaking so necessary for scientific inquiry.[6]

Contemporary historians of religion now seem to agree with Van Harvey that ours is an "age of enlightenment" rather than an "enlightened age."[7] Science and secularization are hardly new phenomena, nor have they erased in any intellectual pursuit the human need for myths and symbols. Indeed, Albert Einstein often is quoted as representing the humility of even the greatest modern rationalists: "As far as the laws of mathematics refer to reality, they are not certain; as far as they are certain, they do not refer to reality . . . . The eternally incomprehensible fact about the universe is that it is comprehensible. The solitary comprehensible fact about human experience is that it is incomprehensible."[8]

The study of religion explores human thought and behavior from pre-historic times until the present. As H. P. Sullivan notes, the history of religions tells "about man—the dimensions of human experience and human expressiveness—and about reality—its mode of manifestation and comprehensibility."[9] Religion, like art, is spontaneous, creative and free. It reflects the qualitative and synthetic aspects of human thought, where rational logic is restricted to the quantitative and analytical. *Mirabile dictu*, we owe to the pioneers of rationalism—the Greeks—our name for what may be religion's central concept, namely *paradox*.

Hans Penner argues that all critical scholars of religion confront what he calls "the paradox of final agnosticism." That is, they describe a religion but cannot know its meaning. If they apply the reductionist techniques of social sciences, this "swallows up the term *religion*." And if they allow for subjective interpretation, this "vaporizes the term *history* in the history of religions."[10] If Paul Ricoeur is correct, this problem is not a hermeneutic one alone; rather, it reflects the nature of reality. "Language says something about being. If there is an enigma of symbolism, it resides completely on the place of manifestation, where the being's equivocality comes to be said in the equivocality of discourse."[11]

Religions not only pose paradoxes; they also embrace them. While in common parlance "paradox" often signifies "self-contradictory," "absurd," or "false," the original meaning of the term is none of these.

Rather παρα (against) δοξον (opinion) denotes something contrary to conventional thinking, thus surprising. Sometimes, as with the classic "Epimenides" [a person says, "I am a liar."], a paradox will paralyze and perplex a hearer. Commonly, however, paradoxes evoked in the ancients wonder and amazement of a religious dimension. In fact, historians of religion have observed that awe of reality's paradoxical nature is often at the root of religious symbolic and mythic systems.[12]

Mircea Eliade's studies persuasively demonstrate the importance of paradox to religion. Drawing on data from South America, North American Indians, and Far Eastern archaic societies, Eliade argues that "religious expression presupposes a bipartition of the world into the sacred and profane." While earlier writers tried to discover social or historical origins for this pattern of religious dualism, Eliade claims that the history of religions approach requires "hermeneutic effort, not demystification."[13]

As in modern psychology, study of abstract art, and philosophical linguistics, contemporary research in religion often focuses on modes of human symbol-forming. According to Eliade, religious symbolism has "existential value," pointing to structures more mysterious and profound than everyday life reveals. "Perhaps the most important function of religious symbolism," he adds, "is its capacity for expressing paradoxical situations, or certain structures of ultimate reality, otherwise quite inexpressible." Symbols thus allow the disclosure of unity in the world despite its polarities "on the plane of immediate experience."[14]

Joachim Wach asserts that while symbols "connect" physical realities with spiritual ones, myths illustrate in narrative form what symbols are able only to imply.[15] Myth relies on experience and intuition rather than speculation, treating the natural as personal. The mythopoeic mind tends to telescope time, so that innovations may be seen as primordial, and space, to emphasize the common lot of humanity in the cosmos. Myths stand behind rituals and are often deeply connected to social and moral rules; thus Bronislaw Malinowski, like others, sees religious myth-making as an "indispensable ingredient of all culture."[16] Wendy Doniger O'Flaherty adds that "good" myths have endless meanings because their psychological value lies in confronting insoluble human problems.[17] Thus Wach concludes a discussion on myths by claiming that "genuine religion involves a paradox."[18] Religion insists on distance between worshippers and God, yet religion also annihilates that distance.

These general comments on religious symbols and myths may serve to introduce Eliade's methodological axiom. "The different types of bipartition and polarity, duality and alternation, antithetical dyads and *coincidentia oppositorum*, are to be found everywhere in the world and at all stages of culture. But the historian of religions is ultimately interested in finding out what a particular culture . . . has done with this immediate datum."[19]

We shall consider some paradoxical aspects of Judaism from three perspectives: early Jewish uses of the word παράδοξος, polarities central to "normal" Judaism, and tensions peculiar to kabbalah.

Forms of the word παράδοξος are found throughout early Greek-language Jewish literature, and their usage readily demonstrates the connection between paradox and a religious sense of wonder or amazement.[20] Some two dozen examples of these forms survive in ancient versions of biblical translations and post-biblical Greek originals, and in all but two cases that which is paradoxical is explicitly attributed to God (rather than to humans or "nature.")[21] In the translations, the Hebrew *Vorlage* is usually from פלא [signifying "extraordinary," "unexpected," or "miraculous"]; this sense is nearly universal in the apocryphal and pseudepigraphic Greek works as well.[22] God is paradoxical [amazing] in diverse ways, from acts of creation (Psalm 139:14; Ben Sira 43:25) to deeds of deliverance (Ps. 31:21, 118:23; Wisdom of Solomon 5:2, 19:5; III Maccabees 6:33; IV Macc. 4:14), and from love of the righteous (Ps. 17:7) to punishment of the wicked (Deuteronomy 28:59; Ben Sira 10:13; Wis. 16:16; II Macc. 3:30).

Post-biblical Jewish tradition contains two other comparable uses of παράδοξος. In Philo's Life of Moses 1:212, the Alexandrian philosopher calls the miracle of water from the rock (Ex. 17:1–7) paradoxical, and he goes on to explain that what is "extraordinary" for human beings is mere child's play for God. A more tenuous example is the only—and at best disputed—rabbinic use of פרדיכסוס. In the oft-repeated midrash, R. Isaac exclaims surprise that a villain in the Torah is called Laban (the "white," rather than Shaḥor, the "black.") R. Isaac thus points out how the Torah (i.e. God) hints that Laban is a deceiver.[23]

Early Judaic literature, in sum, employs the term παράδοξος generally to ascribe to God qualities beyond human comprehension. These paradoxes evoke responses such as awe, humility, wonder, amazement and thanksgiving. Perhaps typical is the attitude of the Psalmist (118.23f) as rendered by Symmachus: "This is the Lord's doing, it is marvelous [παράδοξος] in our eyes. This is the day which the Lord has made, let us exult and rejoice in it."

Paradox in the sense of religous amazement has been characteristic of Judaism since its earliest formulations. In our own time, both historians and theologians of Judaism have found the idea of paradox useful in the explication of basic Judaic myths, symbols, and rituals. Leo Baeck perhaps most consistently of all modern writers utilized paradox as a concept describing Judaism's religious character. Throughout a lifetime of scholarship Baeck maintained that Judaism is built upon three paradoxes: that God is immanent, yet transcendant; that human beings are free, yet dependent; and that life is valuable, yet finite. For Baeck, the Judaic response to life is two-fold; the created human encounters mystery, and the human creator encounters commandment.[24]

This paradox of the human condition and its relation to God and to history has found expression in exegeses of Judaism from its earliest philosophic descriptions until today. Josephus, the first historian of Judaism, points to the Pharisaic acknowledgment of both free-will and determinism, a postion later affirmed by scores of passages in rabbinic literature.[25] In the Middle Ages, all the major philosophers of Judaism struggled to assess the tension between God's will and human freedom.[26] And more recently, Joseph Soloveitchik has devoted one of his rare published works to a confession of the paradoxical faith he derives from the two creation stories in Genesis.[27] Rabbinic tradition, then, reflects continual experience and expression of paradox.

What is true of "classical" Judaism here may be applied *a fortiori* to Kabbalah, in which the whole world becomes a *"corpus symbolicum."* Indeed, Gershom Scholem has ably demonstrated the paradoxical quality of the very term Kabbalah; intimate, personal knowledge that is soteric as well as esoteric paradoxically acquires the name "tradition!" Scholem demonstrates how mysticism develops beyond "normal" Judaism, amplifying the paradoxes of God, human nature, and life that Baeck describes.[28]

For the kabbalist, tension between God's nearness and distance is expressed in the doctrines of *zimzum* and the *sefirot. Creatio ex nihilo* is discarded for creation out of chaos—the abyss between God and the world becomes an abyss within God. In the *Tree of Life* of Hayyim Vital, moreover, *zimzum* is a free act of love that paradoxically unleashes God's powers of stern judgment. Similarly, the Sabbatean concept of "holy sin" illustrates how the mystery of faith is expressed in utterly strange aggadah and bizarre halakhah. So too, Hasidism embraces the notion that communion with God occurs in profane settings; thus the Baal Shem Tov argues that "small talk with one's neighbor can be the vehicle of deep meditation."[29]

These brief comments are construed to introduce, rather than survey, paradoxical elements in classical and mystical Judaism. Historians of religion already have observed that concepts of God, Torah, and Israel set Jewish tradition apart from others. The task that remains is to elucidate how this mythic structure and its derivative symbols and rituals embrace and refine paradoxes present in all of religious life. In this endeavor those who seek wisdom are like those whose quest is for revelation—both labor with the paradox that the human mind is limited by the human condition.[30]

NOTES

1. Thanks are due to the editors for their kind invitation to participate in this venture, and to my colleagues Professors Robert Jones, Dewey Wallace, Alf Hiltebeitel, John Ziolkowski, Robert Hadley, and Ormond Seavey, and my friend Dr. Daniel Polish, for their helpful suggestions.

2. My teacher, Jacob Neusner, has written extensively on the place of Judaic Studies within the History of Religions field. See, e.g., his *The Academic Study of Judaism. Essays and Reflections* (N.Y.: Ktav, 1975) and *The Academic Study of Judaism. Second Series* (N.Y.: Ktav, 1977). See also David Blumenthal, "Where Does 'Jewish Studies' Belong?" *Journal of the American Academy of Religion* 44:3 (Fall, 1976): 535–546, and Jonathan Z. Smith, "Sacred Persistence: Towards a Redefinition of Canon," in William Scott Green, ed., *Approaches to Ancient Judaism: Theory and Practice* (Missoula, Montana: Scholars Press, 1978): 11–28, esp. pp. 11–12.

3. Joseph M. Kitagawa, "The History of Religions in America," and Wilfred Cantwell Smith, "Comparative Religion: Whither—and Why?" in Mircea Eliade and Joseph M. Kitagawa, eds. *The History of Religions. Essays in Methodology* (Chicago: Univ. of Chicago Press, 1959): 1–30, 31–58. Frederick J. Streng, *Understanding Religious Life* (Encino, Calif.: Dickenson, 1969): 1–65. Cf. Paul Ramsey and John Wilson, eds. *The Study of Religion in Colleges and Universities* (Princeton: Princeton Univ. Press, 1970); Claude Welch, *Graduate Education in Religion* (Missoula, Montana: Univ. of Montana Press, 1971); and Claude Welch, *Religion in the Undergraduate Curriculum* (Washington: Assoc. of American Colleges, 1972).

4. Van Austin Harvey, *The Historian and the Believer* (N.Y.: Macmillan, 1966). Bernard Meland, *The Secularization of Modern Cultures* (N.Y.: Oxford Univ. Press, 1966).

5. Meland, p. 110.

6. Harvey, p. 204.

7. Harvey, p. 55. See also Harvey Cox, *The Secular City* (N.Y.: Macmillan, 1979), and Mary Douglas, *Natural Symbols* (N.Y.: Random House, 1973): 19–39. Douglas states (p. 36), "Secularization . . . is an age-old cosmological type, a product of a defineable social experience, which need have nothing to do with urban life or modern science."

8. Ramsey and Wilson, p. 87. Hans Penner, "Reflections on an Ideology. Tradition vs. Modernity" (unpublished): 17.

9. "The History of Religions: Some Problems and Prospects," in Ramsey and Wilson, p. 276.

10. Hans Penner, "Is Phenomenology a Method for the Study of Religion?" (unpublished, 1969); 27ff.

11. "The Problem of the Double-Sense as Hermeneutic Problem and as Semantic Problem," in Joseph M. Kitagawa and Charles H. Long, eds., *Myths and Symbols. Studies in Honor of Mircea Eliade* (Chicago Univ. of Chicago Press, 1969): 79.

12. On paradox in religions generally, see the works of Douglas, Harvey, Meland, Penner, and Sullivan cited above, and those of Eliade and Wach cited below. On paradox in Christianity, see Edmund B. Keller, *Some Paradoxes of Paul* (N.Y.: Philosophical Library, 1974), and Charles W.F. Smith, *The Paradox of Jesus in the Gospels* (Philadelphia: Westminster Press, 1979). Linguistic and philosophic treatments include Marcus Tullius Cicero, *Paradoxica Stoicorum*, trans. by H. Rackham (Cambridge, Mass.: Harvard Univ. Press, 1962); Robert L. Martin, ed., *The Paradox of the Liar* (New Haven: Yale Univ. Press, 1970); John Wisdom, *Paradox and Discovery* (N.Y.: Philosophical Library, 1965); and Elizabeth Hawkins Wolgast, *Paradoxes of Knowledge* (Ithaca: Cornell Univ. Press, 1977). On literature, see Rosalie Littel Cole, *Paradoxica Epidemica. The Renaissance Tradition of Paradox* (Princeton: Princeton Univ. Press, 1966), and David Daiches Raphael, *The Paradox of Tragedy* (Bloomington: Indiana Univ. Press, 1960). On psychology, see Sigmund Freud, *New Introductory Lectures on Psychoanalysis*, trans. by James Strachey (N.Y.: Norton, 1964): 176. On law, see Sidney Hook, *The Paradoxes of Freedom* (Berkeley: Univ. of Calif. Press, 1962).

13. *The Quest: History and Meaning in Religion* (Chicago: Univ. of Chicago Press, 1969): 132f. Cf. Guilford Dudley, *Religion on Trial: Mircea Eliade and His Critics* (Philadelphia: Temple Univ. Press, 1977): 58ff., 139ff.

14. "Methodological Remarks on the Study of Religious Symbolism," in Eliade and Kitagawa, eds., *The History of Religions* (Chicago: Univ. of Chicago Press, 1959): 86–107, esp. 98–102.

15. *The Comparative Study of Religions* (N.Y.: Columbia Univ. Press, 1966): 61–63.

16. "Myth in Primitive Psychology," in *Magic, Science and Other Essays* (N.Y.: Doubleday, 1954): 146. See also Meland, p. 125; W.F. Albright, "The Human Mind in Action: Magic, Science and Religion," in *History, Archaeology, and Christian Humanism* (N.Y.: McGraw-Hill, 1964): 62–82; and H. Frankfort et.al., *Before Philosophy* (Harmondsworth: Penguin Books, 1949): 1–29.

17. *Asceticism and Eroticism in the Mythology of Śiva* (London: Oxford Univ. Press, 1973), esp. Ch. 1.

18. Op. cit., p. 78.

19. *The Quest*, p. 173.

20. S.V. παράδοξος in Henry George Liddell and Robert Scott, *A Greek-English Lexicon* (Oxford: The Clarendon Press, 1968), and Walter Bauer, *A Greek-English Lexicon of the New Testament and Other Early Christian Literature*, trans. and adapted by William F. Arndt and F. Wilbur Gingrich (Chicago: Univ. of Chicago Press, 1957).

21. Ex. 8:22; 9:4; 11:7; Dt. 28:59. Is. 9:6; 28:29; 29:14. Ps. 17:7; 31:21; 90:10; 118:23; 139:14; 145:5. Judith 13:13. Wis. 5:2; 16:16; 19:5. B.S. 10:13; 43:25. II Macc. 3:30; 9:24. III Macc. 2:9; 6:33. IV Macc. 4:14. Exceptions are Arist. 175, and IV Macc. 2:13.

22. Exceptions are Ex. 8:22; 9:4; 11:7.

23. Gen. R. 60:7. For a full discussion of text, variants and parallels see the edition of J. Theodore and Ch. Albeck (Jerusalem: Wahrmann Books, 1965): 647. Their preferred reading is παράδοξως, which agrees with Samuel Krauss, *Griechische und Lateinsiche Lehnwörter in Talmud, Midrasch und Targum* (Hildesheim: Georg Olm, 1964): 479. but Saul Lieberman, *Hellenism in Jewish Palestine* (N.Y.: Jewish Theological Seminary of America, 1962), 6, gives a clearer and more persuasive explanation of the passage by reading παράδοξοσ. Cf. Marcus Jastrow, *A Dictionary of the Targumim, The Talmud Babli and Yerushalmi, and the Midrashic Literature* (N.Y.: P. Shalom, 1967), 1215, where emendation to παραδεξιος is suggested.

24. Baeck's early work is represented by *The Essence of Judaism* (N.Y.: Schocken, 1948), and his later writings by *This People Israel: The Meaning of Jewish Existence* (N.Y.: Holt, Rinehart and Winston, 1965). See also Albert H. Friedlander, *Leo Baeck. Teacher of Theresienstadt* (N.Y.: Holt, Rinehart and Winston, 1968): 141–203; Eugene Borowitz, *A New Jewish Theology in the Making* (Philadelphia: Westminster, 1968): 83f.; William E. Kaufman, *Contemporary Jewish Philosophies* (N.Y.: Reconstructionist Press, 1976): 125–141.

25. See Josephus' B.J. 2:162–166; A.J. 13:171–173, and 18:12–25. The commentaries of H. St. John Thackeray, Ralph Marcus, and Louis Feldman in the Loeb Library editions review many of the well-known rabbinic parallels, as well as some important secondary sources. See also Eugene Mihaly, *Religious Experience in Judaism* (London: World Union for Progressive Judaism, 1957), esp. 3–28. Cf. Ephraim E. Urbach, *The Sages. Their Concepts and Beliefs*, trans. by Israel Abrahams (Jerusalem: Magnes, 1975): 255–285. On rhetorical paradox in rabbinic literature, see Henry A. Fischel, *Rabbinic Literature and Greco-Roman Philosophy* (Leiden: E.J. Brill, 1973): 70–73.

26. Alexander Altmann, "The Religion of the Thinkers: Free-will and Predestination in Saadia, Baḥya, and Maimonides," in S.D. Goitein, ed., *Religion in a Religious Age* (Cambridge, Mass.: Assoc. for Jewish Studies, 1974): 22–52. Cf. S.D. Goitein, "Religion in Everyday Life as Reflected in the Documents of the Cairo Geniza," Ibid., 3–18.

27. "The Lonely Man of Faith," in *Tradition* (Summer, 1956): 5–67. Cf. Abraham Joshua Heschel, *God in Search of Man* (N.Y.: Harper and Row, 1955): 191–199; and Emil Fackenheim, *Quest for Past and Future* (Boston: Beacon Press, 1970): 27–51.

28. On mysticism as a discrete stage in the historical development of Judaism, see Gershom Scholem, *Major Trends in Jewish Mysticism* (Jerusalem: Schocken, 1941): 1–39, esp. 7–8. On Baeck's own debt to Kabbalah, see Friedlander, pp. 154–169.

29. Gershom Scholem, *On the Kabbalah and its Symbolism* (N.Y.: Schocken, 1969): 87–117; and *The Messianic Idea in Judaism* (N.Y.: Schocken, 1971): 49–202, 239–281.

30. See Jacob Neusner, "Being Jewish" and *Studying About Judaism* (Atlanta: Emory Univ., 1977).

Barukh Kurzweil: The Sensibility of Weimar Germany in Ramat Gan[1]

James S. Diamond

B'nai B'rith Hillel Foundation
Washington University (St. Louis)

Barukh Kurzweil, (b. 1907) dean of Hebrew literati of the past generation, flourished as a critic for over thirty years, from 1941, when he published his first article on Agnon, until his death in 1972. During this period he wrote nearly four hundred essays, review-discussions, and causeries. The Kurzweil corpus is exceedingly rich and covers an exceptionally wide range of subjects and concerns: theoretical and practical criticism of Agnon, Bialik, Tshernichovski, Uri Zvi Greenberg, and most of the Hebrew poets and prose writers from the turn of the century until such Sabra figures of the late sixties as Amos Oz and A.B. Yehoshua; criticism of more than twenty major Europeans from Cervantes, Goethe, Stendhal, and Balzac through Tolstoy, Thomas Mann, Kafka, Hesse, Broch, Camus, Frisch, and Dürrenmatt; explorations of the theory of fiction, tragedy, and the modern theater; important critiques of modern Jewish and Zionist theology and philosophy in essays on Buber, Rosenzweig, Ahad ha-Am, Yitshak Breuer, and Gershom Scholem; and scores of polemical and satirical responses to the foibles, pretensions, designs and achievements of those who variously perturbed or opposed him and whom he chose to attack. Of this writing, about half has been collected into eight volumes with specially written prefaces that are indispensable sources for understanding Kurzweil; the remainder lies scattered throughout various newspapers and periodicals and would perhaps fill five or six more.[2]

Implicit in all his writings are two things that are of concern to us here: a consistent, though always developing, methodology, and a coherent theory of modernity. These two unite to allow Kurzweil to develop a theory of modern Hebrew literature and its relationship to the European tradition that is itself remarkably consistent and coherent. It is a serious misperception of Kurzweil to ignore the unity of conception and method that underlies his disparate articles, a mistake which a number of his detractors have made. They point to the fact that he never authored a sustained discussion of a subject or a problem which was not meant to appear in piecemeal fashion in the press as evidence that he was not a *bona fide* literary scholar but a high-grade journalist.

The truth is that if Kurzweil is anything other than a literary critic, he is a philosopher of Judaism, though not a systematic philosopher and certainly not a theologian. Kurzweil can be approached in this way and, from the esthetic standpoint, Schwarcz has laid out the first steps which any such study will have to traverse.[3] Nevertheless, considering that the bulk of Kurzweil's work overtly deals with literature, it is clear to me that if we wish to do it justice, we must apprehend it through literary categories.

In doing so we must not fail to recognize that Kurzweil brought to his reading a distinct hierarchy of esthetic criteria. These criteria are the result of a passionate commitment to specific cultural and religious values which were distilled from two sources: the Central European tradition, particularly the legacy of German classical humanism bequeathed by Goethe, and the German sensitivity to "*Sprachlichkeit*, the linguisticality of man's way of being,"[4] on the one hand; and the world-view of traditional Judaism of pre-Holocaust Central Europe on the other, particularly, but not exclusively, the neo-Orthodoxy that developed in Frankfurt.

The dialectic within and between these two sources enabled Kurzweil to attain to a view of modern Western literature, and modern Hebrew literature in particular, that is, to my mind, definitive and, within its frame of reference, unassailable. Most evaluations of Kurzweil are not only inaccurate in that they seek to measure Kurzweil by the wrong criteria; they are also misleading in castigating Kurzweil's criticism for its subjectivity and in suggesting that an objectively "correct" reading of and approach to Agnon, or anyone else, is possible. Kurzweil, I have concluded, must be understood not within the assumptions of the Anglo-American critical tradition of New Criticism, but within the framework

of Continental phenomenology, specifically that of German phenomenological hermeneutics and its particular epistemology, which attempts,
in its relation to the literary text, to transcend the accepted Cartesian
subject-object dualism. This is an intellectual tradition and a theory of
literature that, to the extent that they are even known, have not fared too
well in the American and Israeli literary worlds. Without taking them
into account Kurzweil is very much a closed book. The following is my
summary of his esthetic and critical philosophy.

I.

Literature is important principally as a discloser of truth about man,
as a human revelation of the human spirit, as the only full, satisfactory,
and dynamic answer to what is judged the most fundamental and pressing of all questions since the waning of the sacral middle ages: What is
man? Literature thus provides what neither philosophy, no matter how
anthropologically oriented it may be (viz., Scheler), nor history nor any
of the other humanistic and social sciences can ever tell us. Further, it
furnishes us with more insight into reality than the natural sciences.
This is because instead of breaking down reality and dissecting it or
manipulating it as an inert object for human control, literature, because
it is art, re-constitutes polysemous reality into a wholeness that relates
man to the cosmos in a way that transcends the Cartesian dualism of
subject-object. In other words, literature, like all art, furnishes man with
that fullness of being that is born of the dialogue between "I and Thou"
as Buber developed it.

This, in turn, is because the act of literary creation is itself the trans-
mutation into language of the encounter between the "I" of the literary
artist and the "Thou" of his world (i.e., his society, his tradition). Dilthey's theory of art as *Erlebnis* is the operative one here, and I have
emphasized, in line with recent Dilthey studies, that this is not an historical, biographical, or psychological matter but an existential-phenome-
nological one.[5] Literature is important because it alone, at its most
sublime, can furnish wholeness of perception and certainty to man now
that religious faith is no longer available, and it must be read to recover
from it this vision, *Anschaung* in the Goethean sense, and not as an
illustration of some arbitrarily defined *Zeitgeist* or as a document of
Geistesgeschichte.[6]

Literary criticism thus partakes of the same process as literary crea-

tion, only it does so from the side of the discerning reader, not of the
literary artist. Criticism is primarily interpretation of the literary text and
evaluation of it in the light of the total human situation of which that
text is a part. Criticism aims at laying bare the *Erlebnis* of a work
through the act of *verstehen*. Such a view has its roots in the hermeneutic theory of Schleiermacher, Dilthey, and Heidegger and it has been
developed in recent years by Gadamer. It sees the critic in a way very different from other approaches such as formalism, structuralism, and New
Criticism. I have brought to bear some evidence that at bottom this difference is an epistemological one. The latter approaches rest on an Aristotelian realism whereby the literary text is seen to exist as an objective
entity susceptible to anatomization and analysis; hermeneutics as understood by Kurzweil and German critical theory rests on the mode of cog-
nition developed by Husserl, whereby the literary text is not reified but
perceived in total subjectivity, out of the "transcendental ego" of phenomenology. More than anything else a literary work contains a human
voice and the task of the critic is to hear that voice and render it audible.
Criticism, then, is as much an art as poesy or narrative, and any attempt
to construe it as a science subverts it. The kind of hermeneutic interpretation Kurzweil espouses seeks after the subjectively—but not arbitrarily—defined truth of a work and renounces the problem of validation.
Kurzweil is much closer to Hans-Georg Gadamer's *Wahrheit und
Methode* than to E. D. Hirsch Jr.'s *Validity in Interpretation.*[7]

As a phenomenological critic Kurzweil seeks to penetrate to the heart
of a work, to reduce it to its undeniable essence. As a hermeneutician he
operates in terms of a cognitive and perceptual circle whereby what he
regards as the essence of a work, its "intrinsic coherence," is related to
even as it is determined by the essence of the total *oeuvre* of its creator,
which essence in turn implies and is implied by the *eidos* of the society
and culture of which he is a part. Kurzweil reduced the problem of
western culutre to the problem of man or, more accurately, to the problem of a proper relationship between man and society. He posits a kind
of spiritual Golden Age when religious faith and practice bespoke a
sacral existence in which this relationship was in balance, and he sees
modernity, beginning about the time of the Renaissance and intensifying with the Enlightenment, as a loss of faith in the living God and the
consequent enfranchisement of man as the ultimate power, throwing the
entire relationship out of balance. This process is commonly termed

secularization but Kurzweil understands this in metaphysical, not socio-logical, terms. Its culmination has come in the twentieth century, "the last days of mankind," when the full absurdity and horror of man, living beyond good and evil, outside the relationship to any values be they of an absolute God or of a relativistic humanism, has manifested itself in two World Wars and the imminent prospect of a final apocalypse.

Modern literature, regardless of its genre or language, of necessity reflects some aspect of this process. Kurzweil sees it all as one large metaphysical field and so is able to relate the various European traditions to it in spite of the fact that he recognizes the individual nature of each. In actuality, however, Kurzweil is not open to substantial areas of modern literature; his holism causes him to see the drama solely in terms of tragedy, where he follows Hegel more than Aristotle, and leads him away from the bulk of modern poetry. Essentially it is fiction that is his focus, but even here he is primarily concerned with the French and German novel from Goethe to World War I.

Modern Hebrew literature is read in the very same way. This allows Kurzweil to account for the manner in which it is linked to the total field of modern literature as well as at the same time to point to its distinctive features. His work here represents a development of Klausner's ideas that secularism is the essential quality of modern Hebrew *belles lettres*— and that their *terminus a quo* is the Enlightenment of the late eigh-teenth century. Kurzweil determines that the absurdity of the human condition as depicted in the literature of modern Europe is presaged by the Jewish condition as modern Hebrew literature at about the turn of the century begins to present it. This is because the collapse of the humanistic ideals of the *Haskalah*, on top of the earlier disintegration of Jewish religious faith, makes the modern Jew a paradigm, if not a har-binger, of the metaphysical nakedness that would pervade all of Europe in the wake of World War I. Kurzweil's readings of Bialik, Brenner, and Tshernichovski are explications of this idea; his interpretation of Agnon and Greenberg affirms the possibility that the dynamic of modernity in the present can be denied and transcended by envisioning a re-sacralized future worthy of the Jewish past; and his rejection of the post-1948 Sabra writers stems specifically from what he sees as their refusal to accept the meta-historical realm, their consequent denial of the ontolog-ical status of the Jewish people, and their resultant embrace of a literary modernism bereft of all cultural values.

II.

This remarkably coherent mosaic of thought and criticism did not come about in any particular stages over Kurzweil's thirty years as a critic. In reviewing his career we find no substantial revisions or dramatic reversals of position. Rather, the outline of the mosaic is already quite visible in his doctoral thesis of 1933,[8] and the treatment of modern Hebrew literature that began after the encounter with Agnon's *Ore'ah natah lalun* in 1939-40 represents but an expansion, not a re-design, of the total structure. In the course of the years one does see a gradual refinement of the total picture; more and more pieces are put in as Kurzweil responds to developments in esthetic and critical theory in Europe and America, absorbing some of them and repudiating others. This is why it has made no sense to deal with the Kurzweil corpus developmentally.

Kurzweil's criticism invites analysis from a different perspective; it coheres only inside the framework imposed by its creator. That is to say, it is most vulnerable outside the pre-suppositions and postulates on which it rests. Once we grant Kurzweil these I think it becomes quite difficult to deny that he has, as Y. Talmon has said of his views on Jewish nationalism, "an irrefutable and hermetically closed case." But no less significant is Talmon's subsequent comment:

> That is the strength of the "case" and that is its weakness, for life is not as logical as logic. Certainly we should believe, but what if we are unable to? And what if faith does not come by itself? It cannot be brought into being by any artificial means [or] by fiat.[9]

As I have shown, in spite of all its claims at an analysis free of pre-suppositions, the phenomenological method has no reference to that which lies beyond what is grasped out of transcendental subjectivity. All Kurzweil's reading flows out of certain specific pre-suppositions about man, God, religion, the Jewish people, and language, and he cannot free himself from these in his criticism. But the pre-suppositions themselves are certainly open to question.

Philosophically, Kurzweil can be seen to combine the legacy of German idealism with German existentialism.[10] He appropriates and synthesizes various elements in the tradition that runs from Goethe through Nietzsche, Dilthey, Buber and Heidegger. The polarity between *Geist* and *Leben*, the central issue of *Lebensphilosophie*, is a fundamental *Erlebnis* out of which his criticism proceeds. Isaiah Tishbi, in an exchange with Kurzweil over the latter's handling of Gershom Scholem and Sabbatianism, comes to wonder "what is the meaning of the satanic quality that pervades Kurzweil's articles?" His observation tells us more about Kurzweil than he might have realized:

> As an authority on demonology I can flatly say: the deep-seated demonism is a basis for his life and work. It is this which has given rise to the bugaboo of making Judaism into demonology, and it is from it that the many weeds that grow in his articles spring.[11]

The demons that torment Kurzweil are the same ones he sees tormenting Faust and all his descendents: individualism, the insatiable demands of the "I" that now understands itself to be living in a universe devoid of an "Eternal Thou" or even a transitory one. There is a distinctly "Promethean" quality in Kurzweil himself, and Abramson has shown the connections between the "true critic" as Kurzweil defines him and the "great individual" of modern fiction that so enchants him.[12] Indeed, an intensive reading of his writings suggests to me that Kurzweil the critic, in a subtle way, insinuates himself as a type of Nietzschean *Übermensch*. It is on this basis that we are really asked to trust his subjective judgments and to accept the violence of his engagement with life.

> Kurzweil's criticism is superb when it is destructive ... It is when he attempts to be constructive that he falls victim to the same wishful thinking which he so skillfully condemns.[13]

Kurzweil is a Nietzschean in another sense too: in his understanding of what modernity is.

> As the man who acts must, according to Goethe, be without a conscience, he must also be without knowledge; he forgets everything in order to be able to do something; he is unfair toward what lies behind and knows only one right, the right of what is now coming into being as the result of his own action.[14]

Modernity in these words is not a matter of fashions, movements, or manifestoes but, as De Man brilliantly shows, the antithesis to history.

This, he feels, is what Neitzsche was trying to teach all along: that there is a fundamental opposition between history and life.

> "Life" is conceived not just in biological but in temporal terms as the ability to *forget* whatever precedes a present situation . . . Modernity exists in the form of a desire to wipe out whatever came earlier in the hope of reaching at last a point that could be called a true present, a point of origin that marks a new departure. This combined interplay of a deliberate forgetting with an action that is also a new origin reaches the full power of the idea of modernity. Thus defined, modernity and history are diametrically opposed to each other in Nietzsche's text. Nor is there any doubt as to his commitment to modernity, the only way to reach the meta-historical realm in which the rhythm of one's existence coincides with that of the eternal return.[15]

This is exactly Kurzweil's perspective. It is this conception of modernity that explains why he defines the modern crisis as one of belief. For if modernity means forgetfulness, then "forgetfulness is the mother of denial,"[16] a line Kurzweil quotes very often. For Kurzweil as a Jew, history can and must be escaped not by forgetting it but by transcending it; the rhythm of one's Jewish existence coincides with that of the synoptic vision.

III.

As an intellectual of pre-World War II Central Europe, Kurzweil from a distance can be seen to bear general resemblances to three other "Goetheans" of that time and place—Georg Lukács, Karl Kraus and Walter Benjamin. Like Lukács he structures his reading around an Absolute; but instead of dialectical materialism he weds existentialism to German idealism. Like Kraus he is an epigone, a stranger to twentieth century reality, imbued with the same sensibility and beset by the same obsessions.

> I was born in the Hapsburg Empire, before the First World War. I write because most of the authors I have loved have already died, and because most of the authors I do not like are alive and continue to write. I write because when I was young I had the strength to hate bad books; now that I am old I am sick of hating bad books. But they are sent to my home, fill up my apartment, and are piled high over the good books which are being choked and which beg mercy from me because they do not want to die.[17]

Like Kraus, Kurzweil

> exposed an age which had lost all faith in absolute values and reminded his readers of ages in which life had not been totally subjugated to commercial purposes, but he did not attempt to show how man could introduce meaning into the modern world. Kraus's message was essentially one of despair. According to him, the world was facing its end.[18]

What is true of Kurzweil is what Janik and Toulmin say of Kraus: "It is a central fact about Karl Kraus that the man and his work are unclassifiable."[19] I regard Kurzweil more or less as a literary critic and refer to his work as literary criticism, which may not be incorrect, but it ought to be noted that his is a criticism that is *sui generis*, in which the boundaries of esthetic theory, textual explication, culturism, and publicism freely intermingle. Kurzweil's singularity comes from the same soil and can be formulated in the same terms as Walter Benjamin's: "Critique is concerned with the truth content of a work of art, the commentary with its subject matter."[20] In this generation it is George Steiner who most closely approximates this approach. In his impassioned espousal of the "old criticism," in his critique of structural linguistics and in such books as *Language and Silence, The Death of Tragedy,* and *In Bluebeard's Castle,* Steiner comes close to what Kurzweil is saying.[21]

What really links Kurzweil with Kraus and Benjamin, however, is what Hannah Arendt describes as "the Jewish question." This she notes as a specific problem of the Jewish intellectual of German-speaking Central Europe before World War II, and one that has been forgotten

> although one still encounters it occasionally in the language of the older generation of German Zionists whose thinking habits derive from the first decade of this century. Besides, it never was anything but the concern of the Jewish intelligentsia and had no significance for the majority of Central European Jewry . . . [But] no matter how insignificant this problem may appear to us in the face of what actually happened later, we cannot disregard it here, for neither Benjamin nor Kafka nor Karl Kraus can be understood without it.[22]

Nor, I would add, can Kurzweil. The "problem" as Arendt describes it has to do with the alienation of these Jewish intellectuals from the Jewish bourgeoisie whom they regarded as living in an "isolation from reality staged with all the devices of self-deception";[23] the "question" itself is one of finding authentic content for one's life as a Jew beyond religious faith. The only available options for such Jews were Zionism or Marxism; "both were escape routes from illusion into reality, from mendacity and self-deception to an honest existence."[24] Both, we may say, supplied the "wholeness" and certainty that religion or metaphysics once did. Now unlike Gershom Scholem, for example, or Lukács, who respectively chose Zionism and Marxism, neither Kraus, Benjamin, or Kurzweil was able to accept either of them wholeheartedly.[25] In this respect, I consider Kurzweil's relationship to Zionism of the same order as Benjamin's to Marxism: there seems to be an apparent embrace but in actuality there is an ambivalence and a thoroughly selective, idiosyncratic appropriation of the ideology. Arendt points out that the "Jewish question" was accompanied by a corresponding crisis of language; the relationship to German as an alien tongue was as problematical as not writing at all. She notes the same despair in all these men:

> The most clear-sighted among them were led by their personal conflicts to a much more general and more radical problem, namely, to questioning the relevance of the Western tradition as a whole . . . Walter Benjamin knew that the break in tradition and the loss of authority which occurred in his lifetime were irreparable, and he concluded that he had to discover new ways of dealing with the past.[26]

So did Barukh Kurzweil. The essay "Self-hate in Jewish Literature,"[27] where he argues that what appears as Jewish self-hate in Brenner, Weininger, Kafka and, above all, Kraus is really an inchoate longing for a higher reality, shows a revealing abundance of intuitive empathy. Hillel Weiss is quite correct in calling attention to the plethora of "meta" prefixes in Kurzweil's writing—"meta-historic," "meta-temporal," "meta-satirical," and his conclusion is noteworthy:

> All these are testimony to Kurzweil's yearning for another reality. He tried to glimpse something beyond reality and above it, as a partner in the tireless struggle of the great artists.[28]

In spite of the facts that he was closer to Jewish sources and less "assimilated" than they ever were, that he professed *halakhic* observance, and that he taught at a "religious" university, I have no hesitation in saying that Kurzweil at the core of his being has more in common with Kraus and Benjamin than with more ostensibly rooted "Jewish" figures. The trajectory of his life and thought is clearly "from vision to the absurd." If he lived like the narrator of Agnon's *Sefer hama'asim*, he died in a Brennerian nullity.[29]

Nevertheless, having defined the European roots, I do not wish to deny or overlook the specifically Jewish roots to Kurzweil's criticism. The decisive difference about Kurzweil is that for him Jewish religious faith and tradition were never ruled out *ab initio* as potential wellsprings of metaphysical certainty as they were by Kraus and Benjamin. All Kurzweil's struggles are within a particular Jewish context. In comparison with him, Kraus and Benjamin were indeed rootless cosmopolitans. But the Jewish nature of Kurzweil's work is *ipso facto* much harder to pin down. As Peter Salm has observed:

> Studies dealing with literary theory call for a more international point of view than those dealing directly with literature ... Poetic and aesthetic theories are justly expected to transcend the special problems of nationality and language.[30]

And the poetic principles of Kurzweil's criticism, as we have seen, derive directly out of European esthetics.

Still I would argue, however speculatively, that there may be a number of Jewish ingredients subtly inter-mixed here. Kurzweil's steadfast refusal to concede the autonomy of the esthetic domain, more than it may be an affirmation of the Kantian ideal of the integration of the beautiful with the good and the true, may be an unwitting adumbration of the classical Jewish fear of the idolatrous possibilities of beauty, especially man-made beauty, when it is made an end in and of itself.[31] In the same way his attitude to the literary text, beyond its grounding in phenomenological hermeneutics, can be seen to have affinities with the attitude of the rabbis to the Biblical text. It was, after all, Buber's approach to the Biblical text that Kurzweil says first opened him up to the art of all reading. In its larger sense what Kurzweil ultimately gives us is an extended *midrash* on modernism, modern man and the modern Jew, a *midrash* which, like its rabbinic forbears, tells us more about its creator than about the text. Criticism in general has been called "a fiction on fiction,"[32] and more than once has attention been called to the manner in which Kurzweil's assumes an independent existence, attached sometimes quite tenuously to the work on which it is based.[33] The most theoretical question that this body of criticism stimulates is the same question that the prose of Agnon and the poetry of Greenberg raise: do they represent a groping toward a particularly Jewish esthetic? Can we even speak of such a thing? It has been noted that there is a correlation between the philosophical and epistemological approaches dominant in a culture and the prevailing critical tendencies.[34] Anglo-American criticism generally is rooted in realism and empiricism and looks for analysis and validity; Continental criticism comes out of phenomenology and existentialism and strives after feeling and depth. Can we, then, speak of a distinctively Hebrew criticism, one grounded in pre-suppositions and an epistemology indigenous to Judaism?[35] The question is more easily raised than answered. In any case I do not claim that Kurzweil's criticism, whose Continental nature is clear, signifies any answer. But it does force the question in a substantial way.[36]

IV.

R. P. Blackmur has written:

> The worst evil of fanatic falsification—of arrogant irrationality and barbarism in all its forms—arises when a body of criticism is governed by an *idée fixe*, a really exaggerated heresy, when a notion of genuine but small scope is taken literally as of universal application. This is the body of tendentious criticism where, since something is assumed proved before the evidence is in, distortion, vitiation, and absolute assertion become supreme virtues . . . But even here, in this worst order of criticism, there is a taint of legitimacy. Once we reduce, in a man like Irving Babbitt, the magnitude of application of such notions as the inner check and the higher will, which were for Babbitt paramount—that is, when we determine the limits within which he really worked—then the massive erudition and acute observation with which his work is packed become permanently available.[37]

This seems to me, when applied to Kurzweil and when such key notions as secularism, the demonic, and primordial wholeness are substituted, to be what a final judgment about him from a minimalist position would sound like.

A maximalist one would go further. He would say, as I would like to, that the central issue of Kurzweil's work is hardly of "small scope." Kurzweil asks the large questions of literature and he therefore should not be called to account if he gives large answers. An encounter with his criticism, with all its limitations and inadequacies, is a unique engagement with the ultimate issues of literature and modernism, a disquieting induction to life and the utter earnestness of the human and the Jewish struggle. It is difficult to read in quite the same way after him. George Steiner says of Lukács:

> It is not the particular omission or persuasive insight that constitutes Lukács' essential quality. His greatness is a matter of inner stance, of *tone*. Wherever we accede to this large enterprise of criticism and philosophic argument, the sense of a supreme seriousness, of a complete trust in the life of the imagination and of thought, overwhelms.[38]

With justice can the same be said of Barukh Kurzweil. If literary criticism is indeed a series of various frameworks and languages devised by critics and, therefore, the individual critic is only as good as the way he uses what he devises, then Kurzweil must be judged a great one.

The Israeli critical scene today, in spite of the proliferation of technical prowess, conspicuously lacks a figure of Kurzweil's mien. It misses him and is all the poorer for his absence. To be sure, his disciples attempt to continue his teaching but most of them are under no illusion that they can do this in quite the same way. What came together in Kurzweil was an induplicable blending of background, temperament, and innate ability. In general, the scope of literary study in Israel seems much reduced now and Israeli critics appear to be content to work within it and answer smaller questions, albeit with proficiency. But when the time will come when this scope and these questions will not satisfy, when once again the fundamental questions of modern literature, especially modern Hebrew literature, will come to the fore, Kurzweil's contribution will have to be dealt with. The eight volumes of his work, and more as they are re-claimed from the pages of fading newspapers and periodicals, will, I am certain, stand, indispensable and unavoidable to all who seek to understand what the word "modern" means.

NOTES

1. This essay is drawn from the final chapter of my doctoral dissertation, *The Literary Criticism of Barukh Kurzweil: A Study in Hebrew-European Literary Relationships*, Indiana University, 1978.

2. References to Kurzweil available in the volumes of collected writings are given in accordance with the following key:

MR[1]   *Masekhet haroman: shenei mahzorei masot 'al Shemuel Yosef 'Agnon ve'al toldot haroman haeiropi [The Course of the Novel: Two Series of Essays on S.Y. Agnon and on The History of European Novel].* Tel Aviv: Schocken Publishing Co., 1953.

S   *Sifrutenu hahadashah—hemshekh o mahapekha? [Our Modern Literature—Continuity Or Revolt?].* Jerusalem and Tel Aviv: Schocken Publishing Co., 1959. Third Enlarged Edition, 1971.

J   *Bema 'avak 'al 'erkei hayahadut [In The Struggle For Jewish Values].* Jerusalem and Tel Aviv: Schocken Publishing Co., 1969.

L   *leNokhah hamevukhah haruhanit shel dorenu - pirkei hagut uvikoret [Facing The Spiritual Perplexity Of Our Time].* Edited with an Introduction by Moshe Schwarcz. Ramat Gan: B. Kurzweil Memorial Foundation, Bar Ilan University, 1976.

Where an article by Kurzweil has not yet been collected, I refer to its original place of publication.

3. See Moshe Schwarcz, "Barukh Kurzweil kehogeh de'ot shel hayahadut," *ha'Arets*, June 13, 1975. Equally crucial is Schwarcz's "Hanahot estetiyot bemif'al habikoret shel Barukh Kurzweil, *Sefer Barukh Kurzweil [Barukh Kurzweil Memorial Volume]*, Schocken Publishing Co., Tel Aviv and Ramat Gan, 1975, pp. 375–397. Both essays are reprinted in Moshe Schwarcz, *Hagut yehudit nokhah hatarbut hakelalit*, Schocken Publishing Co., Tel Aviv, 1976, pp. 165–224.

4. Richard E. Palmer, *Hermeneutics: Interpretation Theory in Schleiermacher, Dilthey, Heidegger, and Gadamer*, Northwestern U. Press, Evanston, 1969, p. 155.

5. See Kurt Müller-Vollmer, *Towards A Phenomenological Theory of Literature: A Study of Wilhelm Dilthey's Poetik*, Mouton & Co., The Hague, 1963.

6. See Erich Heller, *The Disinherited Mind: Essays in Modern German Literature and Thought*, n.p., New York, 1952, pp. 14ff and 65.

7. Gadamer's work has been translated into English by Garrett Barden and John Cumming as *Truth and Method*, The Seabury Press, New York, 1975.

8. *Die Bedeutung bürgerlicher und künstlerischer Lebensform für Goethes Leben und Werk dargestellt am Faust 1. Teil*, Limburg a. d. Lahn, 1933, 114 pp. (This was one of the last, if not the last, doctorates awarded to a Jew before the onset of the Nazi regime.)

9. Response to Kurzweil's paper in the symposium "haLe'umiyut hayehudit bizemanenu," (Jerusalem: World Jewish Congress, 1961), p. 34.

10. See Kurzweil's discussion of the collection of philosophical essays presented to S. H. Bergmann *Hagut*, L, pp. 140–147. See also Moshe Schwarcz, *Hagut yehudit nokhah hatarbut hakelalit* (Tel Aviv: Schocken Publishing Co, 1976), pp. 196–201.

11. "Heker hademonologiah uma'asim demoniyim," *Davar*, Sept. 20, 1957.

12. Ya'akov Abramson, "Sipurei Barukh Kurzweil vezikot hagomelin beineihem levein masotav," (Ramat Gan: unpublished M.A. Thesis, Bar-Ilan University, 1974), pp. 83–87.

13. Ezra Spicehandler, review of S, *Judaism*, X/2 (Spring, 1961), p. 188.

14. F. Nietzsche, "Vom Nutzen und Nachteil der Historie für das Leben," *Unzeitgemässe Betrachtungen*, II, Karl Schlechta, ed., *Werke* 1 (Munich: 1954), p. 216, quoted in Paul de Man, "Literary History and Literary Modernity," Morton W. Bloomfield, ed., *In Search of Literary Theory* (Ithaca and London: Cornell University Press, 1972), p. 245.

15. de Man, op. cit., pp. 243, 245f.

16. Uri Zvi Greenberg, *Rehovot hanahar*, (Jerusalem and Tel Aviv: Schocken Publishing Co., 1953).

17. "haSusah haapokaliptit tsohelet betraklin hasipur hayisra'eli o 'ergat hakisufim shel yisra'el ha'ovedet linesikhim unesikhot," *Ha'arets*, May 31, 1968. Of Kraus, Wilma A. Iggers writes: "Apart from a few isolated instances, Kraus objected very much to the literary movements which continued to spring up throughout his lifetime and was proud to be one of the despised *Epigonen*." *Karl Kraus: A Viennese Critic of the Twentieth Century* (The Hague: Martinus Nijhoff, 1967), p. 27.

18. Iggers, op. cit., p. 228.

19. A. Janik and S. Toulmin, *Wittgenstein's Vienna* (New York: Simon and Schuster, 1973), p. 80.

20. Quoted from Benjamin's *Goethe's Elective Affinities* in Hannah Arendt's introduction to *Illuminations*, Hannah Arendt, ed., Harry Zohn, trans. (London: Jonathan Cape, 1970), p. 4.

21. In *Tolstoy or Dostoevsky: An Essay in the Old Criticism* (New York: Alfred A. Knopf, 1959), Steiner writes: "The old criticism is engendered by admiration. It sometimes steps back from the text to look upon moral purpose. It thinks of literature as existing not in isolation but as central to the play of historical and political energies. Above all, the old criticism is philosophic in range and temper" (p. 6). In the preface to *Extra-Territorial: Papers on Literature and the Language Revolution* (New York: Atheneum, 1971), Steiner directs American criticism to the very sources from which Kurzweil's springs: "I have in mind the phenomenological tradition of Dilthey and Husserl with its stress on the historicity of speech acts, on the time boundedness and mutations of even the most elemental of semantic modes. I am thinking of the investigations into language by Heidegger, of Paul Ricoeur's *De l'Interpretation*, and of the whole hermeneutic approach now so lively in France, Italy and Germany . . . Cut off from these philosophic traditions, contemptuous of the uncertainties and transcendental intimations which they enact, the new linguistics, with its declared meta-mathematical ideals, runs the risk of a powerful triviality . . . The peremptory naivete of a good deal of transformational generative work makes impossible any real access to language when it is in a condition of maximal concentration, when, as Heidegger says, language is total being . . . It is not in transformational grammars, however, but in hermeneutics, in the *Sprachphilosophie* of Walter Benjamin with its unashamed roots in Kabbalistic thought, that the implications of Babel are grasped" (pp. x f.).

22. Hannah Arendt, introduction to Walter Benjamin's *Illuminations*, op. cit., pp. 29f.

23. Ibid., p. 32.

24. Ibid., p. 34.

25. In this connection see Scholem's two letters to Benjamin of Feb. 20, 1930, and March 30, 1931, in *Devarim bego* (Tel Aviv: Am Oved Publishers, Ltd., 1976), pp. 146–151. See also Scholem's insightful paper "Walter Benjamin," *Leo Baeck Institute Yearbook*, X (1965), pp. 117–136.

26. Arendt, op. cit., pp. 37f.

27. S, pp. 331–401.

28. "haYesod hatragi bemishnato shel Barukh Kurzweil," *Yedi'ot aharonot*, Sept. 22, 1972.

29. The resemblances here to the life and death of such more apparently marginal German Jews as Weininger, Toller, and Stefan Zweig cannot be entirely coincidental. See the treatment of these figures in Solomon Liptzin, *Germany's Stepchildren* (Philadelphia: The Jewish Publication Society, 1944).

30. *Three Modes of Criticism: The Literary Theories of Scherer, Walzel, and Staiger* (Cleveland: Case Western Reserve University Press, 1968), p. 1.

31. For a discussion of this issue with important bibliographical material see Steven S. Schwarzschild, "The Legal Foundation of Jewish Aesthetics," *The Journal of Aesthetic Education,* IX/1 (January, 1975), pp. 29–42.

32. See John Caviglia, *Flaubert and Leopoldo Alas: An Essay in Comparative Anatomy,* unpublished doctoral thesis, Indiana University, 1970), p. 2.

33. See S. Alonim's review of MR[1] "Bikoret hai hanose et 'atsmo," *Ha'arets,* Jan. 8, 1954.

34. Elder Olsen has observed that "a given comprehensive philosophy invariably develops a certain view of art." (Quoted in R. Wellek, *Concepts of Criticism,* New Haven and London, 1963, p. 316.) See especially Neal Oxenhandler, "Ontological Criticism in America and France," *Modern Language Review,* LV (1960), pp. 17–23.

35. Northrop Frye suggests that criticism must derive its social context from what he calls the "myth of concern" of a society of a people, that "magic circle drawn around a culture; . . . literature develops historically within a limited orbit of language, reference, allusion, beliefs, transmitted and shared tradition." ("The Critical Path: An Essay on the Social Context of Literary Criticism," Morton W. Bloomfield, ed., *In Search of Literary Theory,* op. cit., p. 105.) Kurzweil's criticism would be very close to a reading of literature from out of what he sees as the Jewish myth of concern. The implicit influence of Tillich on Frye is clear here, but it may also in a less conscious way have permeated Kurzweil.

36. I do not deal with the possibility of holding up Kurzweil as an example of the "German-Jewish symbiosis" that some scholars frequently discuss. Kurzweil himself had great reservations about this concept (see J, pp. 279–281) and its value as a cultural or literary indicator seems to me to be too problematical to be of any use.

37. "A Critic's Job of Work," quoted from *Language as Gesture* (1935) in Morris Weitz, ed., *Problems in Aesthetics: An Introductory Book of Readings* (London: The Macmillan Co., second edition, 1970), p. 802.

38. Preface to Georg Lukács, *Realism in Our Time: Literature and the Class Struggle* (New York: Harper and Row, 1964), p. 15.

Einstein
and the Idea of Freedom*

Isaac Franck

Kennedy Institute of Ethics
Georgetown University
Washington, D.C.

Albert Einstein's life and work reflected, in microcosm, the perennial and ever-reenacted struggle for freedom of the human spirit on the stage of recorded human history. In Einstein's case this dramatic struggle revolved around two pivotal and existentially inescapable aspects of the man: Einstein the scientist, and Einstein the Jew. The two are inseparable. They are inextricably intertwined, not only by virtue of being aspects of the same person, but also, and perhaps even more, because they were welded together by features of the cultural milieu into which he was thrust for the greater part of his career; by the cross-winds of doctrine and dogma that buffeted him thoughout the midspan of his life; and by the unspeakably tragic events, unleashed by the advent of Nazism, that overtook and engulfed the Jews of Europe in the twelve fateful years of Hitler's Third Reich.

In the course of this year's Centennial observances, Einstein's amazing achievements in physical science are being celebrated throughout the world. But it was only a very short time ago that these same achievements were denounced and vilified as putative exemplars of false, fraud-

* A briefer version of this paper was presented at the Smithsonian Institution, in Washington, D.C., on March 29, 1979, as the concluding lecture in a series of six by philosophers and scientists on the subject "Einstein: Master Cosmologist and Humanist," in observance of the Einstein Centennial.

ulent *"Jewish* science," which allegedly had, as its conspiratorial goal, the pollution and destruction of the purity of *"Aryan* science." These attacks on Einstein, in which German "scientists" were among the major actors, epitomized the Nazi assault on the freedom of scientific inquiry, on the freedom of the intellect, and on the very concept of objective truth, an assault that led inexorably to the ghastly culmination of the gas chambers and crematoria.

His vicissitudes not withstanding, or perhaps because of them, Einstein had a wonderful sense of humor; an understated, self-effacing, self-deprecating kind of humor. He was a supreme ironist, perceiving with shrewd, olympian insight many of the follies of the human scene. It will be useful, as a beginning, to single out two of Einstein's witticisms which, when unpacked, and some of their connotations uncovered, may be seen to encapsulate profound reflections on the issues of freedom implicit in the two aspects of his life referred to above. The first of these witticisms is brief. When he was once asked how it was that he came to develop his theories of relativity, his simple reply was: "I dared question an axiom." I have not been able to authenticate this quote. It may be apocryphal. But it is pregnant with implications for our theme.

The other witticism was published in the *London Times* on November 28, 1919. That newspaper had requested from Einstein a description of the results of his theory of relativity, for the benefit of the London public. It was only three weeks after the historic report had been presented at the meeting of the Royal Society about the experimental confirmation of Einstein's theory that light rays are bent in the sun's gravitational field. Let us recall the historical setting. London had just observed the first anniversary of the armistice that had ended World War I, in which Germany had been the enemy. In honoring Einstein, English newspapers tried to ignore every connection between Germany and the scientist they were honoring. Einstein himself deplored this because he hated chauvinistic, narrow-minded nationalism, and he proceeded to twit the *Times* in these words:

"The description of me and my circumstances in the *Times* shows an amusing flare of imagination on the part of the writer. By an application of the theory of relativity to the taste of the reader, today in Germany I am called a German man of science and in England I am represented as a Swiss Jew. If I come to be regarded as a *bête noire* the description will be reversed, and I shall become a Swiss Jew for the German and a German for the English."

Professor Philipp Frank, the distinguished physicist and colleague of Einstein, writing in 1947, supplied this mordant comment on the quote: "At that time Einstein did not anticipate how soon this joke would become true."[1]

Out of these two Einsteinian witicisms we may distill some observations about five aspects of the Idea of Freedom: 1) Freedom of Inquiry; 2) Freedom for Error; 3) Freedom of the Intellect; 4) Socio-political Freedom; 5) Freedom of Religion.

I

Freedom of Inquiry

Einstein was a scientist. Above all, science is dedicated to the advancement of knowledge. To say this is to be neither unmindful nor disparaging of applied science and its contributions to the technological advancement of mankind, and to the improvement of the physical life of man on this planet. But what distinguishes the quintessential idea of science from technology is the pursuit by science of knowledge as an end in itself, over and beyond the application of knowledge to instrumental purposes. Philosophers, historians, and scientists have often reminded us, particularly in the past three generations, that the advancement of knowledge is possible only if scientific inquiry is permitted to follow its own course, as an evolving, self-correcting, trial-and-error process. The making of errors and the freedom to make errors are as integral a part of this process as are the recognition of error, its correction, and the progression beyond any given state of knowledge or ignorance. The advancement of knowledge never proceeds in a confident, rectilinear progression from truth to truth. Significant inquiry in any branch of human knowledge entails and requires questioning of what has appeared to be beyond question, probing, daring, and imaginative projection into the realm of the unknown, often at the risk of being in error.

Such courage and such imagination can obviously flourish only in an atmosphere of freedom in inquiry, and can be hopeful of success in advancing human knowledge only when the various intellectual and scientific disciplines are free to apply their own tests of validity and truth, without outside interference, political or otherwise. When freedom of inquiry is frustrated by fear that errors may be punished; by coerced, slavish assent to any set of preconceived ideas, axioms, or norms outside the immanent canons of logical validity, truth, and the methodology of the sciences; by political orthodoxies; or by appeals to a sanctified something called "common sense" as the final authority and arbiter of truth, then the advancement of human knowledge is sure to be arrested or stopped.

It was the late Alfred North Whitehead who, in one of his many discourses on education, focused his attention on the power of education to liberate man from his unexamined assumptions. Out of minds so liberated, out of free inquiry, out of the free testing of conflicting ideas, new knowledge is born. And in his influential book of half a century ago, *Science and the Modern World*, Whitehead also reminded his readers that "a clash of doctrines is not a disaster—it is an opportunity."[2] The import of what is being said here is dramatically and cogently exemplified in the career of Albert Einstein, the scientist. Indomitably and fearlessly he explored the boundaries of man's knowledge of the physical world, often to the discordant accompaniment of the derision of scoffers, and later under the whiplash of abuse, vilification, and what surely would have become physical persecution had he returned to Germany in 1933. (But to this phase we shall return later.) His relentless probing brought physical science to a confrontation with new frontiers in the exploration of the mysteries of the universe we inhabit. His whimsical answer, "I dared question an axiom," goes to the very root of the matter. For one of the essential features of the growth of knowledge is that the axiom of today so often becomes the error of tomorrow, or, if not an error, at best only *partial* knowledge that was in need of correction and revision. In so much of the history of science and philosophy, the paradigmatic defense of the intellectual or scientific status quo of the day has taken the form of an appeal to the inviolability of "common sense." But as Einstein once observed:

> "Common sense is actually nothing more than a deposit of prejudices laid down in the mind prior to the age of eighteen. Every new idea one encounters in later years must combat this accretion of so-called self-evident concepts."

Einstein's refusal to be intimidated by the accretion of so-called self-evident ideas, his questioning of axioms, his intellectual daring and adventurousness, may have served as stimulus for the remarkable essay by Thorstein Veblen, American economist and sociologist, entitled "The Intellectual Preeminence of Jews in Modern Europe," published in 1919.

It was Veblen's penetrating insight that when the intellectually gifted Jew became "a naturalized, though hyphenate, citizen in the gentile republic of learning," he also became the questioner, the sceptic, the daring prober, and explorer. Having left the "cultural heritage of the Jewish people," and having become "immersed in the gentile culture," the Jew found himself "in the vanguard of modern inquiry" precisely because intellectually he remained an alien, living on the frontiers of European culture. His marginality gave him "the requisite immunity from the inhibitions of intellectual quietism," and "he became a disturber of the intellectual peace . . . a wanderer in the intellectual no-man's-land." The young Jew who entered the intellectual life of Europe was "a sceptic by force of circumstances." The first requisite for constructive work in modern science, said Veblen, ". . .is a sceptical frame of mind," and the young Jew was therefore "in line to become guide and leader . . . in that intellectual development out of which comes the increase and diffusion of knowledge among men." It was this psycho-social analysis that Veblen suggested as explanation of the fact that "the Jewish people have contributed much more than an even share of the intellectual life of modern Europe."[3]

Although Veblen made no reference to him by name, the possibility that Einstein was among those Veblen had in mind in this perceptive essay is not to be discounted. Surely there is an instructive similarity between Veblen's characterization of the young Jew who entered turn-of-the-century European science and Einstein's description of himself in a latter to Max Born: "As a man without roots anywhere . . . I have wandered continually hither and yon—a stranger everywhere." And surely Einstein knew that probing into the recesses of the unknown was bound, as he repeatedly pointed out, "to bring ninety-nine fruitless gropings for one successful grasp." Typically, in connection with a certain feature of one of his theories, Einstein remarked: "That was my biggest blunder. Death alone can save us from blunders."[4] We also know from his own writings, and from the public record, that unlike his experience with the *Special* Theory of Relativity in 1905, he made a number of false starts before successfully developing his *General* Theory of Relativity. We also know that he spent the final third of his life in doggedly, tenaciously—but fruitlessly, as it turned out—pursuing his will-of-the-wisp *Unified Field Theory*. Some future scientist may pick up this trail and succeed where Einstein failed, and, in succeeding, this future scientist may establish that Einstein's vision had reached out toward the correct goal. Contrariwise, it may be shown in the future that his idea of a *Unified Field Theory* was, to use Sir Karl R. Popper's terminology, only another "conjecture" that was unproductive. But seekers after truth in future generations will be able to draw courage and sustenance from his unswerving tenacity, his selfless search for knowledge, his refusal to be diverted from exercising his own intellectual freedom. In spite of fame and world-wide adulation during his life in the United States, he succeeded in avoiding the snares of dogmatism or of the kind of auto-intoxication or self-worship that might have caused a lesser person to try to interfere with, or attempt to restrict, or encroach upon, or be intolerant or contemptuous of the views or of the freedom of others who dissented from his quest.

II
Freedom for Error

But Einstein's gropings, so many of which were so stunningly successful, and the gropings of most scientific inquirers would be discouraged or killed off if the prober lived in an atmosphere of social, ideological, intellectual, or scientific conformity, in which probing and questioning were frowned upon, and unproductive probings or speculations were punishable as heresy, error, or deviation. In his intellectual autobiography which he contributed to the volume called *Albert Einstein: Philosopher-Scientist* (in the series of volumes entitled "The Library of Living Philosophers"), Einstein wrote movingly about what he called "the holy curiosity of inquiry." He said of it the following: "This delicate little plant, aside from stimulation, stands mainly in the need of freedom; without this it goes to wreck and ruin without fail."[5] And again, in a brief essay entitled "On Freedom," Einstein pointed categorically to freedom of inquiry and freedom for error as necessary conditions for the advancement of knowledge.

"... the progress of science presupposes the possibility of unrestricted communication of all results and judgments—freedom of expression and instruction in all realms of intellectual endeavor. By freedom I understand social conditions of such a kind that the expression of opinions and assertions about general and particular matters of knowledge will not involve dangers or serious disadvantages for him who expresses them. This freedom of communication is indispensable for the development and extension of scientific knowledge .... In order that every man may present his views without penalty there must be a spirit of tolerance in the entire population. Such an ideal of external liberty can never be fully attained but must be sought unremittingly if scientific thought, and philosophical and creative thinking in general, are to be advanced as far as possible."[6]

There is an important philosophical point implicit in the notion of "Freedom for Error" that is worth noting here because it forms a natural transition to the connection between Einstein and socio-political freedom. The point becomes discernible when we reflect on aspects of the "history of ideas" in Western thought. It has been developed acutely and instructively by the philosopher of science, Sir Karl R. Popper, principally in his superb book *Conjectures and Refutations.*[7]

The way knowledge in general progresses, and especially scientific knowledge, says Popper, is by "unjustified" (that is, not yet justified) and, as it very often turns out, "unjustifiable anticipations, by guesses, by tentative solutions to our problems, by *conjectures.*"[8] These many *conjectures* in the history of science, most of which turn out to be *false*, are, according to Popper, the lifeblood of the progression of science, and, as part of the life of science, these conjectures are "controlled by criticism, that is, by *attempted refutations.*"[9] *Some* of the *conjectures* propounded by scientists (and we must remember that *all* scientific theories are *conjectures*) do survive the *systematic attempts* to refute them.[10] It is instructive to be reminded that every scientific experiment, every effort to test a scientific theory, if it is a *good* experiment, a *good* test, is in fact an attempt to *refute* the theory, that is to demonstrate that what can be deduced and predicted from the theory is not reflected by the observed facts. I proceed to quote at some length from Popper:

> "Criticism of our conjectures is of decisive importance: By bringing out our mistakes it makes us understand the difficulties of the problem we are trying to solve.... The very refutation of a theory—that is, of any serious tentative solution of our problem—is always a step forward that takes us nearer to the truth. And this is how we learn from our mistakes.... Our own errors provide the dim red lights which help us in groping our way out of the darkness of our cave."[11]

It would seem, therefore, that this fact, namely, that error has a necessary role in the process of the advancement of science, would have been recognized in the world of scientific inquiry, and that such recognition

would have resulted in a concomitant recognition of the indispensability
of freedom for error. And yet, it is a notorious fact of history, more especially of 20th century history, that regimes and societies have been able
successfully, and with fatal effectiveness, to condemn and suppress
opposing ideas, not only of a socio-political nature, but also in the realm
of the sciences, by proclaiming them to be errors, pernicious and
dangerous errors. Such regimes have succeeded in having not only the
masses acquiesce in these condemnations, but in getting the class of
intellectuals to accept them, and in having many of the intellectuals and
scientists even echo them and lead in them. How has this been possible?
How was this *Trahison des Clercs*, this *Treason of the Intellectuals* (to
borrow the title of a book by the French writer Julien Benda), hatched
out of the mainstream of modern Western philosophical and scientific
thought to defile and pollute the intellectual environment of 20th century Europe?

Part of the explanation, Karl Popper suggests, is contained in two
widely held doctrines about the concept of truth. The first is the doctrine
that has come down from Plato, to Aristotle, to Descartes, and in another
way to Francis Bacon, which maintained that "truth is manifest," that
truth is publicly accessible for man to know effortlessly and "once the
naked truth stands revealed before our eyes, we have the power to see
it."[12] For René Descartes, this falsely "optimistic epistemology" was
based on his theory of *veracitas dei*, the theory that the *truthfulness of
God* makes truth manifest to humans. Francis Bacon, according to Popper, held the doctrine of *veracitas naturae, nature is truthful*; it is an
open book and "a pure mind cannot misread it."[13] This doctrine of manifest truth had remarkably beneficent social and cultural consequences,
since it led to the unparalleled intellectual and scientific revolutions of
the 17th century, and to the conviction that through knowledge humans
might become free. However, this same optimistic but clearly false
epistemology also had disastrous consequences. It carried within it the
assumption that, since truth is manifest, knowledge, or the possession of
truth, did not need any explanation. "But how can we ever fall into error
if truth is manifest?"[14] Obviously, the answer lies in a *conspiracy theory
of error*. "There are powers conspiring to keep us in ignorance, to poison
our minds with falsehood, and to blind our eyes so that they cannot see
the manifest truth."[15] That this false epistemology, with its ineluctable
corollary of the conspiracy theory of error, can be the basis of all kinds
of fanaticism, and may both lead to and be utilized by totalitarian ideologies, seems to me amply clear.

III
Freedom of the Intellect

There is another widely disseminated doctrine about the concept of truth that Popper draws to our attention. It is "the strange view that the truth of a statement may be decided upon by inquiring into its sources— that is to say its origin . . . ."[16] It canonizes the *genetic* question, in the belief that a knowledge claim may legitimize itself by its pedigree rather than by objective evidence that supports it. Origins and genesis are substituted for validity, according to this doctrine, and for consistency with objective evidence, as criteria of truth. *Some* sources or origins of knowledge-claims are deemed to be ultimate, absolute, and self-validating, for example, those sources that are racially pure or Aryan, or those that are Marxist-Leninist-Stalinist, in origin. But, of course, as Popper insists, "pure, untainted, and certain *sources*" of scientific knowledge do not exist, and "questions of origin or of purity should not be confounded with questions of validity or of truth."[17] ". . . every source, every suggestion is open to critical examination. . . . The proper epistemological question is not one about sources; rather we ask whether the assertion made is true—that is to say, whether it agrees with the facts."[18]

Thus, when we put together these two doctrines concerning the concept of truth, namely, the theory of "manifest truth" with its corollary "conspiracy theory of error," and the view that the truth of a statement is determined by its source, part of the perverse logic behind the 20th century assaults on intellectual freedoms becomes tragically clear. This perverse, convoluted logic is evidenced in two responses to the experimental confirmation of Einstein's theory, one in the Soviet Union and the other in Germany. In 1922 a Soviet philosopher, A. Maximov, who specialized in the physical sciences, wrote in the official Soviet philosophical journal as follows:

> "[The] idealistic atmosphere [in Germany] has surrounded and still surrounds relativity theory. . . . The impossibility within the limits of bourgeois society for intellectuals to withdraw from these influences led to the circumstance that the relativity principle served exclusively religious and metaphysical tendencies."[19]

Clearly, the "manifest truth" readily perceived by all intelligent and honest Soviet citizens is Dialectical Materialism, and the *error* of relativity theory, which must be banished, has as its degenerate source the conspiracy of the bourgeois intelligentsia to foster religion and metaphysics. And at the very same time in Germany some vociferous opinion characterized Einstein's theory as "Bolshevism in Physics."[20] Germany was experiencing the post-World War I trauma of defeat. Those elements which perceived the loss of war as a "stab in the back" were also hostile to Einstein:

> "We are not surprised to find that the relativity theory soon began to be regarded as 'Jewish' and capable of harming the German people."[21]

Here, in turn, the *manifest truth* is what all good, intelligent and patriotic Germans would automatically recognize in its pristine Aryan purity, namely, "German Physics" (as we shall see forthwith). And there must obviously be no freedom for the insidious *error* of the relativity theory, which has its origin in the conspiratorial anti-German "Jewish Physics" from which Einstein came.

Some years later, in 1929, Einstein reminisced publicly about his own experiences upon his return to Germany in 1914:

> "When I came to Germany 15 years ago, I discovered for the first time that I was a Jew, and I made this discovery through Gentiles more than through Jews. The Jews are a community of people bound together by the bonds of faith and tradition. I saw upright Jews subjected to scorn and contempt, *and my heart bled.*"[22]

It is significant that, under the corrosive impact of the anti-Semitism that pervaded German society during that period, even Einstein's unapologetic dignity and pride in his Jewishness may have suffered some erosion. On the one hand, it was as a proud Jew that he publicly spoke his contempt for the assimilationist, grovelling *Zentralverein Deutscher Staatsbürger Jüdischen Glaubens* (Central Association of German Citizens of Jewish Faith) the adherents of which tried to downplay their Jewishness and to curry favor with the German establishment by speaking disparagingly of other Jews (he did later voice his contempt also for the equivalent "American Council for Judaism"). But, on the other hand, different overtones resonate in Einstein's words at the funeral service for Walter Rathenau, the brilliant Jew who had been the Weimar Republic's Minister of Foreign Affairs, and who was murdered by nationalist German elements on June 24, 1922. In his funeral speech Einstein said:

"I regret that Rathenau accepted an official post in the German government. In view of ideas and acts with reference to Jews in wide circles of the German people, it is my opinion that the natural reaction of Jews ought to be a dignified withdrawal from the public life of Germany."[23]

It is difficult to assess the extent to which Einstein's advocacy of "dignified withdrawal" was in fact a damning indictment of the German people, or a melancholy voice of a Jew who had been inwardly traumatized and humbled, by the hostility he experienced, into advocating retreat.

This was considerably before the advent of Nazism, but the ultranationalists in Germany were already systematically blaming the Jews for Germany's loss of the war. "There suddenly appeared an organization whose only purpose was to fight Einstein and his theories."[24] A literary magazine highly regarded among nationalists published an article under the title "Bolshevistic Physics" which attacked those, "university teachers among them," who "fell for" Einstein's theories, and said:

". . . without mincing words, we are dealing here with an infamous scientific scandal. . . . In the last analysis one cannot blame workers for being taken in by Marx, when German professors allow themselves to be misled by Einstein."[25]

The notion of a Nordic-Aryan philosophy and science that is able to observe and interpret faithfully the reality and profundity of nature was given ever-wider circulation, and by contrast, the "fantastic" theories of the non-Nordic Einstein were vilified. When Einstein, under pressure to reply to these attacks, wrote in a Berlin newspaper that it would be senseless to try to answer in a scientific manner arguments that were not meant scientifically and said simply: "If I were a German nationalist, with or without a swastika, instead of being a Jew with liberal opinions . . ."[26] his opponents were infuriated by his having called the thing by its right name. Einstein began to feel uneasy in Berlin. When he was offered a professorship at the University of Leiden in Holland, and was asked whether he wished to leave Berlin, he replied: "Would such a decision be so amazing? My situation is like that of a man who is lying in a beautiful bed, where he is being tortured by bedbugs."[27]

The most notorious of those who led the attack against Einstein were two fellow physicists, Johannes Stark and the Nobel laureate Philipp Lenard, who blamed the defeat of Germany on an international conspiracy in which the Jews were alleged to have been the actual wirepullers in the background. Lenard had joined the Hitler group in its early days and was one of the long-time members of the Nazi Party. In the preface to his four-volume work entitled *Deutsche Physik* (*German Physics*) (1936), Professor Lenard said: "Jewish physics is a deception (*ein Trugbild*)."[28] Later he said that "Jewish physics," represented by

> "the pure-blooded Jew Albert Einstein, . . . no longer has a leg to stand on. Nor was it intended to be true. In contrast to the desire for truth by the Aryan scientist, the Jew lacks to a striking degree any comprehension of truth."[29]

In a lecture at Munich, in 1937, Lenard spoke of "the gradual development of a Jewish natural science . . . which . . . tried to deprive Aryan physics of its foundations."[30] In 1938, in the *Journal for General Science*, he attacked "the influence of the Jews on the development of natural science" and stated that "Einstein's theory of relativity offers us the clearest example of a dogmatic Jewish type of theory."[31]

One could multiply illustrations of this kind endlessly, and Professor Philipp Frank offers us many in his book on Einstein, including this *obiter dictum* from the same *Zeitschrift für die gesamte Naturwissenschaft*:

> "The Jew would not be himself if the characteristic feature of his attitude, just as everywhere else in science, were not the disintegration and destruction of Aryan construction."[32]

Aryan science is "manifest truth." Einstein's theories are "error," as is self-evident from their non-Aryan, Jewish, source. Such "error" arose as part of the Jewish conspiracy to destroy the "manifest truth" of pure Aryan science, and must be banished. Here the fate of intellectual freedom for error in the progression of science, and of the socio-political freedom of a religio-cultural minority, thus became joined by virtue of the unified barbaric attack against both.

IV
Socio-Political Freedom

When the freedom for error is destroyed, the paradoxical consequence is that a particular kind of error becomes enthroned and *the freedom for truth* is destroyed, as was the case in Nazi Germany and as has been shown in the U.S.S.R. For the suppression of freedom for error is always enforced, as should be clear by now, ostensibly in the interest of protecting the freedom for a claimed higher truth, a manifest truth. Thus, typically, Hitler and his Nazi Party continued to preach Freedom. However, since their foremost principle was the primacy of politics over all fields of human life and thought, Freedom, *true Freedom*, was to be safeguarded for the State alone, with its Aryan philosophy and institutions. The American philosopher, George Santayana, detected this ingredient in German thought even before Hitler. In a 1915 article, later reprinted (1922) in his volume *Soliloquies in England*, Santayana observed:

> "Freedom in the mouth of German philosophy has a very special meaning. It does not refer to any possibility of choice nor any private initiative. German freedom is like the freedom of the angels in heaven who see the face of God and cannot sin. It lies in such a deep understanding of what is actually established that you would not have it otherwise. . . . You are merged by sympathy with your work, your country, and the universe. . . . Your compulsory service then becomes perfect freedom. So that, paradoxical as it may seem, it is only when you conform that you are free, while if you rebel and secede you become a slave."[33]

The dependence of this doctrine on Hegel's metaphysics and philosophy of history will be obvious to anyone familiar with Hegelian doctrine.[34] The practical application of this doctrine of Freedom to German universities under Nazism was explicated unabashedly by E. Kriek, leader in German pedagogy of the Nazi period:

> "It is not science that must be restricted, but rather the scientific investigators and teachers; only scientifically talented men who have pledged their entire personality to the nation, to the racial conception of the world, and to the German mission, will teach and carry on research in German universities."[35]

The same paradoxical consequence has been and continues to be manifested in the Soviet Union. In the years 1937–1964, a Soviet biologist, Trofim D. Lysenko, propounded and, with Stalin's reign of terror supporting him, enforced his phony brand of "Marxist" genetics, with the result that

> "The story of Soviet genetics [during this period] is perhaps the most

bizarre chapter in the history of modern science . . . it was completely incomprehensible that [the U.S.S.R.] could have entrusted its fundamental agricultural resources to exploitation by an obvious quack."[36]

Lysenko's Marxist-Stalinist genetics thus became the "manifest truth." As a consequence, truth and falsity in Soviet genetics ceased to be determined by critical examination of Lysenko's theory, by experiment, or by confirmation or refutation, but rather by Politburo edicts. Was there any freedom left for competent Soviet geneticists to be *right* under Lysenko's suppression of freedom of inquiry for those who, in his view, were guilty of *error?* The answer is writ large in the tortured annals of Soviet genetics in the Lysenko era, and the conclusion is frighteningly clear. *If there is no freedom for error, the consequence is that there is no freedom for truth.* Under the condition of the banishment of freedom for error, the truth or falsity of scientific theories is determined not through the immanent scientific process of search, experimentation, and refutation or confirmation. Truth and error are determined by the ruling political powers and their brand of "manifest truth." The *only* freedom that then remains is the freedom for that error which has become canonized and enthroned by those in power, and freedom for truth is destroyed.

Lest anyone think that the scandalous Lysenko episode is a thing of the past, as was suggested by Zhores A. Medvedev at the conclusion of his book, *The Rise and Fall of T. D. Lysenko*,[37] a sobering report by the Moscow correspondent of the *Washington Post*, dated December 14, 1977, stated that "One year after his death, Lysenko's theories are invoked here by Soviet scientists. . . . This is a stunning development."[38] But, more to the point in relation to the tender treatment of Einstein's Relativity Theory by the Nazis and their "scientific lackeys" is another *Washington Post* report out of Moscow, this one dated March 10, 1979, which, in part, reads as follows:

"Fresh and virulent attacks on Jewish mathematicians in the Soviet Union pose a serious threat to the exchange agreements in science and technology. . . . In the last year, Jewish mathematicians have been forbidden to publish articles and travel abroad to attend international meetings. Jewish students have been barred from universities. . . . We even hear reports . . . that histories of Soviet mathematics are being rewritten to exclude the accomplishments of Jews. . . . One of the two mathematicians allegedly suppressing Jews is identified as L. S. Pontryagin, who . . . directs the editorial Board that decides whose articles get published and edits the journal *Matematicheski Sbornik.*

Pontryagin and a few rabid colleagues of his apparently feel that Jews don't represent Soviet mathematics . . . . These people somehow impute a possible disloyalty of Jews who want to emigrate and see a conflict between this desire and the development of a "true native Soviet mathematics."[39]

Shades of "pure Aryan physics"!

V
Freedom of Religion

We may now conclude this discourse with some reflections on Einstein and religious and cultural freedom, and on Einstein the Jew. That socio-political freedom is a necessary condition for the existence of freedom of the intellect and of scientific inquiry, is axiomatic, and Einstein's many utterances on this subject are so well known that we may limit oursleves to the one quoted earlier in this essay. His refusal to return to Germany following Hitler's accession to power and his publicly demonstrative renunciation of his German citizenship were among his ways of translating his beliefs into actions. His embrace of American citizenship was part of his commitment to political freedom and an exemplification of the ancient apothegm, *"ubi libertas, ibi patria"* ("where there is liberty, there is my homeland"). However, it is of surpassing importance to emphasize that, for Einstein, the imperative need for the Freedom of Inquiry had a religious significance as well. For he saw in that freedom the indispensable safeguard for the experience of religious awe and exaltation that give stimulus to the scientific quest. Einstein often voiced his *amazement* at the rational aspects of the physical universe, and this *rational* amazement, co-mingled with emotional admiration, constituted for him one of the most powerful ingredients in authentic religion. Here too it is worth repeating his own words:

"The most beautiful and most profound emotion we can experience is the sensation of the mystical. It is the sower of all true science. He to whom this emotion is a stranger, who can no longer wonder and stand rapt in awe, is as good as dead. To know that what is impenetrable to us really exists, manifesting itself as the highest wisdom and the most radiant beauty which our dull faculties can comprehend only in their primitive forms—this knowledge, this feeling, is at the center of true religiousness.[40]

Einstein often said that he was not religious in the sense of adherence to observances and rituals. His was what he called "cosmic religion." However, for his entire life following his full rediscovery of himself as a Jew, under the impact of the virulent anti-Semitism he observed and felt in Berlin after his return in 1914, Einstein displayed a deep loyalty to, and was continually involved in, activity on behalf of Jewish communities in need, and later in vigorous support of the Zionist program to establish a reborn Jewish State in the Holy Land for the restoration of freedom, dignity, and justice to the Jewish people.[41] I use the word "rediscovery" advisedly, because earlier in his life, in his early teens, Einstein had gone through a period of devout observance of the ritual practices of traditional Judaism. Moreover, during the two years of his professorship at the German university in Prague he was a member (though only nominally) of Prague's Jewish community, and maintained warm friendships with some of its leading intellectuals, such as Max Brod, Franz Kafka, and Hugo Bergman.

Though it was German anti-Semitism that shocked him into the rediscovery of his Jewishness, his involvements were motivated and reinforced by his discovery and conviction that Judaism had

> ". . . united the Jews for thousands of years [by the bond] of democratic ideal of social justice, coupled with the ideal of mutual aid and tolerance among all men. . . . Even the most ancient religious scriptures of the Jews are steeped in these social ideals. . . . The introduction of a weekly day of rest . . . [and] the unique accomplishments of the Jews in the field of philanthropy spring from the same source."[42]

In addition, he said, what tied him to Judaism is the high place it assigned in its hierarchy of values to the pursuit of learning and development of the mind, within a framework of intellectual freedom and liberty of conscience:

> "A second characteristic trait of Jewish tradition is the high regard in which it holds every form of intellectual aspiration and spiritual effort . . . the esteem in which intellectual accomplishment is held among the Jews . . . at the same time a strong critical spirit prevents blind obedience to any mortal authority."[43]

It is remarkable with what profound insight Einstein, the physicist, who was not a scholar of Jewish thought and relgion, understood the spirit and the ethos of Judaism, and how feelingly he was committed to them. It is in these very features of Judaism that Einstein perceived the explanation of 20th century anti-Semitism. It is only fitting to conclude by quoting his memorable words:

> ". . . today . . . it is just *because* we are the people of the Book that we are persecuted. The aim is to annihilate not only ourselves, but to destroy, together with us, that spirit expressed in the Bible . . . which made possible the rise of civilization in Central and Northern Europe . . ."[44] "Hence the hatred of the Jews by those who have reason to shun popular enlightenment. More than anything else in the world, they fear the influence of men of intellectual independence. I see in this the essential cause for the savage hatred of Jews raging in present-day Germany . . . . The Nazi group sees the Jews as a nonassimilable element that cannot be driven into uncritical acceptance of dogma, and that therefore . . . threaten their authority because of its insistence on popular enlightenment of the masses." "Proof that this conception goes to the heart of the matter is convincingly furnished by the solemn ceremony of the burning of the books staged by the Nazi regime . . ." "[this trend] seeks to base society exclusively upon authority, blind obedience, and coercion. . . . The adherents of this . . . trend are the enemies of the free groups and of education for independent thought. They are, moreover, the carriers of political anti-Semitism."[45]

NOTES

1. Frank, Philipp, *Einstein: His Life and Times,* New York: Alfred A. Knopf, 1949, p. 144.

2. Whitehead, Alfred North, *Science and the Modern World,* (Lowell Lectures, 1925), New York: Macmillan, 1929, p. 266.

3. Veblen, Thorstein, "The Intellectual Preeminence of Jews in Modern Europe," *The Political Science Quarterly,* March 1919. Reprinted in Veblen, *Essays in the Changing Order,* New York: Viking Press, 1934; also in *The Portable Veblen,* ed. by Max Lerner, New York: Viking Press, 1958, pp. 467–79.

4. Quoted by George R. Harrison, "Albert Einstein: Appraisal of an Intellect," *Atlantic Monthly*, Boston, 1955, p. 25. Cf. *Time* magazine, New York, February 19, 1979, pp. 78–79: "Einstein had opted for a stable universe . . . with . . . what he called the Cosmological Constant. A decade later . . . . Einstein reversed himself . . . . The Cosmological Constant, he allowed, was the worst mistake of his scientific career."

5. Einstein, Albert, "Autobiographical Notes," in *Albert Einstein: Philosopher-Scientist*, edited by Paul Arthur Schilpp (The Library of Living Philosophers, Volume VII), Evanston, Illinois: The Library of Living Philosophers, Inc., 1949, p. 17.

6. Einstein, Albert, *Out of my Later Years*, New York: Philosophical Library, 1950, pp. 12–13.

7. Popper, Karl R., *Conjectures and Refutations: The Growth of Scientific Knowledge*, New York: Basic Books, 1962.

8. *Ibid.*, p. vii.

9. *Ibid.*

10. *Ibid.*, p. vii; Introduction, pp. 3–30; and Chapter 1, pp. 33–65.

11. *Ibid.*, pp. vii and 28.

12. *Ibid.*, p. 5.

13. *Ibid.*, p. 7.

14. *Ibid.*

15. *Ibid.*

16. *Ibid.*, p. 18.

17. *Ibid.*, p. 25.

18. *Ibid.*, p. 27.

19. Quoted by Philipp Frank, *op. cit.*, pp. 145–46.

20. *Ibid.*, p. 146.

21. *Ibid.*

22. *Fossische Zeitung*, Berlin, 1929. Quoted in "Einstein *Ha'yehudi V'yahaduto*" ("Einstein the Jew and his Jewishness"), by Z'ev V. Oren in *Hadoar* (Hebrew literary weekly), New York, 7 Nissan, 5728, p. 382 (my translation).

23. Albert Einstein, *Neue Rundschau*, Berlin, 1922, Volume 2, pp. 815–16. Quoted by Z'ev Oren in *Hadoar*, *loc cit.*, above (My translation).

24. Frank, Philipp, *op. cit.*, p. 159.

25. *Ibid.*, p. 160.

26. *Ibid.*, p. 161.

27. *Ibid.*, pp. 161–62.

28. Kneller, George Frederick, *The Educational Philosophy of National Socialism*, New Haven: Yale University Press, 1941, p. 251, Note 14.

29. Frank, Philipp, *op. cit.*, p. 252.

30. *Ibid.*

31. *Ibid.*, p. 253. Cf. *Time* magazine, *op. cit.*, above, Note 4, p. 78: "Einstein and his 'Jewish physics' became the object of increasingly scurrilous denunciations. Fellow German scientists turned their backs on him—with the exception of a few men like [Max] Planck."

32. Frank, Philipp, p. 255. As Frank points out, the history of Nazi attitudes to relativity theory is not without its ironic and amusing elements. In the 1920's there were some among Nazi and pro-Nazi political and scientific writers who tried to appropriate relativity to Nazi doctrine by characterizing it as representative of German Idealism and thus as a useful weapon of National Socialism against materialist philosophy. Later, relativity theory was condemned, on the one hand, as indicative of the alleged preference by Jews for

theoretical deliberations in contrast with the striving by Aryan Germans for concrete action. On the other hand, Nazi spokesmen most frequently branded Einstein's theories as materialistic and therefore linked with Marxism. (Cf. Frank, pp. 250–51 and 253.)

33. Santayana, George, *Soliloquies in England*, New York: Charles Scribner's Sons, 1922, pp. 169–70. (Quoted by Frank, *op. cit*, p. 227.)

34. Hegel, George Wilhelm Friedrich, *Reason In History: A General Introduction to the Philosophy of History*, translated by Robert S. Hartman, New York: Liberal Arts Press, 1953, pp. 50–53: "Law, morality, the State, and they alone, are the positive reality and satisfaction of freedom. The caprice of the individual is not freedom. . . . Only the will that obeys the law is free, for it obeys the law and, being in itself, is free."

35. Frank, Philipp, *op. cit.*, p. 228.

36. Lerner, I. Michael, in the Foreword to *The Rise and Fall of T. D. Lysenko*, by Zhores A. Medvedev (translated by I. Michael Lerner), New York: Columbia University Press, 1969, p. v.

37. *Ibid.*, p. 253.

38. *The Washington Post*, December 14, 1977, p. A25.

39. O'Toole, Thomas, *The Washington Post*, March 10, 1979, p. All.

40. Quoted by Philipp Frank, *op. cit.*, p. 284, and by Barnett, Lincoln, *The Universe and Dr. Einstein*, New York: Mentor Books, The New American Library, 1952, p. 117. Barnett also quotes the following:

"My religion consists of a humble admiration of the illimitable superior spirit who reveals himself in the slight details we are able to perceive with our frail and feeble minds. That deeply emotional conviction of the presence of a superior reasoning power, which is revealed in the incomprehensible universe, forms my idea of God."

One hears here echoes of Psalm 104.

41. "My relationship to the Jewish people," Einstein stated, "has become my strongest human bond, ever since I became fully aware of our precarious situation among the nations of the world." (Quoted in *Science News*, Washington, D.C., March 31, 1979, Vol, 115, No. 13, p. 213). To Kurt Blumenfeld, the distinguished German Jewish leader in the two decades following World War I, Einstein explained his commitment to Zionism as follows:

"I am opposed to nationalism, but I am in favor of Zionism. Today I realized why. The man who has two arms and insists on proclaiming that he has a right arm is a chauvinist. But a man who lacks a right arm must do everything possible to find a substitute for it. As a human being I am therefore opposed to nationalism, but as a Jew I will support from this day the Jewish national aims of the Zionists." (Kurt Blumenfeld, "Albert Einstein," *Jewish Frontier*, New York, May 1955, p. 8.)

42. Einstein, Albert, *Out of my Later Years*, op. cit., p. 249. In an address entitled "Our Debt to Zionism," given in 1938, Einstein stated:

"To be a Jew, after all, means first of all, to acknowledge and follow in practice those fundamentals in humaneness laid down in the Bible—fundamentals without which no sound and happy community of men can exist." *Ibid.*, p. 262.

43. *Ibid.*, pp. 249–250.

44. *Ibid.*, p. 254.

45. *Ibid.*, p. 252–53.

Sabbath as Temple:
Some Thoughts on Space and Time
in Judaism

Arthur Green

University of Pennsylvania
Philadelphia, Pennsylvania

In 1945, just as the European Holocaust (and with it the second great age in Jewish history) was drawing to a close, Abraham Joshua Heschel gave voice to a hope that later Jewish history would one day be recognized and sanctified by the world, as has the history of Biblical Israel:

> When Nebuchadnezzar destroyed Jerusalem and set fire to the Temple, our forefathers did not forget the Revelation at Mount Sinai and the words of the Prophets. Today the world knows that what transpired on the soil of Palestine was sacred history, from which mankind draws its inspiration. A day may come when the hidden light of the East European period will be revealed.[1]

We look at Jewish history throughout the Diaspora period—going here beyond Heschel and extending back from Eastern Europe to the Roman destruction—and ask ourselves what sort of inspiration we hope humanity might derive from the collective experience of the Jew. Surely the basic insights of our religion, moral as well as spiritual, are by now accessible outside of Judaism, whether through her younger sister faiths or altogether independently. The particularizing nuances of Jewish faith and expression, vital as they may seem from within, will not constitute a major new source of understanding. It is rather from the experience of Jewish history, and within this overwhelmingly from the experience of *galut*, that the world has to learn. Homelessness, alienation, permanent insecurity, the feeling of living as unwelcome guests in a society not of our making: these long-known characteristics of life as a Jew are now increasingly the lot of millions of others in a world where the uprooting of populations, the migration of labor forces, and, above all, the ongoing urbanization and de-traditionalization of people are taking place far faster than anyone can record.

Surely the great miracle of Jewish existence is our survival of *galut*. But if we ask ourselves what exactly *galut* is, and what means the Jewish people used to combat its corrosive power, our answer will necessarily be manifold. Our interest here is in the specifically religious quality of *galut*, in distinction (a historical artificiality, to be sure) from its political, economic, linguistic, and other aspects. It was in religious terms, after all, that pre-modern Jews generally and most successfully expressed themselves, and it is around religious symbols, not surprisingly, that a great deal of the discussion of *galut* is focused.

Umi-penei ḥaṭa'enu galinu me-'arẓenu—"because of our sins we were exiled from our land." Such phrases abound in Jewish liturgy, alternating always with the prayers for restoration. If we take such liturgical expression as a standard for the Jews' images of their history, it becomes clear that *ḥurban* and *galut*, the destruction of the Temple and the exile from the land, are invariably treated as one. This is the case despite the fact that they did not come at the same time in the all-important second destruction. Ereẓ Yisrael remained a major center of Jewish life and creativity for four or five hundred years after the Temple was destroyed. The paradigmatic event for classical Jewish self-understanding was the *first* destruction, even though it was in the crucible of the second that rabbinic Judaism had its birth. Sin and prophetic warning, followed by destruction and exile as one event—this is the way the Jewish people chose to remember it.

In order to see the meaning of this exile in religious terms, some patterns perceived elsewhere in the study of the history of religions should be recalled. Israel is a people living in what its God has designated as a holy land, proclaimed as such through the various deeds of revered ancestors in times long gone. In that holy land God has chosen one place "to cause His name to dwell there" (Deut. 12:11) and at that spot has commanded His faithful servant to build a Temple. True, many among Israel had learned, especially by the second Temple period, that their God was not purely a local tribal deity, that the Creator could be worshipped from anywhere and by others as well as Israel. And yet the religion of Israel had never fully abandoned its tribal roots. The Land of Israel, Jerusalem, and the Temple were still the *right* places—if not the only places—for Israel to stand before its God. The clearest expression of this viewpoint in the Bible is probably the prayer of Solomon, with which he reportedly dedicated the House of God. It is worth calling to mind some excerpts:

> But will God really dwell on earth? Even the heavens and their uttermost reaches cannot contain You, how much less this house that I have built! Yet turn, O Lord my God, to the prayer and supplication of Your servant, and hear the cry and prayer which Your servant offers before You this day. May Your eyes be open day and night toward this House, toward the place of which You have said: "My name shall abide there"; may You heed the prayers which Your servants will offer toward this place. And when You hear the supplications which Your servant and Your people offer toward this place, give heed in Your heavenly abode—give heed and pardon . . .
>
> In any plague or in any disease, in any prayer or supplication offered by any person among all Your people Israel—each of whom knows his own affliction—when he spreads his palms toward this House, O hear in Your heavenly abode, and pardon and take action! . . .
>
> When Your people take the field against their enemy by whatever way You send them, and they pray to the Lord in the direction of the city which You have chosen, and of the House which I have built to Your name, O hear in heaven their prayer and supplication and uphold their cause. (I Kings 8:27–30; 38–39; 44–45)

Although this prayer was probably composed long after Solomon, and possibly after the first exile, it shows how central the chosen city and Temple remained in Israelite eyes. Historians of religion have shown that early societies are generally constructed around a geographical "sacred center." Such a center serves to embody the values and aspirations of each society. It is also in one way or another the very real dwelling place of the deity, the locus out of which divine power radiates, or at least the place on earth where humans are most apt to be touched by the Presence. The Bible is somewhat reserved about the expression of this concept, at least in some of its more mythological aspects. The notion that the Temple is the opening to heaven and hell, or stands on the spot with which Creation began, or is located just below a great heavenly Temple, does not find direct narrative expression in Scripture. They are of course indicated by biblical language and terminology: *Beth El* and *Sha'ar ha-Shamayim* are two of the more obvious examples. The fact that these terms grow forth into full and explicit narratives in the post-Biblical sources, where less care was taken with regard to such anti-mythic "orthodoxy," and sometimes in forms quite strikingly parallel to expressions in Mesopotamian literature of more than a millenium earlier, makes it rather likely that these concepts were indeed a part of the unrecorded folk legacy of ancient Israel.[2] This notion of center ties together visions of ideal past or origins and restoration in the harmonious future, which is to say that it stands at the very core of what the Bible understands as both cosmology and history. It has also been suggestively argued that the Biblical narrative itself, taken as a literary whole, may be said to have underlying it an ongoing sense of sacred center, extending from the tree of Eden down through Abraham's discovery of the Holy Land, Jacob's Bethel vision, and the tabernacle in the wilderness, until it receives its final articulation in the city of David and the Temple of his son.[3]

Bearing in mind this view of Temple as the center of cosmic orientation, we can now pose more clearly our question about the religious meaning of *galut* to the Jewish people and how post-Biblical Judaism has been a reaction to it. First, we should reiterate that the destruction of the Temple made *galut* a fact; a visit or even settlement in the Holy Land could not change that. The Land of Israel *sans* Temple and altar was still sacred, to be sure, but it had lost much of its luster in Jewish eyes. Medieval Jewish visitors to the Land, rather than glorying in their return home, joined the land in *its* mourning. It was as though the burning of Jerusalem had caused the land itself to go into exile. Our primary focus, however, should not be upon Judaism's mourning but upon its growth and renewal. Given the role that the Jerusalem center played in the cosmology of ancient Israel, and given the later Biblical insistence that only there could the cult of Israel be practiced, how was the transition made in the religious life of the Jewish people from Temple to synagogue, from a sacrificial cult at the Center to a liturgical faith that could thrive anywhere?[4] To answer this we should look at the attitudes of the early synagogue and its religion, especially as reflected in the liturgy, toward the old cult and Temple. Fortunately, this very question has been addressed in an illuminating study by Robert Goldenberg entitled "The Broken Axis."[5] In examining early rabbinic liturgy the author notes that the rabbis never resolved the dilemma of whether or not their religion of prayer, *halakhah*, and study successfully superseded the Jerusalem cult. They proclaimed with Hosea (14:3) that "We shall render for bullocks the offering of our lips" and they structured their daily *'amidah* prayers as though they were filling the role of sacrifices. But they also made sure, in the midst of those prayers, to express a longing that "the Temple be rebuilt soon, in our own days," that "You restore the priests to their service and the Levites to their song and music," and, quite explicitly, that "there we shall eat of the sacrifices and the Paschal offerings as their blood reaches the side of Your altar, in fulfillment of Your will."[6] Goldenberg reaches the following conclusion:

> The self-conception of rabbinic Judaism is built on the contradictory assumptions that the earlier worship in the Temple has been successfully left behind, but that things will never be quite right until it has been restored. If considered theologically, that amounts to a stark contradiction or at best an ambivalent paradox; seen as an effort to preserve the old religious orientation after its basis has been swept away, it makes sense. We can then see here the outlines of a system which took advantage of the disorientation caused by the fall of Jerusalem, but did not fall victim to it. The continuity of religious life was thus protected, even as all the forms of religious life had to be changed.

This ambivalence toward the sacred center is placed into clearest relief when the position of rabbinic Judaism is contrasted with that of its rival and fellow heir to ancient Hebrew cosmology, the early Church. Classical Christianity took the clear and unambiguous step that the rabbis declined to take: the old Temple has been replaced. Christ has become the center; sacred space has been recast into Christ the Temple. Sacred person completely dominates the cosmological stage; as Jesus the Christ is Torah enfleshed, so is he God's house re-established. His cross and his body are the meeting-place of heaven and hell. His body, through its presence in the eucharist, is able thus to consecrate real sacred space over and over again. It is the clear negation of the old *axis mundi* that allows Christianity the power to symbolically create new sacred space in a way that Judaism was never able (nor did it seek) to do. The cathedral and its architecture seek to recreate and embody the primal world; through the death of sacred space and its rebirth, creation can happen anew. The synagogue, though sometimes called *miqdash me'at*, is viewed so much as a temporary replacement for the only *real* sanctuary that its structure, however loved and sometimes embellished, could not be granted such significance.

Lacking an unambiguous resolution of this question, the Judaism of the rabbis moved on several fronts at once. The Day of Atonement, liturgy, and good deeds all serve in one or another rabbinic pronouncement to replace the altar. Sacred person has a very limited role in early post-exilic Judaism, and assumes major proportions only—to the distress of many—in the Hasidism of the eighteenth century.[7] An area that is less obvious, largely because it is not articulated directly by the rabbis, is our concern here: the transfer of attention from sacred space to sacred *time*. Diaspora Israel are deprived of space; the land they are in is profane in their sight, not capable or worthy of sanctuary. The only truly holy place, far off from most, in any case lies in presently irreparable ruin. What has remained untouched by the conqueror, however, and, moreover, what remains consistently portable for a wandering community, is the realm of time. It is to time, and of course particularly to the Sabbath, that the rabbis sought to turn Israel's attention. The development of the already ancient Sabbath as the central ritual/halakhic institution of rabbinic Judaism was a specific reaction to the era of destruction, and represented an unconscious shifting of primary Jewish allegiance from the spatial to the temporal realm.

It was Heschel, whose words introduced this study, who first called the attention of modern Jews to the Temple-like quality of the Jewish Sabbath. His book *The Sabbath* made frequent reference to *shabbat* as a "palace in time" and went on to describe Judaism as a time-oriented rather than space-oriented way of viewing the world. Heschel did not, however, set the centrality of *shabbat* in historical context, a move that might have been inappropriate to an essentially poetic work.[8] In asserting the superiority of time over space as an eternal Jewish value, however, and in consigning the love of space to the realms of the ancient pagan and the modern materialist, the work inevitably wound up in deprecation of space, despite Heschel's claims to the contrary.

The remainder of this study may be viewed as an extended postscript to *The Sabbath*, a claim that *shabbat*-centered piety belongs specifically to the second era of Jewish history, the result of particular spiritual/ historical circumstances.

Anyone familiar with the life of a traditional Jewish community needs no proof of the centrality of *shabbat* in Jewish religious life. The ongoing love affair between Jew and *shabbat* is so well attested in Jewish folk literature, and has been so beautifully described by Heschel and others, that it would be worse than superfluous to try to capsulize it here. It might be worth noting that there are ways in which the Jewish community actually *defined* itself religiously as a community of Sabbath-observers: one who keeps the Sabbath is part of the group, but one who profanes it (for the Sabbath was proclaimed holy at Creation) is not. A Sabbath-observer may be trusted as a witness before a rabbinic court; a Sabbath-profaner may not. Food served in the home of a known Sabbath-observer may be assumed ritually fit; among others one could take no chances. Probably the closest one could come to speaking of an "Orthodox" Jew in pre-modern Jewish parlance, as used within the community, was *shomer shabbos*. Such evidences are, of course, popular and informal; they reflect general opinion rather than *halakhah*,[9] and are not necessarily early. One might wonder, however, whether the Talmudic tale of the final encounter between Elisha ben Abuya and Rabbi Meir does not represent something similar. It is as Elisha rides off on his horse beyond the Sabbath-barrier, leaving Meir behind, that the final break is made by the heretic who has left the rabbinic fold.[10]

The observance of the Sabbath has always been one of the major concerns of Jewish law: definitons and categorizations of forbidden labors, punishments for Sabbath-violation, and the application of old categories of forbidden labor to ever-new situations of advancing human technology have occupied Jewish legalists since very early times. While we do not know as much as we would like about the observance of the Sabbath in pre-rabbinic times, there is much evidence from the later period of the Second Temple, both internal and external, to indicate that Sabbath rest was a central part, if not actually the defining characteristic, of the religion of the Jews.[11] Evidence from the Dead Sea sectarians shows that their Sabbath was rather like that of the later rabbis in terms of its halakhic nature;[12] some indications are now found that lead scholars to trace later forms of Sabbath observance back to Biblical times, despite the lack of written evidence for them.[13]

Our claim is *not*, then, that Sabbath became *important* only after the destruction of the Temple. This would be foolish; the ten commandments are ample testimony to the contrary. It is rather this: *the Sabbath gradually supplanted the Temple as the central unifying religious symbol of the Jewish people.* This shift took place originally in the context of the sectarian strife of the Second Temple period, and was ultimately confirmed by the destruction of the Temple.

The best symbol for this movement from space-oriented to time-oriented piety is in the formula that the rabbis use to encapsulate the Sabbath regulations; the thirty-nine categories of forbidden labor. According to Talmudic report (originally disputed but later widely accepted by the tradition)[14] the biblical basis for almost the entirety of the Sabbath prohibitions lies in Exodus 31:13: "Moreover you shall keep My Sabbaths . . ." This Sabbath command is inserted, seemingly without reason, in the midst of the ongoing discussion of the building of the tabernacle, the Torah's prototype of an ideal Temple. Since the word *'akh*, with which this Sabbath verse opens, is a term of exception in the technical vocabulary of rabbinic exegesis (i.e. it comes to teach that what follows is an exception to the previously stated rule), the rabbis conclude that all forms of labor involved in any way in the construction of the tabernacle were meant to be forbidden on the Sabbath. These include such general categories, e.g., as planting, shearing, dyeing, sewing, and striking a hammer. The point seems to be obscure and arbitrary, that so much of Sabbath law should be unmentioned in Scripture and derived from a seemingly innocuous two-letter Hebrew word. The rabbis themselves called it "mountains hanging by a hair."[15] But perhaps it is neither arbitrary nor obscure. The commandments for the tabernacle tell how to construct sacred space, elaborating in full and rich detail the place that was to be Israel's center and opening to heaven. Now, because of changed circumstances, a new such center was needed, temporal rather than spatial in character. The ancient and revered institution of *shabbat* is the vehicle, of course, but the detail of *shabbat* observance is lacking in Biblical basis and especially lacking in a coherent structure to lend it meaning. By the deft interpretation of an *'akh*, the rabbis have succeeded in transferring all that Biblical detail from the realm of space, where it had been rendered useless, to that of time. The phenomenon is one of reversal: by *doing* all these labors in the particular prescribed configuration, one creates sacred space. By *refraining* from these same acts, in the context of the Sabbath, one creates sacred time. Here the legalistic device, far from being arbitrary, is used in a highly sophisticated way to effect a basic change in religious modality.

The Talmudic rabbis had not read Mircea Eliade. For them such notions as "sacred time" and "sacred space" hardly existed as categories of thought. There was, of course, no conscious decision taken one fine day at Yavneh to fashion the Sabbath after the fallen Temple.[16] How then, according to our reading, could such a transference have come about? How could Temple and *Shabbat*, two seemingly unrelated institutions of ancient Judaism, be so linked? The question requires a brief examination of the theological rationale provided for these institutions in the Biblical and rabbinic sources, one that will uncover a deep though mostly unspoken link between the two, a link that makes this shift of focus after the destruction considerably more understandable.

Rav Judah in the name of Rav (Babylonia, 3rd cent.) teaches that Bezalel, architect of the tabernacle, "knew how to perform those permutations of letters through which heaven and earth were created."[17] Why should Bezalel, of all people (and not Moses or Aaron), be privy to this secret? The tradition makes sense only if his single task is somehow especialy related to the original Creation. We do not have to go far to see that this is the case:

"These are the accounts of the tabernacle" (Ex. 38:21) . . . Said Rabbi Jacob ben Assi: Why does Scripture say "Lord, I love the habitation of Your House and the place where Your Glory dwells" (Ps. 26:8)? Because it [God's house] is parallel to the Creation of the world. How is this?

Of the first day it is written: "In the beginning God created the heaven and the earth." It is also written "He stretched forth the heavens like a curtain." (Ps. 104:2). And what is written regarding the tabernacle? "You shall make curtains of goatskins" (Ex. 26:7).

On the second day: "Let there be a firmament," and separation is mentioned, as it says: "Let it separate waters from waters." And of the tabernacle: "And the veil shall separate for you between the holy and the holy of holies" (Ex. 26:33).

On the third day water is mentioned: "Let the waters be gathered." And in the tabernacle: "You shall make a brass basin with a brass base . . . and place water there" (Ex. 30:18).

On the fourth day He created the lights, as it says: "Let there be luminaries in the heavenly firmament." And in the tabernacle: "You shall make a gold candelabrum" (Ex. 25:31).

On the fifth day He created the birds: "Let the waters swarm with every living thing and let birds fly." Parallel to them in the tabernacles are sacrifices of lambs and birds. [Alternative reading: "And in the tabernacle: 'The cherubim spread their wings upward' (Ex. 25:20)."]

On the sixth day man was created, as it says: "He created man in His image.

He created him through the glory.[18] Man (Adam) in the tabernacle is the high priest, annointed to serve and minister before the Lord .. [19]

The continuation of this midrash will be quoted below, but there is enough here for our present purposes. The parallel raises to an ultimate height the cosmic significance of the drama that takes place within the tabernacle or Temple. The priest is now Adam or the embodiment of all mankind, the candelabrum gives off the radiance of the sun, and so forth. While the language is that of metaphor, the intent seems clearly symbolic: thus is the cult to be understood. The rabbis speak of sacred space as microcosm, the tabernacle reproducing in a sacralized context the entirety of Creation. In other passages the relationship between Creation and the tabernacle is adumbrated somewhat differently: Creation is not quite complete or secure until it has been "sealed" by the erection of the sacred shrine:

> "Who has established all the ends of the earth" (Prov. 30:4). The tent of meeting, as it says: "It was on the day that Moses completed setting up the tabernacle" (Num. 7:1). The world was set up with it. Rabbi Joshua ben Levi in the name of R. Simeon ben Yohai: It does not say LeHa-QYM Ha-MiSHKaN, but rather LeHa-QYM 'et [with] Ha-MiSHKaN. What was set up "with" it? The world, for until the tabernacle was erected the world trembled; when the tabernacle was set up the world was firmly established ... [20]

Here too we see a theme that is familiar from other cultural contexts. The shrine finally validates (and hence guarantees) the existence of the world itself; only at this point is Creation complete.

Viewing the tabernacle/Temple from this perspective, we understand that the rabbis took it as no coincidence that the Sabbath command of Exodus 31:12 followed immediately upon the details of its construction. Only then is Moses told (31:1ff.) that God has called upon Bezalel and his associates to execute the work. The Sabbath warning comes before work can actually begin. Theologically as well as halakhically, there is no arbitrariness; as God rests on the seventh day after His work of Creation, so do you rest on the seventh of yours. The repetition of the Sabbath command in Ex. 35:1–3, just as the actual work is to get underway, makes it clear that in this case what the rabbis saw was probably peshat, at least the intent of a Scriptural editor.

The Sabbath, according to Genesis, is the apex of Creation. There is no holiness in God's world until He finds rest. Only after Creation has been completed and He ceases from work does He bless and hallow. And it is not the fruit of His labors that is sanctified, but the day of His rest.

The building of a Temple is, for religious societies, the most meaningful of human labors; in it man makes an earthly dwelling-place for the presence of his God or, in Israel's case, a symbol of His presence in their midst. But this labor too remains unhallowed until completion. The laborers who constructed the Temple, we are told, were able to come and go throughout, even walking through what was to become the holy of holies, until their work was done.

No wonder then that the closing chapter of Exodus repeats the step-by-step structure of the opening chapter of Genesis, concluding with the unmistakable refrain *Va-yekhal Mosheh et ha-mel'akhah.*[21] A Biblical redactor, having before him an account that reached from Creation to the tabernacle, sought to "seal" that account with a conclusion that has an appropriate parallel to its beginning. Creation is completed by its repetition as a human act; God's work finds fulfillment only as something of His power to create to imitated by humans. In this linking of sacred-space construction to the original Creation, the Torah also implies a link, spoken only with the subtlety of juxtaposition and linguistic parallel, between Temple and Sabbath.

Now we may proceed with the passage from *Midrash Tanhuma* that we cited above. The six days of Creation, we recall, have already found their match in the tabernacle. And now:

> On the seventh day: "Heaven and earth were completed." And in the tabernacle: "All the work was completed" (Ex. 39:32). Of Creation: "And God blessed [the seventh day]," and of the tabernacle: "And Moses blessed them" (Ex. 39:43). Of Creation: "God completed," and of the tabernacle: "On the day when Moses completed" (Num. 7:1). Of Creation: "And He made it holy," and of the taberncale: "He annointed it and made it holy" (ibid.).

It was the rabbis' sensitivity to this nuance of Biblical meaning, barely hinted at in text but deeply implanted in the structure of the two institutions, that allowed them, in the face of the need of their age, to perform the delicate manipulation of an *'akh*[22] that had so great a meaning for all of the Judaism that was to come.

Jewish thinkers writing under the influence of Kabbalah, beginning in the thirteenth century, were able to articulate most fully this link between Temple and Sabbath. In the works of the Spanish Kabbalists, well known for their deft use of symbols and their ability to rapidly translate from one symbol-system into another, it is frequently made clear either that Temple (or tabernacle) and Sabbath are one or else that they are the classic pair which need to be drawn together. Here we are dealing with a literature of mysticism, one in which both time and space will perforce be relativized. The chief focus of the Kabbalists' interest is the realm of the *sefirot*, seen at once as the stages of divine unfolding or emanation and as the rungs in the ladder of the mystic's ascent to the One. As the adept moves by successive degrees ever "upward" or "inward" toward realization, points along the journey must perforce somehow be designated. These designations, drawn especially by the *Zohar* in a full array of colorful symbols, may be characterized by terms that have their origins either in the temporal or the spatial realm. Either is acceptable for this purpose because neither is quite adequate. The divine effulgence does not first flow through either spatially locatable points or temporarily determined moments; neither does the mystic in his ascent to God. In order to speak of his universe in human language, however, he must designate the stages in symbols taken from one realm or the other. It is not surprising, then, to find in his writings moments in "time" and objects in "space" that turn out to be identical with one another. As symbols of light may turn into water as one proceeds from line to line on the same page of Zohar, so may figures in space "reveal themselves" to be figures in time. What we have here is no merely external literary device, but a representation in symbolic language of an essential characteristic of mystical experience.

The central figures in most discussions of the sefirotic universe are the sixth and the last of these ten manifestations. The sixth *sefirah* represents the deity as generally depicted in the earlier Biblical and rabbinic sources. This is the God-figure, Father and King, who is the source of the written Torah, the object of non-mystical prayer, and whose being represents a constant balance of the potentially warring forces of justice and love, the "Holy One, blessed be He," as He is most frequently called by the rabbis. The tenth *sefirah* is the *shekhinah*, the presence of God indwelling, the hypostatized Community of Israel, and most importantly, the object of divine affection, the bride of the mystical Song of Solomon. The most essential and daring theological innovation of the Kabbalah was the claim that the Canticle, long read by the rabbis as a love-song between God and His people Israel, was now to be seen as

documenting a love that takes place *within* God, between two poles of
the divine self symbolically designated as male and female, a relationship
in which Israel were no longer seen as the direct object of divine *eros*, but
rather as its offspring and devotees.

The association of the Sabbath with the feminine aspect of the divine
world is widespread in the Kabbalah and is quite well known, if only
through its presentation in the Sabbath hymn *Lekha Dodi*. Many Kabbalistic writings speak of two Sabbaths, or of male and female aspects
within the *shabbat* itself (these resting on earlier speculations around
zakhor—"remember" the Sabbath [Ex. 20:8] and *shamor*—"keep" the
Sabbath [Deut. 5:12]. But it is with the *shekhinah* as bride and queen
that the mystics' Sabbath is finally identified:

> The secret of Sabbath: *she* is Sabbath as she cleaves to the mysterious
> One, causing that One to shine upon her . . . When Sabbath comes, she is
> unified and separated from the "other side." All evil forces of judgement are
> removed from her, and she dwells in union with the holy light. She is
> crowned with many crowns as she faces the holy king . . . her face shines
> with a sublime radiance as she is crowned from below by the holy people
> . . .[23]

The tabernacle/Temple too is identified with the *shekhinah* throughout the literature of the Kabbalah. House, Tent, Temple are all classic
symbols of the feminine archetype: that which is entered, gathering
place, womb, etc. It is in this symbolic garb that the last *sefirah* serves as
the meeting-place for God and Israel: the flow of divine energy from the
sefirot "above" and the devotion of Israel's prayers "below" are joined
together in this *bet mo'ed le-khol ḥai*. It was in some of their most daring moments that the Kabbalistic authors allowed Moses (or the adept in
the guise of Moses?) to share with God the role of bridegroom of the
shekhinah. Hence this rather startling passage is made possible:

> "They brought the tabernacle unto Moses" (Ex. 39:33). Why did they *bring*
> the tabernacle? Because that was the hour of Moses' marriage—for this rea-
> son "they brought the tabernacle unto Moses"—just as the bride is brought
> to the bridegroom. First the bride must be brought to her groom, as Scrip-
> ture says: "I have given my daughter to this man as a wife" (Deut. 22:16).
> Only afterwards may he [the bridegroom] come to her, and it says "and he
> came unto her," as is written "Moses came unto the tent of testimony"
> (Num. 17:23). Here, however, what is written? "Moses could not come in to

the tent of meeting for the cloud abode upon it" (Ex. 40:35). For what reason? She was preparing herself for him, as a woman prepares and adorns herself for her husband. At the time when she is adorning herself it is not proper for her husband to come in to her. That was why "Moses could not come in to the tent of meeting" and it was for that reason that "They brought the tabernacle unto Moses."[24]

This rather courtly vignette of Moses and the *shekhinah* as bridegroom and bride is paralleled by a number of passages, particularly in the Zohar, where the lovely damsel or chaste and faithful wife appears as symbolic representation of the *shekhinah*. It is generally understood that these refer in the first place to *shekhinah* as the bride of God, but not exclusively so. With regard to the Sabbath too, it should be recalled, there is reason in old Midrashic sources to think of her as *Israel's* bride: "Israel will be your mate," God says to the lonely seventh day.[25] The poetic genius of Alkabeẓ' *Lekha Dodi* lies in his steadfast refusal to name the *dod* to whom the hymn is addressed, thus maintaining a certain enriching ambiguity in the identity of the Sabbath's bridegroom.[26] This *shabbat*, for whom one must prepare "as one prepares a canopy for a bride," is also the one who is "shut and sealed on the six weekdays," in a passage that quotes from Ezekiel's vision of the restored Temple (46:1): ". . . but on the seventh day she is open to receive her husband."[27] The identification of Temple and Sabbath is sometimes associated with the exegesis of Lev. 19:30: "You shall keep My Sabbaths and fear My Temple." So, for example, Rabbi Bahya ben Asher of Barcelona, a contemporary of the Zohar:

> "'You shall keep My Sabbaths' . . . One is the Great Sabbath, that of 'remember,' and the other is the Temple, the Community of Israel, mate of [the upper] Sabbath. This one is 'keep,' and for that reason it was not proper that the work of [building] the Temple supersede this Sabbath/Temple.[28]

Here the lower Sabbath, that of 'keep' and thus particularly identified with the prohibitions among the Sabbath commands, is identified at once with *shekhinah* and Temple. For the Kabbalist it is perfectly a matter of course that the command of Sabbath was so placed in the Bible as to infer that the work of construction had to cease on the seventh day: anything else would have been self-contradictory, for the Sabbath, and particularly the cessation from labor, *is* the Temple.[29]

If the medieval Kabbalists were able by means of their mystical sym-
bolization of space and time to bring Temple and Sabbath to a state of
identification, the free-wheeling associative patterns of the later Hasidic
homilies were able to do the same. Popular impressions to the contrary,
their method was not at all that of the Kabbalists, but rather an extension, sometimes seemingly *ad absurdum*, of the classical methods of
Midrashic exegesis. Although the rubric of the *sefirot* is formally preserved in Hasidic discourse, its content has been largely vitiated. The
Kabbalistic system is generally used (*HaBaD* is the great exception here)
as only one more device in the hands of the homilist. Thus "Sabbath"
and "Temple" in the following passages are no longer ciphers for the
shekhinah, but once again the real Sabbath and Temple of time and
space, with perhaps just a slight added nuance of Kabbalistic meaning.

The first Hasidic passage comes from the *Degel Mahaneh Ephraim*,
the collected homilies of Rabbi Moses Hayyim Ephraim of Sudilkov,
first published in 1810/11. Ephraim was the grandson of the Ba'al Shem
Tov,[30] and his teachings often reflect the thoughts of the movement's
first central figure:

> "The children of Israel shall keep the Sabbath, observing the Sabbath
> throughout their generations as an everlasting covenant; it is a sign forever
> between Me and the children of Israel" (Ex. 31:13). The *Ba'al ha-Turim*
> notes that the words *'et ha-shabbat le-dorotam* may be abbreviated as *'HL*
> (consonantally) *'ohel*, "tent."

> In commenting on this we must first recall the verse "They shall make Me a
> tabernacle and I will dwell in their midst" (Ex. 25:8). We might then think
> that without such a tabernacle it would not be possible for the *shekhinah* to
> dwell amidst us! But the matter must be understood thus: "A foretaste of
> the world to come is the Sabbath day of rest." The best counsel [since there
> is no tabernacle] is to keep the Sabbath properly. In this way may we merit,
> as it were, the indwelling of the Presence, for the Sabbath is a sort of sanctu-
> ary. In that way too is it a foretaste of the future world [i.e. of the rebuilt
> Temple].

> It was for this reason that the Torah hinted at the word "tent" in the phras-
> ing of this verse, showing that the Sabbath too is a form of tent or taberna-
> cle. The word *le-dorotam* also hints at the notion of "dwelling"
> (DoRoTaM=DiRaTaM), as in the dwelling of a Temple. In this way God
> dwells in our midst, and that is why Scripture continues: "as an *everlasting
> covenant*": by means of the Sabbath, the Lord, blessed be He, dwells in our
> midst . . . and the words *'ot hi' le-'olam* again form the word *'ohel*, showing

that this sign goes on without interruption. Even in times when there is no Temple, the Sabbath has not been negated, *and it is the Temple*.[31]

Operating here outside that symbol-structure that had so utterly relativized space and time, the Hasidic master produces his own spiritualized re-reading of the Scriptural command. His spirituality remains halakhic, to be sure, for it is only by "keeping the Sabbath properly (*kehilkhato*)" that this new Temple is maintained. His essential point, however, is far-reaching, one that goes to the very core of the religious radicalism of the Hasidic movement: The destruction of the Temple does not represent an *essential* change in the relationship of God to His world and to Israel. The Presence remains in our midst as previously; only the medium of primary access to it has been shifted. The immanentism that the Ba'al Shem Tov's religion represented had to find a way to overcome the sense of divine distance that permeates so much of rabbinic and later Judaism.

A second Hasidic example, as likely to have been well-known to Heschel as was the first, is found in the *Mey ha-Shiloah*, by Rabbi Mordecai Joseph Leiner of Izbica (1800/01–1854). Izbica was an important school of Hasidic thought in central Poland; its founder, Mordecai Joseph, had at one point been quite close to Rabbi Mendel of Kotzk, whose latter-day disciples Heschel knew so well in Warsaw. R. Mordecai Joseph writes:

"You shall keep My Sabbaths and fear My Temple" (Lev. 19:30). 'My Sabbaths' [in the plural], for every dwelling of the *shekhinah* at any time, no matter how temporary, is called a Sabbath. The blessed Lord commanded us to honor all the places where His *shekhinah* has dwelt, however temporarily. "And fear My Temple"—the Targum renders this as "be in fear *for* My Temple": you still should long for the deepest [eschatological] good to be found in each of the commandments. The Sabbath as we have it now is much diminished; only in the future will God grant us "the day that is wholly Sabbath," when we shall have no need for any labors. We must long for this, while still giving honor, meanwhile, to that which God has commanded us.

This may be compared to a king who moves from place to place: you show honor to each of his lodgings, while still looking forward to his own resting-place . . .

This was the mistake of Hophni and Phinehas: they saw that God's dwelling in Shiloh was only a temporary one, and therefore they treated it lightly. Of such conduct Scripture says: "You have despised My Temple" . . .[32]

Here we have the lesson drawn out for us in a strikingly modern-sounding formulation: the juxtaposition of Sabbath and Temple teaches us that any place where the glory of God appears, in however transient a manner (and indeed what place is not capable of such description?) is to be treated as God's holy Temple. Yes, Judaism has become a religion of sacred time, learning through the bitter experience of exile that geographical locus alone could not suffice to describe the manner in which God dwells on earth. This time-centeredness, however, also served to expand and "liberate" the notion of sacred space, a process we see reaching its culmination here in the *Mey ha-Shiloah*. The history of exile teaches Israel that a sacred day, unlike a sacred mountain or a sacred shrine, may be carried anywhere and remain safe from outward attack. The hidden lesson here learned also inevitably points to the idea that any place where that Sabbath is proclaimed holy comes to have just a touch of Jerusalem residing within it. The legacy of wandering Israel to the world may lie precisely in this: home does not have to be abandoned as you are forced to leave it. The transformation of space into time may allow us to be bearers of our homes and origins, however far away from them modernity may lead us, so that the values they represented in our lives need not fade into mere pleasant memories of things past.

NOTES

1. *Der Mizrekh-Eropeisher Yid*, New York, Schocken Books, 1946, p. 44f. Expanded translation as *The Earth Is the Lord's*, New York, Schuman, 1950, p. 99.

2. These sources have been collected and discussed by Raphael Patai in *Man and Temple*, London, 1947. See also the dated but still important treatment by Victor Aptowitzer in Bet ha-Miqdash shel Ma'alah" Tarbiz 2 (1931). For the older Mesopotamian parallels see particularly the works of Geo Widengren, including *Sakrales Königtum im Alten Testament und im Judentum*, Stuttgart, 1955, and the various ancillary studies.

3. Michael Fishbane, "The Sacred Center in the Bible," in *Texts and Responses: Studies Presented to Nahum N. Glatzer*, Leiden, 1975, p. 6ff. See also his *Text and Texture: Close Readings of Selected Biblical Texts*, New York, Schocken, 1979. I am grateful to Pro-

fessor Fishbane for several suggestions he has made in connection with this article.

4. I do not mean to oversimplify a long and complex process. Of course I am aware that the synagogue began to come into being before the Temple was destroyed, etc. The question is asked from a long-range historical vantage-point.

5. Robert Goldenberg, "The Broken Axis," in JAAR 45 (1977) 353ff.

6. The phrases are all from the liturgy: daily 'amidah, festival mussaf 'amidah and Passover haggadah.

7. See the author's "The Ẕaddiq as Axis Mundi in Later Judaism," in JAAR 45 (1977) 327ff.

8. It is perhaps noteworthy, however, that the tale of Rabbi Simeon ben Yohai and his son plays so prominent a role in that volume, certainly serving to focus the reader's attention on the generation immediately after the destruction.

9. As to witnessing, for example, Maimonides' Mishneh Torah, Laws of Testimony 10:2 makes it clear that a violator of any Torah law of a certain magnitude may not testify; no special point is made of the Sabbath.

10. Yer. Ḥagigah 2:1 (77b).

11. The Sabbath attracted a good deal of attention among Latin writers, and not only those who had a particular interest in the Jews. For the sources see Radin, The Jews among the Greeks and Romans, p. 245ff. and J. Hugh Michael, "The Jewish Sabbath in the Latin Classical Writers" AJSLL 40 (1923/24) 117ff.

12. See the thorough treatment by Lawrence Schiffman, The Halakhah at Qumran, Leiden, 1975, p. 77ff.

13. See the treatment by Y.D. Gilat, "Le-Qadmutam shel 'Issurey Shabbat 'Aḥadim" in Bar-'Ilan 1 (1963) 106ff. A summary of Sabbath ritual in the Second Temple is found in EJ 15, col. 977. See further M. Fishbane's "Revelation and Tradition as Religious Categories in the Bible" in a forthcoming JBL.

14. The "derivation" of the 39 labors from the construction of the tabernacle is given in Shabbat 49b; see also 96b. It is clear that this is a rubric added later to an accumulation of forbidden labors of diverse origins. Tosafot ad loc. seems nearly to admit as much. On the 39 labors see further Y.D. Gilat, "39 'Avot Mel'akhot Shabbat" in Tarbiz 28 (1959/60) 226ff.

15. Ḥagigah 1:8, Tosefta Ḥagigah 9:9 and 'Eruvin 11:23. The actual derivation from 'akh is not found in the extant rabbinic sources, but only in the Middle Ages: RaSHI to Ex. 31:13. We do have a source in the Mekilta (ed. Horwitz/Rabin p. 345) that derives the relationship from the similar juxtaposition in Ex. 35:1ff. On the question of 'akh, see the extended discussion by M.M. Kasher in Torah Shelemah, v. 21, p. 58, n. 34.

16. But consider the parallel between our matter and the decision recorded in Rosh Hashanah 4:1: "When the holiday of Rosh Hashanah occurs on the Sabbath, the shofar is blown in the Temple but not in the town. When the Temple was destroyed, Rabbi Yohanan ben Zakkai decreed that it should be blown wherever there is a bet din." Here is a rather clear symbolic statement that the seat of rabbinic authority takes on something of a Temple-like quality. On this see Neusner, A Life of Yohanan ben Zakkai. Second edition, Leiden, 1970, p. 205f and Development of a Legend, Leiden, 1970, Index s.v. Sabbath.

17. Berakhot 55a. The Biblical text itself already seeks to link Hiram, architect of Solomon's Temple, with Bezalel. Note the linguistic parallel of I Kings 7:14 with Ex. 31:3. Further material on Bezalel of a similar sort is found scattered in rabbinic sources. See Ginzberg, Legends, s.v. Bezalel.

18. I am emending bi-khevod yoṣero to ba-kavod yeṣaro, which seems to make more sense, particularly if the phrase is a medieval gloss. I find no way of understanding the text as it stands.

19. Tanhuma, *Pequdey* 2. A parallel version is found in *Leqah Tov*, ad loc., and a somewhat better text of the Tanḥuma is preserved in R. Bahya to Ex. 38:21. A rather different version is found in *Midrash Tadshe'* 2 (*Bet ha-Midrash* 3, p. 164f.) See also the sources discussed in Ginzberg's *Legends*, v. 6, p. 67, n. 346, and by Chavel *ad loc.* in his edition of the Bahya commentary. See Bahya also on Ex. 40:16.

20. *Pesikta de-Rav Kahana*, ed. Buber 5b–6a, as emended by the editor. Perhaps an even stronger statement is found regarding Solomon's Temple in *Pesikta Rabbati* 6, ed. Friedmann 25a. There it is suggested that Solomon's very name SHeLoMoH) indicates that it was he who completed (hiSHeLyM) the making of heaven and earth.

21. This has been noticed by Cassutto, *Commentary on the Book of Exodus:* Jerusalem, 1967, pp. 476 and 483. Cassutto does not mention that he had been preceded by the Midrash and especially by R. Bahya in this insight. M. Fishbane informs me that "there is an ancient Near Eastern pattern, embedded in Enumaelish, that the end of Creation is construction of a temple for the victor god." Fragments of this, he notes, appear in the Bible (Ex. 15, Ps. 29) and this concluding pattern of Exodus is to be seen as a transformation of that pattern.

22. Taken symbolically; see note 15 above.

23. Zohar 2:135a-b. On the two Sabbaths in early Kabbalah see Nahmanides on Ex. 20:8 and 31:13. His comments are based on those in Bahir 181–2 (ed. Scholem 124). See further Tishby's *Mishnat ha-Zohar*, v. 2, 487ff. Sabbath as bride in the Kabbalah is of course also based on earlier motifs; the figure of Sabbath as queen is mentioned occasionally in rabbinic literature. Much is made of this theme in the Falasha treatise *Ta'azaza Sanbat*, but that development seems entirely unrelated to the Kabbalistic expansion of this idea.

24. Zohar 2:235a. "And he came unto her" is not part of the verse in Deut. 22:16, but has slipped into the author's mind from elsewhere.

25. Bereshit Rabbah 11:8. Elsewhere, however (Shemot Rabbah 25:11, for example), shabbat is taken as a token of the intimacy that exists between God as King and His lady Israel.

26. See the extended discussion of the bride and queen motifs in Heschel's *Sabbath*, p. 126ff., n. 4. The rabbinic sources to which I refer in n. 23 above are there listed in full.

27. Zohar 3:272b; Tiqquney Zohar 36, ed. Margaliot 78a.

28. Bahya to Lev. 19:30; ed. Chavel v.2, p. 532.

29. One cannot help but wonder also whether the Safed Kabbalists did not have this association somehow in mind when they chose Psalm 95 as the opening to Kabbalat Shabbat. The closing line of that Psalm stands before the Sabbath as a liturgy of entry: "So I vowed in My anger that they would not come in to my *menuḥah*." Of course in the context of the Psalm *menuḥah* clearly refers to the Land of Israel. Here, however, it cannot but refer to the Sabbath, and the Psalm then challenges the worshipper, much as does Psalm 24, to examine whether he is ready to "enter" the Sabbath as *Sanctum*. This same verse, by the way, was used earlier, exactly as one might expect, with regard to the Temple. See *Yalqut Shime'oni*, 2:189. I am indebted to Rabbi Jack Riemer for this insight.

30. On R. Ephraim, see the references in my *Tormented Master*, a study of his nephew, R. Nahman of Bratslav. The sources on him have been collected by M. Y. Guttman, *Geza' Qodesh*, Tel Aviv, 1950/51, and in Horodezky, *Ha-Ḥasidut weha-Ḥasidim*, v. 3, p. 7ff.

31. *Degel Mahaneh Ephraim, Ki tissa'*, ed. Jerusalem, 1962/63, p. 131f.

32. *Mey ha-Shiloah*, part one, *Qedoshim* 38b. The verse with which he concludes is not to be found in Scripture. He seems to be misquoting from I Samuel 2:29ff.

Jewish Particularity from Ha-Levi to Kaplan: Implications for Defining Jewish Philosophy

Raphael Jospe

University of Denver
Denver, Colorado

The attempt to define Jewish philosophy—what is specifically Jewish about it, and who may accordingly be considered to be a Jewish philosopher—is clearly a prerequisite for any study of this field. There seem to be two ways of approaching the problem: essential and formal. The first way is to establish criteria for the content of what may constitute Jewish philosophy; the second way is to begin (but not necessarily to end) with the Jewishness of the philosopher, whatever his topics and positions may be.

The essentialist approach has been followed by many of the leading scholars of Jewish philosophy. Its main advantage is that it provides clear criteria for what may or may not constitute Jewish philosophy, on the basis of which we may decide which philosophers deserve the label "Jewish" and which aspects of their works are part of the chain of Jewish philosophy.

The essentialist position is clearly stated by Julius Guttmann in the beginning of his monumental *Philosophies of Judaism:*[1]

> The peculiar character of Jewish existence in the Diaspora prevented the emergence of a Jewish philosophy in the sense in which we can speak of Greek, Roman, French, or German philosophy. Since the days of antiquity, Jewish philosophy was essentially a philosophy of Judaism. Even during the Middle Ages—which knew something like a total, all-embracing culture based on religion—philosophy rarely transcended its religious center. This religious orientation constitutes the distinctive character of Jewish philo-

sophy . . . . In this respect the philosophy of Judaism, whatever the differences in content deriving from the specific doctrines and the concepts of authority of the religions concerned, is formally similar to that of Christianity and Islam.

Thus, for Guttmann, philosophy is Jewish only if it focuses on religious issues, specifically within the context of Jewish religion. Accordingly, Guttmann begins his study with a survey of "the basic ideas of biblical religion" (Chapter 1) and "the religious ideas of Talmudic Judaism" (Chapter 3), and divides his book into "Jewish religious philosophy in the Middle Ages" and "Jewish philosophy of religion in the modern era." Colette Sirat articulates a second essential criterion:[2]

> To the extent that philosophy would relate to the Bible and would draw its justification from it . . . it is Jewish philosophy. It is not sufficient that the philosopher himself be a Jew; Spinoza, for example, whose theory is perhaps the most original of all philosophies formed by Jews, was certainly a Jew, but his philosophy is not Jewish, because it does not rely at all on the Jewish tradition . . . . As has been said, the Jewish origin of a philosopher is not sufficient; to the contrary, Jewish philosophy is not derived from Jewish sources . . . Medieval Jewish philosophy is philosopy which was adapted to the Jewish tradition by finding agreement or similarity of expression between it and Jewish religious tradition . . . . Only the combination of philosophy and Jewish tradition forms Jewish philosophy . . . . The essence of Jewish philosophy is the harmonizing of a particular system of thought with the Jewish Sources.

In other words, not only must Jewish philosophy deal with Jewish religion, but it must also be in agreement with the religious tradition. Dr. Sirat therefore rejects Spinoza as a Jewish philosopher. According to her view, Spinoza was a Jew and a philosopher, but not a Jewish philosopher. Guttmann accords Spinoza a similar treatment. His chapter on Spinoza is carefully titled "The influence of Jewish philosophy on the system of Spinoza," and he begins his discussion of Spinoza with the following disclaimers:[3]

> Spinoza's system belongs more properly to the development of European thought than to a history of Jewish philosophy . . . . His philosophy stands in profound opposition to the Jewish religion . . . and he abandoned the attempt to reconcile this opposition through harmonization . . . . Separated

from any connection to the Jewish religion, his philosophy is no longer directed to believers in Judaism, but to the community of European thinkers. . . . Spinoza consciously placed himself within this European movement of thought, and sought to develop his system within it. His influence was exclusively beyond the boundaries of the world of Judaism . . . . Spinoza was involved with Jewish philosophy only insofar as the latter served as one of the formative causes of his thought . . . . The historic roots of Spinoza's philosophy, however, extended far beyond the Jewish sphere.

Spinoza's qualifications as a Jewish philosopher are debatable, and not all agree with Guttmann and Sirat. But the point here is clear: the essentialist position requires not only that the Jewish philosopher limit himself to Jewish religious questions (at least in those aspects of his interests that he would wish to qualify as essentially Jewish), but also that his position be in accord with Jewish religious tradition either directly or through harmonization with the tradition.

It seems, moreover, that from the essentialist perspective, Jewish philosophy may no longer exist, since the qualifying conditions cannot be met. As Isaac Husik sorrowfully concludes in his *History of Medieval Jewish Philosophy:*[4]

There are Jews now and there are philosophers, but there are no Jewish philosophers and there is no Jewish philosophy.

Guttmann was only slightly more positive:[5]

Jewish philosophy, which had been renewed in the last decades of the nineteenth century, has now reached its nadir. If it once more arises to continue its work, it will develop under entirely new conditions.

Like Leopold Zunz and others, who thought that *Wissenschaft des Judentums* should provide "an accounting from that which is closed," since they regarded Judaism as dying or dead and "the Jews in our day . . . (as) carrying post-Biblical Hebrew literature to its grave,"[6] without foreseeing the contribution their "accounting" would make to the renewal of Jewish creativity, Husik and Guttmann may have contributed to a renewal of Jewish philosophy by facilitating its study.

By searching for the Jewishness of the philosophy rather than the Jewishness of the philosopher (as the formalist approach does), the essentialist approach would seem to fulfill the mandate of the Jewish

philosopher of thirteenth century Spain, Shem Tov ibn Falaquera: "It is
not proper to consider the speaker but rather what is said."[7] However,
the medieval philosopher was concerned not with the *Jewishness* of a
proposition but rather with its *truth*. *Ad hominem* calculations certainly
are irrelevant to the truth—but they are quite as certainly relevant to the
criteria for defining the Jewishness of a philosopher or philosophy. For
we are not asking if a philosopher is right or wrong, or whether his
philosophy is true or false (which was Falaquera's concern). We are
simply asking if the philosopher and his philosophy are *Jewish*, which is
an entirely different question.

Here we come to a fundamental problem with the essentialist
approach, despite its clarity: it is prescriptive rather than descriptive. It
mandates what Jewish philosophy should be, rather than understand
what it is and has been. It limits one to a pre-defined or pre-conceived
notion of what is legitimate within the context of Judaism. How can such
an approach take into account the varied and even opposing positions
that we find throughout Jewish literature (in this case philosophical)—a
richness of points of view that is manifested even in the Bible and Talmud? Is Hasdai Crescas to be excluded from the ranks of Jewish philosophers because he affirmed a deterministic theology in opposition to
most of the other Jewish philosophers, including Maimonides, who
affirmed human free will? Crescas' position was not normative; shall we
therefore conclude that it was not Jewish?

The essentialist position presumes that Judaism has an essence by
which philosophers and philosophies can be judged to be Jewish. But to
state that Judaism has an essence seems to have proven consistently
easier than to define that essence. Like the negative way of describing
God, of whom all we can say is that He exists and not what He is,
not Christianity) than to state definitively what it is. Like Maimonides'
God, of which all we can say is that He exists and not what He is,
Judaism's essence seems to be there, somewhere, but to defy commonly
acceptable definition. In short, the essentialist position does not work.
Has anyone ever defined the essence of Judaism to the satisfcation of all,
or even many, educated Jews? And without such a definition, the essentialist approach has no basis.

Finally, the essentialist position obligates us to create artificial dicho-
tomies within works of thinkers who are universally recognized as
Jewish philosophers. Take, for example, Maimonides' four proofs of the
existence, incorporeality, and unity of God (in Part II of the *Guide of the*

Perplexed). Such proofs presumably meet the two conditions the essentialists posed: the subject (God) is part of Jewish religion and the philosophical position taken (that God exists) is in accord with Jewish tradition. Aristotelian physics and metaphysics presumably fail to meet these conditions: in the first case, because principles of motion are scientific questions extraneous to Jewish religious interest and, in the second case, because they may not necessarily be in accord with at least some of Jewish tradition (if, for example, one concludes philosophically that motion must be eternal, but also accepts the view that the Torah teaches *creatio ex nihilo*).

So we are left with the following paradox: a supposedly "Jewish" proof consists entirely of non-Jewish elements. And what if we find similar or identical proofs in Muslim, Christian, or other thought, either by coincidence or due to direct or indirect influence in the one direction or the other? Can the same proof be essentially (i.e., in terms of its content) Jewish and non-Jewish? We shall presumably then have to conclude, following this same line of reasoning, that the *Guide of the Perplexed*, which is generally considered to be a Jewish book (Leo Strauss questioned whether it is philosophy but not whether it is Jewish), is both a Jewish and a non-Jewish book; the proofs of God are both Jewish (in their conclusion) and non-Jewish (in the Aristotelian principles upon which they are based and in their line of reasoning), and Maimonides is thus both a Jewish and a non-Jewish philosopher.

At this point, we may question the helpfulness as well as the accuracy of an approach which forces us to dissect a man's thought and work, perhaps sentence by sentence, to separate the Jewish from the non-Jewish elements. We may legitimately point out that some of Maimonides' works deal with more explicitly Jewish subjects, while others (such as his scientific or medical works) deal with subjects of more general interest, just as one may distinguish his efforts in the area of Jewish law from his efforts in Jewish philosophy. But can we really say that the one is Jewish and the other is not, when (as in the proofs of God) the two are so intimately interwoven and are the product of one man's mind? Where should we draw the line between the Jewish and non-Jewish aspects of Maimonides' proofs of God—and is this even a useful question, helping us to understand Maimonides better?

The essentialist approach, however successful or unsuccessful it may prove to be, assumes that Judaism defines the Jewish people, and in this case Jewish philosophy. The essence of Judaism, whatever it may be, shapes the Jewish people and provides the criteria for judging the Jewishness of a philosopher and philosophy. The formalist approach, on the other hand, assumes that the Jewish people shapes Judaism, and, by extension, that it is the Jewishness of the philosophers that determines the Jewishness of their philosophies. In a way, this position goes back to Judah Ha-Levi's concept of Jewish distinctiveness and particularity.

For Ha-Levi, the Jewish people, biologically descended from Abraham, possesses a unique and divine faculty for prophetic revelation, the 'amr 'ilahi (Hebrew: 'inyan 'elohi), divine power or influence. All living things have the faculty of nutrition, growth, and reproduction. But only some of them, the animals, have the faculties of sensation and voluntary motion; and of the animals, only humans have the capacity to reason.[8] The historic phenomenon of prophecy, however, cannot be attributed to the rational faculty; if it were a rational function, all peoples could have experienced divine revelation, whereas in fact prophetic revelation was historically manifested only among the people of Israel and in the land of Israel.[9] In sharp disagreement with the rationalists (like Maimonides) who saw prophecy as the highest stage of intellection, Ha-Levi points out that there never was a prophet among the philosophers or a philosopher among the prophets.[10]

Ha-Levi denied that Jewish distinctiveness could be associated with ethics or rationality, which must be universal, and without which even a band of robbers could not exist. These universal rational and ethical principles are the foundation of any just society, and are necessarily prior to the specifically Jewish laws, both in nature and in time. That which makes Israel unique among the nations is accordingly neither rational nor ethical, but divine.[11]

And here we come to the crucial point in Ha-Levi's theory. One cannot maintain that the Torah gave the Jews their distinctive divine faculty. The Jews, and only the Jews, were able to receive prophetic revelation because they already possessed the 'amr 'ilahi ('inyan 'elohi). This special faculty, with which Adam was endowed, passed initially from generation to generation among individuals, until it reached Abraham, Isaac, and Jacob, from whom it passed to the latter's twelve sons and thus to the entire people of Israel. It is part of the biological structure of every Jew, although it has become actualized only in a few, the prophets.[12] Therefore, "without the children of Israel there would be no Torah; moreover, they did not derive their uniqueness from Moses, but

Moses derived his uniqueness from them."[13] Thus, according to Ha-Levi, it is not the Torah that makes the Jewish people possible, but the people that makes the Torah possible.

Ha-Levi's "racial" theory of Jewish distinctiveness was revived in the nineteenth century by Abraham Geiger, who saw the Jewish people as endowed with a "religious genius," as other nations manifested genius in other areas of endeavor. Geiger wrote that

> Judaism . . . does not speak of the God of Moses, or of the God of the prophets, but of the God of Abraham, Isaac, and Jacob, and of the God of the whole race . . . It is the revelation which lay dormant in the whole people and was concentrated in individuals.[14]

Even if he had accepted such a "racial" concept of Judaism, Moses Mendelssohn, who argued more than a generation before Geiger for Jewish integration into European society while retaining traditional Jewish practice, could scarcely have propounded such a theory publicly at the same time as he was attempting to demonstrate Judaism's compatibility with religious liberty and freedom from coercion. Mendelssohn did not follow Ha-Levi's "racial" doctrine, but his structure of Jewish particularity was clearly based on Ha-Levi. Like Ha-Levi, Mendelssohn rejected the equation of Jewish identity with rational truth. The truth, knowledge of which is essential for salvation must be universally accessible to all people through reason. According to Mendelssohn, there is a universal "natural" religion of reason on which all positive religion must be based, and Judaism, unlike Christianity, claims no truths necessary for salvation in addition to those of natural religion.

The truths of natural religion were not, and could not have been, revealed:[15]

> The voice that was heard at Sinai on that great day did not proclaim, "I am the Lord your God, the necessary autonomous Being, omnipotent and omniscient, who rewards men in a future life according to their deeds." This is the universal religion of mankind, not Judaism; and this kind of universal religion—without which man can become neither virtuous nor happy—was not and, in fact, could not have been revealed at Sinai.

The notion of "revealed religion" or "revealed truth" is a contradiction in terms; a person capable of understanding the truth does not need revelation (in which case revelation is superfluous), and a person un-convinced of the truth "demands rational proofs, not miracles" (in which case revelation is ineffective).[16]

For Mendelssohn, therefore, Judaism is not revealed religion but revealed law, and these revealed laws "refer to, or are based on, eternal verities, or remind us of them, or induce us to ponder them."[17]

> Laws, precepts, commandments, rules of conduct: they were to be peculiar to this people, and their observance was to bring happiness to the entire nation as well as to its individual members . . . These laws were revealed, that is, they were made known by God through the spoken and written word . . . they guide the seeking mind to divine truth—partly eternal, partly historical—on which the religion of this people was based. The ceremonial law was to be the link between thought and action, between theory and practice.[18]

Thus, Jewish particularity has nothing to do with doctrine; a proposition is in itself neither Jewish nor non-Jewish. It is either true or false. The specifically Jewish factor lies not in the rational content of what is taught, but in the manner in which it is taught—in this case, in the rein-forcement the doctrine receives through the observance of the revealed ceremonial law. Granted that the observance of the cremonial law depends on the truth or facticity of the revelation of that law at Sinai (as Mendelssohn clearly maintains), that historic truth is not specifically Jewish. A believing Christian would accept the facticity of Sinai, but neither the Christian nor the Jew would regard the ceremonial law as applying to the Christian. The particular Jewish quality still lies in the observance of the law, and not in the acceptance of truth, be it historical or rational.

For Mendelssohn, then, the universal is the foundation of the par-ticular, and the particular supports and guides people to the universal. For Ha-Levi and Mendelssohn, as for some later Jewish thinkers, the problems of essentialism versus formalism and the universal versus the particular seem to be related and to function analogously. In both Ha-Levi and Mendelssohn, as we have seen, the rational teachings of Judaism, which some others would call its essence, are seen as universal and not particularly Jewish, and Jewish particularity is therefore for-mal—it lies in the non-rational or supra-rational ceremonial law, which for Ha-Levi activates the Jew's *'inyan 'elohi*, and which is for Mendels-sohn the link between thought and action.

Conversely, the essentialist would seem to regard Jewish particularity as a function of Judaism's essence. That which is specifically Jewish is its essence, but that essence may have universal implications and importance (such as messianic goals or theories of Jewish mission). If what is particular to Judaism is its ultimately universal teachings, then it is by this essentialist standard that we should judge the Jewishness of a philosopher or a philosophy.

The formalist, of course, cannot define Jewish particularity in terms of essence: such essence may not exist, or may not be readily and meaningfully definable, or it may be identified with rational truth which is regarded as universal and not particular, and thus not "Jewish." Having rejected the possibility of an essential Jewish particularity as tantamount to a contradiction in terms, the formalist must turn elsewhere for Jewish particularity, by which standard a philosopher or philosophy could be judged purely formally to be Jewish or not.

The essentialist would agree that the essential teachings of Judaism are ultimately universal, but he would see the relationship of particular and universal as basically chronological: the Jews are the particular source of a universal truth in which all humanity will ultimately somehow share. The formalist, while not necessarily denying the chronological relationship, would regard the particular and universal as inherently correlative: that Judaism provides particular expression of universal truth, and that the universal and particular cannot exist without each other.

Such a relationship of the universal and the particular is evident in several of Aḥad Ha-Am's essays, although, unlike Mendelssohn, he did not generally identify the particular element with Jewish law. In "Ha-'Adam Ba-'Ohel" (1892), written in reaction to Y.L. Gordon's poem "Haqiẓah 'Ami," in which the poet said "heyeh 'adam be-ẓetekha vi-yehudi be-'ohalekha" ("be a man when you go out and a Jew in your home"), Aḥad Ha-Am asserted:[19]

> A man when you go out—but when the man goes out he does not remain merely an abstract man; he must put on some form. And if he is not a Jew, he is a Russian, a Pole, a German, etc.

Aḥad Ha-Am rejected the dichotomy between universal humanity and particular nationality as false; he saw no contradiction between these two concepts. Humanity, he maintained, is an abstraction, and nationality is its concrete form; universal humanity is revealed in every nation in accordance with its conditions of life and its particular needs. The "internal spirit" requires expression in the "external form." Thus, the two principles are not opposites; they complement each other. But, as a result of diaspora conditions, the Jewish law and spirit have become petrified and, accordingly, have lost their ability to deal flexibly with human problems and needs. Therefore, Ḥibbat Ẓiyyon (as opposed to political Zionism, which could only deal with the material problem of the Jews and not the spiritual problem of Judaism) "stands for a Judaism which shall have as its focal point the ideal of our nation's unity, its renaissance, and its free development through the expression of universal human values in terms of its own distinctive spirit."[20]

In "Ḥiqui Ve-Hitbolelut" (Imitation and Assimilation; 1893), Aḥad Ha-Am distinguished between imitation, which is a positive principle on which individual learning and cultural development are based, and the negative principle of assimilation. Imitation aims at self-expression, at which the imitated model excelled. However, when one takes over from the model not only the pattern of self-expression but also the particular content expressed, one negates or effaces one's own distinctive identity and assimilates the identity of the model.[21]

Aḥad Ha-Am similarly argued in "Shinui Ha-'Arakhin" (Transvaluation of Values; 1898) against uncritical Jewish adoption of Nietzsche's concept of the *Uebermensch*. Aḥad Ha-Am found room in Judaism for the formal concept, but not for its content, which he saw as specifically Teutonic in its glorification of physical power and brute force. But in formal terms he argued that Judaism had a concept of the *Uebermensch* in the *ẓaddik*, whose superiority is spiritual and moral rather than physical.

> It is not enough for us simply to import the foreign material; we must first of all adapt and assimilate it to our national spirit . . . Let us analyze these ideas, and divide them into their constituent parts, in order to discover what it is in them that attracts, and what it is in them that is at variance with Judaism . . . Then we shall be able to give these ideas a new form; to free the human element from its subordination to the German form, and subordinate it instead to our own form. Thus we shall have the necessary synthesis, and we shall be importing into our literature ideas which are new, but not foreign.[22]

Here Aḥad Ha-Am is calling attention to the need for an appropriate relationship between the universal content (the ideal leader) and its particular form (spiritual as opposed to physical superiority); certain ideas may lend themselves more appropriately to one form of expression than to another. But he does not define this relationship precisely, and his repeated references to the Jewish "spirit" and national "genius" may have blurred the distinction between form and content. When Nietzsche's *Uebermensch* is translated into the spiritual terms of the ẓaddik, have we merely changed its external form, adapting it to Jewish forms, or have we possibly changed the very essence of the concept? Is there something—an essence perhaps—in Judaism (in Aḥad Ha-Am's terms, its spiritual genius and moral superiority[23]) which requires us to adopt only certain forms and to reject others? This ambiguity may well be the major disadvantage of the formalist approach to Jewish particularity.

But the essentialists also fail to resolve this problem. Leo Baeck, in his *Essence of Judaism (Wesen des Judentums)*, virtually restates the formalist position, with the same ambiguity as to what constitutes "a uniquely Jewish character" or "Jewish genius" and makes something "genuinely Jewish" and in accord with Judaism's "essential character":[24]

> For as the Jews breathed the air of the countries in which they lived, they also participated in their histories. And thus a variety of alien influences entered through the gates of Judaism. The ability of Jewish genius to absorb within itself varied elements of civilizations with which it has contact bears witness to its creative power; for it has proved itself capable of digesting and completely assimilating them . . . The influences were subsumed into the Jewish tradition and given a uniquely Jewish character . . . Only that which could be made genuinely Jewish became part of the permanent heritage. However much the Jewish religion exposed itself to alien influences, it never changed its essential character, nor abandoned itself to those influences.

At times, Baeck's "essence of Judaism" seems to give way completely to formalism. Baeck equates "essence" with a certain "constancy" that Judaism manifested, despite its many changes and variations.[25] Pointing out that rabbinic Judaism identified the "principles of the Torah" with proper deeds and not creed, and that this emphasis on the "good deed is one of the strongest possible checks against dogmatism,"[26] Baeck commented that

> even if a need had been felt for dogmas, there were no bodies with authority to establish them. *The will to belong and the conviction of adherence were the decisive criteria for Judaism.*[27]

The "essence" has now become formal. The "decisive criteria for Judaism" no longer lie in some essential doctrine but in the identification with the Jewish group. Like the parable of the wicked son in the *Haggadah shel Pesaḥ, she hozi et 'aẓmo min ha-kelal ve-khafar ba-'iqar* (who removed himself from the group and thereby denied the fundamental principle), it seems that the *'iqar* (which the second son denies) consists of identifying with the Jewish people and not with any set doctrine or set of doctrines.

Such formalism becomes most explicit in the thought of Mordecai Kaplan. For Kaplan, "in Judaism as a civilization, 'belonging' is prior to 'believing,' although meaningless without 'believing.'"[28]

> The common denominator in the different stages of the Jewish civilization is not to be sought in the tenets and practices, but in the continuous life of the Jewish people.[29]

For Kaplan, as for Aḥad Ha-Am, no human exists independently of a particular group and its culture.[30] The abstract universal never exists independently of the concrete particular. For example, "there are languages, English, French, German, etc., but language in general is only an abstract concept, not a reality."[31] Just as individual languages are necessary to provide particular expression for universal ideas, without implying that one language is better than any other, so do individual civilizations provide particular expression for universal values. Therefore, if "Judaism as a civilization is not a form of truth but a form of life,"[32]

> when we are asked: 'Why remain Jews,?' the only reason we should feel called upon to give is: 'Because the Jewish people is here and we are part of it.'[33]

Or, as Aḥad Ha-Am put it:[34]

> I at least have no need to exalt my people to Heaven, to trumpet its superiority above all other nations, in order to find a justification for its existence. I at least know 'why I remain a Jew'—or, rather, I can find no meaning in

such a question, any more than if I were asked why I remain my father's son.

Therefore, according to Kaplan, "the value of Judaism is in no wise dependent on its ability to demonstrate superiority to other ways of life."[35]

> The difference in character between one civilization and another is not so much in the ideals they profess as in the social institutions they evoke as a means of expressing their ideals.[36]

Each civilization absorbs elements from other civilizations. Kaplan differentiates between "active assimilation" (Aḥad Ha-Am's "imitation") and "passive assimilation" (Aḥad Ha-Am's "assimilation"), or *assimilating* (in which the civilization's uniqueness and individuality are preserved and enhanced) and *being assimilated* (which involves self-effacement).

> Jews must discover what there is in western civilization that has universal import, must relate those aspects of it to the traditional sancta of Judaism, and thus integrate them in the very fabric of Jewish civilization.[37]

In such a formal structure, uniqueness and distinctiveness imply no superiority, as already stated, but merely the fact that each civilization (like each language) differs from all others. For just as each language has a distinct way of expressing universal concepts, each civilization has "sancta"—

> those institutions, places, historic events, popular heroes, all other objects of popular reverences to which superlative importance, or sanctity, is ascribed.[38]

Sancta focus attention on universal ideals and values, and provide for their particular reinforcement and expression. Kaplan's "sancta" thus function anthropologically, as Mendelssohn's "revealed law" functioned theologically. For Kaplan, as for Mendelssohn,

> these truths and values . . . are universal. They are not the monopoly of the group that discovers them. They may be discovered by other groups as well.

> Religions are distinct from one another not so much ideationally as existentially ... What is important is that the sancta of each people or church help to humanize all who belong to it, by implementing those universal values which it should share with all other peoples and churches.[39]

Since truth is universal, and what is particular is only the sancta through which it is expressed, one cannot claim that Judaism possesses any unique or distinctive essential truth, but rather that

> Jewish religion is Jewish only because of its functioning in and through the Jewish people.[40]

Such a theory of Jewish particularity, as it has evolved from Ha-Levi to Kaplan, has clear implications for the criteria of defining Jewish philosophy. The formalist approach begins not with the Jewish content of the philosophy but with the Jewishness of the philosopher. Obviously, the accident of Jewish birth is only a necessary and not a sufficient criterion.

Another contemporary writer, Isaac Franck, in two recent articles on Spinoza,[41] has proposed three formal criteria for determining who is a Jewish philosopher: first, that the philosopher's ideas grew out of the collective experience of the Jewish people; second, that the philosopher aimed at a Jewish audience, and sought to advance Jewish thought; and third, that the philosopher did in fact contribute to the advance of Jewish thought.[42]

These or similar formal criteria, especially the third, necessarily entail some degree of subjective judgement when applied to specific cases (such as Spinoza), and we may well find any number of philosophers who fulfill one or two of them, but not all three.

Formalism affords far greater flexibility than does essentialism. What, for example, will happen if we find diametrically opposing points of view among several Jewish philosophers? Maimonides categorized as a heretic (*min*) anyone who affirms that there is one God, but that God has a body,[43] and later asserted that a person who believes in a corporeal God is worse than an idolator.[44] To this, Ravad (Rabbi Abraham ben David of Posquières) took strong exception:

> This is impossible. Why did he call such a person a heretic, when some who were greater and better than he fellowed this opinion, according to what they saw in the Bible and even more according to what they saw in *aggadot* which corrupt opinions.[45]

And what, for example, if we find similarities or even identity between the positions of "Jewish" and non-Jewish philosophers? The common Jewish denominator can thus not lie in the positions themselves (since Jews may disagree with each other but agree with non-Jews), in an essential manner. The positions must be Jewish (whether true or false) not because of what they are intrinsically, but because of their being held by Jews, in accordance with the formal criteria we have mentioned. When it comes to truth, Falaquera was right: we must consider only the statement, and not the speaker (whether Jewish or non-Jewish). But when it comes to determining Jewishness, we must consider the speaker and not what is said.

Let us consider another possibility. What if the Jews of his time had accepted Jesus as Christ? Christianity would then have been Judaism (or a part of it), or Judaism would have been Christianity, for better or for worse. It seems rather obvious that the split between Judaism and Christianity was inevitable, and from many perspectives, desirable. Most Jews regard Judaism and Christianity as totally incompatible, and Aḥad Ha-Am devotes a major essay ("'Al Shetei Ha-Se'ipim," called "Judaism and the Gospels" in English) to this theme. But without regard for the substantive issue, was not the Jewish people's historic and continued rejection of Jesus and all that came after him the decisive factor here, whatever the reasons for the rejection may have been and may be today? In other words, what the Jewish people historically accepts and affirms is Judaism, and what the Jewish people historically rejects is not Judaism.

Such total acceptance or rejection, however, with virtual if not total unanimity over the ages, is surely limited to overwhelming life and death issues that affect the very survival of the Jewish people and Judaism. On a similar magnitude, we saw debate over the need for a Jewish State virtually eliminated with the threat, and then the reality, of the Holocaust, which made the need for a homeland so obvious as to render opposition to it obscene and limited to the tiny lunatic fringes of the right and left of the Jewish spectrum.

But on other questions, many of which are highly abstract, theoretical, and speculative, and on which immediate Jewish survival does not obviously depend, there always has been great latitude in Judaism. The formal approach mandates such latitude, whereas essentialism limits, and may even preclude it.

If we think of other areas of Jewish cultural creativity, such as art and music, the problem is the same as in the case of Jewish philosophy.

Should Jewish art be restricted essentially to what we predetermine to be legitimate and authentic Jewish themes? Are only pictures of Jerusalem (with its Roman, Arabic, and Turkish features), or pictures of rabbis wrapped in *talit* and *tefillin*, poring over heavy tomes of the Talmud, to be accepted as "Jewish art?" Is Jewish music outside the synagogue to be limited essentially to "Fiddler on the Roof" *schmaltz?*

In fact, music is a good example of how the formalist approach may prove more successful than the essentialist position. The same basic melody (the content) can be given radically different expression by changing its form: Beethoven's Fifth became a "disco" hit in the movie "Saturday Night Fever," and a famous tune of the Beatles was transformed into a baroque "Fifth of Beethoven." In both cases, the same melody took on the sound of a different era or culture by changing its form and retaining its essential content.

Cannot, then, the same be said of Jewish philosophy? The idea, if it has any merit, may not originally have been Jewish at all, but it became Jewish by being incorporated into the thought of Jews, struggling with their Jewish past, confronting their Jewish present, and attempting to contribute to the Jewish future.

Perhaps the differences between formalism and essentialism have been exaggerated. Like the particular and the universal, form and essence may well be correlative in reality, and our abstract dichotomy between them may be artificial. Analogous to the futile question of whether the chicken or the egg came first, it may not be very productive for us to weigh the degree to which the Jews shape Judaism or Judaism shapes the Jews. Jews are certainly as much products of Judaism as they are its producers. As Aḥad Ha-Am put it, *yoter mishe-yisra'el shamru et ha-shabbat, shamrah ha-shabbat 'otam* (more than Israel preserved the Sabbath, the Sabbath preserved them).[46]

In this sense, neither formalism nor essentialism alone is entirely adequate. Nevertheless, when attempting to define Jewish philosophy, and when developing a theory of Jewish particularity as the basis for such a definition, the formalist approach, even with all of its admitted limitations, may ultimately prove far more effective than the essentialist approach. The formalist position, for example, does not preclude our making descriptive statements about Jewish teaching in an attempt to find normative positions in Jewish teaching. But it does preclude our making prescriptive statements about those teachings. The existence of a normative position (such as is alluded to by Baeck's term "constancy''),⁴⁷ if it can be documented and demonstrated, does not imply that non-normative positions were not in their day, or may not be even today, legitimate forms of Jewish expression (as might be implied by Baeck's term "essence").

Even in *halakhah*, let alone in non-halakhic literature, the minority view is respected as legitimate, certainly with regard to those belonging to that particular community or observing its minhag. *Kal va-ḥomer* in matters of opinion, such as philosophy. Majority rule determines the *halakhah*, as well it should. But the majority cannot decide what is true or false, and by excluding non-normative opinions from Jewish philosophy, we do a greater disservice to ourselves than to the philosophers whom we treat in this manner. To exclude them is to preclude any possibility of our learning from their mistakes within the context of our own tradition. And who knows—perhaps they were right after all?

NOTES

1. Julius Guttmann, *Philosophies of Judaism* (N.Y., 1964), p. 4; *Ha-Pilosofiah Shel Ha-Yahadut* (Jerusalem, 1963), pp. 9–10.

2. Colette Sirat, *Hagut Pilosofit Bi-Yemei Ha-Beinayim* (Jewish Philosophical Thought in the Middle Ages) (Jerusalem, 1975), pp. 7–8. My translation.

3. Guttmann, *Philosophies of Judaism*, Eng. pp. 265–266, Heb. p. 241. Guttmann's statement here that Spinoza's "influence was exclusively beyond the boundaries of the world of Judaism" is contradicted by his own essay "Mendelssohn's *Jerusalem* and Spinoza's *Theologico-Political Treatise*" ("Yerushalayim Shel Mendelssohn Veha-Masekhet Ha-Te'ologit Ha-Medinit Le-Spinoza") in *Dat U-Mada'* (Religion and Knowledge; Jerusalem, 1955).

4. Isaac Husik, *History of Medieval Jewish Philosophy* (N.Y., 1916, 1973), p. 432.

5. Guttmann, *Philosophies of Judaism*, Eng. p. 397, Heb. p. 354.

6. Quoted in Michael Meyer, *Origins of the Modern Jew* (Detroit, 1967), p. 161.

7. Falaquera, *Sefer Ha-Ma'alot*, pp. 11–12. Cf. *De'ot Ha-Pilosofim*, Introduction, p. 12. This was said in the context of accepting the truth from any source, Jewish or non-Jewish. Maimonides had similarly prefaced his work on ethics and psychology (*Shemonah Peraqim*, the *Eight Chapters of Maimonides on Ethics*, ed. Joseph Gorfinkle, N.Y., 1912, 1966, Arabic and Hebrew text p. 6, English p. 36) by stating: "Listen to the truth from whoever says it."

8. Judah Ha-Levi, *Kuzari*, I:31–35.

9. *Kuzari*, I:95, 103; II:12–24, 32–45, 48.

10. *Kuzari*, I:4.

11. *Kuzari*, II:48, III:7.

12. *Kuzari*, I:95.

13. *Kuzari*, II:56.

14. Quoted in Gunther Plaut, *The Rise of Reform Judaism*, p. 126.

15. Moses Mendelssohn, *Jerusalem and Other Jewish Writings*, edited and translated by Alfred Jospe (N.Y., 1969), p. 69.

16. Mendelssohn, *Jerusalem*, p. 69.

17. Mendelssohn, *Jerusalem*, p. 71.

18. Mendelssohn, *Jerusalem*, pp. 98–99.

19. "Ha-'Adam Ba-'Ohel" (1892) in *Kol Kitvei Aḥad Ha-Am* (Jerusalem, 1965), p. 50.

20. "Torah Sheba-Lev" (1894), in *Kol Kitvei Aḥad Ha-Am*, p. 53.

21. "Ḥiqui Ve-Hitbolelut" (1893), in *Kol Kitvei Aḥad Ha-Am*, p. 86ff.

22. "Shinui Ha-'Arakhin" (1898) in *Kol Kitvei Aḥad Ha-Am*, p. 155. The translation is based on Leon Simon's *Selected Essays of Aḥad Ha-Am* (Philadelphia, 1948), p. 224. Simon, however, renders *ruḥenu ha-le'umi* (our national spirit) as "our national genius," which is inaccurate, especially since later in the essay, Aḥad Ha-Am does refer to "our genius" (*ge'onutenu*) (Hebrew, p. 156, English p. 228). Simon also translates *harkavah* (synthesis) as "assimilation," which is misleading in light of Aḥad Ha-Am's opposition to assimilation (*hitbolelut*). On *harkavah* as "synthesis," cf. Joseph Klatzkin, *Oẓar Ha-Munaḥim Ha-Pilosofiim*, Vol. I, p. 215.

23. Cf. "Shinui Ha-'Arakhin," pp. 154–156 (Eng. pp. 228–232.)

24. Leo Baeck, *The Essence of Judaism* (N.Y., 1948), pp. 17–18.

25. Baeck, *Essence of Judaism*, p. 9: "Such constancy, such essence, Judaism does possess despite the shifting phases of its long history."

26. Baeck, *Essence of Judaism*, p. 14.

27. Baeck, *Essence of Judaism*, p. 15. Italics added for emphasis.

28. Personal correspondence.

29. Mordecai Kaplan, *Judaism as a Civilization* (N.Y., 1934, 1957), p. 381.

30. Kaplan, *Judaism as a Civilization*, p. 342.

31. Kaplan, *Future of the American Jew* (N.Y., 1949), p. 512.

32. Kaplan, *Judaism as a Civilization*, p. 521.

33. Kaplan, *A New Zionism* (N.Y., 1955), p. 115. Cf. *Future of the American Jew*, p. 47: "We are faithful to Jewish religion, not because we have chosen it as the best of all religions, but because it is ours."

34. Aḥad Ha-Am, "'Avdut Be-Tokh Ḥerut" (1891) in *Kol Kitvei Aḥad Ha-Am*, p. 69 (Eng. pp. 193–194).

35. Kaplan, *Judaism as a Civilization*, p. 100.

36. Kaplan, *Judaism as a Civilization*, p. 419.

37. Kaplan, *The Meaning of God in Modern Jewish Religion* (N.Y., 1962), p. 351. Cf. p. 339.

38. Kaplan, *Future of the American Jew*, p. 46. Cf. p. 220.

39. Kaplan, *Future of the American Jew*, p. 220.

40. Kaplan, *Future of the American Jew*, p. 209.

41. Isaac Franck, "Spinoza's Onslaught on Judaism" in *Judaism*, Vol. 28, No. 2, Spring, 1979; and "Was Spinoza a 'Jewish' Philosopher?" in *Judaism*, Vol. 28, No. 3, Summer, 1979.

42. For the full discussion, see Franck, "Spinoza's Onslaught on Judaism," pp. 179–180. Franck maintains that Spinoza did not fulfill the second criterion (aiming at a Jewish audience and seeking to advance Jewish thought). But Spinoza clearly did fulfill the first criterion (Jewish sources influenced his thought), and, Guttmann's comment (quoted above; see note 3) notwithstanding, Franck maintains that Spinoza also fulfilled the third criterion (contributing to the advance of Jewish thought), so that Spinoza should qualify as a Jewish philosopher (although not unqualifiedly so, according to Franck).

43. Maimonides, *Mishneh Torah*, Sefer Mada', Hilkhot Teshuvah 3:7.

44. Maimonides, *Guide of the Perplexed*, I:36.

45. Ravad, Hasagah (gloss) to Hilkhot Teshuvah 3:7. Ravad himself did not affirm any corporeal notions about God, but he rejected the view that such belief constitutes heresy, or that Maimonides had the right to make such a determination.

46. Aḥad Ha-Am, "Shabbat Ve-Ziyyonut" (1898) in *Kol Kitvei Aḥad Ha-Am*, p. 286.

47. See note 25, above.

Pre-Zionist Jerusalem

David Polish

Congregation Beth Emet
Evanston, Illinois

Before there was a Zionist Movement or a Zionist ideology, there was a form of anticipatory activity best referred to as embryonic Zionism. Unlike the later development of Jewish nationalism, this had its origins in Eretz Yisrael and, while rudimentary, nevertheless contained certain components on which Zionism was to be founded—political action and settlement on the land. This essay will outline certain beginnings of embryonic Zionism which originated in the religious community of Jerusalem early in the nineteenth century.

As early as 1623, the Kehillot of Lithuania were collecting funds in behalf of Jews living in Eretz Yisrael. At periodic intervals the Lithuanian Vaad would issue a call for contributions to "the poor of the Holy Land." A courier system was set up by which *meshulachim* (messengers) passed back and forth between Eretz Yisrael and Lithuania, collecting and disbursing funds. In 1623, the Pinkas of Medinat Litta records that Jewish leaders seeking to assist "our brethren from the Golah who are scattered in the Holy Land" decreed that there should be collections in their behalf on every New Moon. In addition, special appeals should be made each Rosh HaShanah or Yom Kippur. "The money to be collected from all over the land should be brought to Lublin during the Gramnitz Fair and from here it is to be taken to its destination. This decree has the force of law, the violation of which is a penalty of a hundred gulden to be imposed on the heads of the national Kahal, to be paid to the poor of Eretz Yisrael." Eleven years later, the application for assistance by Yosef ben Eliezer from Brisk seeking to make Aliyah was approved. "It is known how difficult and long and expensive it is to go to the Holy Land, and what a heavy personal burden it is. We have decided to grant him eight thaler as soon as his wagons set out for the Holy Land. In addition we have decided to send him forty thaler annually throughout his life in the Holy Land. This shall be distributed by the Gabbaim of the Lublin community in Eretz Yisrael." Fifteen years after that action, Freidel the widow of Koppel from Lotzk loaned the community nine hundred and forty gulden on condition that the sum accruing from investing the funds be sent to her in Eretz Yisrael throughout her life. After her death the principal was to be distributed as stipulated in her agreement with the leaders. (That occurred in 1649, one year after the massive pogroms in the Ukraine.)

The appeals for funds were perennial, and they referred generally to Eretz Yisrael rather than to any specific locality. Except for one reference to Jews in Hebron, there is no specific reference to other cities, including Jerusalem, although it did contain a Sephardic community.

Some time during the 1780's a Jew from Vilna arrived in Jerusalem. That was a historical occasion, for he was the first Ashkenazi during that era to settle in Jerusalem. He was Shlomo ben Yisrael Rosenthal, also called Pach, a mnemonic for Pituchey Chotem, seal maker. We do not know whether he acquired the seal-making skill in Vilna, although his craft had gained currency among some European Jews and had given them status, but the designation Pach, which was to be transmitted to his son, Yitzchak, was in all probability acquired in Jerusalem. What brought him to Jerusalem rather than Safed, Tiberias, or Hebron where the Ashkenazim gathered? According to some sources, local Moslem law forebade Ashkenazim from living there because of an unpaid debt incurred by earlier Ashkenazic settlers. (More on this later.) Why was he admitted or tolerated? We can only speculate that, as somewhat later sources indicate, a few Ashkenazim were admitted subject to heavy restrictions or through bribes. Reconstructing similar journeys, we can theorize that he travelled to Mohilev on the River Dniester, proceeded through Wallachia (Rumania) to the port of Galatz where he boarded a ship to Constantinople, arriving after about six months in Jaffa or Acre. Since his own son was born in Jerusalem in 1789, we know that he came to the Land of Israel no later than the 1780's.

The city at that time was a dismal and forsaken place. In his "Ir B'Rei Hatekufah," Yehoshua ben Aryeh describes Jerusalem at the beginning of the nineteenth century. It could not have presented a more favorable appearance toward the close of the eighteenth century. The overall impression was of decay, desolation, disease. Carcasses of camels and donkeys littered the dark and narrow streets. The accumulation of winter's refuse was locked up in storage rooms within the city. Water wells were contaminated. Periodic eruptions of pestilence drove people out of the city walls until the pestilence would subside. Sunset brought added dreariness to the place, for the gates would be locked for the night as precaution against intruding Bedouins and only armed sentries and bandits were abroad in the blacked-out city. A colony of about thirty lepers huddled together in make-shift hovels near the Zion Gate and they subsisted on whatever coins or leavings came their way. The Jewish population lived in a special state of fear. There were robberies of Jewish homes by Moslem invaders who threatened the dwellers if they resisted, and who sometimes murdered as well as pillaged. There was religious fanaticism. An incident is recorded of a Moslem compelling an aged Rabbi to bow to him and then beating him because "he denied the Prophet Mohammed." Taxes were heavy, violence was rampant, and Jews did not dare to protest lest they be accused of blaspheming Islam. Local judges accepted testimony only from Moslems. When Moslems had merchandise they could not sell, they would deliver it to Jewish homes and demand payment. Water carriers, bringing water to town fifteen times a day, would spill it on the ground in Jewish courtyards if Jews did not want water or if vessels were not available to receive the water, and they would then demand payment. All this was especially hard on the Ashkenazim who did not know Arabic and did not understand Arab customs.

Even in the second quarter of the nineteenth century, Jerusalem was desolate. Many of the houses, including the inner courts and the cisterns where rain water was collected, were in ruins. The remaining homes were tiny, narrow, low, dark—their windows shut and covered by lattices in order to protect women from the prying eyes of passers-by. Shops were in a similar state. In a few of them "merchants" sold coarse, black earthenware vessels made in Gaza. There were a few shoemakers who produced crude shoes of red and yellow hides. Most of the Ashkenazim lived in the eastern quarter, known as Bab Khutah, while fewer lived with the Sephardim in the southern quarter. The Sephardim allowed their Ashkenazic neighbors to worship in a small synagogue known as Bet Ha-Knesset Ha-Tichon, located between the Yochanan ben Zakkai Synagogue and the Synagogue of the "Stambuli" (migrants from Constantinople).

In 1820 an event occurred which precipitated not only a symbolic act but a political claim to Eretz Yisrael, and it took the form of organized political intervention. Some time after Ashkenazim began to settle in small numbers in Jerusalem, they occupied and established a claim to an area known as the Churvah of Yehudah Ha-Chassid, who had come from Poland around 1700 with a small band of followers that soon after began to drift away from Jerusalem. In a short time, heavy debts had been incurred by Jewish leaders, for which the community continued to be held responsible. In 1720 the area was destroyed by Moslems who demanded payment, and the section was thereafter known as the Churvah (the ruin).

In 1820 the Sultan decreed invalid all debts over forty years, thus lifting all Jewish debts, including those that had been incurred by Rabbi Yaakov Ashkenazi. But the Moslems who held as security all Jewish shops in the section known as Dir El Ashkenaz seized the Churvah area. Rabbi Suzin intervened, claiming that this was illegal, since part of the property was used for worship and study. According to the subsequent testimony of Moslem elders, the earliest Ashkenazim had indeed paid a full price for the land and had established a legitimate claim to it. However, the more recent Ashkenazim were not permitted to rebuild the Churvah, because this required the approval of the government and ratification by the Sultan. Two efforts, one in Jerusalem, the other from Jerusalem to Constantinople, were undertaken for the purpose of securing such approval. It is unclear whether these efforts were concerted or independent of one another. In the first instance, in 1823, the heads of the Jerusalem comunity turned to Shlomo Pach with a request, issued on the first of Adar, to undertake a mission to Constantinople. It reads in part:

> "We, the undersigned designate . . . the Chacham Shlomo Pach Ashkenazi to travel to Constantinople in order to secure a firman from our lord the King for the purpose of building the Churvah in Jerusalem for the Ashkenazim . . . . We have agreed with the aforementioned emissary that he will go on our mission according to the following conditions: From now on, Shlomo Pach must try energetically and faithfully to secure the firman . . . . He shall try to achieve this with all his might, not once or twice or three times, until he brings us decrees from the leading people in the Kingdom to the officials residing in Jerusalem, ordering us to build without hindrance. . . . When Rav Shlomo fulfills our request . . . we are obligated to pay him for his expenses, cost of travel and the cost of his effort, a total of 3,000 grush, whether this is less or in excess of his outlay . . . . If the terms of the firman are not carried out, then we are obligated to pay him 2,300 grush. When the firman is issued, Rav Shlomo Pach shall receive a document wit-

nessed by the [Jewish officials], residents of Constantinople, Avraham Fuah and Yitzchak Khitim . . . Shlomo Pach is required to give [the document] to someone who can copy the firman letter by letter in Hebrew . . . and to make two or three copies, and to send to us the first copy with a reliable man. Then we are obligated to pay the [remaining] 2,300 grush."

For Shlomo Pach, who must have been in his middle fifties or early sixties, the task was both arduous and dangerous. Shlomo Pach traveled by way of Safed, where he was met by leaders of the Ashkenazim who urged him to undertake a special mission in their behalf in Constantinople. Their request was sufficiently urgent to unite Chasidim and Mitnagdim (both known as Perushim as distinguished from Sephardim). In 1823, Safed had a sizeable Ashkenazic community, but its rights and privileges derived from the Sephardic community which was the only Jewish authority recognized by the Turkish government. Shlomo Pach was asked to secure full government recognition of the Ashkenazim as an independent community. The Safed mission was authorized on the twenty-second of Adar. It is reported that he succeeded in both missions. Frumkin reports having seen a letter of thanks to Shlomo Pach from the Ashkenazim of Safed.

In the second instance, a decree, issued in Constantinople, stated that the Chacham Mendel Vakil had come before the Chief Judge in Jerusalem, Said Al Kadi, and intervened in behalf of the Churvah area (Dir Al Ashkenaz) "which was destroyed and is deteriorating from day to day . . . This Dir is in the street of the Jews, it is in ruins and has no value. It belongs to them and they have lived there since ancient times. [According to one source, from the time the Moslems conquered Jerusalem from the Crusaders, D.P.] Since their debts have mounted heavily they were compelled to abandon those places since over eighty years ago, and the Dir was left without dwellers, thus causing the ruin, and it is now known by old and young as Dir El Ashkenaz . . . . Therefore the aforementioned Chacham requested that a document be given him for the time of need. We have therefore written and sealed it in the month Muharam in the year 1240."

It is possible that the plea by the Chacham Mendel Vakil was transmitted to Constantinople by Shlomo Pach. The relationship of both missions is difficult to determine since about eight months elapsed between Yitzchak Pach's assignment in Safed and the promulgation of the abovementioned decree.

The Turkish firman was to be invalidated by political events which engulfed Eretz Yisrael in waves of conflict. In 1832 Ibraham Pasha of Egypt rebelled against the Sultan, conquering Syria and Palestine. This was a time of chaos during which Arabs terrorized the land, also conquering and pillaging Jerusalem and compelling its Jews to flee to Safed. But the Sultan soon subdued the revolt, broke the tyrannical rule of Abdullah Pasha, ruler of Acre who oppressed the Jews, and imposed peace on the land. He then made treaties with European rulers and their consuls who would thereafter represent their subjects in Eretz Yisrael, so that they would no longer be at the mercy of Moslem judges. Evidently, the authorization to rebuild the Churvah had been suspended during the new conquest; in 1836, after the turmoil had subsided, a new effort was made by Zalman Tzoref to secure consent to rebuild it, this time from the Egyptian ruler. Tzoref interceded with the Russian and Austrian Consuls in Egypt, who prevailed upon the Pasha to order the return of the land to the Ashkenazim and its restoration by them. The work of rebuilding and the erection of new homes and shops began after the granting of the permit. However, in 1840, England conquered Acre, the Egyptian armies were routed, and the territories formerly belonging to the Turks were restored. Consequently, permission to continue building was annulled, and consent for completion of the work was not secured until 1864.

Shlomo Pach's son, Yitzchak, was born in Jerusalem in 1789, and according to one chronicler, "achieved greatly for the Ashkenazim in all the cities of their habitation in Eretz Yisrael." He underwent the privations which all the early settlers suffered, but he proved to be a man of great courage and resources. Together with his father, he was held in high esteem, and in his earlier years was granted an extra portion of *chalukah* on condition that he would engage exclusively in study. He pursued his studies for a while and then followed his father's craft of seal-making. He learned Arabic and the laws of the land. "He did not permit Jacob to be plundered, he often struggled with the oppressors—wild men—and he overcame them. He was the right-hand man and confidante of Rabbi Yeshayahu Bardaki, the leader of the community and a wealthy man who was close to the local government and also the representative of the Austrian Consul in Jerusalem. Yitzchak Pach was also Bardaki's interpreter in his dealings with Moslem officials. The scholars and rabbis honored and respected him. He was highly esteemed by Sir Moses Montefiore." Yitzchak Pach lived in the house of his birth throughout his ninety-six years; there his first wife was killed when she resisted bandits who broke in during his absence and seized his equipment for making seals.

During the life of Yitzchak Pach and others, especially Joseph Rivlin and Yehoshua Yellin as well as their associates, there began a movement to settle beyond the city walls. The Christian community had already begun to move out, and with the growth of the Jewish community, both as a result of Aliyah and the influx of refugees from the devastating Safed earthquake, the congestion and squalor within the walled city made living conditions increasingly difficult. In 1864 Moses Montefiore built the first houses for Jews outside the walls. The project was identified with Judah Touro of New Orleans, who willed $50,000 for the Jews of Eretz Yisrael and who designated Montefiore to carry out the request. The original intention was to build a hospital, and Montefiore requested the British Foreign Minister, Lord Clarendon, to secure a permit from Constantinople for the acquisition of land. Together with Touro's executor, Gerson Kors, Montefiore saw the Sultan and received the permit. On July 18, 1856, they arrived in Jerusalem and for a thousand liras bought a tract of land to the west of the city, on the road to Hebron, consisting of 66,225 square cubits.

Having learned that the Rothschild family was planning to build a hospital in Jerusalem, Montefiore decided to convert his project into dwellings for the poor. Upon returning to England, he also commissioned the building of a windmill on the tract so that future residents could grind their own grain, thus reducing the cost. The housing for the poor began in 1859, when Montefiore sent a British architect who put up twenty homes for six hundred liras each. This prompted Jerusalem Jews to complain that at that cost three or four times as many dwellings could have been erected by a local contractor. The area was called Mishkenot Shaananim (dwellings of those at ease), a euphemism to spare humiliation to the poor and a derivation from "Neveh Shaananim" in Isaiah 33:20. It was also decided that the houses would be given to families of scholars, eight each for Ashkenazim and Sephardim, one to each community as a synagogue, one for a weaving school, and one for a dispensary. Upon the completion of the houses, it was difficult to find occupants because of the fear of bandits who roamed freely outside the walls. Those who did accept were given the homes for life as well as annual stipends from Montefiore. Joseph Rivlin claims that, as a representative of Montefiore, he did not have the heart to tell him that the people occupied their homes only for a few hours during the day and returned to the inner city before dusk. Ben Zion Gat denies this, claiming that Yitzchak Pach was in fact Montefiore's local representative, and if such a situation did prevail, it was only for a short period.

In 1866, on his sixth trip to Eretz Yisrael, Montefiore visited Mishkenot Shaananim and found the settlers content and the area clean. (By 1875, sixty-five people were living there.) Before leaving Jerusalem, Montefiore laid the cornerstone for Kerem Moshe V'Yehudit for the purpose of building additional dwellings for the poor. The task of overseeing this work was assigned to Montefiore's agent, Yitzchak Pach, who hired a local builder; the result was that the cost of construction was much cheaper than in the first project. In the Journal *Levanon*, Elul 1866, appears the following: "Sir Moses Montefiore has requested his wise and esteemed overseer, Yitzchak Pach, to build more houses on a broad tract which he has in Kerem Moshe V'Yehudit where for many years there are twenty lovely homes for Sephardic and Ashkenazic Jews. The righteous lives by his fidelity because he had promised the Rabbis who had asked him that the most important thing for the inhabitants of Jerusalem is for people to live in houses at low cost, and he fulfilled his promise."

The place stood vacant until Montefiore's return in 1875, when he allowed three Sephardic and one Ashkenazic family to settle there. An American publication, *The Jewish Messenger*, complained that unworthy people were living there, neglecting the premises and subletting them, while deserving scholars could not get in. The *London Jewish Chronicle* suggested that the interlopers should be expelled and that the chief supervision should be put into the hands of a resident of Jerusalem. Nevertheless, writes Gat, despite the excessive trust that Montefiore placed in the administrative competence of his representatives, "it was because of them that the way out of the walls was broken open, and they served as an example for the conquest of other areas."

Indications that matters were not in order are found in a letter from Dr. Louis Loewe, Chief Adminsitrator for Montefiore, to Yitzchak Pach. The letter, which came into the hands of Chayim Michael Michlin, was written from Brighton, England, 22 Tammuz 1866: "Life and uninterrupted peace for my friend, the distinguished Yitzchak Pach Rosenthal in the Holy City, Jerusalem. I wish to ask two or three questions which I would like him to answer truthfully. Is it true that the ruler of the city has ordered the suspension of construction of the houses in Kerem

Moshe V'Yehudit? For what reason did he order the stoppage of a worthy work? What can be done to change his evil intent? How many people are working under the chief builder? Is it true that he has a hundred workers? Have the stones been prepared for all the houses? Have the pits for washing and the wells for drinking water been dug for all the occupants of houses? Have the roads leading to the houses been constructed and repaired? It is necessary to know all this for the benefit of our brethren. Please answer me soon and give me an opinion. I am writing, not at the request of Sir [Moses] but on my own initiative, because I am concerned lest precious funds be lost. I am happy to hear that your dear son has returned home in peace. May God remove all anguish and grief from us and lead us from darkness to light."

The Montefiore settlement projects were a philanthropic and benevolent boon to the Jewish community. However, they were induced from abroad. What was soon to follow was self-initiating and the result of internal efforts, not by an individual but by a group of settlers. This was the work of men like Yehoshua Yellin (born 1843) whose father, David, came to Eretz Yisrael in 1834 from Lomza. The Yellins' efforts in behalf of Jewish settlement fall into three categories—the acquisition of land by the father and his son-in-law; the daring but aborted effort by Yehoshua and others to acquire most of the land around Jericho; and, finally, the creation of a settlement, the first of its kind, by Yehoshua and a group of Jerusalem Jews. The acquisition involved the purchase, in 1859 or 1860, of land in Motza, about seven kilometers northwest of Jerusalem. The acquisition entailed legal complications because Turkish law did not permit the purchase of land by foreign subjects. (It will be recalled that Montefiore's purchase required special approval from the Sultan.) The elder Yellin and his son-in-law consulted with the British Consul, who helped them work out a legal fiction by which they could get around the Turkish restriction. When word got around, the elder Yellin was approached by other would-be sellers who wanted to dispose of their land, which was undergoing a time of drought. Many of the landowners in the area had moved to Syria or east of the Jordan, leaving their land to relatives who stayed behind. As a consequence, David Yellin and his son-in-law were able to acquire extensive tracts. All this was done with the help of the British Consul, whose influence was so great that during his term of office he succeeded in having some local Pashas removed. "In those days the influence of England in Constantinople was greater than that of any other government, and even the Sheikh Mustafa

Abu Gosh, who ruled all the villages around Jerusalem, turned a blind eye to us and did not interfere with us." Motza was the site of a station for travellers from Jerusalem to Jaffa, where they would stop to rest and to feed and water their animals. From Motza they would continue on an eight hour journey to Ramle. There Yellin eventually built a hotel to accommodate the travellers.

In 1866, the Turkish government granted British citizens permission to buy land in Eretz Yisrael and in Syria, and Yellin was officially apprised of this by the office of the Khadi, Abd El-Rachman Effendi Al-Kaldi. Yellin now had the opportunity to convert his quasi-legal claims to the land to fully authorized, official ownership. This involved a long process of validating all the prior bills of sale, with the cooperation of the original sellers. This was done officially through Yehoshua Yellin's father-in-law, Shlomo Ezekiel, who, as a native of India, was a British subject while Yellin was only under British protection.

In 1872, the government put up for auction two thirds of a tract adjoining Jericho. The tract, known as Jur, called Arvot Yericho in the book of Joshua, consisted of four thousand dunam. According to Turkish law all the territory outside the cities belonged to the government, and occupants of the land could only lease it, subject to their working the soil. They also had the right to sell or bequeath their leases. But if an occupant were to discontinue cultivating the land for three years, the land would revert to the government, which would then auction it off. In 1872, when government officials came to survey the land around Jericho, the Bedouin settlers complained that they were deriving benefit from only a third of the land while they were being taxed for all of it. This was reported to Constantinople, which ordered the auction. Two leading opponents in the auction were the wealthy effendi Musa Pasha el-Husseini and an Armenian, residing in Egypt, who wanted to acquire the land for the Armenian community in Jerusalem. "Then a few sons of Zion whose love of the land of our ancestors burned within them were stirred up . . . . We organized a company with shares of a hundred napoleons each, for the purpose of buying the land." In the company were Yellin, Ben Zion Leon, his partner Nathan Gringert, Beinish Salant, his brother-in-law Leib Salant, Yoel Moshe Solomon, Moshe Yitzchak Goldschmid and Leib Lomzir, Yellin's brother. About forty others joined them in the enterprise. The executive committee of the group consisted of Yellin, Leon, and Solomon.

The group began its work with an appeal by its representatives to the head of the Armenian community to discourage any effort to outbid the Jews. They contended that the Armenian community was prospering and had no need of the desolate and torrid Jericho territory, while the Jewish poor of Jerusalem were in need of land on which to settle. The Armenian notable acquiesced, just as Musa Pasha bowed out when he promised not to outbid the Yellin group in return for a promise to receive one tenth of the land at no cost. The group then increased its bid by 1800 Turkish liras, the amount which the Armenian had stipulated. Both Musa Pasha and the Armenian publicly withdrew from the bidding and, after an official waiting period of three months, it was announced from Constantinople that the Yellin group was authorized to consummate the purchase.

> "Our goal in this purchase was very great. It was our aim not only to acquire the four thousand dunam but in the course of time to acquire tens of thousands of dunam of desolate land on our border up to the Jordan, which according to law we could acquire for nothing if we would convert it from uncultivated to cultivated land. We planned to use it for planting orchards and gardens where even fifty dunam could support a large family comfortably . . . . We believed that in the course of time thousands of families could find sustenance there. In addition we discovered that the land of the Jordan and the Dead Sea contained great sulphur deposits from which many families could make a living."

After three months the Pasha dispatched his interpreter to inquire in his behalf who the purchasers were, who were foreign subjects and who were Turkish subjects. The group met to take counsel as to whether to list only the Ottoman subjects or the others. The members of the executive committee and other older settlers stressed that the inquiry by the government implied that it was not well disposed toward foreigners; therefore, the signatories to the notice of sale should be Ottoman subjects. The vital factor was to get the land out of the hands of the government, after which the Ottoman subjects could transfer it to the foreigners without requiring further approval from Constantinople. The majority, however, argued that under no circumstances would they place the land under exclusively Ottoman jurisdiction. Rather, the various nationalities should be listed "so that if it should prove necessary, the various Consuls could come to their aid, and if the government were to see that there were no other buyers, it would agree to our purchase."

After much debate, it was decided to give the Pasha the names of

Russian, Austrian, German, and British subjects for transmission to Constantinople. After a month, word came back that Sultan Abd El-Chamid would not permit the transfer of any of his land to strangers and that he would acquire the land for himself by adding five hundred liras to the cost. The Pasha was ordered to send a bill of sale to him, attesting to the consummation of the royal sale. "Then I said to myself, 'Your destroyers will come from your midst' and 'Jericho was closed and fore-closed because of the children of Israel.' . . . The hearts of many in the company ached over the folly of a single mistake."

The first indigenous Jewish settlement in Eretz Yisrael was established in 1869. Yellin writes: "In those days there was no sign of a settlement and no house had yet been built outside the walls of Jerusalem . . . except for many rest houses for Russian tourists who would come annually for their holidays, and the Montefiore homes near the railways station." In that year, seven natives of Jerusalem bought land near the Russian compound, for the purpose of establishing a new settlement. It was called "Nachalat Shivah," after the seven founders—Michael Ha-Cohen, Chayim Ha-Levi, Beinish Salant, Leib Horvitz (Lomzer), Yoel Moshe Solomon, Yosef Rivlin, and Yehoshua Yellin. Every square cubit cost twenty-five prutot. They approached leaders of the various Kollelim with a request for help:

> "Our fathers sinned by refusing to buy houses cheaply in the city, while the Christians are acquiring entire streets with many houses, giving free homes to their people . . . . Now, however, a new settlement is arising outside the walls and the Christians have already begun to buy tracts near the Russian Compound . . . . Do not lose the opportunity while land is still cheap . . . Build houses for the poor who over the years will repay you the same sums that they are now paying gentiles for rentals that go up from year to year."

The plea was ignored.

The founders of "Nachalat Shivah," to whom was added Leib Salant, agreed that every pair would live on adjoining tracts. A well was dug, houses were built, and settlers moved in, following the building of a main road to Jaffa, ordered by Constantinople in anticipation of a visit by the Austrian emperor who was to stop in Jerusalem on his way to the opening of the Suez Canal. The first builders were Michael Ha-Cohen and Yosef Rivlin. The rest followed, except Yellin, who was involved in his Motza project. The cost of building proved to be excessive and the settlers had to borrow at exorbitant rates, compelling them to sell their homes and part of their land at a loss. The only exception was Yoel Moshe Solomon, who was to be one of the founders of Petach Tikvah.

Anticipatory Zionism in Jerusalem met with obstacles and setbacks, which were to be replicated even more intensively with the rise of Jewish nationalism. But the events accompanying it and its historical personalities yielded promising seed.

Bibliography

Ben Aryeh, Yehoshua. *Ir B'Rei Ha-Tekufah (Yerushalayim Ba-Meah Ha-T'sha-Esreh)* Jerusalem, 1977.

Frumkin, Aryeh Leib. *Toldot Chachmay Yerushalayim.* Jerusalem, 1929.

Gaon, Moshe David. *Yehuday Ha-Mizrach B'Eretz Yisrael B'Avar U'V'Hoveh.* Jerusalem, 1928.

Gatt, Ben Zion. *Ha-Yishuv Ha-Yehudi B'Eretz Yisrael Bishnot 1840–1881.* Jerusalem, 1962.

Grayevsky, Pinchas ben Zvi. *Zikkaron L'Chovevim Ha-Rishonim.* Jerusalem, 1928.

Tidhar, David. *Encyclopedia L'Chalutzay Ha-Yishuv U'Vonav.* Tel Aviv, 1958.

Yaari, Avraham. *Igrot Eretz Yisrael.* Jerusalem, 1971.

Yaari, Avraham. *Masaot Eretz Yisrael.* Jerusalem, 1976.

Yellin, Yehoshua. *Zichronot L'Ven Yerushalayim.* Jerusalem, 1924.

Diaries of Sir Moses Montefiore, edited by Louis Loewe. Chicago, 1890.

The 'Minhag':
Some Examples of Its Characteristics*

Herman Pollack

B'nai B'rith Hillel Foundation
Massachusetts Institute of Technology (Emeritus)

In *Yosif 'Omeṣ*, a book of *Minhagim* relating to the religious, cultural, and social life of the Jews of Frankfort-on-the-Main durng the late Middle Ages, the author, Joseph (Yosef) Yuspa (Juzpa) Hahn,[1] relates: "At large banquets it was the practice to eat cheese [a milk product] after meat, which was called a lesser meal, [namely] *nokh tsekh*.[2] The cheese must have served as a dessert."[3] This custom was previously referred to in my *Jewish Folkways*: "We have adopted a lenient position by waiting one hour to eat cheese after meat—concerning which *qinnuach* (removing particles of meat in the mouth by chewing bread, something abrasive) and *hadachah* (washing the hands before eating) are not required before eating the cheese. However, when meat is felt between the teeth, it is to be removed."[4] In this connection, we cited the gloss of Moses Isserles (Rema, Ramo: d. 1572, Cracow), who lived sixty years before Hahn, and who incorporated customs of Ashkenazi Jewry that embrace Germanic and Slavic areas in Central and Eastern Europe: ". . . There are those who say it is not necessary to wait six hours before eating cheese after meat . . . . And in these lands the custom is simply to wait an hour before eating cheese after meat."[5] If there is just a transition

Appreciation is expressed to Professor Salo W. Baron, my former teacher, Dr. Haym Soloveitchik, and Rabbi Mordecai Feuerstein for the helpful suggestions they offered.

*The term *minhag* (sing.; *minhagim*, pl.) may be translated as custom, practice, or usage.

from meat to cheese, then what is required is "to remove the meat particles from the mouth," "wash the hands," and recite the *birkat ha-mazon*, "the blessing after the meal." The *birkat ha-mazon* would not be recited a second time after eating cheese as this would not be regarded as a meal. The practice as described by Hahn differs from that as stated by Isserles in that *qinnuach* and *hadachah* are not necessary. Isserles concludes his gloss by stating: "And there are those who punctiliously wait six hours between eating meat and cheese . . ."[6]

That food customs were not uniformly the same may be illustrated further by referring to the practice cited by Joseph Kosman (Kosmann), the grandson of Joseph Hahn, in his *Noheg qa-Ṣ'on Yosef*, a book of *Minhagim* that presents special customs and ritual observances of Frankfort. Kosman states that he would wait six hours before eating cheese after meat, and for his authority cites Maimonides.[7] Obviously, in the case of Hahn and Kosman, both of the same region, we have divergent practices based on differing views or interpretations.

We are thus prompted to go beyond the account in *Jewish Folkways* by endeavoring to trace the background of the custom bearing on the time that is to elapse before eating cheese after meat. Like any historical phenomenon, a practice must be viewed in the context of its own development in order to be fully understood. In short, behind the custom is a body of explanation that we shall strive to uncover as a phase of daily life on the grass-roots level.

I

In the *Ṭur* or Code of Jacob b. Asher (d. 1340, Toledo), which served as the basis for the *Shulchan 'Arukh* of Joseph Karo (d. 1575, Safed), we read of the practice of eating cheese shortly after meat: "It is written in the *Halakhot Gedolot* that if one has eaten meat it is permissible to eat cheese afterwards by means of *qinnuach* and *neṭilah*, that is removing the meat that remains in the mouth and washing the hands . . . . And I [learned from] my father and master (teacher), the Rosh of blessed memory, the people did not make it a practice to eat cheese after meat even if it is the meat of the fowl. And the *minhag* [they established] has not been changed in any way. Hence cheese is not eaten after meat until a specified period of time [has passed], from the morning meal until the evening meal."[8]

Fearing that he might experience the same fate as that of Meir of

Rothenburg—who was held in prison as a hostage for ransom—the Rosh came with his son to Spain from Germany in order to escape the persecutions instigated by Rindfleisch, one of the nobility. The Rosh, who was interested in maintaining the Ashkenazi tradition,[9] transmitted to his son Ashkenazi *minhagim*, among which was the custom that we are discussing. As the passage from the *Ṭur* shows, the people not only chose a more stringent regulation, but they evidently exercised an influence on rabbinic opinion.[10]

While the authorship of the *Halakhot Gedolot* has not been confirmed with certainty, there is a measure of agreement that Simeon Kayyara of Sura, Babylonia, wrote this "summary of Talmudic laws" around 825. Concerning the question as to when cheese may be eaten after meat, the *Halakhot Gedolot* restates the two differing opinions in the Talmud. There is, first of all, the opinion of R. Nachman, who said that cheese may be eaten after meat providing the hands are washed. Although he stated that ". . . the washing of the hands between courses is a matter of choice," nevertheless, ". . . between a [meat] course and cheese it [the washing of the hands] is obligatory."[11] *Qinnuach*, eating something hard to remove meat particles before one may eat cheese after meat, which is required in the *Ṭur*, is not mentioned in the Talmudic passage. Then, in the second place, the *Halakhot Gedolot* refers to the contrasting opinion of R. Chisda: To eat meat after cheese is permissible, but cheese after meat is forbidden.[12]

In his explanation of the Talmudic opinion cited above, ". . . it is forbidden to eat cheese after meat . . ." (. . . *'asur le-'echol gevinah* . . .), Rashi, the noted commentator (d. 1104, Troyes), explained: "The reason [for the prohibition] is because meat produces a fatty taste that stays in the mouth afterwards."[13] Maimonides (d. 1204, Fostat-Cairo), eminent as legal codifier, philosopher, and scientist, based his position on the grounds that "*qinnuach* does not remove meat particles between the teeth"; time must therefore elapse before eating cheese.[14] Both Rashi and Maimonides wanted a period of time to pass so as to digest the meat before eating cheese. Merely removing meat particles from the mouth was no assurance that meat would not remain and would therefore be eaten with cheese.[15]

Among the contemporaries and successors of Rashi there were those whose views differed. His opinion, while scholarly and authoritative, must not have been regarded as absolute or final; otherwise, Rabbenu Tam, his grandson, would not have permitted cheese to be eaten after

meat.[16] The *Tosafot*, disciples of Rashi who succeeded him as interpreters of the tradition, likewise did not agree with him, but commenting
on the practice of Mar 'Uqba who did not ". . . eat [cheese] in the same
meal but in [the] next meal," they state: It does not matter how soon you
eat cheese after the meal, for it can be [eaten] immediately afterwards;
the requirement is to ". . . clear the table, recite the blessing after the
meal, and there is no differing among the authorities."[17] We mention
again the passage of Isserles because of its relationship to the position
taken by the *Tosafot*: Once the blessing after the meal has been said, the
meal can be considered completed and a new meal is begun: ". . . It is
[then] permitted to eat [the cheese after the meat], according to the
opinions of those who take a lenient position; the *birkat ha-mazon* (the
blessing after the meal) does not have to be recited. It does not matter if
the one-hour waiting period is begun before or after the *birkat ha-
mazon*."[18] Custom (the *minhag*) thus impinges on law (*halakhah*), interacts with it, and, as in this instance, has the effect of shaping and
influencing the direction that it takes.[19]

Built into the pattern of Jewish religious and social life is the recognition that there can be differences in practice on the local level without
disrupting communal unity. That local customs were accepted as far
back as ancient times, during the Talmudic period, as an integral part of
the community is cogently demonstrated by Hugo Mantel:

> So a Baraita [a teaching of the first Talmudic sages not included in the
> Mishnah] relates that "in the city of R. Eliezer they cut wood on the Sab-
> bath in order to make charcoal in which to forge the iron-knife for cir-
> cumcision. In the place of R. Jose the Galilean, they ate the flesh of fowl
> with milk." In the Mishnah we find that "where the custom is to do work
> until midday on the day before Passover, they may do so; where the custom
> is not to do work, they may not work." The local Bet Din in each city was
> the authority on all religious and civil matters, deciding which customs to
> retain and which to innovate. The schools of Shammai and Hillel were
> courts as well, their full names being probably Bet Din Shel Hillel and Bet
> Din Shel Shammai. Every student and scholar lived and taught in accor-
> dance with the decisions of his respective school-court. The differences
> between the schools of Hillel and Shammai ranged over such matters as
> prayers, benedictions, holidays, marriages, damages, et cetera. As long as
> these differences were not resolved by the Great Bet Din, the court in each
> city could legislate at its own discretion.[20]

Since the days of the Second Temple there appear to be no signs of a hierarchy in order to regiment communal behavior and establish conformity by reducing diversity in procedure.

II

In our attempt to trace the background of the custom *noch tsekh* we went back to the *Ṭur*, thereby covering a period of some 350 years, from about 1250 to 1600. While *halakhah* is Jewish law in its abstract, theoretical state, we saw how the *minhag* has an effect or influence on the role of *halakhah* in relation to the area of dietary practice. From the Geonic period, in the ninth century, onward, local customs were recognized to have "autonomous validity."[21] Inasmuch as rabbinic authority was obliged to yield to a practice that became entrenched in the life of the people, for a fuller understanding of the role of custom, our curiosity is aroused to give consideration to the earliest Books of *Minhagim* that are closest in time to that of the *Ṭur*. The Books of *Minhagim* are: *Sefer ha-Manhig*, by Abraham ha-Yarchi of Lunel (ca. 1155–1215)[22] and *Sefer ha-Minhagot*, by Asher B. Sha'ul (d. ca. early 13th cent., Narbonne).[23] They are described as a bridge between the period of the Men of the Great Assembly (ca. 350 B.C.E.) and the *Ṭur* because they helped transmit customs that had developed over the centuries. Thus books of *Minhagim* served as a means of handing down the oral tradition from the Talmudic period and thereafter.[24]

When he visited Toledo (Spain), ha-Yarchi had been encouraged by his teachers and scholars of the time to observe as much as he could in his travels. He discerned that there were multiple customs with no apparent meaning underlying each one and, as a result, the people were bewildered and knew not what to do.[25] Prompted by this situation, he wrote *Sefer ha-Manhig* as a guide and reassurance that for each custom there is a halakhic basis, a valid reason. Yet he recognized in the variants in observance a common core of spiritual striving, and he therefore would not wish for differences to be blotted out in order to attain arbitrary uniformity:

> . . And I saw that their customs [lit., laws, procedure] differed; they were divided into seventy tongues; there was confusion and all kinds of vessels [that is, *minhagim*] . . . [Yet] all of them are built on the foundation

of truth. These and these are the words of the living God . . . . One person may arise in the middle of the night, another may awaken in the morning. Still what is done stems from a common source [lit., from a leader, shepherd]. Whether one has decided to make a light or not to do so, they are inclined to a single goal.[25]

The Books of *Minhagim,* in providing instruction as what to do, also dealt with variations of practice, as in the case of "covering the head." In *Sefer ha-Manhig* ha-Yarchi adjures the people that it is *"a minhag* not to pray if one's head is not covered," that is, *gilluy rosh.*[26] That there were times when they did pray bareheaded is confirmed—as we shall show—by Asher b. Sha'ul in his work on *minhagim.*[27] Ha-Yarchi quotes passages from the Bible and the Talmud as substantiation for the practice of "covering the head." He begins with the verse, "I have always set the Lord before me" (Psalm XVI, 8), which is then followed with the statement in the Talmud that the covered head is a sign of respect, "humility and reverence for the Rulership of the World," while the uncovered head represents haughtiness (*qomah zequfah,* "proud carriage").[28] He urges the Jews of Provençe to emulate *'anshe Sefarad,* "the residents of Spain, who always keep their heads covered—and may they grow from strength to strength [lit., their strength (health) be firm]."[29] We suggest that the head-covering worn continuously in Spain was influenced by the Moorish surroundings.[30]

Thus the Jews of Spain and France did not follow the same *minhag* with regard to covering the head during prayer. Asher b. Sha'ul relates that in the Morning Service ". . . it is not our practice to recite 'Who crowns Israel with glory,'" the reason being, ". . . that not everyone has the head covered, but is bareheaded."[31] To cover the head, either a hat (*kova*) or a *misnefet* (turban, beret) would be worn. The *misnefet* was probably a forerunner of the *yarmulke.*[32]

In the *responsa* of Isaac b. Moses of Vienna (ca. 1180–ca. 1250), there is further evidence that Jews of France prayed without covering their heads. He points out that the practice does not have his approval.[33] Although rabbinic opinion was decisive, the voice of authority, as in this instance, did not always sway the people.[34]

Instead of being arbitrarily imposed, a regulation would be changed if conditions of life prevented individuals from fulfilling it.[35] The *minhag* that was then introduced under such conditions served to bend, modify, or alter *halakhah,* established procedure.[36] To illustrate, when days were longer, as in the summer when the *'Omer* is counted, after reciting the *minchah*, afternoon, service, there were those not inclined to wait in the synagogue for *ma'ariv*, the evening service; perhaps the supper was ready for them, they would wish to go home "to eat and drink," and in so doing, "they would forget to say the evening service," which included the *Shema'*.[37] To cope with a practical situation, arising from longer summer days, it was decided that it would be preferable to hold the evening service before the stars appeared—which is not the designated time—and in this way assure the saying of the *Shema'*. And when it is the period of *Sefirah*, the ceremony for the *'Omer* could be said at home when it became dark.[38]

III

While our study is not intended to be a history of medieval Jewish society, it should be mentioned nevertheless that the feudal system was conducive to the establishment of self-governing Jewish communities. Regional self-contained religio-cultural enclaves developed thereupon. Although the overall relationship between one community and another was on the basis of a shared tradition, local customs developed as a result of the autonomy in each area. On the one hand, the *minhagim* reflected the general, external environment, and, on the other, the moods and aspirations of individuals or the local community as a whole.

Variations in religious and cultural life were reinforced by the stress placed on local autonomy as a basic requirement for communal life. The pattern of the Jewish community entailed different types of practices that became an indigenous part of its institutions.[39] The Maharam (Meir of Rothenburg: d. 1293), for instance, followed the procedures established in Talmudic times,[40] by emphasizing that each locality exercise its own authority. And so he declared: One should not reject the court (*bet din*) of his or her community in favor of a higher court (*bet din ha-gadol u-vet ha-va-'ad*).[41] Referring to the Maharam, Joseph Colon (ha-Riq) of Padua (d. 1480) gave special attention to the local rabbinical court in its domain by pointing out that it is equal to the greatest authorities of the generation.[42] The emphasis of Colon on settling disputes by the local court was to prevent a wealthier person from going to another court outside his community, thereby placing a poorer person at a disadvantage.[43] Such autonomy throughout the Middle Ages resulted in the development of practices unique to specific locales and thus fostered regional differences.[44]

With regard to variations in communal customs, in Germanic lands, for instance, *Shabes* (*Shabbat*) bread was known as *barkhes* (*berkhes*) and in eastern Europe it was called *khalleh* (*challah*). In the Rhine area, before a circumcision ceremony, women arranged the *yidish-kerts* ("circumcision candle") ceremony. After a wedding the Dance of the Dead (Dance of Death, *la danse macabre*, *toytn-tants*, *meysim-tants*) was staged in the Hamburg area.[45] It is suggested that the *toytn-tants* could have been a forerunner of the Beggars' Dance in Ansky's play *Der Dybbuk*.[46]

Often it is said that the pluralistic views and practices in Jewish life today—whether on the college campus or in the adult community—are the outgrowth of development and events since Jewish Emancipation. The objective of our study was to present evidence that diverse interpretations and practices are not a modern or contemporary phenomenon but have been characteristic of the Jewish traditions through the ages. Such differences, instead of being disconcerting and troublesome, should be welcomed as the underpinning for self-expression and creativity.

NOTES

1. Hahn was born in Frankfort, died in 1637. The first edition of *Yosif 'Omeṣ* was published in Frankfort, 1723.

Dr. Solomon B. Freehof asked Dr. Alfred Jospe if his name was related to Yuspa in Hahn's name. See in this regard Ephraim Zalman Margoliyot (Margoliyoth), *Ṭiv Giṭṭin* (Names Derived from Deeds of Betrothal, Divorce, and Responsa: Bucharest, 1819), no. 18, fol. 27b, for names Yosel, Yuzpa as forms of Yosef.

2. *Yosif 'Omeṣ*, no. 136: לכן בסעודות גדולות שרגילים לאכול גבינה אחר בשר וקורין סעודה קטנה ההיא

נוך (צעך) .... נוך (צעך) = prob. *nokh tsekh* (Yiddish); cf. *nach Zech* (German), "after the banquet," that is, the main meal.

3. Cf. *Nachspeise*, *Nachtisch* (Ger.); *nokhshpayz*, *nokhgerikht* (Yid.), (lit.) "after the meal," dessert.

4. *Yosif 'Omeṣ*, no. 136. Trans. based on my *Jewish Folkways*, p. 107, n. 87. For *qinnuach*, see *Chullin* 105a and for *hadachah*, *ibid.* 107b.

5. Trans. based on *Jewish Folkways*, p. 106. See gloss of Isserles, *Yoreh Deah*, LXXXIX, 1. cf. above, n. 9.

6. Isserles, *ibid.*

7. *Jewish Folkways*, p. 280, n. 88: cit. of *Nogeh qa-Ṣ'on Yosef*, "Hil. Se'udah," sec. 60, fol. 29a, no. 4. Cf. *Mishneh Torah*, "Hil. Ma'akhalot 'Asurot," IX, 28; *Chullin* 105a.

8. *Ṭur: 'Orach Chayyim*, "Hil. Berakhot she-be-Se'udah," sec. 173: כתב בה״ג [בהלכות גדולות] שהאוכל בשר מותר לאכול אחריו גבינה מיד ע״י קינוח ונטילה . . . וכן א״א [אבי אדוני] הרא״ש ז״ל ולא נהגו העולם כן אלא נוהגין שלא לאכול גבינה אחר הבשר אפי׳ הוא בשר עוף ואין לשנות המנהג הילכך אין לאכול גבינה אחר הבשר עד שישהה בשיעור מזמן סעודת הבוקר עד זמן סעודת הערב . . . . Cf. *Shulchan 'Arukh: Yoreh De'ah*, "Dine Basar be-Chalav," sec. 89, which summarizes the passage above in the *Ṭur.*

9. See [n.n.] "Asher ben Yehiel, " *Encyclopeadia Judaica*, III (1972), 707.

10. As yet, we are not able to confirm what prompted the adoption of this position.

11. *Halakhot Gedolot*, ed. A. Hildesheimer (Berlin, 1892), "Hil. Berakhot," p. 66, based on *Chullin* 105b. Cf. *ibid.*, ed. S.A. Traub (Warsaw, 1874), p. 18.

12. *Ibid.*, ed. Hildesheimer, p. 67, cit. of *Chullin* 105a. Cf. *ibid.*, ed. Traub, p. 18.

13. Based on S.Y. Zevin, *Entsiklopedia Talmudit*, IV (1956), 713, n. 339.

14. *Mishneh Torah*, "Hil. Ma'akhalot," IX, 28. See also "Bayit Chadash" on *Ṭur: Yoreh De'ah*, "Hil. Dine Basar be-Chalav," sec. 89, regarding the waiting period of six hours before eating a milk product after meat.

15. That dairy foods are not to be eaten immediately after meat, which is a rabbinic injunction ('issur de-rabbanan), see *Chullin* 104a and M. 'Eduyyot, V, 2; *Ṭur: Yoreh De'ah*, "Dine Basar be-Chalav," sec. 87.

16. Cf. *Ṭur: Yoreh De'ah*, sec. 87.

17. Comment on לסעודתא: *Chullin* 105a: אלא אפילו לאלתר וברך מותר דלא אם סילק השולחן לאלתר אפילו אלא . . . פלוג רבנן.

18. Isserles, gloss no. 3 on *Shulchan 'Arukh: Yoreh De'ah*, "Hil. Basar be-Chalav," LXXXIX, 1: . . . דמותר לאכול לדברי המקילין אבל בלא ברכת המזון לא מהני המתנת שעה ואין חילוק אם המתין השעה קודם ברכת המזון או אח״כ. For the origin of the *birkat ha-mazon*, see, among others, Deut. VIII, 10; *Berakhot* 48a-b. Cf. Eisenstein, "Birkat ha-Mazon," *'Oṣar Yisra'el*, III (1909), 209, col. 1, cits.

19. Cf. *Baba Meṣia* 59b; *Yevamot* 14a. And also Roscoe Pound, *The Spirit of the Common Law* (Francestown, N.H., 1921), p. 173: "A developed legal system is made up of two elements, a traditional or habitual element and an enacted or imperative element."

20. Mantel, *History of the Sanhedrin* (Harvard Univ. Press, 1961), p. 86. Passage is based on *Shabbat* 130a (not 130b as cited), *Chullin* 116a, *Yevamot* 14a, M. *Pesachim* IV, 1. See below, p. 347.

21. Salo W. Baron, *Social and Religious History* (rev. edit.: Columbia Univ. Press, 1958), VI, 126.

22. His name ha-Yarchi is related to Lunel; cf. *lune* (Fr.), "month, moon"; *yerach* (Heb.) = "moon, month." For the meaning of his name, see J.D. Eisenstein, "Abraham b. Natan ha-Yarchi" (Hebrew), *'Oṣar Yisra'el*, I (1906), 98, col. 1; *Sefer ha-Manhig* (Jerusalem 1978), ed. Yitzhak Raphael, I, Intro., 11.
That ha-Yarchi visited Toledo in 1304, according to his account, must be an error.
See I. Twersky, *Rabad of Posquières* (Harvard Univ. Press, 1962), pp. 240–42 for the importance of *Sefer ha-Manhig* ". . . in the genre of 'customs of literature' . . ." *Idem.*, "Soc. and Cult. Hist. of Provençal Jewry," *Jewish Society through the Ages*, eds. H.H. Ben-Sasson and S. Ettinger (New York, 1969), pp. 188ff., for cultural life in the Provençe; and also I. Zinberg (Tsinberg), *Geshikhte fun der literatur bay yidn* (Vilna, 1930), II, 103–106; *idem., Toledot Sifrut Yisra'el* (Tel-Aviv, 1955), II, 287–88.

23. Pub. in *Sifran shel Ri'shonim* (Jerusalem, 1938), ed. S. Assaf, pp. 123ff.

24. Based on Assaf, *op.cit.*, p. 130. Books of *Minhagim* used Talmudic, Geonic, and medieval sources (*poseqim*).

25. *Sefer ha-Manhig*, ed. Raphael, I, Intro., p. 8, lines 27-36: וארא והנה דתיהם שונות . . .
מחלקות לשבעים לשונות המונים המונים וכלים מכלים שונים . . . כולם על יסד האמת בנויים, ואלו ואלו דברי אלהים
חיים . . . . זה יקום חצות הלילה וזה שחרית יעיר, וכולם ניתנו מרועה אחד, ובין שאמרו (שלא) להדליק ובין שאמרו
שלא להדליק שניהם לא נתכוונו אלא לדבר אחד.
Cf. *Sefer ha-Manhig* (pub. with *Sefer ha-Roqeach* by Eliezer of Worms: Warsaw, 1880), Intro., fol. 2a [p. 3].

The Raphael edit. comprises a more complete and critical text.
For הן חיים אלהים דברי ואלו ואלו, see Raphael edit., *ibid.*, line 30, cit.: *'Eruvin* 13b.

See cit. from *Sefer ha-Manhig* in Eisenstein, "Ha-Yarchi," *'Oṣar Yisra'el*, I, 98, col. 1.

26. *Sefer ha-Manhig*, ed. Raphael, I, no. 45, lines 13, 14 (p. 84). Cf. Warsaw edit., 1880.

27. "Sefer ha-Minhagot" in *Sifran shel Ri'shonim*, p. 141.

28. See *Qiddushin* 29b, 30a. Also, *Qiddushin* 30a for the opinion of R. Huna who ". . . would not walk four cubits bareheaded, saying, 'The *Shekhinah* (Divine Presence) is above my head.'" The statement of Huna is one of the sources frequently cited to substantiate the practice not to go with an uncovered head.

29. *Sefer ha-Manhig*, ed. Raphael, no. 45, lines 13, 14 (p. 84). Cf. Abrahams, *Jewish Life in Middle Ages*, ed. Cecil Roth (London, 1932), p. 301, n. 4, cit.

30. See Abrahams, *op. cit.*, p. 301, n. 3.

31. *Sefer ha-Minhagot*, p. 141: שהמנהג שלנו שאין אנו מברכין משום דאין כל ישראל מכסין . . .
ראשיהם והולכין בגלוי הראש.

32. *Yarmulke* could have been derived from the two words: *yore* + *malkhut*, "reverence for the Heavenly Rulership."

33. *'Or Zarua'* (Zhitomir, 1862), "Hil. Shabbat," II no. 43, fol. 10b, col. 2: נראה ואין . . .
בעיני . . . Cf. cits. in Jacob Z. Lauterbach, "Should One Cover the Head?" [A Reply to a Query], *Central Conf. Amer. Rabbis Yearbook*, XXXVIII (1928), 599; *idem*, *Studies in Jewish Law* (New York, 1970), p. 235; *Sefer ha-Minhagot*, p. 141, n. 5.

34. See account of Purim in my *Jewish Folkways*, p. 187. Also my "Historical Inquiry concerning Purim Masquerade-Attire," p. 11 (to be published in vol. on Hist. of Europe, Proceed. Seventh World Congress of Jewish Studies, Jerusalem, Aug. 1977): The public had an influence on rabbinic opinion to hold a tolerant attitude toward Purim festivities; the Biblical injunction that a woman should not dress as a man and a man as a woman (Deut. XXII, 5) was waived.

35. Cf. *Baba Batra* 60b: יכולין הצבור רוב [כן אם [אלא א"כ הצבור על גזרה גוזרין שאין . . .
בה לעמוד . . . . We do not issue a regulation for the community that the majority cannot fulfill . . . ."

36. For the way in which "custom annuls law," הלכה מבטל מנהג, see my "The *Minhag* in Its Bearing on a Communal Controversy," *Proceed. Amer. Acad. for Jewish Research*, XLIII (1976), 193–97, includ. nn.

37. *Sefer ha-Minhagot*, p. 137.

38. *Ibid.* That the 'Omer is counted at night, see *Shulchan 'Arukh: 'Orach Chayyim*, "Hil. Pesach," 489:2. Cf. Jacob Katz, "'Alterations in the Time of the Evening Services': An Example of the Interrelationship between Custom, Halacha and their Social Background," *Zion*, XXXV (No. 1–4, 1970), pp. 37, 39: The time for the *ma'ariv* service was not set. When days were longer, the custom developed in Geonic times to recite the evening

service immediately after *minchah*. Hai Gaon was consulted about this practice and he recommended that the evening prayers continue to be said in the afternoon by those who so desire. The others could then say the *ma'ariv* service later; in this way the *minyan* would be kept intact.

39. Cf. Baron, *Soc. and Relig. Hist.*, VI, 126, concerning the ". . . rise of independent cultural centers throughout the dispersion . . ." *Ibid.*: The authority of "Postgeonic leaders . . . rested on the recognition of local diversity."

40. See above, p. 344.

41. *She'elot u-Teshuvot* (Prague, 1605), no. 523, fol. 55b. Cf. Irving Agus, *R. Meir of Rotheburg* (Philadelphia, 1947), no. 394, cit.: Rothenburg, *Responsa* (Prague, 1605), no. 290.

42. *She'elot u-Teshuvot* (Lemberg, 1798), no. 1, fol, la, col. 2: הרי הן בבית דין גדול כמו שכתב מהר"ם . . . שפירש רבינו מאיר שטובי העיר בעירם כמו גדולי הדור בכל מקום.

43. *Ibid.*, no. 21, fol. 11a, col. 1. Cf. Louis Ginzberg, "Joseph b. Solomon Colon, *Jewish Ency.*, IV (1903), 170, col. 1, cit.: *She'elot u-Teshuvot* (Warsaw, 1884), no. 21, fol. 17a. See my "Minhag in Its Bearing on Communal Controversy," *Proceed. Amer. Acad. for Jewish Research*, XLIII (1976), 190, nn. 26, 28.

44. This is an area for further research.

45. *Jewish Folkways, passim.*

46. Comparison is made by Professor Richard J. Fein.

The Achievement of American Yiddish Modernism

David G. Roskies

The Jewish Theological Seminary of America
New York, N.Y.

Modernism, that most Promethean and elusive of movements, has left its unmistakable imprint on Jewish life, yet the temper of postwar revisionism has blurred and all but obliterated it. In Yiddish circles, modernism has become either a term of opprobrium, something akin to Jewish self-hate, or is applied imperialistically to include all of modern Yiddish writing from the time of the Haskalah.[1] A more judicious, though still inadequate usage, divests the word of its moral implications and locates it more specifically in time. Modernism, according to this scheme, marks the entry of Yiddish writers from Russia, Galicia, and America into the European cultural mainstream, albeit a century late. Indeed, Yiddish writers who made their debut in the decade before World War I can be located, stylistically at least, in one or another of the dominant European movements: the romantic, lyric poets Dovid Einhorn, S. I. Imber, Yitskhok Katsenelson, and Ber Lapin; the impressionists Lamed Shapiro and Dovid Bergelson; the symbolists Mani Leyb and Der Nister. A thematic dialectic, propelled by Romanticism on the one hand and Naturalism on the other, prevented any one movement from holding sway for very long. I. L. Peretz in Warsaw and Yoel Entin in New York wrote manifestoes calling on the new generation to transcend observable reality by exploring the realms of Jewish history and religious tradition.[2] But in the fledgling Yiddish art theater, Naturalism was the order of the day, with Dovid Pinsky, Sholem Asch, Peretz Hirschbein, and even Peretz himself depicting the lives of starving workers and fallen women.[3]

The sudden onrush of European trends also coincided with the rise of modern literary journals: *Yugend* (Youth; N.Y., 1907), *Literarishe monatsshriftn* (The Literary Monthly; Vilna, 1908), Chaim Zhitlovski's influential *Dos naye lebn* (The New Life; N.Y., 1908–1914, 1922–23), *Yugend-klangen* (Sounds of Youth; N.Y., 1909), and *Literatur* (N. Y., 1910), the official organ of a group soon to be known as *Di Yunge* (the youngsters).

Still, to call this belated literary outburst "modernism" would be anachronistic. It was, for lack of a better term, the European Connection, when a hundred years of cultural development were compressed into ten. Even Estheticism, espoused by the so-called "youngsters" in America, began to take on momentum just when its European counterpart had been proclaimed dead.[4] Yiddish modernism broke with that eclectic tradition in response to the great upheavals of the early twentieth century which brought an end to so much else. Vast destruction and unprecedented mobility—these were the Jewish fruits of the Great War and Russian Revolution. In literature and art, the new age had already been heralded by the Futurists in Italy and Russia; the Expressionists in Germany; the Vorticists and Imagists in England and America. Yiddish modernism, a postwar phenomenon, was influenced by all of the above. Characteristically, its various groups are associated with the great Jewish urban centers of the period: the *Inzikhistn* (Introspectivists) in New York, the *Khalyastre* (Gang) in Warsaw, and the Kiev Circle. Of the three, only the New York based modernists remained true to the ideals and consistently upheld their movement. For our intents and purposes, Yiddish modernism is virtually synonymous with America.[5]

By 1940, even the American movement was dead, and before we examine its achievements, we would do well to ask why and how it sank into oblivion. To begin with, the whole undertaking was dismissed as an artificial (or "goyish") appendage to an otherwise "organic" cultural manifestation. The Europeanizers, of course, had also borrowed heavily from foreign models, as is lavishly attested to, for example, by the eight-volume deluxe edition of Heinrich Heine's collected works (New York, 1918), produced with the collaboration of over seventeen poets. Even without this testimony, Heine's impact can easily be detected in the work of Peretz, Avrom Reisen, Moyshe-Leyb Halpern, Moyshe Nadir, and Itsik Manger. But Heine, after all, was almost one of us and can hardly be reckoned a "foreign influence!" Be that as it may, this edition and similar efforts brought European culture into the home of the intelligent Yiddish reader. When the same reader, however, picked up a poem by Jacob Glatstein or Mikhl Licht, it all seemed disjointed and contrived. The reader lacked a proper frame of reference, never having heard, let alone read anything of Pound or Joyce.

The American Yiddish modernists, in contrast to their precursors and most certainly to their readers, had received an English academic training: Leyeles in London University and Columbia, Licht in City College and The New School for Social Studies, and Glatstein met Minkov in a class at N.Y.U. Law school. Though open to European trends, the modernists were particularly influenced by English and American literature—its traditions, tonality, and especially its new orientation since 1912. Put in less exalted terms, the modernists drank a toast with that new American invention, the cocktail, while their older colleagues enjoyed delicate French wines and 90-proof vodka.

The English influence manifested itself most clearly in the phenomenon of "little magazines." Glatstein made his poetic debut in the first issue of *Poezye* (Poetry, New York, 1919). New Yiddish journals with such names as *Literature, Literature and Life, The Free Muse, The New Land, The New Home, The Island*, had been appearing for quite some time, but the name *Poezye* derived from Harriet Monroe's Chicago-based journal, the first tribune of English modernism (founded 1912). *In zikh*, "a monthly of introspective literature," whose dates of publication (Jan. 1920 - Dec. 1940) define the time span of American Yiddish modernism, is closely related, in name and content, to Ezra Pound's *The Egoist*.

As in the English sphere, most of the Yiddish little magazines were short-lived and their editorial boards tended to split and regroup. In 1921, Glatstein and Licht, the most avant-garde of the *In zikh* group, put out their own journal, *Loglen* (Vessels) with a press run of 150 copies. With the characteristic hubris of youth, the editors almost boasted that there weren't even 150 candidates "who have been given the unique opportunity to be counted among the chosen few to discover us intuitively before our time has come."[6] Licht expressed the modernists' indifference to the masses when he compared *Loglen* to the London literary journal *The Germ* (1849), published by the Pre-Raphaelite Brotherhood. Just as the British intelligentsia took some fifty years to recognize their greatest contemporary poets, so too, Licht prophecied, would the Yiddish readership realize its mistake in ignoring their own poetic innovators.[7] Though Licht's prediction still has not been borne out in fact, *Loglen* resembled its British counterpart in that only four issues of both journals appeared. Licht, undeterred, founded a new journal with N. M. Minkov. Despite its derivation, the new name *Kern* (Germ) did not help sustain the journal beyond three issues.

In the phenomenon of the short-lived, non-commercial literary journals, with its direct parallel in the American little magazines, we see another reason for the public's disdain for Yiddish modernism. The modernists were an elite group who compensated for their isolation with reciprocal disdain. Ideology was another factor that set them apart from everyone else. Drawing from various programmatic statements, we arrive at the following composite literary manifesto:[8]

1. Reality already exists.
   I, the poet, must express it, not describe it.
   I must not recreate reality into something else, something artificial, more beautiful than reality itself.

2. Individuality is the measure of truth.
   External reality exists only insofar as it is reflected within myself.

3. The psyche of a person is chaotic. My poetry must therefore be kaleidescopic and fragmentary.

4. I, the poet, am an intellectual.
   Whatever I experience I must first subject to scrutiny and analysis.
   I must filter experience through the intellect.
   I must strive for psychological realism.

5. I, the poet, am a cosmopolitan.
   Of course I am a Jewish poet, but I am a Jewish poet in that I write in Yiddish.
   Whatever a Yiddish poet writes in Yiddish is *ipso facto* Jewish.

To be sure, there was nothing particularly original in any of this. Bergson and Freud are as much in evidence as Pound and Eliot. What makes the credo unique in the annals of Yiddish culture is that, for once, a group of its writers was perfectly synchronized with the prevailing *Zeitgeist*. Unfortunately, this credo, flaunted openly and loudly, flew in the face of the mainline of secular Jewish culture. Article one was a calculated repudiation of the symbolist, esthetic school of the "young-sters." Articles two, three, and four, emphasizing the primacy of intellect and the psyche, ruled out any espousal of social causes, or any catering to the masses. Cosmopolitanism, finally, did not sit well with those who demanded that literature reflect the national struggle of the Jewish people.

Many defected from these articles of faith, and in practice the poetic discourse of the loyal modernists was more flexible than their theory. It should be noted that, with only two exceptions that I know of, modernist experimentation did not extend to prose.[9] The Holocaust brought an end to most of this. Modernism was lumped together with all the other movements that had courted strange gods and were thus guilty of collaborating in our own destruction. The modernists themselves were fast becoming part of the establishment, and Yiddish culture now turned inward to recoup its incalculable losses.

Anglo-Saxon influence, ideological incompatability, and the trauma of history all conspired to rob Yiddish modernism of its audience. Today, long after the *Kulturkampf*, its achievement can finally be retrieved. What emerges, in the forefront of both its theory and practice, is a new awareness of the I: in its individuality, its relation to the other sex, to the world, and to the word. Selected works of only two poets, Jacob Glatstein and A. Leyeles, will have to suffice in way of illustration.

The poetic I was always a persona. An ever-changing mask was needed to reveal the different and contradictory aspects of the modern individual. Glatstein's first volume of collected poems was called *Yankev Glatshteyn* (N.Y., 1921), as if to say, there is nothing real outside of the psychological being. From Bergson came the teaching that the human mind receives external reality through static frames, splinters of reality, or, to use Virginia Woolf's phrase, "an incessant show of innumerable atoms."[10] But the mind also contributes appropriate memory images that give to what is perceived a completed, meaningful form. In one of the poems in his inaugural collection, Glatstein explored what happens when external reality is in a state of utter chaos, and the mind is thus incapable of integrating its disparate parts.

1919

Lately there remains hardly a trace
of Yankl the son of Yitskhok,

just a small round dot
rolling insanely around the street
with fly-away clumsy arms and legs.
The Lord-on-high has ringed the whole world round
with sky blue
and there's no escape.
Everywhere newspaper extras fall from above
and flatten out my watery head.
One with a long tongue
smeared my glasses forever with a long smear
and red, red, red.[11]

The "rain of splinters" is objectified by the screaming headlines of
the daily papers which *physically* beat him to death. The world is a
closed system, ruled by an impersonal "Lord-on-high," and the individual, here depicted in his Jewish aspect, is being destroyed by modern
life.[12] The poem concludes with a vision of the small round dot whirling
forever in the ether of the great unknown.

The poetic I of Leyeles' early poems is a split personality, just as a
dualism pervades the poetry itself. Psychological realism and free
rhythms follow the Introspectivist credo, but Leyeles also mastered the
most complex Renaissance forms—rondos, villanelles, tercinas, and sonnet cycles—in which a mystical, philosophical tone predominate. His
exquisite "Villanelle from the Mystical Cycle" (1924) concludes with a
vision of the poet, at the midpoint in his life, hoping to discover the
divine source of inspiration:

Brighter and brighter. By the grace of love.
In search of the light that redeems and is white—
Mystical cycle of seven times five.
The husk is gone and the kernel survives.[13]

The full complexity of the Leyeles persona was revealed in the figure
of Fabius Lind. Fabius is the Latin equivalent of Fayvl or Fayvish. As
Glatstein understood it,

The name Fabius Lind with its surface sound of foreignness symbolizes the
full scope of foreign influences that the modern poet has absorbed in order
to enrich the original, inherited Jewish sources. The sound of Fabius Lind is

intimately tied to new form and innovative content and represents no less an achievement than the Jewish-sounding names Mendele, Sholem Alei-chem, Yitskhok-Leybush (Peretz), Avrom, and Moyshe-Leyb.[14]

Besides the profound insight that the history of modern Yiddish litera-ture is the history of its personae, Glatstein alerts us to the centrality of Fabius Lind, the title of Leyeles' fourth and perhaps most important col-lection of poems. In "Fabius Lind's Diary," 33 poems dated January 27 to February 28, poetry is not a search for transcendence, as in the vil-lanelle. True to the modernist requirement of conveying the varying impulses of everyday life, Leyeles provides the biography of a poetic consciousness through a variety of forms, tones, and themes. Other kindred souls, who can be recognized by their exotic names, are Mikhl Licht's *Velvl Goth* (1929, 1934–5), which resonates with the German barbarians, the English foolstown Gotham, Gothic, and even God; Minkov's *Our Pierro* (1927), and Aaron Kurz's *Figaro* (1924).

The modernists, then, introduced a new I to Yiddish poetry: intellec-tual, introspective, and dispassionate; a multi-faceted personality in a constant state of flux. One poem or one consistent mask would not suf-fice to express the fragmentary nature of modern life. The problem, however, is that profound self-knowledge seemed to preclude effective action in the real world. Here is an individual too sophisticated to believe in any escape from the labyrinth. It never occurs to Yankl son of Yits-khok to resist the bombardment of splinters. Leyeles' I waits in anticipa-tion of a mystical revelation and fervently hopes that the struggles of life lie behind him. His Fabius Lind is a lonely, suffering poet. Can such a passive, resigned I establish any contact with the outside world, say, with a woman? How does this I fare in the realm of love and sex?

Not too badly. In Leyeles we find the familiar dualism: a quasi-reli-gious tone of sadness and longing on the subject of love; an analytic, highly "unpoetic" approach on the subject of sex. In "Eladea," a charac-teristic poem of the first group, the romantic ideal is never achieved. A poem of incantations and word-associations, it tells of two lovers who set out for the river where they will cast forth their jewels, but their love is not consummated.[15] In "Fabius Lind's Diary," on the other hand, we find a poem that treats the male sexual impluse. Through language, which translation can only approximate, the poet expresses the concrete physicality of the sexual act.

Yanuar 28 (January 28)

Fintsternish.
Gedikhte, knoylike,
Uralte, groylike, umheymlekhe, moylike.
Un plutsling—funken vayse, gantse pasn.
Magnium-gli—vays, vays.
A kni—varem, veykh un shtayf.
A reyf arum mir, vi der ring arum Saturn.
Shtayf arum mir. Vays. Muterlekher nokturn.
Sumne reytsenish.

Markh-farfleytsenish. Fal-fli. Fal-fli.
Kni. Magnium-gli. Un vider—
Knoylike, koylike fintsternish
Farfalenish.[16]

(Darkness./Dense,   tangled,/ancient,   horrible,   eerie,   mouthy./
suddenly—white sparks, whole streaks (of them)./ Magnesium glow—
white, white./ A knee—warm, soft and stiff./ A hoop around me, like the
ring around Saturn./ Stiff around me. White. Motherly nocturn./
Gloomy teasing./ Brain flooding. Fall—flight. Fall—flight./ Knee. Magnesium glow. And again—/Clumpy, coaly darkness./ Lostness.)[17]

Leyeles often associates sex with a cave, with darkness, and the primitive
raw passions of primeval man. He even wrote a one-act verse play on
the sexual struggles of prehistoric men and women![18]

   For Glatstein, only the second, negative side of Leyeles' vision exists.
In his early poetry, Glatstein describes sexual relations as a game in
which one or both players are destroyed.[19] In this game of love, the She
either assumes gigantic proportions or is reduced to the size of a dot.
When played by three, the game becomes particularly dangerous.
"Evening Bread" depicts the eternal triangle as a sexual ritual performed
every evening. The three characters, the husband, his wife and his lover,
are described abstractly, mechanistically. We know them only as pro-
nouns, that is, in terms of their sexual identity. Objects, in contrast,
assume a religious aura and are endowed with the strongest human
emotions.

   A fresh bread on the table, pregnant, whole.
   Unspeaking guests at table—

I and she and one more she.
The mouths silent yet the hearts strike.
Like small golden watches strike the hearts of the guests.
And by the bread, a keen knife, quieter still than the guests
Whose striking is more restless
Than mine, than hers, than the other hers.

The door lies open to the setting sun.
Flies, day-worn, drowse on the ceiling
And the windows glow astonished, expectant and afraid
Afraid and expectant of evening bread.

Tightly, the knife and I embrace each other's fright.
I flap around the bread with trembling hands,
And I think of my warm love of them.
Of my deadly hatred of them.
The knife faints in the grip of my hand
From fear and danger of evening bread.

She takes up the knife and looks at me, at her:
Two dead guests sitting silent at table.
And in the heart of she the knife blade sings
A song of danger of evening bread.

The other she plays with the blade of the knife
Lightly, joyfully, and with words that have no life;
And her love of us and her hatred of us
And her love of me and her hatred of her
Sings out through the gaping door
To the setting sun, to the sun, to the sun
With longing for evening bread.

Windows flooded with song and color.
The knife exhausted from red desire.
Unspeaking guests sit at table—
I and she and one more she.
The knife dances from me to her, from her to her.
And unspeaking we eat of love and hatred.
Evening bread.[20]

   The knife, an obvious symbol of sexual desire, unites all three people. The man is almost paralyzed, so great is his fear of impotence. The

wife is stolid and self-assured, ready to take on the lover, while the latter views the whole enterprise as a capricious game. With the setting of the sun, the three of them prepare to devour the sacrifice. The battle of the sexes is somewhat mitigated by the almost religious aura of the final tableau. Both Glatstein and Leyeles attempted a strict analytical, individualistic approach to interpersonal relations. As in its state of isolation, so too in the face of a woman, the I often felt powerless. But love, whether viewed as transcendent or primordial, also revealed hidden powers which ultimately defied a purely rational analysis.

If the presence of a woman could render the I powerless, the world at large could most certainly incapacitate it. Yankl son of Yitskhok is reduced to nothingness by the pressures of everyday life. The poet, for his part, could not subscribe to any political or national platform if external reality existed only insofar as it was reflected within himself. As if in defiance of this stance, the creative years of American Jewish modernism, 1919–1940, were a period of unprecedented turmoil. Some biographical information is now in order to help explain the political allegiance of our two representative poets.

Leyeles was politically active from early youth and remained an ardent Territorialist throughout his life. At age 17 he became London correspondent for a Vilna paper and at 25 a regular columnist for the *Tog*, a position he kept for 52 years. Glatstein considered himself a radical but refused to join any of the existing parties.[21] Out of necessity, not choice, he accepted a column in the *Morgn-zhurnal* at age 30 which proved to be a valuable outlet for his polemical mind. This difference is reflected in their poetry. In Leyeles, the collective invariably asserts its claim on the individual, but it took Glatstein some twenty years to integrate his private, poetic self into the context of modern Jewish history.

As Jews and as cosmopolitans, the modernists were at home in the world, or at least in that part of the world called Manhattan. And none as much as Leyeles. His celebrated cycle "In the Subway," a tour de force of free rhythm in modern poetry, expresses the psychic levels experienced simultaneously by a person riding the subway. Leyeles' embrace of the city—its bridges, stock exchange, and nationalities—is especially impressive when compared to the 45 other Yiddish poets collected in Mani Leyb's anthology *New York in Verse* (1918) who are drawn to the periphery or see only the broadest contours of the city.[22]

Leyeles also took on the great historical upheavals of the period, trying in each case to find a poetic form appropriate to the content. *Di mayse fun di hundert* (The Story of the Hundred, 1921) treats the Ukrainian pogroms of 1918–1919 in a pseudo-biblical epic style, and he retells the October Revolution as a *bylina*, a medieval Russian hero-epic. This last, called "Di almone un er" (The Widow and He, 1935), centers on Lenin's widow who was party to all the struggles, but now, under Stalin, is alone, afraid, and full of despair. Through her Leyeles expresses his familiar dualism: the messianic vision pitted against the individual who is helpless within a prison of loneliness.[23]

For Glatstein, the world, insofar as it impinges upon individual freedom, is as dangerous an enemy of the I as are women. All isms are equally suspect. The scientific truths they preach are nothing but empty rhetoric. Glatstein addressed one of his most bitter poems to those parties, of the right and the left, who were out to redeem the blood of the suffering worker:

> Oh, arise, arise, arise
> To the battle which is red.
> To red-battle and battle-red
> To bread-battle, to battle-battle.
> With the flag which is red
> (With the shirt that is black
> Black-red, red-black)
> For the first, for the twelfth, for the umteenth—
> And sorrow is his closest companion.[24]

The poem, called "Shpigl-ksav" (Mirror Script), is included in Glatstein's second volume, *Credos* (1929). I have my own script, the poem argues, the mirror-image of yours. My credo is the absolute inviolability of the word.[25]

Indeed, the word for the modernist poets is the sole measure of truth and falsehood. For Glatstein, the absolute freedom of the word is the only possible response to the screaming lies of society. The question is: where will this word come from? The modernists, contrary to popular belief, did not reject all literary traditions out of hand. Inspired by Eliot's famous essay "Tradition and the Individual Talent," which he translated in 1927, Mikhl Licht explored the poetic range of Old Yiddish literature and was the first modern poet to actively appropriate the model through imitation.[26] Leyeles wrote an ode to Yehoash's Bible translation, not to mention his own use of the biblical epic mode in *The Story of the Hun-*

dred. In the tradition, the modernists sought not old themes, but new expressive forms that would generate new possibilities for Yiddish poetry.

There was one tradition, however, that all the modernists were united in rejecting: that of *folkstimlekhkeyt.* For Leyeles, writing in the folk-vein was the chief criterion of anti-modernism:

> "Heart," "feeling," and "mood"—this is the three-dimensional. At best, it is an outpouring of emotion . . . and stands on the lowest rung of the artistic ladder. They ask for a song or a tune to be "sung," that it may rock and cradle them. Such as they have not advanced beyond the level of a folksong. If they speak of modernism, they are merely paying lip service to the times. Actually, what they want are songs like "Hartsenyu, kroynenyu, lyubt-shenyu mayn lebn, shvayg shoyn a bisenyu shtil, oy ven vestu mir shoyn gebn, oy dem vemen ikh vil."
>
> This is the meanest level of poetry: mono-tonal, mono-rhythmic, superficial and idyllic. It is the poetry that the masses feel is true poetry, the kind that "grabs" them.[27]

The indictment is clear. The stylized folksong is the epitome of falsehood because it denies and obscures the labyrinth of self-contradictions which is the true state of the modern person.

The most profound and far-reaching statement on the problem of language appears in Glatstein's fourth collection of poems, *Yidish-taytshn* (Yiddish Meanings, 193[6]). All the old themes—sex, politics and literature—are dealt with here, but are not broken down into impressions as experienced by a persona or individual poetic voice (as in "1919"), are not dramatized through situations (as in "Evening Bread"), but are interpreted through language. Glatstein examines the games words play; the medium is the message and vice versa.

The only true words, it seems, are those of an infant reacting to its sensory perception, to its mother. These words on the borderline of consciousness express authentic needs and are a true index of a person's psychic state. In exploring the mind of the child, Glatstein translated Piaget's discovery about child development into poetic form.

Clock and Mama

a clock ticks and she ha
is warm and eye

and eye and boo and hand and hand
and dress and click
click click click[28]

In an infant, the senses are not yet differentiated. The sound and feel of an object are perceived as identical to the object itself. The older one gets, however, the greater the gap between subject and object, as between the sexes; hence, the greater the need of language to cover the abyss.

In a carefully structured progression, Glatstein condemns all forms of false language: the empty slogans of political leaders, the musical, pleasant-sounding words of professional poets, and the *kheynevdike yidishtaytshn*, the charming, folksy phrases that evoke the cheapest emotions in the reader. Instead he offers Yiddish in *all* its meanings, i.e., a new analytic language in which each syllable and letter carries potential meaning. Aided by this new medium, the I can achieve a new synthetic understanding of its relation to the world, and the poetic word, in turn, can become not a *refuge* from the world, but a response to it.

The climax of Glatstein's affirmation and indictment comes at the end of the volume, in his most brilliant word-extravaganza, "Tsum kopmayster" (To the Brainmaster, 1929). The poem is an encyclopedic attack on all factions of Jewish society: the sentimental poets from Frug to Ber Lapin; the professional critics from Yoel Entin to S. Niger; the pseudo-modernists, and especially Chaim Zhitlovsky, to whom the crowning title apparently belongs. Glatstein counters their claims of moral, artistic, and political leadership with the achievement of Yiddish modernism. The modernists, he rebuts, don't have the answers, but they encompass more and with greater honesty, than anyone else. He rejects the accusation that their preoccupation with sex is pornographic. Sex, or more specifically, the male sexual organ, is, after all, the source of life, art, and individual identity:

Dos shteyndike vunder vos vert mert un gebert.
Dos eyntsike dos monishe
Dos konishe poligonishe un poligomishe
Dos komishmonogomishe dos zomishe
Un tsart lirish shtromishe
(Der khirik fun lirik)
        Der egotsenter—

(The standing miracle that becomes, breeds, and begets./ The one-and-only, the claimer/ the abler, polygonimal, and polygaminal/ the comic-monogominal the germinal/ and delicate lyrical fluvial/ (the pin-point of lyric)/ the egocenter—).[29]

Those who claim to speak for the Jewish people in this age of national upheaval decry the elitism and non-involvement of the modernists. Glatstein counters by accusing the leaders of being impotent, cynical, self-satisfied, and themselves well on their way to assimilation:

> Di idvund farlatet, farzatet.
> Keyn mamet keyn tatet.
> Der funvanet farvyanet
> Glat azoy a vuks a vegituks.

(The Id [or Jew] wound patched and placated./ No mothered no fathered./ The wherefrom wasted/ just a growth a vegitoth.)[30] It is worth mentioning that the rhetorical power of this no-holds-barred declaration of independence was appreciated, if not by its intended opposition, then at least by a contemporary audience of ordinary Jews.[31]

American Yiddish modernism, in conclusion, was a function of self-imposed exile, a deliberate attempt to uproot the self from its native soil in order to rebuild the world anew. Rejecting political panaceas and popular poetic conventions, the modernists' ideal was to achieve a unique synthesis of literature and life using only the means they had within themselves and those traditions, ancient, medieval, and contemporary, which afforded new, expressive possibilities. Modernism, they recognized, meant being strangers among one's own people. Many of the English modernists travelled to foreign lands—Pound and Joyce to Italy, Eliot to England—in order to establish a new artistic identity. The Yiddish modernists, by the same token, welcomed their American *goles* (diaspora). By a selective adaptation of modern English and American culture they forged their own language and tradition.

The murder of European Jewry brought in its wake a profound revision of Yiddish culture, particularly in America.[32] The modernists, ever-sensitive to change, were in the forefront of this process of re-traditionalization. Now, in their added capacity of poet-critics, Glatstein, Minkov, and to a lesser degree, Leyeles, became the arbiters of current literary taste and of the traditional canon. Though adopting a more public mode of discourse they continued, at their best, to experiment, to struggle with the contradictions in themselves, with the other sex, with the world, and with the word.

NOTES

1. The Soviet-Yiddish poet Ziama Telesin, on being awarded the Glatstein Prize for Yiddish literature for 1974, used the occasion to equate modernism with decadence. Though he invoked I.B. Singer, Yiddish culture's most celebrated debunker of modernism, Telesin unwittingly revealed himself as a true son of Socialist realism. See *Yerusholaimer almanakh*, No. 2/3 (1974), 234–5. For the "imperialist" view, see Y. Hirshhoyt, "The Paths of Jewish Literature: Tradition or Modernism" (Yiddish), *Di tsukunft* (Feb. 1978), 46.

2. I.L. Peretz, "What Our Literature Needs" (1910) in Irving Howe and Eliezer Greenberg, eds., *Voices from the Yiddish. Essays, Memoirs, Diaries* (Ann Arbor, 1972), pp. 25–31; Yoel Entin, "A Yiddish Romanticism" (Yiddish), *Troymen un virklekhkeyt* (New York, 1909), pp. 14–24. For a later Romanticist manifesto, see B. Grobard, "Tradition in Yiddish Literature" (Yiddish), *Nay-yidish*, No. 6/7 (Jan. 1923), 1–11.

3. See *Isaac Sheftl* by Dovid Pinsky (1899), *God of Vengeance* by Sholem Asch (1907), *In The Dark* by Peretz Hirschbein (1907) and *Bashefl* (also *Sisters*) by I.L. Peretz (1904–1906).

4. Ruth R. Wisse, "*Di Yunge* and the Problem of Jewish Aestheticism," *Jewish Social Studies*, XXXVIII (1976), 265–276.

5. On the Khalyastre, see Melekh Ravitsh, *Dos mayse-bukh fun mayn lebn* (The Storybook of My Life 1921–1934) (Tel Aviv, 1975); on The Kiev Circle, Ch. Shmeruk, "Yiddish Literature in the U.S.S.R." in Lionel Kochan, ed., *The Jews in Soviet Russia since 1917* (London, 1970), pp. 237–243.

6. *Loglen* (Jan.-Feb. 1922), 10.

7. *Ibid.*

8. Jacob Glatstein, A. Leyeles, N.B. Minkov, "Introspectivism" (Yiddish), *In zikh A zamlung introspektive lider* (Introspectivist Anthology) (New York, 1920), pp. 5–27; Mikhl Licht, "Answer to a Critic" (1934), in *Af di randn. Vegn literatur* (Marginalia. Literary Essays) (Buenos Aires, 1956), pp. 115–125; A. Leyeles, "A Forgotten Manuscript," intro. to his *Fabius Lind* (New York, 1937), pp. i-xvi.

9. The exceptions are: Mikhl Licht, *Nit tsu dertseyln* (Not To Be Recounted) (Buenos Aires, 1955), short stories written between 1919 and 1930; *idem, Velvl Goth: Poem-memoir* (Buenos Aires, 1955), part II; and Jacob Glatstein's stories of 1926–1931 which have never been collected. Glatstein's two published novels are somewhat experimental in

technique. Outside America, Dvoyre Fogel applied Cubist theories of montage to her prose as well as poetry.

10. Virginia Woolf, "Modern Fiction" (1919), reprinted in Miriam Allott, ed., *Novelists on the Novel* (New York, 1959), p. 77.

11. Jacob Glatstein, *Yankev Glatshteyn* (New York, 1921), p. 14; translation by Ruth Whitman, *The Selected Poems of Jacob Glatstein* (New York, 1972), p. 27, with slight revisions.

12. For the interpretation of this poem and its relation to Bergson's thought, I am indebted to Professor Dan Miron.

13. A. Leyeles, *Rondos un andere lider* (New York, 1926), p. 27. My translation.

14. Jacob Glatstein, "The Figure of Fabius Lind" (Yiddish) *In zikh* (April, 1937), 107.

15. A. Leyeles, "Eladea" *In zikh* (Anthology), pp. 111–113.

16. Leyeles, *Fabius Lind*, p. 14.

17. Translation by Uriel Weinreich. See Benjamin Hrushovski, "On Free Rhythms in Modern Yiddish Poetry," *The Field of Yiddish: Studies in Language, Folklore and Literature* (New York, 1954), p. 248.

18. "A halbe sho" (Half an Hour) in *Fabius Lind*, pp. 167–177.

19. Janet Hadda, "The Early Poetry of Yankev Glatshteyn" (unpublished Ph.D. dissertation, Columbia University, 1975), chap. two.

20. Jacob Glatstein, *Fraye ferzn* (Free Verses) (New York, 1926), pp. 22–3. Translated by David G. Roskies and Hillel Schwartz.

21. Jacob Glatstein, "To All Those Who Demand Allegiance" (Yiddish), *In zikh* (April, 1934), 2–10. This was a quixotic effort to organize a new radical Jewish movement along the lines of the American Worker's Party.

22. Mani Leyb, ed., *Nyu-York in ferzn* in *Der indzl* (New York, 1918) part two, separate pagination.

23. Leyeles, *Fabius Lind*, pp. 99–112.

24. Jacob Glatstein, *Kredos* (New York, 1929), p. 79. My translation.

25. Again, the interpretation is Miron's.

26. Mikhl Licht, "Dize sheyne naye tfile" (1927) in his *Gezamlte lider* (Buenos Aires, 1957), pp. 85–6. On the limitations and irretrievability of Old Yiddish literature, see Licht's "Fragments of An Essay" (1929), *Af di randn*, pp. 13–25. Compare also, Ch. Shmeruk, "Medresh Itsik and the Literary Tradition" (Hebrew) *Hasifrut*, II:2 (1970), 347–354, and especially n. 12.

27. A. Leyeles, "Rhythm, Form, Technique" (Yiddish), *In zikh* (June, 1923), 229–230.

28. Jacob Glatstein, *Yidishtaytshn* (Warsaw, 193[6]), p. 7. Translated by Ruth Whitman, p. 50. The poem was written in 1929.

29. Glatstein, *Yidishtaytshn*, p. 109. My translation.

30. *Ibid.*

31. A. Leyeles, "Yidishtaytshn," *In zikh* (Oct., 1936), 109. I derived the publication date of the book from this review.

32. David G. Roskies, "The Emancipation of Yiddish," to appear in *Prooftexts: A Journal of Jewish Literary History*, No. 1 (1981); Khasye Cooperman, "Why Tradition" (Yiddish), *Di tsukunft* (Feb., 1978), 48–50.

Messianic Expectations
in Kastoria on the Eve of Sabbateanism

Leon J. Weinberger

University of Alabama
Tuscaloosa, Alabama

In their study of the Sabbatean movement and its wide popularity throughout the Jewish world, historians continue to seek the causes for this remarkable phenomenon. The consensus in modern research is that no one factor, including the Chmielnicki massacres of 1648, was decisive.[1] It is here suggested that the most productive results would be gained from a study of each individual community in which the Sabbatean movement not only gained a wide following but also retained its popularity long after the apostasy and death of its founder.

Kastoria in Greece is such a community. In the middle of the seventeenth century, Kastoria had a sizeable Jewish population made up largely of wealthy fur dealers. The Sabbatean movement gained acceptance among the Kastoreans and soon was in the majority. Its followers included some of the leading community figures such as Shemaya de Mayo, Rabbi of Kastoria and a member of its Rabbinic Court, and Rabbi Israel Ḥazzan. The latter visited Sabbatai Ṣevi in 1667 and was so impressed that he was moved to pronounce the benediction on seeing a king in Israel. Israel Ḥazzan later became the disciple and secretary of Sabbatai's prophet, Nathan of Gaza, and a leading writer on the Sabbatean movement, carefully preserving recollections of Sabbatai's life and justifying the latter's apostasy. In line with this, it is noteworthy that another of Kastoria's Sabbateans, Jacob Kohen, went so far as to convert to Islam in imitation of the movement's founder.

Kastoria's leading luminary at this time was Nathan of Gaza, the prophet of Sabbatai Ṣevi. Nathan arrived in Kastoria and remained there for a considerable time. His major work *Sefer ha-Beriah* (Book of Creation) was written in Kastoria where he was held in great esteem and was frequently asked to arbitrate internal disputes. Although he would often make visits to the Sabbatean faithful in Adrianople, Salonika, and Sofia as well as go to secret meetings with Sabbatai, now exiled in Dulcingo, Albania, he would always return to Kastoria. There his authority was uncontested and his commands obeyed on pain of excommunication. Such were the deep roots struck by Sabbatean messianism in Kastoria, which remained a stronghold for the believers even after Sabbatai's death and after the Sabbateans in neighboring Adrianople had disbanded.[2]

Why was Sabbateanism so warmly embraced in Kastoria? Undoubtedly, a decisive factor is the long history of intense messianic expectation in this region. Already in the eleventh century, on the eve of the First Crusade, there was the well-known messianic agitation in which a leading role was played by Rabbi Tobias b. Eliezer of Kastoria and Salonika. The approach of a huge army on its way to Jerusalem incited the messianic hopes among the Jews of Byzantium, many of whom left their homes as they prepared to greet the Messiah. According to a letter circulating among Jewish communities in Palestine and Egypt and probably written not long after the events described, all the congregations in Byzantium "have been stirred and have repented before God with fasting and almsgiving" amid reports that Elijah, precursor to the Messiah, had revealed himself "openly, and not in a dream, to certain men of standing," including Rabbi Eliezer b. Judah, nephew of the aforementioned Rabbi Tobias. Whereupon Rabbi Tobias sent a letter to the Jews of Constantinople "to apprise them of the good news" and of "the signs and miracles [that] have taken place among us" and that "Elijah has manifested himself to us." Among the "wonders" described in Rabbi Tobias' letter was that "a totally blind man . . . [had] regained his eyesight." Even the Christians in the region were seized by the messianic fervor as reflected in the words of the local archbishop: "O Jews, sell your homes and property [and go to greet the Messiah] . . . we have definitely learned that your Messiah has appeared." Rabbi Tobias was apparently a central figure in this messianic movement, since he not only informed the Jews of Constantinople of the said events but also made the rounds of other communities in Greece, including Thebes, with the good news.[3]

Not as well known is the intensity of the messianic expectation in Kastoria in the thirteenth century, following the Fourth Crusade and the later rise of the Palaeologues. References to this messianism are preserved in the liturgical writings of Kastoria's leading synagogue poets: Menaḥem b. 'Elia, 'Elia b. Abraham he-'Aluv, David b. Eliezer and Mordecai b. Shabtai Longo. From David b. Eliezer we learn that the Kastoria community was acutely aware of living in the time of the "birth-pangs of the Messiah," given the increase in lawlessness in his day:

> Men have been emboldened to act violently
> Their activity extends even to the court of the king
> The rate of sin has risen
> Even the travail of these days.[4]

It was a time when men were anxious to know when the redemption would come, as indicated in a *seliha* by Mordecai b. Shabtai:

> I inquired of the seers and visionaires who have prophesied for me:
> "Do you know how long it shall be to the end of the wonders when the redemption will come?"
> And they replied: "Wherefore do you ask seeing that it is hidden?"[5]

Although the exact hour of the end-time is not revealed, there is the conviction that God has heard the prayers of Israel and that the Redeemer is on his way as expressed in the following lines from Menaḥem b. 'Elia:

> Behold the Redeemer, riding upon an ass, is coming and a mighty host accompanies him.
> Ruddy and pre-eminent above ten thousand, seeing how he stirs up love . . .
> You shall be sated with the good things that my servants have prepared for you
> Even the fatted Behemoth and Leviathan that they have preserved for you
> Know this, understand it and believe it . . .
> The time of the exile has ended and the rule of the wicked has been abolished
> For Judah has emerged victorious even as the decree has gone forth from the Lord.

> Behold the Prince Michael and with him the Prince Gabriel
> And between them the annointed Redeemer;
> Let Jacob rejoice, let Israel be glad![6]

In view of the Redeemer's imminent coming, the poet 'Elia b. Abraham urges his congregation to emigrate to the Holy Land in order to greet the Messiah, since God has instructed the earthly ruler of the land to relinquish Palestine to the people of Israel:

> Therefore we have come into the court of the garden [the synagogue]
> To pray [for the fall] of the persistent enemy
> For without your help [O God] we cannot make the ascent into the fortified cities because of the inhabitants of the land.[7]

And although the congregation is prepared to make the journey to the Holy Land trusting in God's might ("Thereupon your children respond: 'There is none like unto God, O Jeshurun, who rides upon the heavens [as your help] and God is with us.'"),[8] there remain the skeptics who counsel against making the perilous voyage. And against them the poet cries out:

> Wherefore will you turn away the hearts of the children of Israel from going into the land.[9]

And, continuing, he charges the skeptics:

> You are destroying my people with your counsel;
> This has been your doing by bringing up an evil report against the land.[10]

The model and the language for this skepticism is taken from the report of the spies in the Book of Numbers (Chapter 14). The reasons for the opposition's unwillingness to migrate to the Holy Land are not given although they probably were not different from those stated by the "learned" Jews of thirteenth century France and England who counselled their children not to remain in Palestine. From a responsum by the thirteenth century R. Me'ir b. Baruch of Rotenburg we learn that the French and English sages ordered their children to leave the Holy Land

and return to their homes in Europe (which they did) because of a lack of unity among Palestine's Jewish leaders, coupled with the difficulties in securing a livelihood and the absence of Torah learning in the ranks of the general population.[11]

What were the factors that made for the intensity of Kastorian messianism in the thirteenth century and is there evidence of one figure that might have served as catalyst for Israel's hopes for redemption at that time?

Although not a sufficient cause by itself, the disabilities suffered by Jews under Paleologue rule following the disruptions of Jewish communities after the Fourth Crusade (1204) and the succeeding period of warring states (from 1204 to 1259) undoubtedly served to fuel the rising messianic hopes in this period. Although there is no evidence of attempts by the royal houses to force the conversion of the Jews, as was the case during the reign of Basil I, founder of the Macedonian dynasty (ninth century), there are several references in the writings of Kastoria's Hebrew poets to the pressures brought upon the Jewish congregations to accept the Christian faith. In a *seliha* by Menaḥem b. 'Elia we read the revealing lines:

> The flock of sheep [Israel] called: Borne [by God from birth] say to Esau [the Christians]: "Israel belongs to its Maker and waits for His wonders . . ."
> They cry in agony, wander in exile, and even die preferring not to heed those who portray You in images.[12]

Another hint of the Jewish defense against the efforts of Christians to convert them is suggested in these lines from the David b. Eliezer:

> God alone by His power shall redeem [lit. lead] him [Israel]
> And no [strange] god is with him.[13]

Jews lived in almost constant anxiety and fear as reflected in the lines of Eliezer b. Judah:

> We grievously fear
> The decrees of the children of arrogance
> Filled with venomous hatred
> Under their lips.[14]

They also suffered under the heavy yoke of special taxes levied upon them by the government, as indicated in the following statement from the thirteenth century poet Abraham b. Isaac b. Moses:

> We cry out to You on account of the violence we endure
> And we wail because of the heavy taxes [laid upon us].[15]

Moreover, it is of no avail to try to reason with the ruling powers since, in the words of the poet Shemarya b. 'Elqanah, they:

> . . . deny the law of the God who established heaven and earth
> Persuaded that there is no truth, nor righteousness, nor knowledge
> of God['s will].[16]

It is likely that Abraham Abulafia, self-proclaimed messiah and propounder of the doctrine of prophetic Kabbalism, was the catalyst for the messianic fervor in Kastoria in the thirteenth century. It is known that Abulafia spent some ten years in Greece and Italy during his wanderings abroad and his doctrine of the search for ecstacy and prophetic inspiration was apparently known to the Kastorian poet Menaḥem b. 'Elia. According to Professor Gershom Scholem, meditation on the letters of the Hebrew alphabet provided for Abulafia the ideal object to aid the soul in becoming free from preoccupation with its natural self and enabled it, in Abulafia's words, "to untie the knots which bind it." The layers of meditation on the alphabet include articulation (*mivta*), writing (*miktav*), and thought (*maḥshav*). By renouncing his attachment to the phenomenal world, the individual proceeding on the steps of the mystic ladder is ultimately able, with the aid of meditation on the letters of the Divine Name, to attain prophetic inspiration.[17]

In describing the preparations for meditation and ecstacy, Abulafia, commenting on the verse (in Amos 4:12) "Be prepared for thy God, O Israelite," writes: "Make thyself ready to direct thy heart to God alone . . . begin to combine a few or many letters, to permute and to combine them with rapidity until thy heart be warm . . . then turn all thy true thought to imagine the Name and His exalted angels in thy heart as if they were human beings sitting or standing about thee . . . And know, the stronger the intellectual influx within thee, the weaker will become thy outer and inner parts. Thy whole body will be seized by an extremely strong trembling, so that thou wilt think that surely thou art about to die, because thy soul, overjoyed with its knowledge, will leave thy body. And be thou ready at this moment consciously to choose death, and then thou shalt know that thou hast come far enough to receive the influx . . ."[18]

Similarly, in his *seliha* "'Ayahedkha Bemorah," Menahem b. 'Elia states that "the attainment of awe-inspiring prophecy is dependent upon the proper articulation [of the letters of the alphabet] by one seeking [to attain this goal]," even as he refers to the discipline of placing (in imagination) the permuted and combined letters on the threshold (of the Divine Throne) among the adoring angelic host. The poet then closes with the revealing line: "God hearkens to the supplicator whose imagination prepares him and who, in his own eyes, considers himself as if he did not exist and is about to die."[19]

Given Menahem b. 'Elia's familiarity with Abulafia's teachings on ecstasy and prophecy, it is reasonable to assume that he was also familiar with the latter's messianic claims and his prophecy that the Redemption would come during his own lifetime,[20] and it is this conviction regarding the imminent coming of the Redemption time that Menahem b. 'Elia expresses in his *seliha* "'Amarti Ladonai 'Eli."[21]

Historically, Kabbalistic lore has been intimately bound up with the messianic hope. Gershom Scholem has correctly observed that "Kabbalistic contemplation is a kind of individual anticipation of eschatological messianism."[22] While the Sabbatean movement relied heavily on the Lurianic writings, the thirteenth century messianism was undoubtedly influenced by the Kabbalists of Gerona in Spain. This is clear from the *seliha* for the Ten Days of Repentance "Hallelu 'Et 'Adonai 'Emunai" by 'Abrekh b. Isaac preserved in the Book of *Selihot* for Romaniote congregations.[23] The burden of his work is that by means of proper contemplative concentration during prayer aided by the letters of the alphabet, the human will cleaves to the divine will and to the world of the *sefirot*. This view derives in part from the Rabbinic statement "great is repentance . . . for it leads to the throne of Glory" which R. Yehudai Gaon regarded as an equation of repentance with the ecstatic ascent of the soul. It is thus described in a statement by R. 'Aqiba to R. Ishmael in the Hekhalot literature: "When I ascended to the first place I was devout, in the second place I was pure . . . in the seventh place I . . . spoke the following prayer . . . Praise be to Thee . . . Sublime in the chambers of grandeur."[24]

In the said *seliha* of 'Abrekh b. Isaac mention is made of the ten *sefi-*

rot beginning with the "thought" (maḥashava) after the manner of the Sefer ha-Bahir and the writings of Isaac the Blind, "the father of Kabbalah." 'Abrekh sometimes refers to the sefirot by the term middot in the same way as does the author of Sefer ha-Bahir—whose writings influenced Isaac the Blind—as well as by the term sefirot. Following the views of Ezra and 'Azriel of the Gerona school of Kabbalists, 'Abrekh divides the sefirot into three stages ('olamot) comprising "the intellectual" (ha-muskal), "the psychic" (ha-murgash), and "the natural" (ha-mutba'). This division is probably based on the neo-platonic model wherein the movement from the one to many is achieved by the successive transition from the intellect through the universal soul to nature.

Like Isaac the Blind, 'Abrekh speaks of the hidden heavenly essences (havayot nistamot) and gives instructions on how to attain communion with God and the world of the sefirot through meditation on the letters of the alphabet.[25]

Occasionally the Hebrew poets in Byzantium reveal that with the aid of the requisite esoteric knowledge such a communion with God was actually achieved, as is indicated from the following lines by Benjamin b. Samuel Qushtani:

> My beloved [God], hidden and concealed from human eyes,
> I shall sing of His wonders with thanksgiving [that He has revealed Himself to me] like the angels on high,[26]

and from the twelfth century Moses b. Ḥiyya:

> He [God] who abides with unobserved might . . . and is concealed from view . . .
> In holiness I have beheld Him, and though He is hidden, He dwells before me.[27]

To summarize: the popularity of the Sabbatean movement in Kastoria is best understood against the wider background of earlier messianic activity in that region. Those events, plus the Kastorians' active interest in Abulafia and Gerona mysticism as well as the continuing disabilities endured by the Jewish community, set the stage for the region's wide acceptance of Sabbatai Ṣevi and his prophet Nathan of Gaza.

NOTES

1. Cf. G. Scholem, *Sabbatai Ṣevi*, (Princeton, 1973), pp. 2ff.

2. *Ibid.*, pp. 779–922.

3. Cf. J. Starr, *The Jews in the Byzantine Empire*, (Athen, 1939), pp. 74–75.

4. Ms. Oxford, 1168, fol. 182: ופעולותי ומרייהם/ודרכיהם בימים ההם/כשבת המלך. יספתי הבלי/זדון וחבלי/הימים האלה.

5. Cf. I. Davidson, *Thesaurus of Medieval Hebrew Poetry* (=D), New York, 1923–1933), 4 volumes, Mem 106: שאלתי נביאי וחוזי הנבאים בגללי: "הידעתם מתי קץ הפלאות אשר אמר לגאלי?" ויענו אותי: "למה זה תשאל—והוא פלאי?"

6. The text as preserved in *Maḥzor Romania*, Constantinople, 1510, Seliḥa 28, in Ms. Oxford, Opp. Add. 4V 96 and 283 reads: ורכב על חמור הנו בא/חליפות עמו וצבא/אדום דגול מרבבה/ומה תעוררו את האהבה . . . תשבעו הטובות הזמינו/לכם משרתי והטמינו/בהמות וליתן תשמינו/תדעו ותבינו ותאמינו . . . קץ הגלות עבר/ומטה-רשע נשבר/כי יהודה גבר/מה' יצא הדבר הנה השר מיכאל/ועמו השר גבריאל/וביניהם משיח הגואל/יגל יעקב ישמח ישראל.

7. Ms. Oxford, 1168, fol. 176: אכן אנחנו באים לחצר/ביתו לחנן על הצורר כי בלתך לא נוכל לעלות בערי המבצר/מפני יושבי הארץ.

8. *Ibid.*: לכן בניך יענו אין כאל/ישורון רכב שמים ועמנו אל.

9. *Ibid.*: ולמה תניא את לב בני ישראל מעבור אל הארץ.

10. *Ibid.*: כי אתם הַמִיתם את עמי בעצתכם/ומידכם היתה זאת לכם/להוציא דבה על הארץ.

11. Cf. MAHARAM, *Sefer Sha'arei Teshubot*, M.A. Bloch ed., (Berlin, 5651), #79, p. 187.

12. *Maḥzor Romania*, Constantinople, 1510, Seliḥa 74, *loc. cit.*: טלאי כבשיו קרואי עמוסיו יאמרו לעשו: ישראל לעושיני יחכה לנסיו . . . ירועו ינועו יגועו בל ישמעו אשר בדמין יערכוך.

13. Ms. Oxford, 1168, fol. 178: יוצרם בדד באונו ינחנו ואין עמו אל (נכר).

14. The author is the said nephew of R. Tobias b. Eliezer of Kastoria and Salonika. The text (cf. D.'Alef 7841) reads: נפשנו זוחלה/הנחלה מדיני בני עולה/אשר חמתם נתמלא/תחת שפתימו סלה.

15. D. 'Alef 3258: צועקים אליך חמס/צורחים מכובד המס. The term *mas* preceded by the definite article would suggest that the poet has reference to a special tax on Jews in Byzantium. This would cast doubt on the view of A. Sharf (in his *Byzantine Jewry*, Shocken: New York, 1971, p. 189) that the "evidence for a special tax . . . is inconclusive."

16. D. 'Alef 4665: מכחישים בדת אל ארץ ושמים יסד/חושבים בלבבם לאמר אין אמת ואין חסד/ואין דעת אלהים.

17. Cf. G. Scholem, *Major Trends in Jewish Mysticism*, (New York, 1941), pp. 126ff.

18. Cf. Abraham Abulafia, *Ḥayye 'Olam Habah*, cited in A. Jellinek, *Philosophie und Kabbala*, (Leipzig, 1854), pp. 44–45 and G. Scholem, *ibid.*, pp. 136–137.

19. *Maḥzor Romania, ibid.*: נבואה נוראה תלויה בקריאה נאה מופלאה מפי דורש ושואל . . . סחופים, דחופים, שפופים שימם (האותיות) בין שרפים צופים . . . קשבת אזנו למתחננו אם רעיונו מכינו וכאינו בעינו נחשב ובא כמת.

20. Cf. Abulafia's statement in his *Sefer ha-'Ot* cited by A. Jellinek in H. Graetz, *Jubelschrift*, (Breslau, 5648), p. 79: וקץ התשועה ויום הגאולה בא ואין איש אשר שים לבו היום לדעת זאת.

21. Cited above, from *Maḥzor Romania, ibid.*, Seliḥa 28, see note 6, above.

22. G. Scholem, *Sabbatai Ṣevi*, p. 16.

23. *Maḥzor Romania, ibid.*, Seliḥa 34.

24. G. Scholem, *Major Trends etc.*, pp. 78–79.

25. Cf. *Encyclopedia Judaica*: "Kabbalah," p. 571. Following is the text of Abrekh's Seliḥa:

הללו את ה' אמוני דרשוהו בהמצאו בעתה רצויה/נצח שחרוהו ספרו מדותיו במגדלי ציון הבנויה. יחי נפשכם כי משם תוצאות חיים,—ולכן כל מבקשי תחיה/הללויה.

הללו אל אלהי הרוחות אשר המציא והאציל מאין עולמו וחדשו/וטובו הגדול מעשהו בכל יום מחדשו ומקדשו.

מיום העלהו במחשבה עד יום מלאת ימי קצו וחלשו/הללו אל בקדשו

הללו בורא הויות נסתמות ואמרו נוראות עזוזו/וגדלו ספרו ומללו פלאיו ועזו

בהפכו משורש הרים ויאורים בקע במדת חכמה זו/הללוהו ברקיע עזו.

הללו ראשון ואחרון הנאור בפעלותיו/בחרוט רשימות דקות בלב נתיבותיו בבינה חקקם הנספרת שלשית בספירותיו/הללוהו בגבורותיו.

הללו כבד ראשון הנחלק לכמה גוני אורה בגבולו/כנמצא במתן הדמים הנותן כל איש בגללו.

וכלם זוכים בחסד כזכה אב המון עמד בהיכלו/הללוהו כרוב גדלו.

הללו בשיר שם אלהים וגדלוהו בתודה ושירכם יושפר/ותטב לה' משור פר

ונאמן בגבורה במורא שחרוהו, עבדוהו לבל בריתכם תפר/הללוהו בתקע שופר.

הללו נורא ואיום ובקשוהו בכל יום ואולי במדת אור/הנשמרת לחוכיו ינחילכם האדיר והנאור.

ולחננכם עת יחכה, מתפארתו ישפיעכם שופע חיים כצנור/הללוהו בנבל וכנור.

הללו יה הנורא במורא, עזרה בצרה,—מפניו כל יזחול זחול/לכן יראו ואליו סברו וקוו למחול.

עונותיכם, וטוב נצחו עליכם עת ירב כחול/הללוהו בתוף ומחול.

הללו צדיק וישר אל אמונה ואין עול הנשא על גב/גב חיות הקדש ונעלה ונשגב

ואת זיו הודו בהרבותו עליכם בהתמד כמעין בל ינוגב/הללוהו במנים ועגב.

הללו חנון ורחום מבטיח בנחום עמו להסיר מני דמע/עינימו ומימי ראש בל נגמע

וליסד עולם עת אזנכם כזאת תשמע/הללוהו בצלצלי שמע.

הללו קדוש הנקדש במדה הידועה/לכל היא בכל מעין הישועה

ועטרת מלכות קרואה,—ולכן בקידה וכריעה/הללוהו בצלצלי תרועה.

הללו חזק ואמיץ לה' המפורש המורה היה/אשר הוה הווה ויהיה,

לכן כל מתאוה יהודה כנאם איש עליה:/כל הנשמה תהלל יה.

הללו לעד לשוכן בתהלה, משכוי שכויה/מנויה ממוטבע, בנויה ממורגש וממושכל עטויה,

ועל זאת התהללו והללו יה/ואמרו: כל בֶּן זאת,—התושיה, הללויה.

דודי טמון וחבוי מעין כל נפוחי נשמות/אני :104 .p ,606 ,Paris ,Nationale Bibliothèque .Ms .26
נוראותיו אשרשר בברוך כאופני מרומות.

יושב יתלונן בעוח חביון/ . . . ומסתתר בלי חזיון/ . . . בקדש :25 Seliḥa ,.ibid ,Romania *Maḥzor* .27
חזיתיו והוא פלאי/יושב ממולי.

Changing Pattens of Relationship Between Campus and Community: A Personal Retrospective

Philip M. Klutznick

Chicago, Illinois

Alfred Jospe's career with the B'nai B'rith Hillel Foundations, a pioneering program that brought the Jewish experience to university campuses of this and other lands, is the most prominent part of a lifetime of distinguished service to the Jewish people and the campus community. His career also spans a period of multiple and significant changes on the campus, in the Jewish community, and in the patterns of relationship between them. Since Alfred and I are approximate contemporaries (although I am the elder), many of our insights on this period emerge from personal experience. In one particular I have an advantage—my college years were spent in America and in the varying environments that in some respects foreshadowed the post-war evolution of the American campus.

In our lifetimes the opportunity for young people to go to a university and the character of the campus have undergone significant metamorphosis. The democratization of accessibility of college education is one of the most remarkable developments of the past generation or two. I matriculated at a university in 1924. With the exception of a modest number of urban campuses and long-established schools like New York University or the University of Chicago, going to college then meant leaving home. For the overwhelming majority of college youth, it involved breaking ties with home and community and with the atmosphere they induced. For some young people, this was one of the attractions to continuing their education—the opportunity to be on their own. For many, if not most, it also presented psychological and fiscal barriers.

There was another, more subtle, aspect that in some measure has disappeared. As late as the 1920's and even later, the prospect of being a college or university graduate meant entering a financially select and socially exclusive segment of society. This does not imply that only the sons and daughters of the wealthy matriculated, although it was certainly easier for them. There were countless Horatio Alger stories acted out by the offspring of the poor, students who waited on tables, or peddled papers, or held menial jobs in order to get a college degree.

What was true of society generally had special impact on the Jewish youth of the 20's and 30's. Jewish students were largely either first generation Americans or immigrants themselves. The "world of our fathers," so brilliantly portrayed by Irving Howe, was the milieu out of which a considerable number of Jewish youngsters sought to achieve the goal of higher education. Those were the days when *kashrut* and Jewish educational and cultural opportunities did not exist in the small towns where state or private universities were situated. The clash between home and campus made many of us frequent recipients of "care" packages from home and accompanying reminders of the Jewish holidays.

At Lawrence, Kansas, where I first went to college, there was a Menorah Society to which seven to ten of us were normally attracted. Later, when I was in Lincoln, Nebraska, the presence of a synagogue and temple and a fair-sized Jewish community offered social and religious contacts that only a few students welcomed. But, when I finished up in Omaha, Nebraska, a Midwestern metropolis with a vital and unusual Jewish community (10,000 people in those days), a Jewish community center, a Jewish federation, and all of the trappings of multiple Jewish organizations, the campus lost its importance. It was the community which provided a Jewish life akin to what I had at home in Kansas City.

My impressions from the late 20's and early 30's, underscored by extensive travel across the United States and Canada as a national Jewish youth executive, were that the number of Jewish young people who were educationally upward bound was relatively small—most who were headed for college and with whom I came into contact felt themselves destined for an exclusive position in society, and any other considerations were of little or no interest.

In sum, the number and character of institutions of higher learning were limited compared to today; the number in percentage and absolute terms of Jewish youth who reached for these opportunities was small compared to today; and the on-campus facilities for Jewish experience were few. To this must be added the observation that the number of Jews who held high administrative or professional posts in colleges and universities was relatively small.

The sad and disturbingly apparent phenomenon at that time was the large percentage of that small number, whether students, administrators, or faculty, who felt it advantageous to either hide their Jewish identity or neglect it. A minority people, with religious and cultural customs strange to the majority society of the 1920's and 1930's, when the "melting pot" theory and 100% Americanism were dominant, could hardly expect anything else. Neither the country nor its people accepted ethnic pluralism as a worthy norm. Although anti-Semitism was not rampant, the Ku Klux Klan was then at the height of its power. As a student, I saw crosses burnt on campus.

As our nation moved into World War II and the events that followed, a revolution occurred in our society and its economy. The United States emerged from the War as a "colossus," accounting for as much as 40% of the total productive capacity of the world. What is especially pertinent was the triumph of science and higher education. The United States and its allies won the War because of the superiority of their scientific knowledge which, overcoming a late start, made possible the accelerated production, in both quality and quantity, of needed war materials.

Higher education, science, and learning have been enthroned at the pinnacle of our national concerns. Some claim that in our times the only major progress in research and development has been the fallout from defense and security activity. It is true that the extraordinary changes in higher education can be traced in large part to the defense and war efforts attendant to World War II. The GI educational program, the competition for scientists, and the expanded need for educated persons increased facilities and campuses at a geometric rate of growth. After World War II a college education was no longer the exclusive privilege of youngsters whose parents could afford it or who were prepared to pay the price of drudgery, hard work, and little sleep to go to school.

Among Jews, traditionally dedicated to learning, the heightened accessibility to the university, the improved capacity to meet the costs, the availability of low-interest scholarships, and other inducements stimulated a tremendous response. Eighty percent and more of Jewish youngsters of college age now matriculate at institutions of higher learning. Since World War II they have sought not only an education, but also, in large numbers, to be educators and administrators. Today, at some of the most prestigious campuses of the nation, Jewish personalities occupy posts as presidents, deans of faculty, deans of colleges, professors, and lesser but significant teaching positions. An estimated 60,000 Jews hold administrative and teaching appointments at American universities.

The transformation in numbers, both general and Jewish, has been accompanied by a change of setting. Now that more than 70% of the American population lives in or near cities, the urban college or university is no longer a rarity. Today they are found everywhere, from small towns to large cities, and in great numbers. This increase of opportunities in higher education could not have been satisfied without a large scale shift from privately financed and endowed instruction to public funding. The impact has been so immense that the adjustment caused a number of fatalities among smaller and less viable private institutions. State universities have grown larger and the newer urban campuses have achieved ever higher attendance records.

While this massive change was taking place in higher education, the Jewish community did not stand still or regress. As a boy, I remember the settlement house, later replaced by a Y.M.-Y.W.H.A. in an old mansion and still later by a fully-equipped Jewish Community Center. One of the significant contributions of the American Jewish community to Jewish life all over the world has been this institution.

My first contact with Jewish philanthropy was the "pushke" in my father's home and the Yom Kippur appeal in our synagogue. The frequent calls from distinguished bearded emissaries from overseas, representing every cause, most often a yeshiva, were a regular part of the scene. Many were upset by this type of activity, but others enjoyed the contact. The "landsmenschaften" and their preservation of the shtetl atmosphere from which their members had come were everywhere, even in small Midwestern communities. Whenever I encounter traces of this "dying breed" of American Jewish community life, I feel the warmth of friendly nostalgia for that beautiful dimension of the Jewish community.

With increased affluence there was a declining need for Americanization programs and a new need to keep Jews Jewish. New institutions and new types of personnel were required. There were increased efforts to consolidate local fundraising efforts; national domestic charitable activities were joined and, as Zionist activities increased, they too were absorbed into the community framework. I remember the personalities who were among the pioneers in what was to become a highly professionalized Jewish civil service. At the outset, with notable exceptions, they came from the laity—lawyers, businessmen, or teachers, who laid the groundwork for an influential element in our Jewish communal structure. Early in the process the idea of federation also began to spread.

In the field of Jewish education the *heder* gave way to the Sunday School, the three-day-a-week school, the more dignified Talmud Torah and the Day School. Religion moved from Orthodoxy or Reform to an orthodoxy divided into several camps, Conservativism, Reconstructionism, and various gradations of Reform. We evolved into a minority full of pluralisms, a minority with its own smaller minorities.

There were great debates over how to handle anti-Semitism—by vigorous outspoken attack, by a "sha-sha" approach, or something in between; debates were also reflected in the divisions over the issue of a Jewish national homeland. The differences between Zionists, non-Zionists, and anti-Zionists are still vivid to those to us who regarded ourselves as Zionists and who, nevertheless, worked with all sectors.

All of this was magnified, and eventually exploded, by the Holocaust, which went too long unrecognized, and by the birth of Israel. Since 1946, and certainly since 1948, the unorganized, confused, and competitive Jewish community has taken on a more orderly form and shown an increased sense of priority. Greater unity has emerged for the support of Israel, rescue work, fighting anti-Semitism, Jewish education and even religion. The community had grown in numbers and affluence. Many relatively small communities federated and managed sizeable budgets. Hundred thousand dollar campaigns became million dollar efforts, and campaigns for several million dollars are now drives for hundreds of millions. Even with the effects of inflation, which magnify numbers, it is no small miracle that voluntary giving by the Jewish community of the United States has long since passed the billion dollar level. All things included, it is probably near or past the two billion dollar mark.

How important has the campus been, and what has it become, during this period of remarkable change? Some call it progress and in many respects this is correct. But revolutionary change is not a respecter of values. It can wreck as well as build. Some values get lost in the wake of the momentum for change. When higher education was reserved for the "elite" and when it offered an almost automatic grant of leadership and distinction, our society and communities reflected a more simply defined set of values. As industrialism and high technology became the distinguishing elements of our national life, it was inevitable that the masses would be affected by the tempo of a new world and a new environment.

For the Jew, there have been additional traumatic impacts which arose out of ancient causes and yearnings. Starting in the late nineteenth century, the burden of anti-Semitism, both physical and psychological, provoked the largest voluntary Jewish migration in history from the indignity of Eastern Europe to new homes, principally in America. The tragedy of the Holocaust depleted this reservoir of imported Judaising influences and manpower. And the rebirth of the State of Israel inspired a new orientation for Jewish life everywhere. We Jews, especially in the West, have been the beneficiaries or the sufferers of these revolutionary developments. The long-range impact on the community has been matched by turbulent changes on the campus.

In the 1920's, the beginnings of Hillel were stimulated by the need to keep the leadership elite of the Jews from hiding or abandoning their heritage. Hillel's birth at the University of Illinois in an upstairs facility over a commercial establishment was the hesitant and reserved response to a surfacing challenge. Budgets, then as now, were a great problem. It is an axiom of human behavior that important and growing needs tend to exceed available resources. Champaign, Illinois, was unknown to the community, and Hillel, prior to being adopted by B'nai B'rith or even afterwards, was known to relatively few. B'nai B'rith itself numbered less than 50,000 members. When the irrepressible and unforgettable Dr. Abram L. Sachar took hold of Hillel leadership, he dramatically transformed the needs of a weak infant into a noble cause. But even he saw it as a function that dealt with the leadership potential for tomorrow's community. I recall his plea for a budget and the needed approval to establish Hillel at Princeton. One of his convincing arguments was that this was a "prestige campus" which we could not ignore. The other argument that he used with telling effect was that Hillel had to be on certain campuses with full or partial operations in order to "co-opt" the field and preclude the tendency toward wasteful competition which typified so much Jewish activity.

There were other campus programs, but as the Jewish body was relatively small and the number of campuses a fraction of what it is today, he nearly accomplished this goal. It required statesmanship and a careful selection of rabbis and directors with varied Jewish orientations, but with a relatively docile life on campus and a general community only passively concerned, Dr. Sachar's vision and energy produced results. This was enhanced in great measure by his unique ability to recruit talented individuals who were infected by his enthusiasm and commitment. Not the least among these was Alfred Jospe.

But that was yesterday. It was a time when virtually the only courses in Jewish studies were at the Hillel Foundation and the primary social meeting ground for Jewish college students (except fraternities and sororities) was the Hillel house. Many Jewish couples acknowledge that they met at Hillel. This too was one of Dr. Sachar's great selling points in his appeal for more funds.

The stirring events of the last forty years have compelled the Jewish community to expand its horizons. Alongside the pressure to raise money for Israel and overseas relief, the fundraising enterprises have sought to satisfy domestic needs as well. Resources have been made available to cope with a variety of demands, not the least of which is the need to serve college youth. There were always a few Federations that responded to this demand with genuine understanding. This was especially true in communities where the challenge was physically apparent and the large numbers of Jewish students were not faceless. But as colleges and universities multiplied, it became apparent in many additional places. Federations that had been content to make a grant and nothing more became concerned with what was happening and even sought direct involvement.

When the 60's produced violence and sit-ins, minority students seeking their rightful opportunities, and student bodies seeking to influences public policy, the campus acquired new significance. College students were no longer "kids" as far as their influence and importance were concerned. Even though the hyper-activity of the 60's has now subsided (perhaps even too much), the aftermath of commitment remains, especially in the Jewish community.

Although hundreds of institutions of higher learning have made Jewish studies a part of the curriculum, there is major concern within Jewish communities as to whether or not the programs for Jewish life for the large population of students are adequate. The B'nai B'rith Hillel Foundations and the Association for Jewish Studies have just published a major survey of *Jewish Studies at American and Canadian Universities*. The World Jewish Congress and the World Zionist Organization are producing a study of the competence and adequacy of Jewish studies and teaching on campuses around the world. The Memorial Foundation for Jewish Culture has tabled a report on more general aspects of the community commitments to the college student, in which it suggests programs to supplement what is now going on.

So it is that the seeds sown by the late Rabbi Benjamin Frankel at the University of Ilinois and nurtured by Dr. Abram Sachar and loyal and devoted co-workers like Alfred Jospe have borne fruit. Hillel is the keystone of Jewish university life, even as we acknowledge the centrality of the teachings of the great sage whose name it bears. But the vital and comparatively miniscule beginnings have been supplanted by huge demands and unmet needs. The community whose lukewarm commitment of yesteryear reflected a lack of understanding and capacity has been brought by cataclysmic events to a growing appreciation that our college youth must not suffer further neglect.

All this cannot be attributed only to external events; had it not been for an organization, B'nai B'rith, which provided the seed and through difficult times and at great sacrifice nourished and protected the Hillel Foundation movement, our hopes for Jewish youth on campus might have vanished long ago.

We appropriately single out Alfred Jospe for his lengthy and effective leadership in this great mission among our people. His career with Hillel, begun at the University of West Virginia and Indiana University, reached its most influential heights during his long tenure at the top levels of Hillel's professional leadership. His service as the Director of the Department of Program and Resources and, later, as the International Director, has influenced the lives of hundreds of Jewish leaders in all walks of communal life. The contributors to this Festschrift and its publication in his honor are but one expression of the affection and esteem in which he is held. May his influence and productive capacities be sustained for many years to come.

Appendix

Alfred Jospe's Writings

Die Unterscheidung von Mythos und Religion bei Hermann Cohen and Ernst Cassirer in ihrer Bedeutung für die jüdische Religionsphilosophie, Berlin 1932

"Das religiöse Problem im Zionismus," *Der jüdische Wille* III 5/6, July-August 1935

"Religion und Erziehung," *Lessler Schule Festschrift*, Berlin 1938, 21–26

"Ein Gespräch im Lehrhaus," *Jüdisches Gemeindeblatt für Berlin*, January 23, 1938

"Hitler and the German People: A Warning," *The Torch*, November 1942

"Torah and the Jewish State," *The Indiana Jewish Chronicle*, September 1946

"Adjustment Tests for Students," *Guideposts* II, 2, January 1947, 12–16

"Some Reflections on Religious Unity," *The Indiana Jewish Chronicle*, September 1947

"Introducing the Book of Books" [review], *Commentary*, July 1950

"The Program of the Hillel Foundations," *Living as a Jew Today*, New York, N.Y. 1950, 46–51

"A New Primer of Judaism" [review], *Commentary*, June 1951

"On the Meaning of Jewish Culture in Our Time," *The Jewish Heritage and the Jewish Student*, New York, N.Y. 1951, 14–30

"Israel Avraham Rabin" [necrologue], *Historia Judaica* XVI, 1952, 170–171

"The B'nai B'rith Hillel Foundations," *Religious Education*, July-August 1953, 1–7

"The Role of Student Leadership in the Hillel Foundation," *Towards a Program of Jewish Living*, New York, N.Y. 1953, 67–73

"The Individual Jew: Identity and Adjustment," *American Freedom and Jewish Identity*, New York, N.Y. 1954, 12–25

"The 'Roles' of the Hillel Director," *Who "Belongs" to Hillel?*, New York, N.Y. 1954, 24–35

The B'nai B'rith Hillel Foundations: An Academic Catalogue, compiled and edited by Alfred Jospe, New York, N.Y. 1955

"Blueprint for a 'Successful' Hillel Foundation," *Judaism for the Modern Age*, New York, N.Y. 1955, 61–73

"The Philosophy of Hillel Work: A Historical Re-Examination," *The Philosophy of Hillel Work in the Light of Experience*, New York, N.Y. 1955, 1–13

"The World of Moses Maimonides" [review], *Jewish Heritage*, 1957, 49–50

"Religious Perspectives in Higher Education (with Special Reference to the Concerns of the Hillel Foundation)," *Aspects of the Hillel Program: Principles and Practices*, New York, N.Y. 1957, 14–27

"The Hillel Foundation and the Jewish Heritage," *Judaism and Ethical Choice*, New York, N.Y. 1957, 75–88

United Jewish Student Appeal: A Campaign Manual, Washington, DC 1958

"Religious Perspectives in Higher Education," *The Reconstructionist*, XXIV # 3, 1958, 7–14

"The Jewish Student and the Hillel Foundation," *On Being Jewish Today*, Washington, DC 1958, 3–16

"The Hillel Foundation and the Transmission of the Jewish Heritage," *On Being Jewish Today*, Washington, DC 1958, 86–99

"Increasing Jewish Content in Youth Movements," *Proceedings of First World Jewish Youth Conference*, Jerusalem 1959, 117–123

"After the Institute—What?", *The Jewish Image of Man*, Washington, DC 1959, 79–87

"The Outlook for Religion in the State Universities," *Religious Education*, March-April 1959, 141–143

Films and Film Forums in the Hillel Program, Washington, DC 1959

"The Three-Fold Rebellion: Some Observations on a Recent Visit to Israel," *The Way of Judaism*, Washington, D.C. 1960, 50–68

"The Jewish Student and His Sense of Jewish Identity," *Jewish Identity and The Jewish College Student*, Washington, DC 1960, 18–28

"Challenges Confronting Hillel on the Campus Today," *Jewish Identity and the Jewish College Student*, Washington, DC 1960, 56–71

The Counselorship Program: An Orientation Manual for Hillel Counselors, (three editions), 1960–1965

"The Jewish Image of the Jew," *Jewish Heritage*, vol. 2 # 4, Spring 1960, 5–12

"Some Observations on Student Life in Israel," *Changing Patterns of Jewish Life on the Campus*, Washington, DC 1961, 51–64

"What Makes Jews What They Are?" [review], *The National Jewish Monthly*. March 1961, 59–60

The B'nai B'rith Hillel Foundations: A Guide to Hillel Purposes, Program, Policies, Washington, D.C. 1962

Israel as Idea and Reality: A Sourcebook for Study and Discussion, ed. by Alfred Jospe and Daniel Thursz, Washington, D.C. 1962

"The Hillel Foundation and the Role of the Educated Jew," *The Sabbath as Idea and Experience*, Washington, D.C. 1962, 92–112

Judaism on Campus: Essays on Jewish Education in the University Community, Washington, DC 1963 (second printing 1965)

"On Reason and Revelation: Moses Mendelssohn," *Judaism*, vol. 12 # 4, Fall 1963, 476–478

"Faculty and Students 1904–1938: Biographies and Bibliographies," compiled with an introduction by Alfred Jospe, Guido Kisch, ed., *Das Breslauer Seminar*, Tübingen 1963, 381–442

Faith and Reason: An Introduction to Modern Jewish Thought, by Hugo S. Bergmann, transl. and ed. by Alfred Jospe, New York 1963

—Spanish edition: *Fe Y Razon*, Buenos Aires, 1963

—Portuguese edition: *Fe e Razao*, Sao Paulo 1965

"Religious Issues on Campus: Some Observations on the Religious Attitudes of Jewish College Students," *Living Legacy: Essays in Honor of Hugo Hahn*, New York 1963, 95–104

"Religion in Higher Education," *CCAR Journal* 1963, 14–22

"The Legacy of Maurice Pekarsky," *Challenges to Jewish Education on the Changing Campus*, Washington, DC 1964, 81–98

"Jewish College Students in the United States," *American Jewish Yearbook*, vol. 65, 1964, 77–99

"Mos'dot Hillel la'Studentim," *Bit'futzot Hagolah*, VI, 3/4, Jerusalem 1964, 138–141

"Challenges to Jewish Education on the Changing Campus," [condensed], *The Jewish Digest*, June 1964, 27–36

"Intermarriage: The Crucial College Years," *Intermarriage and the Future of the American Jew*, New York 1964, 77–94

Jewish Students and Student Services at American Universities, Washington, DC, 1965 (mimeographed, publ. by B'nai B'rith Hillel Foundations)

Experimental Worship in the Hillel Foundations (Program Monograph), Washington, DC, 1965

Hanukkah in the Hillel Foundation: A Guide to Hanukkah Programs and Resources, Washington, DC 1965

The Legacy of Maurice Pekarsky, edited with an introduction by Alfred Jospe, Chicago 1965

"Challenges to Jewish Life on the Changing Campus," *The Jewish Teacher*, *vol. 34 # 2*, December 1965, 23–32

"Intermarriage and the Jewish College Student," *Jewish Heritage*, Spring 1965, 5–13

"Profile of an Ideal Hillel Graduate," *Dimensions of Jewish Existence Today* (Proceedings of the National Hillel Summer Institute), Washington, DC 1965, 101–120

"Moses Mendelssohn," *Great Jewish Personalities in Modern Times*, Washington DC, 1960, 11–36 (reprinted in *Molders of the Jewish Mind*, Washington D.C. 1966, 123–147

"Jewish Youth and the Jewish Community: Challenge and Counter-Challenge," *Proceedings of the Founding Convention, North American Jewish Youth Council*, Nyack, NY, 1966

"New Perspectives for the Hillel Program," *Campus 1966: Change and Challenge*, Washington, DC 1966, 85–99

"Intermarriage and Conversion: Issues Confronting the Hillel Director," *Campus 1966: Change and Challenge*, Washington, DC 1966, 28–46

A Handbook for Student Leaders, Washington, DC 1967

"Varieties of Jewish Belief," [review] *In Jewish Bookland*, April 1967

"Religious Issues on the Campus," *Working with College Students: A Handbook for Rabbis*, Central Conference of American Rabbis, New York 1967, 1–7

"Changing Frontiers in the Campus Ministry," *New Frontiers for Jewish Life on the Campus*, Washington, DC 1967, 16–42

College Guide for Jewish Youth, prepared and edited by S. Norman Feingold and Alfred Jospe, Washington, DC [fifth revised edition] 1968

Campus '68—Labels and Facts [brochure], Washington, DC 1968

"The Teenager and Jewish Education," ed. by Eli Grad [review], *Religious Education*, November/December 1968, 495–496

"Challenge on Campus: Some Proposals for Counter-Action against Arab Propaganda," *The National Jewish Monthly*, June 1969, 13 ff.

Free Jewish University: An Experiment in Jewish Study (Program Monegraph), Washington, DC 1969

Outreach Programs: A New Approach to Student Involvement (Program Monograph), Washington, DC 1969

Issues of Faith: Two Letters of Theological Concern, Washington, DC 1969 [brochure]

Jerusalem and Other Jewish Writings by Moses Mendelssohn, translated and edited with an introduction by Alfred Jospe, New York 1969

"A Fundacao Hillel de B'nai B'rith," [excerpted from *Handbook for Student Leaders*], Sao Paulo, May 1969

"The Jewish Student Today: A Portrait," *Jewish Heritage*, Fall 1969, 21–26

"Youth in Turmoil" [review], *Journal of Jewish Communal Service*, vol. 46 #2, Winter 1969, 193–195

"Innovation or Traditionalism in Worship?", *Campus '70: Agenda for Critical Renewal*, Washington, DC 1970, 36–42

"In Memoriam—Harry Kaplan," *Campus '70: Agenda for Critical Renewal*, Washington, DC 1970, 63–67

Jewish Studies in American Colleges and Universities (Program Monograph), Washington, DC 1970 and 1971 (second revised and enlarged edition).

"Hebrew Houses on Campus: A new Approach to Intensive Jewish Studies," condensed from *Clearing House*, September 1970, *The Jewish Digest*, December 1971, 11–14

Tradition and Contemporary Experience: Essays in Jewish Thought and Life, ed. by Alfred Jospe, New York 1970

"On the Meaning of Jewish Culture in Our Time," *Tradition and Contemporary Experience: Essays in Jewish Thought and Life*, New York 1970, 35–50

"The Jewish Image of the Jew: On the Meaning of Jewish Distinctiveness," *Tradition and Contemporary Experience*, New York 1970, 126–150

"The Three-Fold Rebellion: Some Reflections on Israel Today," *Tradition and Contemporary Experience*, New York 1970, 293–310

"Tradition and Innovation in Worship: Some Fundamental Issues," *CCAR Journal*, October 1970

The Campus: Conflict or Challenge?, Washington 1970 [brochure]

"A Generation without Memories," *The National Jewish Monthly*, May 1970, 25–30

"Moses Mendelssohn," *Encyclopaedia Judaica* XI, 1971, 1328–1342

"Jews in American Universities since the End of the 19th Century," *Encyclopaedia Judaica* XV, 1971, 1679–1683

"Farewell to a Colleague," *Continuity Plus: Changing Perspectives on Jewish Life on the Campus Today* (Annual Conference of Hillel Directors), Washington, DC 1971, 13–15

"A Nation of Creative Rebels," *Jewish Heritage*, Spring 1971, 5–13

"The Campus: Conflict or Challenge?", condensed in *The Jewish Digest*, October 1971, 23–28

"Free Jewish Universities," *The Jewish Spectator*, April 1971, 9–11

"Generation without Memories," [condensed from *The National Jewish Monthly*], *The Jewish Digest*, January 1971, 57–65

"The Issues Before Us," *Jewish Policy Issues on the Campus Today: A Staff Report*, Washington, D.C. 1972, 3–18

Jewish Studies in American Colleges and Universities, ed. by Alfred Jospe, Washington, DC, 1972, [monograph]

"Jewish College Youth at the Crossroads," *Jewish Heritage*, Fall/Winter 1972, 37–41

"Religion in Higher Education—A Terminal Case?" *Religious Education*, vol. 57 #2, March-April 1972, 123–130

Bridges to a Holy Time: New Worship for the Sabbath and Minor Festivals, ed. and with an introduction by Alfred Jospe and Richard N. Levy, New York 1973

"A Nossa Juventude Universitaria," *Heranca Judaica*, #15, vol. 1, Sao Paulo, 1973, 17–21

"Rabbi Nathan Gaynor," [eulogy] *Beneynu*, May 1973, vol. III, 38–41

"To Leave Your Mark," *The National Jewish Monthly*, June 1973, 15–18

"Objectivity Versus Advocacy in Jewish Studies," *Conservative Judaism*, vol. 27, # 2, Winter 1973, 20–24

"The Test of Time," *The Test of Time* (*A Commemoration and Celebration of Hillel's Fiftieth Anniversary*), Washington 1974, 1–21

"A Profession in Transition: The German Rabbinate 1910–1939," *Yearbook of the Leo Baeck Institute*, London 1974, 51–59

"Prelude to Modernity," *The Thought of Moses Mendelssohn*, trans. and ed. by Eva Jospe, with an introduction by Alfred Jospe, New York 1975, 3–46

"Estrangement and a Search for Roots," *The National Jewish Monthly*, June 1975, 16–20

"A Guiding Spirit of Hillel," *The Legacy of Philip W. Lown; A Memorial Tribute*, Brookline, Mass. 1976, 6–71

"The Jew on the College Campus," *Judaism* Vol. 25 # 3, Summer 1976, 270–280

"A Guide to the 'Guide'," [review essay] *The National Jewish Monthly*, March 1977, 34–39

"German Jewry Was Different," [review essay] *Judaism*, Spring 1979, 237–247

"Youth," selected and introduced by Alfred Jospe, *The Turbulent Years: Jewish Communal Service 1958–78*, ed. by Graenum Berger, to be published in 1980

Studies in Jewish Religious and Philosophical Thought: From the Writings of Wissenschaft des Judentums, selected, edited, and with an introduction by Alfred Jospe, Wayne State University Press, to be published in 1980

Editor

Clearing House, a professional bulletin for Hillel Directors and Counselors (1949–1971).

Hillel Little Books, a series of publications dealing with issues of fundamental importance to Jewish college students, intended to stimulate further study and discussion. Five volumes.

Hillel Library Series, written by men of variant points of view; the books in this series are selected with special regard to their value as literary and educational resources at the university level, in the hope that they will stimulate further discussion and study of issues in the foreground of Jewish concerns. Eight Volumes.

Proceedings of the National Hillel Summer Institute, ed. by Alfred Jospe
Living as a Jew Today, New York, N.Y. 1950
The Jewish Heritage and the Jewish Student, New York, N.Y. 1951
Towards a Program of Jewish Living, New York, N.Y. 1953
American Freedom and Jewish Identity, New York, N.Y. 1954
Judaism for the Modern Age, New York, N.Y. 1955
Education for Jewish Living, New York, N.Y. 1956
Judaism and Ethical Choice, New York, N.Y. 1957
On Being Jewish Today, Washington, D.C. 1958
The Jewish Image of Man, Washington, D.C. 1959

The Way of Judaism: The Sabbath as Idea and Experience (I), Washington, D.C. 1960

The Sabbath as Idea and Experience (II): The Ways of Judaism in Our Time, Washington, D.C. 1961

The Sabbath as Idea and Experience (III): On the Meaning of Jewish Identity in Our Time, Washington, D.C. 1962

Tradition as Idea and Contemporary Experience, Washington, D.C. 1963

Dimensions of Jewish Existence Today, Washington, D.C. 1964

Proceedings of the Annual Conference of Hillel Directors, ed. by Alfred Jospe

Who "Belongs" to Hillel? New York, N.Y. 1954

The Philosophy of Hillel Work in the Light of Experience, New York, N.Y. 1955

The Hillel Program: Principles and Practices, New York, N.Y. 1957

Religious Issues on Campus, Washington, D.C. 1958

Jewish Identity and the Jewish College Student, Washington, D.C. 1959

Changing Patterns of Jewish Life on the Campus, Washington, D.C. 1961

Challenges to Jewish Education on the Campus, Washington, D.C. 1963

Campus 1966: Change and Challenge, Washington, D.C. 1966

New Frontiers for Jewish Life on the Campus, Washington, D.C. 1968

Campus '70: Agenda for Critical Renewal, Washington, D.C. 1969

Continuity Plus: Changing Perspectives on Jewish Campus Life, Washington, D.C. 1971